Applications for
Distributed Systems and Network Management

Kornel Terplan
Jill Huntington-Lee

JOHN WILEY & SONS, INC.

New York   Chichester   Weinheim   Brisbane   Singapore   Toronto

Copyright © 1995 by John Wiley & Sons, Inc. All rights reserved.

Published by John Wiley & Sons, Inc.

Published simultaneously in Canada.

This publication is designed to provide accurate and authoritative information in regard to the subject matter covered. It is sold with the understanding that the publisher is not engaged in rendering legal, accounting, or other professional services. If legal advice or other expert assistance is required, the services of a competent professional person should be sought.

Library of Congress Cataloging-in-Publication Data:

Terplan, Kornel.
    Applications for distributed systems and network management / by
Kornel Terplan and Jill Huntington-Lee.
      p. cm.
    Includes bibliographical references and index.
    ISBN 0-471-28639-7
      1. Electronic data processing—Distributed processing.
  2. Client/server computing.   3. Computer networks—management.
  I. Huntington-Lee, Jill.   II. Title.
  QA76.9.D5T47   1994
  004'.36—dc20
                                              94-19593
                                                CIP

Printed in the United States of America.

10 9 8 7 6 5 4 3

Contents

Preface vii
Acknowledgments ix

Chapter 1 Harnessing the Downsized Network. 1
   1.1 Transitioning from Legacy Systems to Client/Server Architectures 1
   1.2 How Downsizing has Changed the Requirements of Systems
       and Network Management. 4
   1.3 How Distributed Systems are Managed Today 9
   1.4 What is Covered by Standards. 17
   1.5 The Changing Scope of Systems and Network Management. 26
   1.6 Summary. 29

Chapter 2 Management Functions and Processes. 30
   2.1 Introduction. 30
   2.2 Business Model of Managing Systems and Networks 30
   2.3 Management Tools 36
   2.4 Management Database. 39
   2.5 Change Management Processes. 50
   2.6 The Fault Handling Process. 54
   2.7 The Tuning Process. 60
   2.8 The Security Control Process 63
   2.9 The Costing and Billing Process 67
   2.10 Summary. 71

Chapter 3 Typical Management Problems and How to Solve Them 72
   3.1 Introduction. 72
   3.2 Remote Configuration of Routers. 72

3.3   Software Version Control in Client/Server Environments 76
3.4   Isolating Faults Using Smart Hubs 80
3.5   Are Expert Systems Worth the Cost? 84
3.6   Turning Reams of Data into Concise, Useful Information 90
3.7   Applying Kerberos to Increase Security 95
3.8   License Management in the Distributed Systems Environment 98
3.9   Summary 100

Chapter 4   Management Platforms **101**
4.1   Network Management Tools 102
4.2   Basic Management Platform Services 107
4.3   Examples of UNIX-Based Network Management Platforms 115
4.4   Examples of DOS/Windows-Based Network
       Management Platforms 148
4.5   Examples of UNIX Systems Management Platforms 152
4.6   Integrating Applications onto Management Platforms 164
4.7   Summary 190

Chapter 5   Network and Systems Management Applications **191**
5.1   Overview of the Status of Management Applications Market 191
5.2   Levels of Integration 195
5.3   Application Shipments 196
5.4   Application Examples 198
5.5   Summary 257

Chapter 6   Management Solutions from IBM **258**
6.1   IBM Product Families 259
6.2   Applications for the Principal Product Families 271
6.3   Communication Alternatives Between and Within IBM
       Product Families 287
6.4   IBM's Directions 293
6.5   Summary 299

Chapter 7   HP OpenView Integration **301**
7.1   Introduction 301
7.2   OpenView Platforms 301
7.3   Integrating HP OpenView with Applications 302
7.4   Summary 315

Chapter 8   Application Integration Case Studies **317**
8.1   Customized Network Management Integration Using
       NetExpert from Objective Systems Integrators 318
8.2   Network Management Integration Using AT&T StarSENTRY 325
8.3   Integrated Applications for Managing WAN Services Using
       WilTel and SunNet Manager 334
8.4   Integrating Network and Systems Management: a Case Study
       of Integration at the U.S. Army 341
8.5   Summary 352

Chapter 9   Managing Client/Server Structures **355**

9.1   Definitions... 355

9.2   Special Problems with Client/Server Management 358

9.3   Convergence of Network and Systems Management 361

9.4   Summary.. 363

Chapter 10 Trends **364**

10.1 Management Frameworks 364

10.2 Smart Agents.. 365

10.3 ATM and Switching Technologies 365

10.4 Improved Network Management Protocols........................ 367

10.5 Increased Use of Object-Oriented Technology..................... 367

10.6 Expert Systems 368

10.7 Cost Constraints 368

10.8 Summary... 370

Appendix A. Abbreviations 372

Appendix B. Vendor Names and Addresses 376

Bibliography 381

Index.. 386

Other VNR Communications Books . . . .

- EDI Guide: A Step by Step Approach. *By Edward Cannon*
- NetView: IBM's Network Management Product. *By Alfred Charley*
- Doing Business on the Internet. *By Mary J. Cronin*
- Routing in Today's Internetworks. *By Mark Dickie*
- EDI: A Total Management Guide, 2nd Edition. *By Margaret A. Emmelhainz, Ph.D*
- Digital Signal Processing in Communications. *By Marvin E. Frerking*
- Broadband Networking. *By Lawrence Gasman*
- Data Communications Test and Troubleshooting, 2nd Edition. *By Gilbert Held*
- Mastering PC Communications Software. *By Gilbert Held*
- Working With NetWare: For Network Supervisors and Users. *By Gilbert Held*
- The Complete Cyberspace Reference and Directory. *By Gilbert Held*
- Low-Cost E-Mail With UUCP: Integrating Unix, DOS, Windows and Mac. *By Thomas Wm. Madron*
- Analyzing DECNET/OSI Phase V. *By Carl Malamud*
- Analyzing Novell Networks. *By Carl Malamud*
- Analyzing Sun Networks. *By Carl Malamud*
- The Handbook of International Connectivity Standards. *Edited by Gary R. McClain*
- Networking NT: Using Windows NT in the Corporate LAN Environment. *By Christopher Monro*
- The Illustrated Network Book: A Graphic Guide to Understanding Computer Networks. *By Matthew G. Naugle*
- Making Telecommunications Happen: A Guide for Telemanagers and Telecommuters. *By Jack M. Nilles*
- JPEG Still Image Data Compression Standard. *By William B. Pennebaker and Joan L. Mitchell*
- X.500 Directory Services: Technology and Deployment. *By Sara Radicati*
- SNA: IBM's Systems Network Architecture. *By Stephen J. Randesi and Donald H. Czubek*
- Using Wireless Communications in Business. *By Andrew M. Seybold*
- Network Topology Optimization. *By Roshan Lal Sharma*
- Communications Standard Dictionary, 2nd Edition. *By Martin H. Weik, DSc.*

Preface

New information technologies and networking architectures continue to emerge while price-performance rations change rapidly. This creates tough challenges for the communications industry and for corporations as they seek to stay competitive. Many corporations that rely on aging networking technology, applications, and systems believe that distributing power, databases, and applications may help them to compete better, to protect their investment in technology, and simply to survive in today's very complex systems and networking environments.

Client/server structures represent the physical and logical distribution of computing and networking functions. In such environments, the client typically initiates a service request to a server across local, metropolitan, and/or wide area networks. The server responds to the client's request by performing printing, database, communication, electronic mail, security verification, and other services. Actions can also be initiated by the server if the network requests the execution of certain tasks on behalf of the client.

A single server can simultaneously provide service to multiple clients; a client can access the services of multiple servers. No standard rules govern the distribution of tasks between servers and clients.

Despite the fact that client/server structures and distributed computing environments are gaining in popularity, several misconceptions about these technologies are widely held. The most important of these misconceptions are:

Client/server computing will soon dominate the market.
Because of the heavy use of interprocess communications in client/server structures, multiple interfaces are required. Some of these interfaces may be open, while others are not—locking users into manufacturers' proprietary solutions.

Client/server computing guarantees openness.
Because of the heavy use of interprocess communications in client/server structures, multiple interfaces are required. Some of these interfaces may be open, while others are not—locking users into manufacturers' proprietary solutions.

Client/server and distributed systems always cost less than legacy systems.
Downsizing and replacing legacy applications by a number of value-added functions will increase product quality and user productivity, but the requirements for more complex management/client server structures may significantly increase operating costs.

To truly benefit from client/server and distributed computing, organizations must be realistic about the challenges associated with these technologies. To that end, this book addresses the management requirements—and management solutions in general—for distributed systems. In particular, this book looks at client/server architectures and provides answers and solutions for the following management challenges:

How to define and quantify management requirements
What are the critical success factors of management
How to redesign single management functions and processes
How to determine the qualifying attributes of management platforms
How to classify and integrate management applications
What are the alternative levels of integration available
How to select applications and management platforms
How to embed solutions from IBM and Hewlett-Packard into customized management products
How to customize existing products into integrated solutions
What are the peculiarities of managing client/server structures
Assessment of management protocol directions
Assessment of the importance and applicability of recommendations from standards bodies

Acknowledgments

The authors would like to acknowledge the support of the following persons in supplying information for the contents of this book:

John Burnham: Cabletron Systems, Inc.
Sanjiv Ahuja, James Rich, Gale Meyers, Ron Vaughn: IBM Corp.
Gordon MacKinney, Thomas Nebe, Scott Safe: Hewlett-Packard Company.
Matt Russell: Hewlett-Packard Company
Sally Brandon: Hi-Tech Communications
Jim Corrigan: ki Research
Rob McGovern: Legent Corp.
Ellis Gregory: NetTech, Inc.
Tom Johnson, Dick Vento: Objective Systems Integrators, Inc.
Eric Olinger: Peregrine Systems
Dave Mahler, Atta Rasehki, Tim Lee-Thorpe: Remedy Corp.
Asheem Chandna: SynOptics Communications, Inc.
Steve Morgenthal: Unified Systems Solutions, Inc.
Ted Collins: ViaTech Development, Inc.
Russ McQuire: WilTel
John Lunny: the Wollongong Group, Inc.
Lenny Liebman

We would also like to than Rick Sturm (US West) for the valuable comments that helped make this book more useful for network managers. The production of the manuscript would not have been possible without the assistance of Melissa Morales. We are especially grateful to Adam Szabo for doing an excellent job producing the graphical figures illustrating key points throughout each chapter.

And, finally, we are very, very thankful for the patience of our friends and families who spent many hours anticipating the time when this project would be completed!

This book is dedicated to Adele Terplan, mother of Kornel Terplan, who has encouraged and motivated her son to consolidate his knowledge and experience in publications.

This book is also dedicated to Jessie Oberholtzer, whose love for books and long career in education has been an inspiration to her granddaughter, Jill Huntington-Lee.

1

Harnessing the Downsized Network

Client/server. Distributed computing. Open systems. What is the true meaning of each of these phrases—and what impact will these technologies have upon the manageability of business systems and networks? Today, many data processing and data communications professionals occupy positions of responsibility that include overseeing these areas of rapidly-changing technology. Pressures to "work smarter" with fewer resources make this challenge even more difficult.

This chapter outlines key management problems that arise in the transition from older networking and data processing technologies to newer environments. In older environments, "proprietary" or "legacy" systems revolved around mainframe and minicomputer-based terminal-to-host networks. Now, these structures are being replaced by smaller, faster, and less expensive computers that are capable of communicating and sharing applications processing. This chapter discusses the current line of demarcation between network and systems management in most organizations and the driving factors behind the convergence of network and systems management. It concludes with a brief discussion of the primary standards that apply to network and systems management in today's world. (For more information on the subtle distinctions between client/server systems, distributed systems, and open systems, see Chapter 9.)

1.1 TRANSITIONING FROM LEGACY SYSTEMS TO CLIENT/SERVER ARCHITECTURES

Downsizing (or rightsizing) is the process of porting existing applications to, and writing new applications for, client/server structures. Typically, this means moving applications from centralized mainframe computers to distributed PCs or UNIX workstations. This trend will not change the enterprise environment overnight. Distributing both processing power and databases requires industrial-strength local area networks (LANs), servers, and workstations, as well as embedded systems management capabilities in these components. Client/server structures create new and complex networking interrelationships. These require higher-quality network design techniques and, as a result, more sophisticated network and systems management applications. Despite the rapid advance of client/server networking, legacy systems will remain a part of the enterprise network scene for some time to come.

At first glance, the problem of managing legacy systems seems trivial. Many applications and tools that cover the traditional functions of fault, configuration, performance, security, and accounting management are available. While these legacy system tools and applications may not be state-of-the-art (they often lack sophisticated user interfaces), they work.

Fitting legacy system management applications and tools into new client/server structures, however, is not a trivial problem. Porting them to newer hardware and software platforms, leaving the "server" part of them untouched, is often a weighty question.

When porting legacy management applications to client/server implementations, the "server" part remains in charge of collecting and preprocessing data. In other words, the legacy system (e.g., mainframe) acts as the server. Several examples of this slow migration can be found in industry. In particular, IBM now allows several management applications, such as trouble ticketing, asset management, and network topology display, to be off-loaded from its NetView mainframe-based management system to the NetView/6000, which is a UNIX-based program for client/server environments. (For more information on IBM NetView/6000, see Chapters 4 and 6.)

Porting existing mainframe applications to LANs, servers, and workstations significantly increases the number of computing devices on the network. This is particularly true in remote sites, where there is often a shortage of on-site technical personnel. Consequently, there is a growing demand for improved remote systems management.

As servers and workstations become more powerful, breakdowns and performance degradations can seriously impact the business goals of the enterprises they serve. The need to avoid performance and availability problems is driving a demand for more sophisticated proactive management applications.

Distributing critical applications on LANs can increase the vulnerability of an enterprise to security violations. As a result, security protection in client/server-structures requires more sophisticated security applications than centralized legacy systems, where access is easy to control. The increased number of systems significantly impacts network security. It's much more difficult to maintain security in a distributed computing environment simply because there are so many managed (as well as unmanaged) PCs, workstations, and other objects to be protected.

This problem of scale also affects the management database. The scope of various asset, inventory, and configuration databases must increase, necessitating an increase in the number of databases or the distribution of a database into various segments. Distributed databases are, however, not without problems. With the exception of only very few new products, truly distributed databases do not yet exist.

Legacy systems have been monitored, measured, and studied for many years. In most cases, organizations have optimized the performance of their legacy systems to reasonable limits. Load and utilization profiles of legacy systems are typically predictable and stable. The nature of legacy system applications communication (batch file transfer, etc.) makes sudden changes in traffic patterns unusual.

In client/server structures, however, performance predictions are very difficult to make. In LAN-to-LAN connections, for example, bursty traffic samples are not unusual. As a result, it can be extremely difficult to optimize the sizing and configuration of wide area network (WAN) and metropolitan area network (MAN) segments.

In legacy environments, change management is a periodic—rather than a real-time—activity. That is often sufficient, because legacy environments rarely require configuration modification. Client/server structures, however, require moves, adds, and changes more frequently, primarily because there is less centralized control and users may take their PCs with them when their offices or job assignments change. Such frequent network reconfigurations mandate very dynamic change management procedures. Change requests in client/server networks are typically organized as trouble-tickets, requesting real-time responses. Another result of the dynamic nature of client/server structures is that electronic software distribution is virtually a necessity.

In client/server environments, the exchange of information between servers and clients is common. If these exchanges occur over the wide area, the cost of bandwidth quickly becomes excessive. Dynamic bandwidth management is, therefore, a critical factor in the success of managing client/server interaction over the wide area. Both "production" and management data are transmitted over the WAN, requiring even more bandwidth. The volume of management information will only increase if the organization increases the frequency with which it checks the status of managed objects.

The phrase, "the network is becoming the computer" accurately implies that servers, clients, network interface cards, and communication facilities are working seamlessly together. Most likely, a new discipline called "service management" will emerge, integrating all systems- and network-management functions and tools.

In summary, in a downsized or rightsized environment, management will play an even more important role than in legacy system networks. Expenditures on management applications will be increasingly justified by the critical need for controlling complexity, improving service quality, reducing outages and downtime, and improving change control management.

1.2   HOW DOWNSIZING HAS CHANGED THE REQUIREMENTS OF SYSTEMS AND NETWORK MANAGEMENT

Network and systems management requirements are continuously changing. Depending on their business' proprietary needs and priorities, users must revisit their product purchase selection criteria several (or even many) times a year.

The advent of widely accepted management protocol standards, such as the Simple Network Management Protocol (SNMP), has helped users establish important product selection criteria. Also, equipment and software vendors are under increasing competitive pressure to try to better understand their users' needs. This is certainly good news for users.

Organizations should focus on seven key areas when assessing the impact of client/server migration on their management strategies. These areas are listed in the top half of Table 1-1.

1.2.1   Support for Principal Management Functions

The need to support principal management functions will not change after an organization has ported its important business applications to client/server structures. These functions, outlined in Chapter 2, include fault, configuration, performance, security, and accounting management.

In client/server environments, however, the importance of certain management functions will be greater than in legacy networks. Specific areas requiring greater emphasis include remote configuration of servers, software version control, isolating faults to the port level, and controlling moves, adds, and changes.

Effective management of client/server networks requires a higher degree of automation for both backup and recovery procedures. It also requires an ability to reroute network traffic using scripts. Tuning the performance of internetworks becomes extremely important and difficult, as the great volume of management data coming from a wide variety of sources must be compressed and processed locally.

In client/server networks, security is also a much greater problem. Organizations must pay particular attention to access control, network partitioning, evaluating security audit trails, and usage registration in distributed systems. Figure 1.1 shows the layers of a management solution in the client/server environment, including managed objects (network devices, systems, and software), applications, and management functions.

1.2.2   Integrated Configuration Database

Client/server structures are heavily distributed. However, a single inventory of all resources is necessary. This central, logical repository supports construction of a comprehensive network map, for example; however, physical distribution of data may be desired.

1.2.3   Integration of Management Applications

Because device-specific applications must forward information to generic, process-specific applications, some level of application-to-application integration is

TABLE 1-1   Assessing the Impact of Client/Server Migration

Primary Areas of Focus	Impact
Support for principal management functions	Management functions stay the same, with increased emphasis on certain functions.
Integrated configuration database	Client/server structures are heavily distributed. However, a single inventory of all resources is necessary. This central, logical repository supports construction of a comprehensive network map, for example. Physical distribution of data may be preferred for performance reasons.
Integration of management applications	Device-specific applications must forward information to generic, process-specific applications. Some level of application-to-application integration is required to reduce redundancy of polling and data storage.
Alarm handling	Alarms from all management applications should be received by a single application that has access to the integrated configuration database.
Trouble ticketing	This must be automated and consolidated.
Centralized change management	In client/server environments, changes are frequent, and their administration can be costly if it is not automated and controlled. A centralized change management system receives information about clients and servers from a variety of applications, storing it in a common format.
Scalability	Upward scalability of all management platforms and applications is much more essential in dynamic client/server environments, where growth is often rapid and unpredictable.

Secondary Areas of Focus	Impact
Shared management knowledge	Because management functions are distributed between multiple managers and multiple agents, both managers and agents need to have the same semantic level of understanding about the management information model, managed objects, and naming.
OmniPoint conformance	The NM Forum's OMNIPoint recommendations specify interoperability of management systems using Open Systems Interconnect (OSI) and other standards. OmniPoint specifications for managed object attributes may be particularly useful in distributed systems and networks.
Representation of managed objects	The number of managed objects and object attributes multiplies rapidly in client/server networks. Graphical representation of managed objects is absolutely essential, as is autodiscovery of network and system components. Objects are described by attributes, operations, behavior, and notifications. Objects are grouped into classes for easier management.

TABLE 1-1 Assessing the Impact of Client/Server Migration *(continued)*

Multilayered control (security)	Client-server structures require tougher control mechanisms to ensure security. Controls must be put in place at the end-user server layer, the management server layer, and management client layer. Controls include restricting access to servers and clients as well as restricting functions and span of control.
Audit trail	Audit trails logging system- and operator-initiated events and commands are necessary to support after the fact analysis of potential security violations of servers and clients.
Authentication	Access to management information should be limited to authorized clients—additional authentication services are necessary.
Security alarms	The impact of local security violations is often more severe than in hierarchical structures. The ability to automatically trigger active or passive actions based on alarms is important.
Diagnostic and test procedures	The management system must support predefined diagnostic and test procedures for determining where faults are and why they occurred. Diagnostic and test procedures may be on-line or off-line and local or remote. In complex client/server environments, there is a greater need for on-line diagnosis as well as support for remote diagnostics.
Management protocol support	Support of multiple management protocols is a necessity in client/server environments. Management platforms should support SNMP at minimum, and preferably also SNMPv2, the Common Management Information Protocol (CMIP) and CMIP over TCP/IP (CMOT).
Use of published test results	Support for de facto or open standards is not always clear-cut; many products claiming to support SNMP, for example, exhibit interoperability problems in production networks. Users should look for vendors that publish results of conformance tests. Independent test groups such as Interworking Laboratories are important sources of information.
Initial population of management databases	Because of the tremendous volume of management data accrued in client/server networks, initial population of management databases should be supported by batch import, with support for automated format changes where necessary.
Data entry/editing	The dynamic nature of client/server environments dictates a tremendous amount of data entry and editing of configuration data and network topology maps—automated procedures will never do it all. User-friendly procedures for data entry and editing are imperative.
Support for query languages	Requests for information could be initiated from any client in the network. The management database should support interpretation of English-like syntax—specifically, structured query language (SQL).

TABLE 1-1   Assessing the Impact of Client/Server Migration *(continued)*

Management database performance	Database performance is critical to effective management. Because the management database may be distributed, access is flexible and response time is difficult to quantify. Measurements such as database updates, reads, writes, searches using various masks, processing of records, and opening/closing of trouble tickets must be measured and reported.
User interface	The user interface to the management platform should shield operators from the differences in language, terminology, and methods of identifying resources that are employed by various management applications.
Support for graphics and windowing	The operator interface should display alerts generated by management applications using high-definition graphics. Windowing allows simultaneous display of data from multiple management systems.
Color-coded displays	Resources in the client/server network should be displayed using a color coding scheme to represent administrative and operational status, including alerts. Color coding should be user-customizable.
Multiple management views	The management system should support the creation and display of multiple management domains and views. Grouping objects into domains can help administrators deal with the complex client/server environment.
Interaction between fault diagnosis and inventory management	Because of the variety of systems and components in the typical client/server network, the ability to automatically display inventory data about failed components can accelerate troubleshooting.

required to reduce redundancy of polling and data. Management applications are expected to work seamlessly with the platform. Failure of one management system to perform its assigned task in a defined time scale should generate an alert.

1.2.4   Alarm Handling

Alarms from all management applications should be received by a single application that has access to the integrated configuration database. Correlation of alarms is needed to suppress a flood of secondary alarms in interconnected client/server networks. Using algorithms or rules (or both), correlations should be made among all the alarms within a definite time window with the most likely source of the problem(s) identified.

1.2.5   Trouble Ticketing

When multiple trouble tickets are issued to correct a problem affecting numerous clients and/or servers, the tickets should reference each other to ensure that

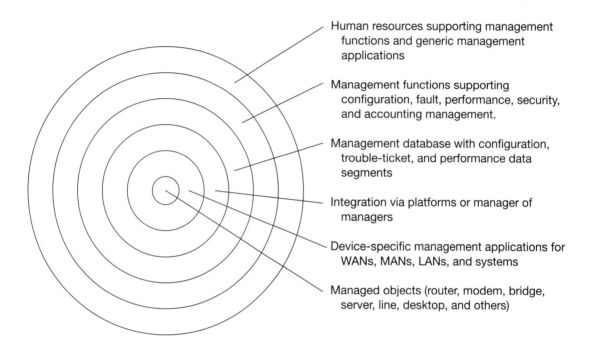

Human resources supporting management functions and generic management applications

Management functions supporting configuration, fault, performance, security, and accounting management.

Management database with configuration, trouble-ticket, and performance data segments

Integration via platforms or manager of managers

Device-specific management applications for WANs, MANs, LANs, and systems

Managed objects (router, modem, bridge, server, line, desktop, and others)

Figure 1.1 Management objects, applications, and functions

all problems can be properly cleared before a particular component is restored to service. Trouble ticketing must be generated automatically upon detection of predefined fault conditions. The trouble ticketing application should be distributed in implementation, with relevant components accessible to both users and administrators. Trouble ticketing applications should be integrated with the inventory/configuration databases. Figure 1.2 depicts the life-cycle of trouble tickets.

1.2.6   Centralized Change Management

In client/server environments, changes are frequent and their administration can be costly if it is not automated and controlled. A centralized change management system receives information about clients and servers from a variety of applications, storing it in a common format. From this inventory, a network map can be developed to show the entire network and to point out where connectivity gaps exist.

1.2.7   Scalability

Because client/server-structures change and grow continuously, upward scalability of all management platforms and applications is essential. Management solu-

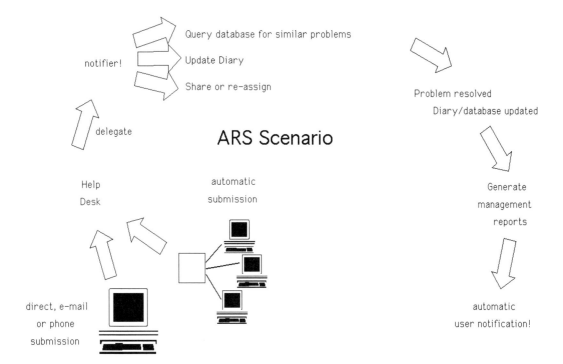

Figure 1.2 Life cycle of trouble tickets (Action Request System from Remedy)

tions must guarantee the accommodation of growth in terms of number of managed objects, number of alarms to be correlated, number of clients to be supported, and the volume of management information distributed in the network. Other requirements and their impacts are listed in the bottom half of Table 1-1.

1.3   HOW DISTRIBUTED SYSTEMS ARE MANAGED TODAY

This section reviews the status of distributed systems management in today's client/server networks. Three aspects of distributed systems management are: the fragmentation of management; management applications, and staffing (human resources).

1.3.1   Fragmentation of Management

The complexity of client/server structures makes it difficult to view the entire information infrastructure as a whole. However, achieving an integrated view is the only way to harness the downsized network. There are both technological and organizational barriers to obtaining management integration. Many of these barriers are steeped in traditions established during the growth of legacy systems. Eight major barriers to achieving integrated management of client/server structures are listed in Table 1-2.

1.3.1.1   Separation of Network and Systems Management

Traditionally, network management and systems management have been separate disciplines. However, in today's client/server environments, there are no clear lines of demarcation between systems and networks management. Sometimes the network interface card is considered the boundary.

In many organizations, management of the network is more advanced than management of the distributed systems that are attached to the network.

When network and systems management are viewed as separate functions within an organization, the network management group usually views systems as black boxes with the status "on" or "off." Systems management targets all components on the other side of the interface card, such as processors, power supplies, memory, input/output subsystems, processes, and applications.

Figure 1.3 shows the demarcation line of systems and network management within a hub.

1.3.1.2   Separation of Logical and Physical Management

Physical management involves detecting failures of physical components, isolating the problems, and resolving them. Logical management focuses upon the logical connection between the user and the ultimate network destination, generally the application. Two principal components of logical network management are session awareness and traffic flow visibility. Traditionally, separate tools and procedures have been used for logical and physical management. While it is certainly possible, it is not necessary to support logical and physical management in a single, integrated database. In most cases, the existence of SQL links are adequate for meeting troubleshooting, performance optimization, and capacity plan-

TABLE 1-2 Barriers to Achieving Integrated Management of Client/Server Structures

1. Separation of network and systems management

2. Separation of logical and physical management

3. Separate management of active and passive components

4. Separation by network architecture

5. Separate management of WANs, MANs, LANs, systems, and desktops

6. Lack of integrated alarm management

7. Lack of integrated trouble ticketing

8. Lack of clear understanding of Application Programming Interfaces (APIs)

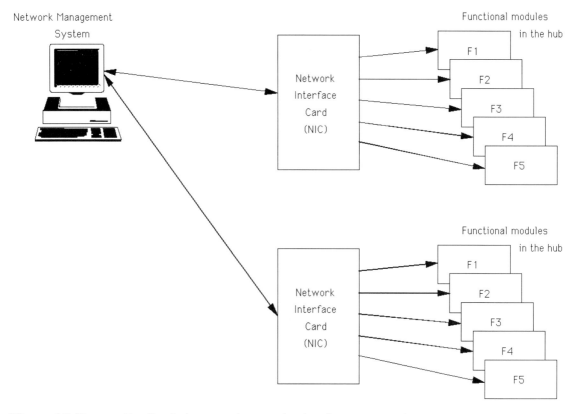

Network Management
System

Functional modules
in the hub

Network
Interface
Card
(NIC)

F1
F2
F3
F4
F5

Functional modules
in the hub

Network
Interface
Card
(NIC)

F1
F2
F3
F4
F5

Figure 1.3 Demarcation line between systems and network management

ning requirements. In many organizations, however, even these minimal links
are not in place.

1.3.1.3   Separate Management of Active and Passive Components

The intelligence of networking components varies greatly from device to device.
Some components are able to report their status, while others cannot. Managers
must take these differences into account, when configuring polls or reacting to
events, for example. Figure 1.4 shows an example from the LAN-area highlighting a number of various systems and network components. Advanced management platforms use artificial intelligence to infer the status of non-intelligent
components from connected devices. This capability is particularly valuable in
large enterprise networks.

1.3.1.4   Separation by Network Architectures

Each leading architecture, such as IBM's Systems Network Architecture (SNA),
Digital Equipment Corporation's DECnet, the Xerox Networking System (XNS),
Novell's Netware, Microsoft Windows NT, and Banyan Vines, etc., has a propri-

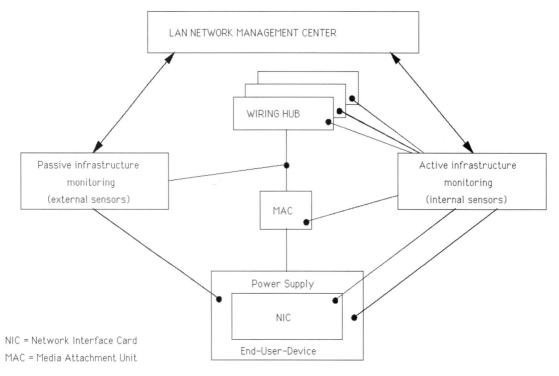

Figure 1.4 Managing active and passive LAN components

etary solution for logical network management. Unfortunately, the solutions are hardly interchangeable. While gateways are available to achieve interconnectivity, there are few applications for exchanging management data. However, new applications for managing legacy environments under SNMP-based frameworks are emerging, including OpenDNM from Ki Research for DECnet environments and various SNA management applications from IBM and third parties. For more information on this topic, see Chapters 5 and 6.

1.3.1.5   Separation by WANs, MANs, LANs, Systems, and Desktops

Management solutions for WANs are stable and available. While WAN management applications are typically proprietary in nature, they are well-defined and mature. Solutions for MANs and LANs are still fragmented and very labor intensive.

Similarly, while mature applications for management mainframe systems are abundant, comparable solutions for client/server networks are just starting to appear. Servers and some clients are typically managed by individual methods without much standardization. Finally, desktops are not yet enabled for management, although this will change with anticipated market acceptance of the Desktop Management Interface from the Desktop Management Task Force (DMTF). (For more information on DMTF, see section 1.4.)

1.3.1.6   Lack of Integrated Alarm Management

Users are looking for standardized alarms to detect problems. What they get today are a vast array of messages and events generated by almost all network elements. Most management systems offer weak support for alarm filtering, differentiation by severity, on-site interpretation, and alarm correlation. As a result, management operators in client/server networks are often overloaded and problem determination is slower than required. The results are low productivity and inefficient trouble-shooting. Figure 1.5 illustrates one result of the lack of integrated alarm management. A communication resource shares the bandwidth between multiple logical architectures. Due to the lack of alarm correlation, a resource failure starts four separate troubleshooting actions.

1.3.1.7   Lack of Integrated Trouble-Ticketing Applications

Many of the existing trouble ticket applications are mainframe based. Only a few—including Remedy Action Request System (AR System) and Legent Paradigm—support client/server implementations. While these two applications support message filtering and links to alarm management, they are more the exception than the rule. In many other products, even routine types of information must be entered manually.

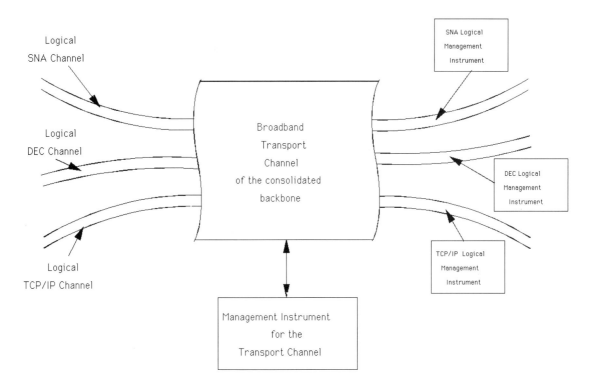

Figure 1.5 Consolidated backbone with segmented logical management

1.3.1.8   Lack of Clear Understanding of APIs

Management system Application Programming Interfaces (APIs) allow users and third parties to write management applications. However, users very rarely take advantage of platform APIs due to a lack of time and the skills required for Unix, OS/2, and, likely, for C and C++ programming. Some third parties take advantage of these APIs when writing management applications, but generally most vendors just loosely integrate their applications with management systems and platforms. For more information on management platforms and their APIs, see Chapter 4.

1.3.2   Networks and Systems Management Applications

Today's network and systems management products exhibit many weaknesses. Table 1-3 lists six major barriers to integration of network and systems management applications.

1.3.2.1   Multiple Management Databases

Managers of client/server networks must wrestle with numerous files, file formats, and databases storing management applications. Although management applications may interface with a common management platform, each application still maintains its own database. These multiple databases are not connected or synchronized. In many organizations, data is also grouped along departmental lines, such as the purchasing department, technicians or trouble-shooters, administrators, or planners. All too often, asset and inventory data is maintained separately from configuration data.

1.3.2.2   Fragmented Products and Too Many Consoles

Compounding the database problem, each product has its own domain of management which may overlap with others. While SNMP-based management platforms provide some level of consolidation, there are many areas (such as desktop, LAN, and proprietary systems) that are not yet manageable by SNMP applications. As short-term solutions, many organizations use terminal emulation to

TABLE 1-3   Barriers to Integration of Network and Systems Management Applications

1. Multiple management databases

2. Fragmented products and too many consoles

3. Lack of reporting capabilities

4. Limited support for customization

5. Lack of good support for expert systems

6. Lack of security features

reduce the large number of consoles. On the screen, each console is represented as a window.

1.3.2.3 Lack of Reporting Capabilities

In dynamic client/server environments, an urgent need for particular performance statistics or data may not be anticipated. In many organizations, these ad-hoc needs cannot usually be satisfied because the performance database is not accessible in real-time. For LANs in particular, system and desktop performance data is not collected on continuous basis.

1.3.2.4 Limited Support for Customization

Only a few vendors, including Objective Systems Integrators, Teknekron, and Network Managers, Ltd. offer both a truly customizable platform framework and customization services. This combination has been very successful with phone companies and with companies operating large and complex global networks.

1.3.2.5 Lack of Good Support for Expert Systems

There are only a few good expert system prototypes and operating expert systems in the management industry. The majority of working expert systems have been designed and implemented for WANs, rather than for client/server LANs and internetworks. The reasons for this slow progress include the high initial cost of designing and operating the expert system and the lack of personnel with skills sufficient to maintain them. Also, the complexity of the networks they are supposed to automate is another barrier to implementation.

1.3.2.6 Lack of Inherent Security Features

Some of the most severe security violations occur as a result of unauthorized persons using management products. At this time, most management platforms and applications for client/server networks provide only the limited protection that is built into the operating system of the network management platform. Typically, this means the very vulnerable scheme of UNIX permissions.

1.3.3 Staffing Issues

Staffing the organization's various network and systems management departments can, in itself, present a challenge in complex, client/server environments. Eight critical staffing challenges that create barriers to network and systems management integration are listed in Table 1-4.

1.3.3.1 High Turnover

High turnover always affects the consistency of services rendered to users. The result is an additional need for hiring, cross-education, and training. Transition and training inevitably affect the high quality level expected by users. Frequent

TABLE 1-4   Staffing Issues that Create Barriers to Achieving Integration of Network and Systems Management

---

1. High personnel turnover

2. Lack of technical know-how

3. Inexperience in selecting management applications

4. Increased need for staff

5. Low productivity of management operations staff

6. Unclear distinctions concerning ownership of management functions

7. Changing responsibilities and assignments

8. Salary and benefits expense

---

reasons for turnover include lower than expected salaries, lack of motivation, lack of job security, unclear career paths, lack of recognition, inadequate tools and applications, little challenge, no job rotation, and unpleasant working conditions.

1.3.3.2   Lack of Technical Know How

The art and science of managing client/server structures is a new area. It is not possible for even seasoned managers to translate the experience of years in legacy environments to newer client/server structures. To compound this problem, current desktop systems have been designed without embedded management features. This is a sharp contrast to many mainframe and minicomputer systems, which include such features.

The typical management control center's support staff may be overloaded, overworked, and poorly equipped. Operations and help desk staff are sometimes treated impolitely by end users. Products that could make the operations staff's job easier—such as automated call distributors, large screens, speaker phones, mature trouble ticketing features, short-code for check-lists, and comfortable chairs with legroom—are often missing. Space in the management control center may be cramped and uncomfortable for the staff.

1.3.3.3   Inexperience in Selecting Management Applications

There are many applications available for managing systems and networks. But the integration level between the applications and the platform or manager of managers is very low. (For definitions of "platform" and "manager of managers," see Chapter 4.) Many network managers and systems administrators are too busy to take time to learn to differentiate between APIs, command line interfaces, and simply launching an application from the platform. Additional and continuous education is absolutely necessary.

1.3.3.4   Increased Need for Staff

Systems and networks show no signs of getting smaller or less complex, and the demand for human resources is growing rapidly. It is extremely difficult to find, train, and keep qualified staff. As systems and networks become more complex, people who are really able to operate them are becoming more scarce. Automation and better instrumentation are the keys to controlling staffing requirements. However, until more automated and better integrated management applications emerge, reductions in staffing needs will be rare.

1.3.3.5   Low Productivity of Management Operations Staff

Due to lack of both motivation and the proper tools, productivity of management personnel may be low. Productivity varies from organization to organization, and from country to country. Productivity can be measured by the length of time required to resolve problems, number of fault referrals, reaction times to fault notification, and similar statistics.

1.3.3.6   Unclear Distinctions Concerning Ownership of Management Functions

Management responsibilities are often split among arbitrary lines between different people and even different organizational units. The result is the delay of problem ownership leading to lower network availability. Unfortunately, this problem is often carried over when management functions are automated.

1.3.3.7   Changing Responsibilities and Assignments

The ever-changing client/server environment requires frequent changes in job assignments and responsibilities. This may add to instability in the organizational structure unless job rotations have been planned in advance. Unfortunately, ad hoc decisions dominate, and many managers react rather than act. At the present, the ideal role assignments for managing LANs, servers, clients and workstations are not clear.

1.3.3.8   Salary and Benefits Expense

The operation of networks and systems is becoming increasingly costly. Even when the right people are found for the job, the expenses are considerable. Practical experience suggests that human resources consumes more than 40 percent of the management-related expenditures.

1.4   WHAT IS COVERED BY STANDARDS

Network and systems management product solutions are greatly affected by emerging standards. These include proprietary solutions, such as IBM's Network Management Vector Transport (NMVT); de facto standards for TCP/IP-based networks, including the Simple Network Management Protocol (SNMP) versions 1 and 2; and open solutions, based on OSI and CCITT recommendations, including Common Management Information Protocol (CMIP) and Telecommunication Management Network (TMN).

In addition, there are organizations promoting application programming interfaces (APIs) between standards and frameworks that include these standards. These groups and interfaces include the Network Management Forum's OMNIPoint, the Open Software Foundation's (OSF) Distributed Management Environment (DME), Unix International's ATLAS framework, the Object Management Group's (OMG) Common Object Request Broker Architecture (CORBA), and the Desktop Management Task Force's (DMTF) Desktop Management Interface (DMI). In general, standards covering protocols (such as SNMP and CMIP) are more concrete and mature than API standards such as OSF DME and DMTF DMI.

Finally, groups with special interests in particular technologies have been established to support Asynchronous Transfer Mode (ATM), Fiber Distributed Data Interface (FDDI), and desktop management (Desktop Management Task Force).

1.4.1   SNMP and CMIP

The use of standards will help accelerate widespread acceptance of management applications, providing some measure of future-proofing. Specific management functional areas and services have been defined by the International Organization for Standardization (ISO) in documents concerning Open Systems Interconnect (OSI). The primary OSI management protocols are the Common Management Information Services/Common Management Information Protocol (CMIS/CMIP). However, performance of CMIS/CMIP standards have not yet been widely proven in the marketplace. OSI management encompasses both WAN and LAN management, but the estimated overhead scares both vendors and users away.

The Internet Engineering Task Force (IETF) in the United States has also defined standards for the management dialog in networks using the Transmission Control Protocol/Internet Protocol (TCP/IP). Among these standards is the Simple Network Management Protocol (SNMP). The market rapidly embraced SNMP after its introduction in 1988, and the protocol is now a common denominator for management. It will continue to be so for the remainder of this decade.

Figure 1.6 shows an overview of processes and communication links between managers, agents, subagents, and managed objects. These processes are almost the same for all types of protocols; differences occur in respect of the initiator of the communication exchange, contrasting polling- and event-based techniques.

Both SNMP and CMIP are defined as application-layer protocols that use the underlying transport services of the protocol stack. Both protocols use the manager-agent paradigm, whereby an agent, a passive software process residing on a managed device or system, collects data and reports it to the manager, an active software application that typically supports a graphical user interface (GUI). The manager process is user-initiated.

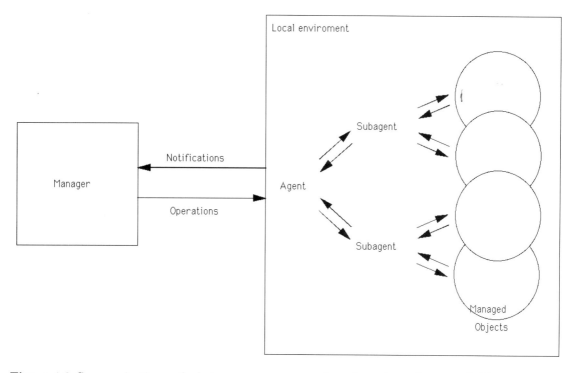

Figure 1.6 Communication paths between manager, agents, subagents, and managed objects

In the SNMP environment, the manager can obtain information from the agent by polling managed objects periodically. Agents can transmit unsolicited event messages, called "traps," to the manager.

 The management data exchanged between managers and agents is called the management information base (MIB). The data definitions outlined in the Structure of Management Information (SMI) must be understood by both managers and agents.

The manager-agent paradigm is central to both SNMP and CMIP architectures. A manager is a software program housed within the management station. The manager has the ability to query agents using various SNMP commands. The management station is also in charge to interpret MIB data, construct views of the systems and networks, compress data, and maintain data in relational or object-oriented databases.

The MIB is a virtual database of managed objects, accessible to an agent and manipulated via SNMP to achieve network management. In addition to the standard SNMP MIB-II defined in Request for Comment (RFC) 1213, the IETF has defined a number of adjunct MIBs covering bridges, repeaters, FDDI networks, AppleTalk networks, and frame relay networks. One of the most important adjunct MIBs is the Remote Monitoring MIB (RMON), which standardizes management variables for monitoring network traffic. The RMON MIB is defined in RFC 1271. (For more information on RMON, see Chapter 3.) Figure 1.7 shows a generic SNMP-based management structure.

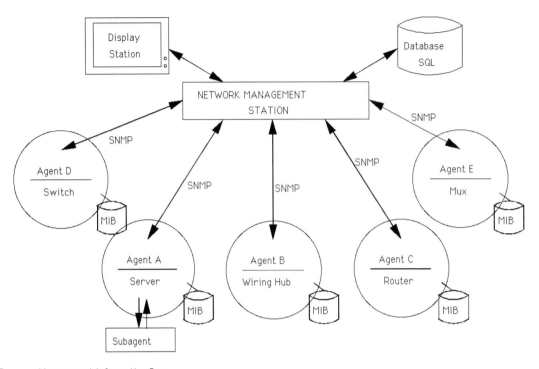

MIB   = Management Information Base
SNMP   = Simple Network Management Protocol

Figure 1.7 Structure of SNMP-based management solutions

For standardizing the manager-agent dialog of enterprise network management, the following items must be carefully considered:

- How will the management information be formatted and how will the information exchange be regulated? This is actually the protocol definition problem.
- How will the management information be transported between manager and agent? The OSI standards employ the OSI protocol stack, and the TCP/IP standards use TCP/IP protocol stack. This is no longer the only solution. Several protocols demonstrate the emerging independence of management protocols from underlying protocol layers. These protocols include CMOT (Common Management Information Protocol over TCP/IP), CMOL (Common Management Information Protocol over Logical Link Control, or LLC), and CMOS (Common Management Information over SNA).

 Both SNMP and OSI employ the concept of managed objects. Managed objects are defined by their attributes, operations that may be performed upon them, and the notification that may result. The set of managed objects in a system, together with their attributes constitute that system's management information base (MIB). In addition to MIBs, the structure of management information (SMI) defines the logical structure of OSI or SNMP management information. The MIB can be extended to include private variables for describing devices or components offered by vendors or developed by users.

In terms of SNMP, the following trends are expected. SNMP agent-level support, already widespread, will be provided by an even greater number of vendors. SNMP manager-level support will be provided by only a few leading vendors in the form of several widely-accepted platforms. Management platforms provide basic services, leaving customization and the development of additional applications to vendors and users. (For more information on platforms, see Chapter 4.)

Wider use of intelligent agents—also called "smart agents," "dual-role agents," or "mid-level managers"—is also expected. Intelligent agents are capable of responding to a manager's request for information and performing certain manager-like functions, including testing for thresholds, filtering, and processing management data. Intelligent agents enable localized polling and filtering on servers, workstations, and hubs, for example. Thus, these agents reduce polling overhead and management data traffic, forwarding only the most critical alerts and processed data to the SNMP manager.

The RMON MIB will help bridge the gap between the limited services provided by management platforms and the rich sets of data and statistics provided by traffic monitors and analyzers. RMON defines the next generation of network monitoring with more comprehensive network fault diagnosis, planning, and performance tuning features than any current monitoring solution. It uses SNMP and its standard MIB is designed to provide multi-vendor interoperability between monitoring products and management stations, allowing users to mix and match network monitors and management stations from different vendors.

The strengths of SNMP include:

- Agents are widely implemented
- Simple to implement
- Agent-level overhead is minimal
- Polling approach is good for LAN-based managed objects
- Robust and extensible
- Offers the best direct manager-agent interface

It met a critical need; it was available and implementable at the right time

In addition, Version 2 of SNMP (SNMPv2) now being implemented in vendor offerings, offers significant security improvements over SNMP version 1.

The weaknesses of SNMP include:

- Too simple, does not scale well
- No object-oriented data view
- Unique semantics make integration with other approaches difficult
- High communication overhead due to polling
- Many implementation-specific (private MIB) extensions
- No standard control definitions
- Small agent (one agent per device) may be inappropriate for systems management. (However, the use of intelligent agents will improve the applicability of SNMP to systems management.)

In contrast, the strengths of OSI-CMIP include:

- General and extensible object-oriented approach
- Support from the telecommunications industry and international vendors
- Support for manager-to-manager communications
- Supports a framework for automation

Weaknesses of OSI-CMIP include:

- It is complex and multilayered
- It incurs high overhead
- Few CMIP-based management systems are shipping
- Few CMIP-based agents are in use

1.4.2   OMNIPoint

A consortium of vendors and users known as the Network Management (NM) Forum is seeking to overcome market resistance to CMIP by promoting a comprehensive integration plan called the OMNIPoint program. These "Open Management Interoperability Points" (OMNIPoints) offer an industry solution to the worldwide problem of managing heterogeneous networks. An OMNIPoint is an agreed approach to the development and procurement of interoperable management systems and their components. OMNIPoints include:

- Standards and profiles
- Industry agreements
- Object definitions
- Supporting technologies

The goals of the OMNIPoint program are to establish intercepts at specific intervals of standards development, to standardize migration rules, to reduce upgrade costs, and to foster technological changes as early as reasonable. (See Figure 1.8.)

OMNIPoint-deliverables concentrate on:

- Guidelines for purchase and development decisions
- Library services including object definitions and object catalogues
- Specification for standards
- Test procedures and tools.

OMNIPoint clarifies communications between management systems using CMIS/X.700 and to managed objects using SNMP, CMIS/X.700 and proprietary protocols. The transport itself is supported by OSI, TCP/IP, UDP/IP, LAN LCC and over proprietary protocol stacks. The internal interfaces include APIs for the user interface, APIs for the Management Information Base, APIs for the communication with CMIP and SNMP agents, and APIs for network management applications.

OMNIPoint does not differentiate between WAN and LAN management; OMNIPoint 1 offers, in particular, the following services:

- Security management
- Problem management

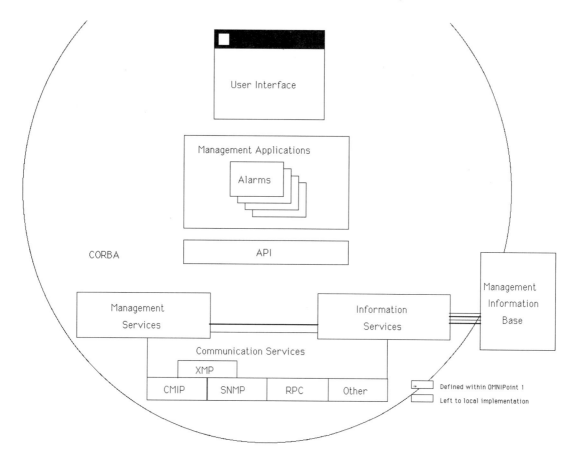

Figure 1.8 OMNIPoint example with services, applications, and interfaces

- Status management
- Alarm and event management

1.4.3   Telecommunications Management Network (TMN)

The NM Forum is also coordinating its OMNIPoint program with the Telecommunications Management Network (TMN) architecture. TMN may be defined as an organized architecture for achieving interconnection between various types of operations support systems and/or telecommunications equipment. TMN incorporates functional information and physical architectures. The Q-interface plays a key role in TMN. Specifically, the Q-reference-point is between two physically separate functional blocks. It is defined by the protocol it uses and the information carried across it.

The TMN management services are different from those recommended by OSI-bodies. In the case of TMN, products have been developed for switching management, tariff and charging administration, management of customer access, materials management, management of transport networks, management of circuits and routes, and staff work scheduling.

TMN plays an important role in offering a standard umbrella for all networks operated by phone companies and network services providers.

1.4.4   Systems Management Standards

Standardization in the area of distributed systems management has been slow. The Open Software Foundation first introduced its Distributed Management Environment (DME) architecture in September 1991. While OSF has been able to deliver some functionality for distributed printing, software licensing, and related services, it was unable to form a consensus on the key object-oriented management framework that was desired in the industry. DME now promotes an API called XMP. Originally designed by Group Bull, XMP does not include support for object request brokers. The Object Management Group (OMG) is working on a Common Object Request Broker Architecture (CORBA) which may yield a standard for object-oriented management communications.

Finally, desktop management has yet to come under the umbrella of enterprise network and systems management in most organizations. An important emerging standard for desktop management is the Desktop Management Interface (DMI). The Desktop Management Task Force (DMTF) had defined the DMI to accomplish the following goals:

- Enable and facilitate desktop, local and network management
- Solve software overlap and storage problems
- Create a standard method for management of hardware and software components
- Provide a common interface for managing desktop computers and their components
- Provide a simple method to describe, access and manage desktop components.

The scope of management under DMTF includes PC CPUs, BIOS, mother boards, video cards, network interface cards, faxes, modems, mass storage, and application software. Figure 1.9 shows the structure and the position of DMI.

1.4.5   Application Programming Interfaces (APIs)

As more network management application software gets written, it is important to define standardized APIs so that the software can be easily ported to different management platforms, and so that software developed by different vendors can be easily combined on a single platform. The management platforms provide a standardized environment for developing and implementing applications, and they also separate management application software from the usual system-level services.

Many independent companies are now offering network and system management applications designed to provide real multi-vendor solutions while taking advantage of the system-level services of platforms. This allows third-party vendors to concentrate on their specific hardware and software while users can focus

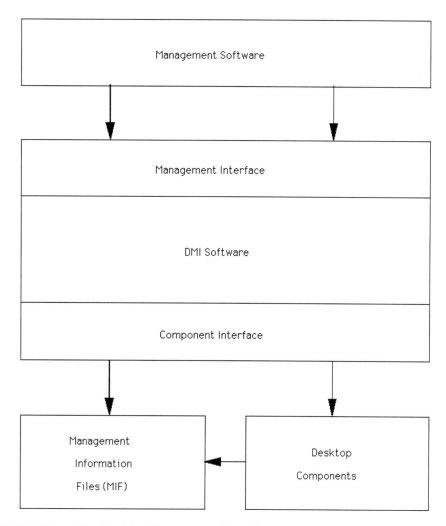

Figure 1.9 Definition of the Desktop Management Interfaces

on the customization and fine tuning of management applications. For more information on these applications, see Chapter 5.

Figure 1.10 shows how applications, platforms, and protocol interface modules work together.

In summary, standards will work together in various combinations. SNMP and CMOL are very important for manager-agent-subagent communications. CMIP and SNMPv2 can serve to support peer-to-peer manager communications. For user interfaces, vendors are implementing Motif, X-Windows, Openlook, and DOS/Windows. In distributed implementations, Remote Procedure Calls (RPC) or object invocation techniques may be used. OSF DME implements XMP (X/Open Management Protocol) in order to shield developers from the specifics of underlying protocols, such as CMIP and SNMP.

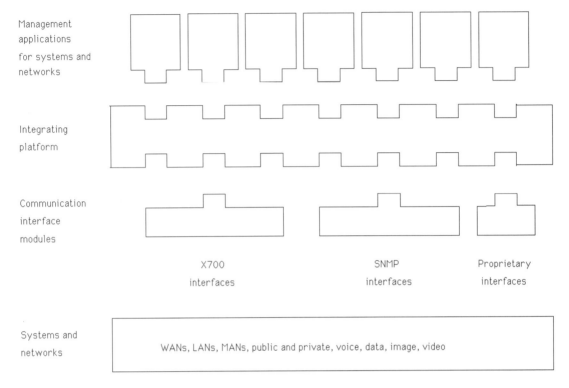

Figure 1.10 Applications, platform, and communication interfaces

1.5   THE CHANGING SCOPE OF SYSTEMS AND
NETWORK MANAGEMENT

Network and systems management have similarities and differences. In both disciplines, a dialog exists between the manager and the managed systems. The manager or supervisor collects alarms, events, status indicators, traffic statistics, and raw accounting data. The manager also issues commands in the form of configuration changes, parameter changes, priority communication resets, authorization changes, activation and deactivation requests, and restart notifications. Managers occasionally distribute software updates, as well.

The basic requirements of network and systems management are also the same: remotely manage fault, configuration, performance, security, and accounting functions. The manager model may be different due to the requirement of distributing parts of the manager to each system. The distributed managers communicate with each other using remote procedure calls (RPCs).

As mentioned previously, the demarcation line between network and systems management is not really clear in client/server environments. In legacy environments this line was a bit more apparent; as in IBM Systems Network Architecture, where the "network" was everything from the front-end processor out.

Figure 1.3 tries to find the demarcation line within networked systems. In this case, the hub's network interface card (NIC) can be defined as the demarcation line, indicating facilities, cables, and NICs as part of the network. Consequently, the other components of the hub are parts of the system. Similar considerations maybe made for routers, bridges, repeaters, extenders, servers, modems, multiplexers, generic gateways, front-end-processors, PBXs, and generic switches.

In general, systems management encompasses a much greater number of managed objects than does network management, owing to the many internal software and hardware components on each managed system. Thus, distributed systems management necessitates powerful and low-overhead management protocols or distributed management architectures.

There are big differences between the level of management intelligence embedded in various systems. Some are quite limited (DOS), while others are quite powerful (large workstations and servers). Usually, users start with server management. Systems management is more sensitive than network management. As a result, there is more emphasis on security issues and more support for users who have the ability to alter system parameters.

Key status and performance indicators for network management are very different than those for systems management. Network management focuses on statistics and indicators such as line status, line utilization, component status, error rates, echo, cross talking, beaconing, collision rate, response time, transfer time, sent/received messages and packets, queue length for facilities, overhead, polling rates, retransmission rates, etc.

Key systems management indicators include CPU utilization, file utilization, disk space availability, memory assignments, process status, application directory, application traffic, active queues, sent/received packets, error rates, inventory data of hardware and software.

Figure 1.11 simplifies the visualization of the management tasks for both systems and network management. The agent is responsible for initiating local supervisory functions, such as data collection on status and traffic monitoring. Depending on the agent's intelligence and sophistication, on-site data compression, filtering, interpretation, and local displays may be supported. Information is exchanged with the manager or managers, either periodically or on-demand. Further processing, correlation, databasing, and displays are supported at the agent level.

The convergence of network and systems management is being driven largely by user organizations. Users are seeking to improve the uptime, availability, and efficiency of their networks and systems without adding staff. Integrating the network and systems management functions under a common technological and organizational framework promises to reduce both staffing requirements and the need to maintain redundant databases and management applications. Chapter 5 describes emerging UNIX systems and PC/LAN systems management applications that can be integrated into an SNMP-based network management framework. Chapter 8 includes an important case study in which the integration of network and systems management is the primary goal. Also, Chapter 9 discusses the convergence of network and systems management in detail.

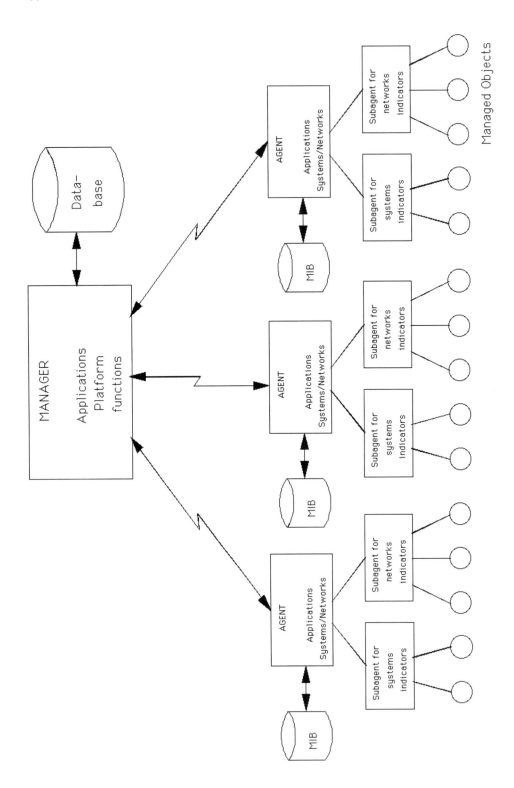

Figure 1.11 Managing systems and networks by sharing the same platform

1.6   SUMMARY

Client/server structures will bring new challenges to the management of systems and networks. Server systems, wide area networks, local area networks, and desktop systems are currently managed very differently (Figure 1.12). By concentrating on critical success factors, such as integrating fragmented solutions, evaluating leading-edge management applications, and targeting staffing issues, organizations can better set priorities for designing, developing, and implementing acceptable solutions.

Despite the current fragmentation of network and systems management solutions in most organizations, the future will bring better integration of management applications under a single management platform and concentration of technical personnel at key networking locations. Applications will play the most important role in meeting challenges. Management applications are expected to become platform-independent, to use application programing interfaces, to be scalable, and to support the ability to communicate not only with the platform, but also with other applications.

To ensure successful management over the next decade, each business must have strategies in place for integration, automation, centralization, database implementation, and outsourcing. These items will be addressed in the following chapters.

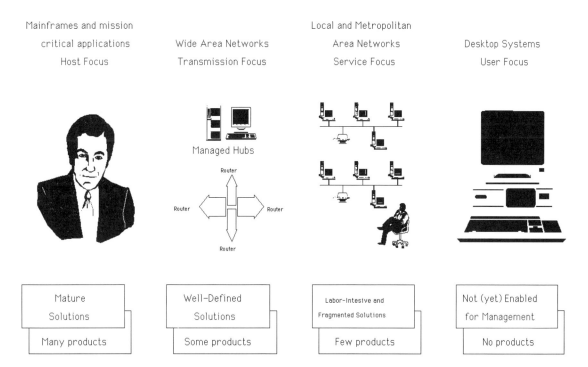

Figure 1.12 Status of current management solutions

2

Management Functions and Processes

2.1 INTRODUCTION

Management processes are critical to the successful operation of systems and networks. This chapter describes a logical business model of management and key management processes involved, including those for change, troubleshooting, performance, security, and accounting. Functions as well as products and applications are introduced.

The starting point for reengineering each management process is the consolidation of the management database. To avoid volume and performance problems, management data describing the logical and physical aspects of the network can be maintained in separate databases. In the future, object-oriented technology will support integration of these segments into one logical database, supporting the use of masks to ensure secure access to data by different applications.

2.2 BUSINESS MODEL OF MANAGING SYSTEMS AND NETWORKS

This chapter discusses principal management functions within the context of a logical business model. This logical model shows the cause-and-effect relationships of key management activities. Ideally, an organization should distribute responsibility for management functions among different groups in a manner that follows this model.

To avoid redundancy, organizations should allocate responsibility for each management function to a single group. However, individuals may be members of more than one group, particularly if the organization is small—although this is not ideal. Data integrity between these business areas or management groups can be guaranteed by implementing the concept of shared management knowledge—for example, use of a common data model or common database.

Figure 2.1 shows the logical model, highlighting management groups within an organization and the information flow between them (*OSI/NM Forum,* 1992). The scope of business areas is based on a hypothetical "average" corporation—it is not the model of a particular corporation.

The logical model identifies eleven key business areas or groups responsible for principal management functions:

- Client contact point
- Operations support
- Fault tracking
- Fault monitoring
- Change control
- Planning and design
- Performance monitoring
- Finance and billing
- Implementation and maintenance
- Security management
- Systems administration

The client or end user is the entry point into the model. The client represents internal or external customers or any other users who make use of management services. Clients may report problems, ask for changes, or request information. Their point of interface is the client contact point—a single point of contact for handling all client problems, changes, and inquiries. The Client Contact Point may be implemented as a help desk, providing "first level" support for users. The primary functions of the Client Contact Point are listed in Table 2-1.

The Operations Support group receives trouble-tickets from the Client Contact Point. The principal responsibilities of the Operations Support group are listed in Table 2-2. The Operations Support group provides both second and third level

TABLE 2-1   Client Contact Point Functions

Separation of network and systems management

Separation of logical and physical management

Separate management of active and passive components

Separation by network architecture

Separate management of WANs, MANs, LANs, systems, and desktops

Lack of integrated alarm management

Lack of integrated trouble ticketing

Lack of clear understanding of Application Programming Interfaces (APIs)

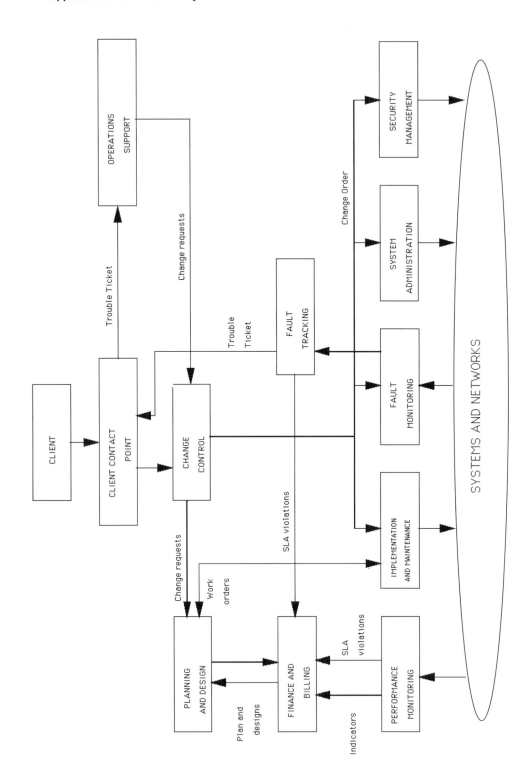

Figure 2.1 Model of managing systems and networks

TABLE 2-2   Responsibilities of the Operations Support Group

Problem determination (handling trouble tickets)

Problem diagnosis

Taking corrective actions

Repair and replacement

Referring to third-party maintenance providers or vendors when necessary

Backup and reconfiguration

Recovery

Logging events and corrective actions

---

support. Second-level support involves problem determination and a limited amount of troubleshooting. Third level support is required when it becomes necessary to involve equipment vendors, service providers, or third-party maintenance organizations in the resolution of the problem.

Once troubleshooting and problem diagnosis are complete, change requests are sent to the Change Control group. In some instances, management software may automatically report problems to Operations Support. When this occurs, automatically-generated trouble tickets are opened and forwarded to Operations Support via the Fault Tracking group. The goal of this group is to proactively detect problems, opening and referring trouble tickets when necessary. Principal responsibilities of the Fault Tracking group are listed in Table 2-3.

Supervising and correcting service quality-related problems is the central activity of the entire management process. The Change Control group plays a key role in maintaining service quality. The principal responsibilities of the Change Control group include the following:

- Managing, processing, and tracking service orders
- Routing service orders
- Supervising the handling of changes

TABLE 2-3   Principal Responsibilities of the Fault Tracking Group

---

Tracking manually reported or automatically detected faults

Tracking the progress and escalating problems if necessary

Distributing information

Referring problems to technicians when necessary

The end result of these activities is the creation of validated change requests, which are forwarded to the Planning and Design group. The functions of the Planning and Design group are listed in Table 2-4. The Planning and Design group distributes its output (including purchase orders, implementation plans, etc.) to the Finance and Billing group and the Implementation and Maintenance group.

The Finance and Billing group acts as a focal point for receiving high-level information about network status, Service Level Agreement violations, plans, designs, changes, and invoices from vendors and third-party maintenance organizations. The responsibilities of the Finance and Billing group are listed in Table 2-5.

The Implementation and Maintenance group implements the changes and work orders sent by both the Planning and Design and Change Control groups. In addition, the Implementation and Maintenance group is in charge of:

- Maintaining resources
- Conducting inspections
- Maintaining configuration database(s)
- Provisioning components

TABLE 2-4 Planning and Design Group Functions

Needs analysis

Projecting application load

Sizing resources (planning and design)

Authorizing and tracking changes

Raising purchase orders

Producing implementation plans

Establishing company standards

TABLE 2-5 Responsibilities of the Finance and Billing Group

Asset management

Costing services

Billing clients

Collecting reports on usage and outages

Calculating rebates to clients

Verifying bills

Throughout the entire cycle of events, the Performance Monitoring group is collecting status and performance information by using software and probes to continuously monitor the systems and networks. The primary responsibilities of the Performance Monitoring group are listed in Table 2-6. The Performance Monitoring group informs the Finance and Billing group about the status of service quality. In some cases, Performance Monitoring may be further subdivided into Fault Monitoring. In this case, Fault Monitoring opens trouble tickets and sends them to Fault Tracking.

The Security Management group is responsible for insuring secure communications and for protecting the management systems. The specific responsibilities of the Security Management group are listed in Table 2-7.

Finally, the Systems Administration group is responsible for administering the whole distributed processing environment. The responsibilities of the Systems Administration group are listed in Table 2-8. Systems administration is a key activity that requires the coordination of many tools and utilities. Systems administration in the distributed computing environment is a nascent technology.

The level of technical sophistication may vary widely between management groups. Consequently, the activities of each group are supported by a wide variety of management systems and software. Figure 2.2 shows what types of products and applications assist the various groups in this logical business model of management.

TABLE 2-6   Responsibilities of the Performance Monitoring Group

Monitoring system and network performance

Monitoring Service Level Agreements

Monitoring third-party and vendor performance

Optimizing, tuning, and modeling networks and systems

Reporting (usage statistics and trends)

TABLE 2-7   Responsibilities of the Security Management Group

Threat analysis

Administration (access control, partitioning, authentication)

Detection (services, solutions)

Disaster recovery (services, solutions)

Protecting management systems and applications

TABLE 2-8   Responsibilities of the Systems Administration Group

---

Software version control

Software distribution

Systems management (upgrades, disk space, jobs)

Administering user-definable tables and structures (e.g., user profiles, route tables, security levels)

Local and remote resource configuration

Directory services

Name and address management

Applications management

2.3   MANAGEMENT TOOLS

Most organizations currently use some combination of the products described below. Eventually, as organizations transition to the platform/applications model of management, many of these stand-alone products will take the form of applications integrated onto an open management platform. (For more information on platforms and applications, see Chapters 4 and 5.)

Management Integrators
   These products supervise and control multiple element management systems and management objects, using a variety of management applications, standardized user interfaces, and multiple gateways to communicate with SNMP, CMIP, and proprietary agents.

WAN Element Management Systems (EMSs)
   These products supervise and control a homogeneous family of managed objects in the WAN area, such as modems, multiplexers, switches, cellular units, cable television, ATM, and Sonet, by using a variety of device-specific management applications, standardized user interfaces, and multiple gateways to communicate with SNMP, CMIP, and proprietary agents.

LAN Element Management Systems (EMSs)
   These products supervise and control a homogeneous family of managed objects in the LAN area, such as Ethernet segments, Token Ring segments, routers, bridges, repeaters, brouters, and hubs using a variety of device-specific management applications, standardized user interfaces, and multiple gateways to communicate with SNMP, CMIP, and proprietary agents.

WAN monitors
   These special-purpose tools continuously measure key fault and performance indicators in various locations of the WAN.

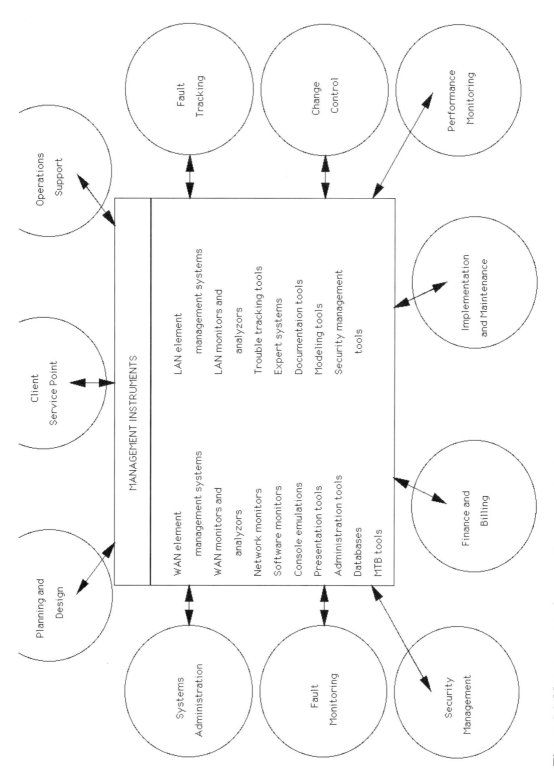

Figure 2.2 Management tools supporting various business areas

WAN analyzers

WAN analyzers are dedicated to diagnosing faults and performance bottlenecks in various locations of the WANs.

LAN monitors

These special-purpose tools continuously measure key fault and performance indicators in various locations and segments of the LANs.

LAN analyzers

LAN analyzers, also called protocol analyzers, are designed to diagnose faults and performance bottlenecks in various locations or segments of the LANs.

Network monitors

These products extract, process, and report collected traffic information utilizing published data communication interfaces. They target the continuous supervision of complete networks, usually using sampling technology.

Software monitors

These products are software-based utilities that extract, process, and report collected traffic information utilizing published data communication interfaces. They target the continuous supervision of complete networks, usually using sampling technology.

Console emulators

This special-purpose software can represent multiple element management systems, monitors, and analyzers as windows on state-of-the-art workstations, supporting some degree of centralized management. If necessary, the windows allow operators to cut through to the systems experiencing problems.

Presentation tools

This is a generic term for all tools that process data stored in various databases and present it to users in various forms such as lists, tables, graphs, pie charts, or other user-customizable forms.

Administration tools

A generic term for all tools that are responsible for administering components of networks and systems. Included are tasks like asset management, software distribution, documenting changes, and information distribution services.

Databases

This generic group of tools supports the maintenance of configuration, performance, trouble tickets, contracts, and other data in relational or object-oriented databases. Products in this category include database management systems (but populating them remains the responsibility of the users).

MIB tools

This group of tools helps populate MIBs and retrieve information from MIBs using a browser.

Trouble tracking tools

These are special-purpose applications that open, dispatch, track, and close trouble tickets. Also included are processing, notification, and reporting features.

Expert systems

These tools automatically determine and diagnose complex management-related problems using rules and actual input from various measurement and management systems. Both off-line and on-line operational alternatives are supported.

Documentation tools

These products are tightly coupled with administration and configuration management tools. Their principal goal is to maintain the actual status of managed objects, their connectivity, and their dynamic indicators.

Modeling tools

These tools predict future service quality and utilization of networking and systems resources using simulation, emulation, or applied queueing technology.

Security management tools

These tools help with the authorization and authentication of usage of systems and networking resources to protect against viruses and to protect the network and systems management products.

The general applicability of each tool for various management groups is shown in Table 2-9.

2.4   MANAGEMENT DATABASE

Documentation of networks and systems is the basis for practically all other network and systems management functions. Network documentation is particularly critical for effective configuration management and change control. The next section describes the present status of typical management database implementations.

2.4.1   Contemporary Management Database Implementations

In most organizations, network and systems documentation is often segmented according to geographical location, communication forms, network architectures, and vendors. There may be separate databases for each type of information. As a result, there is a high level of redundancy of data elements in different databases and files.

To compound the problem, many organizations maintain network and systems documentation manually. Documentation is usually out of date due to lack of automated change management procedures. For example, cable management software is rarely integrated with other network management applications. In many cases, cable management applications do not even support relational database management systems (RDBMSs) or an object-oriented database.

2.4.2   The Configuration Database: A Better Solution

To better support network and systems management functions, a configuration database with a relational or object-oriented structure should become a central component in an organization's management strategy (See Figure 2.3). The ele-

TABLE 2-9 Management Tools and Groups

Tools	Client Point Contact	Planning and Design	Finance and Billing	Implementation and Maintenance	Systems Administration	Change Control	Performance Maintenance	Security Management	Fault Monitoring	Fault Tracking	Operation Support
Integrators	✓						✓	✓	✓	✓	✓
WAN EMS	✓						✓	✓	✓		✓
LAN EMS	✓			✓			✓	✓	✓		✓
WAN Monitors				✓			✓		✓		✓
LAN Monitors				✓			✓		✓		✓
WAN Analyzers				✓			✓		✓		✓
LAN Analyzers				✓			✓		✓		✓
Network Monitors				✓			✓		✓		✓
Software Monitors					✓		✓		✓		✓
Console Emulators	✓				✓		✓	✓	✓	✓	✓
Presentation Tools	✓				✓		✓				
Administration Tools	✓				✓					✓	
Databases	✓	✓	✓	✓	✓	✓	✓	✓	✓	✓	✓
MIB Tools					✓						
Trouble-Tracking Tools	✓					✓				✓	
Expert Systems							✓		✓	✓	✓
Documentation Tools	✓	✓	✓	✓	✓	✓					
Modeling Tools		✓		✓	✓						
Security Mgmt. Tools								✓			

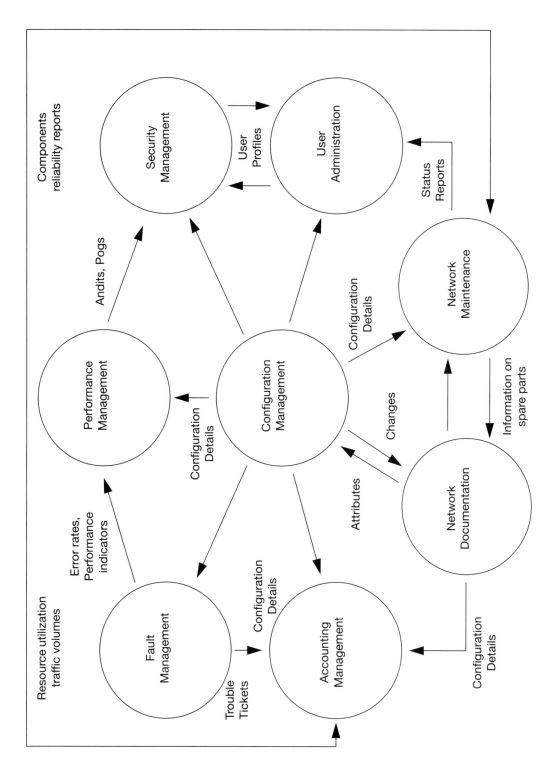

Figure 2.3 Central role of configuration management

ments in the configuration database can be described as "instances of predefined objects" residing in a standard library of network and systems objects. Examples of these objects include hubs, multiplexers, modems, servers, cables, routers, bridges, desktops, media access units, disks, CPUs, and software components. Ideally, the configuration database supports links to a performance database, providing some degree of history of the state of network and systems configuration. Of particular importance is the capability to create a report or display showing the network state immediately after the execution of approved changes, as well as network state immediately prior to those changes.

The configuration database may be considered a subset of the inventory database. An inventory lists attributes of all network and system components including hardware and software. Attributes may include component ID, user phone, vendor contact, etc.

The third type of a database, called asset database, may also be incorporated into an integrated database structure.

2.4.2.1   Populating the Configuration Database

There are various methods for populating the configuration database, including manual data entry, use of default templates, automatic discovery, augmenting discovery, and importing data.

Manual entry involves typing in data object information via keyboard. While this is time consuming, the process can be accelerated by using graphical user interfaces (GUIs) and Application Programming Interfaces (APIs.) Default templates for specific network elements have certain attributes prespecified so that repetitive typing can be avoided.

Automatic discovery facilities of various network management platforms and applications electronically survey a network to detect the presence or absence of particular resources. If a resource is discovered, a special application may automatically generate an object based on its template, and fill in the discoverable attributes. Information obtained from discovery processes often is augmented by manual entry of certain attributes that cannot be discovered automatically.

Import tools allow object information to be transferred from existing or external management systems or databases.

Table 2.10 lists examples of certain managed objects, including the generic definition for each object and the most frequently used attributes. Examples of managed objects include:

- Equipment
- Facility
- Service
- Circuit
- Application and systems software
- Location (site)

The Network Management Forum publishes periodical updates to recommended objects and attributes typically used in OSI systems. In official documents, Abstract Syntax Notation-1 (ASN.1) is used to describe the details of

TABLE 2-10 Managed Object Attributes

Class Name	Class Definition	Data Elements
Equipment	A physical unit. Equipment may be nested within equipment, thereby creating a parent/child relationship. A facility is supported by equipment at each end. Equipment may also connect or terminate circuits. Equipment includes telecommunication systems that provide a service to an end-user, the management systems that are used to manage such systems, and the end-user hosts and terminals. Equipment also includes physical units of functionality within these systems (e.g.,CPU).	Equipment type Equipment ID Equipment alias Equipment status Equipment release Parent equipment ID Child equipment IDs Location ID Network IDs Customer IDs Provider IDs Service IDs Vendor IDs EMS IDs (= equipment IDs) Contact IDs Effective time
Facility	A physical connection between equipment in two different equipments without any intervening equipment. A facility is geographically distributed functionality and excludes the equipment within the associated equipments. The function of a facility is to support the transport of circuits (0 or more).	Facility type Facility ID Facility alias Facility status Endpoints (= 1 or, if known, 2 equipment IDs) Network IDs Vendor ID Effective time EMS IDs Contact IDs
Service	An offering from a single provider which supplies a specific network functionality to one or more customers.	Service type Service ID Service alias Provider ID Contact ID

(continues next page)

attributes. Attributes are classified as mandatory (e.g., what attributes an object must contain), optional (e.g., what attributes an object *may* contain), and the operations performed on the object (e.g., create and delete notifications).

2.4.2.2   Integrated Database

To maximize efficiency and levels of automation of management functions, multiple configuration databases should be merged into an integrated database. An

TABLE 2-10 Managed Object Attributes *(continued)*

Class Name	Class Definition	Data Elements

Circuit	A logical point-to-point connection between two end equipments which traverses one or more facilities and possibly one or more intermediate pieces of equipment. Circuits may be simple or complex. A simple circuit is supported by two end pieces of equipment and an interconnecting facility. A complex circuit is supported as well by intermediate equipments and additional facilities. In general, a complex circuit consists of an ordered sequence of (1) less complex circuits of the same bandwidth and (2) associated cross-connects within any intermediate equipments.
	A parent/child relationship may also exist between circuits in that a circuit may share the bandwidth of another circuit.
		Circuit type
		Circuit ID
		Circuit status
		Circuit bandwidth
		Endpoints
		  (= equipment IDs)
		Facility IDs (1 or more)
		Parent circuit ID
		Child circuit IDs
		Component circuit IDs
		  (for complex circuits)
		Cross-connect IDs
		  (for complex circuits)
		Circuit group ID
		Network ID
		Customer ID
		Provider ID
		Service IDs
		Effective time
		EMS IDs
		Contact IDs

Application and system software	Program having responsibility for executing applications and systems-related tasks.	Software type Software ID Versions and level Options Fixes Warranty information Date installed/removed
Location	A place occupied by one or more managed objects or persons associated with object management.	Location type Location ID Location alias Customer ID Provider ID Parent location ID

integrated database is capable of generating all configuration views of various network and systems software and hardware components. If the integrated database is properly implemented, organizations can realize the following benefits:

- Less redundancy
- Synchronized change management
- Unique names and addresses
- More efficient troubleshooting
- Easier capacity and contingency planning

International standards committees have been trying to make progress in the area of integrated databases. In particular, ISO has defined four aspects of managing elements in an object-oriented, integrated database, including the following:

Existence A managed object exists if it has an object identifier and an associated set of management information that is accessible through OSI Management services. Managed objects can be created or deleted. To create a managed object, the user places the object's identifier and a set of information appropriate to the object's class into the MIB.

Attributes These describe properties of the object, such as operational characteristics. An attribute has an ID and a value. During the object's existence, only the values can be changed; the attributes themselves can neither be created nor deleted.

State This represents the instantaneous condition of the object's availability and operability. For example, a multiplexer's state may be represented as 11, meaning available and operable. Conversely, state 10 may indicate available, but inoperable.

Relationship These define the interdependence between the managed object in question and other managed objects. For example, a relationship exists between an OSI terminal and the OSI packet switch that provides protocol processing and routing for that terminal.

The management information base (MIB) represents a virtual store of all managed object data. However, it is not under ISO's purview to physically or logically define MIBs.

In the TCP/IP world, the MIB concept has been implemented in many products that support the Simple Network Management Protocol (SNMP). For OSI environments, CMIP-based MIB updates are available from the Network Management Forum.

2.4.2.3   Structure of Management Information

Both CMIP and SNMP incorporate a defined structure of management information (SMI) for specifying how a MIB should look. While the CMIP SMI and the SNMP SMI share some similarities, they differ markedly in their implementations. Understanding these SMIs is essential for constructing an integrated management database.

The OSI SMI standard is called the Guidelines for the Definition of Managed Objects (GDMO), and it is defined in ISO 1064. The GDMO defines the logical structure of OSI management information—that is, any information exchanged in OSI management communications. This information is structured in terms of managed objects, their attributes, the operations performed on them, and the notifications that objects may issue. The GDMO standard defines managed object concepts within the OSI information model and sets out the principles for naming the managed objects and their attributes. Objects must be named in order to be identified in OSI management protocols, such as the Common Management Information Protocol (CMIP).

The GDMO also defines a number of subobject types and attribute types that are, in principle, applicable to all classes of managed objects. These definitions include the common semantics of the object/attribute types, the operations performed upon them, and the notifications they issue. The definitions also cover the relationships that may hold between the various types.

The SNMP SMI standard is described in Request for Comment 1442 (RFC 1442). The SNMP SMI defines how information is structured and the rules for writing a Management Information Base (MIB). Like the GDMO, the SNMP SMI also uses ASN.1 to specify the schema for the SNMP MIB database. However, that is essentially where the similarity ends. The SNMP SMI describes generic information types including integer, octet string, object ID, and null. This is but a subset of the generic information types defined by the OSI GDMO. SNMP MIB attributes are defined differently by the SNMP SMI. Each SNMP MIB attribute supports access levels of read-only, read-write, write-only, or not accessible. The implementation requirement for MIB objects is either mandatory, optional, or obsolete. Finally, object identifiers (names) are described in integer notation (Rose, 1990).

2.4.2.4   Manipulating the Database

To use the configuration database, operators must be able to query the database and set attribute values. For both queries and setting of values, database access is supported by standard Remote Procedure Calls (RPCs). Finally, all database queries and sets must be logged.

The query function allows operators to obtain information about any attribute of any object. Queries are directed to the database or/and to the managed object depending on where the attributes are instantiated.

Setting functions are limited by attributes and by the user's authorization. Only writable attributes can be set or reset. When attributes are modified, changes are made first to the managed object (e.g., networking device) and then to the device's internal management database. To facilitate this process, many vendors provide guidelines for setting managed objects' attributes. Changes to device attributes may occur simultaneously, in a specific order, or within a timing window. Successful setting is the prerequisite for initiating networks and systems operations.

Logging records all modifications to the network. Logged data may include the ID of the user making the change, the management station from which the change was made, the time of change, the substance of the change, and any comments made during the change. Event synchronization is required for appropriate event time stamping and for understanding the sequence of occurrences. It is also required for coordinating changes.

Network topology changes may be executed by manipulating the database in the same way as systems attributes changes. Topology can be "instantiated" in (described by) the attributes of the managed elements. Network device vendors typically support mechanisms allowing users to add, delete, and modify the relationships among network resources. Also, many devices can be upgraded or expanded without taking all or part of the network down. This is particularly important because many network conditions (such as congested routes, disaster recovery priorities, backup capabilities, etc.) necessitate connectivity or relationship changes.

2.4.2.5   Directory Services

Directory services provide a more or less temporary solution for accessing and updating configuration management information stored in various systems, databases, and files. These systems may be network elements, or they may be management systems that maintain data about the specific network elements they control and manage. These systems may also be applications that run on a variety of processors and operating systems. Although applications do not control or manage network elements directly, they play an integral part in managing information about these elements.

A directory service is needed to maintain a centralized logical view of the data stored in the attached network management systems. The view is "logical" because the data may actually physically reside in many different systems. A directory service supports "location independence," whereby applications can be written without regard to a specific DBMS. Database calls are simply made to the directory in a standard format. The directory then forwards the data request to the appropriate system for processing. Each remote system participating with the directory translates the data request into the correct database call for its particular DBMS and its particular schema. For example, the addition of a performance management application to the integrated network management system would require interfaces to multiple systems.

Some organizations use products such as Boole and Babbage Command/Post to gather network-related performance data. In SNA environments, products such as Legent's NetSpy perform the same function. (For more information about Command/Post, see Chapter 5. For more information about NetSpy, see Chapter 6.) These products support interfaces to the integrated network management system, allowing the sending of performance threshold alarms. However, these products to not transfer the entire volume of performance data generated; rather, this data is accessed only when needed by the performance application. A directory service provides a standard way to access this data from each performance monitor.

Another requirement for this type of directory services is to facilitate interfaces to other customer applications, such as inventory and change management.

Many large organizations have inventory applications supporting the administration of the network elements comprising their corporate networks. The more than 100 different inventory applications available store data in a multitude of relational and proprietary database management systems. In the past, these inventory applications were usually mainframe based, since they support more than 100 simultaneous users. New client/server inventory applications are starting to appear.

Integrated network management systems, particularly SNMP-based management platforms, do not include inventory applications as part of the base product. However, organizations are increasingly demanding the ability to pass configuration information obtained from the management system directly to inventory applications in real time. When configuration changes are made to one system accessing the director the update is automatically propagated to all other systems requiring the data.

A directory service should also support the concept of multiple directories in a shared environment. This would allow for another copy of the directory to be running on mainframes. These shared directories communicate any and all directory changes to each other. The shared directory concept allows users to write and access integrated network management applications without affecting the performance of the integrated network management system.

An example of this would be a user-written program to obtain a listing of all the terminals in the network that had less than 10 percent utilization for the last 30 days from the performance database. The same program could then extract location and contact information from the inventory database. This may allow the user to reallocate underutilized corporate assets. By accessing a copy of the directory, this program can obtain all the information it needs without adding any processing constraints to the processor of the integrated network management system.

A directory service should provide reasonable response times to users accessing data. Access to the directory and forwarding of requests to the appropriate system should not add significantly to the response time. The response time incurred when accessing any system directly should only slightly increase when accessed through the directory.

A directory service should manage updates to multiple systems. If an update requires records stored in several systems to be updated, some type of integrity locking must be performed on those records in each system. These locks should not be released until confirmation of a successful update has been returned from each system or until some time threshold has been exceeded. If a successful acknowledgment is received from each system participating in the update, the locks should be released. Otherwise, the update should be aborted and backed out from each of the systems participating in the update.

A directory service should also incorporate a security scheme. This allows customers to define which terminals, user IDs, and applications may access different types of data. The security scheme also defines what type of access they can have: read, update, add, or delete.

Directory services include the OSI X.500 standard, de facto schemes such as Sun's Yellow Pages (now called Network Information Services, NIS), and the Internet Domain Name Service (DNS).

It is important for users to stay current on the progress of directory service standards. Various standards committees are currently working to define how directory services attributes can be used to support distributed database access.

2.4.2.6   Import/Export

Database import/export facilities must be defined very clearly to avoid blocking and performance bottlenecks while the facilities are in use. The database import/

export feature is intended to allow customers to load and extract data from the database of the integrated network management system. This feature should be designed to allow customers flexibility in determining which fields they want to load and extract.

Import. Many users have information about their network elements stored in a variety of inventory and other databases. Much of this information makes up the optional fields and attributes in the configuration message set and in the configuration database. In many cases, this information (such as user or vendor contact and location) already exists in other systems. By using import features, customers avoid having to enter the data again. For example, customers can write an extract or unload program against these databases to create a file with the information needed to populate these fields in the database of the integrated network management product. This file can then be sent to the integrated network management product with some type of file transfer program. Operators can then load the file into the database using some type of load program or utility.

Export. This is the ability to extract fault and configuration information from the database of the integrated network management system. This information can then be transmitted for input into an inventory application or problem tracking and availability application. To export data, users need access to an internally developed user interface to download the tables, records, and fields they need into a file. Again, this file is transmitted to the server, where additional customer-written programs process the data into new files for loading into these other systems.

Logging. An integrated management system should also keep a log of any changes made to the configuration database, allowing operators to extract information on changes. The log should keep track of changes for a user-defined time frame (i.e., 24 hours, three days, or one week).

2.4.2.7   Other Database Applications

State-of-the-art management protocols allow operators and applications to examine the attributes associated with resources and the current values of these resources. For example, SNMP-based management platforms and applications can interrogate the status of specific MIB attributes. The ability to compare the actual status of networks and systems with the specified/expected status stored in the database is very important. The differences may be periodically reported or alarmed, based on the significance of the difference. This feature supports security management by identifying and reporting unknown stations on the network.

One of the biggest problems today is controlling software versions in client/server structures. Organizations are increasingly distributing software releases and new versions electronically throughout the network. This requires facilities to permit software loading requests, to transmit the specified versions of software, to notify operators at the completion of the software loading, and to update the configuration management database.

   If the downline loading fails, it is necessary to return a previous software version. This change must be controlled remotely from the management system. This function is usually continued with software licensing, helping the organization honor user agreements. Licensing is a typical accounting function. The Open Software Foundation (OSF) has specified solutions for both distribution and licensing functions.

   Finally, notification of configuration changes must be distributed to users and clients. This is usually accomplished electronically, with remotely printed configuration change status reports. Reports focus on network connectivity, network topology, systems, attributes, and actual values after settings. These reports maybe combined with notifications informing clients about preventive maintenance actions. Table 2-11 lists typical database and documentation applications.

2.5   CHANGE MANAGEMENT PROCESSES

   Change management is a near-realtime activity. The quality of this process impacts many related activities, such as configuration and fault and perfor-

TABLE 2-11   Typical Database and Documentation Instruments

Tools	Primary Use	Secondary Use
Integrators		
WAN EMS		
LAN EMS		
WAN Monitors		
LAN Monitors		
WAN Analyzers		
LAN Analyzers		
Network Monitors		
Software Monitors		
Console Emulators		✔
Presentation Tools		
Administration Tools		✔
Databases		
MIB Tools	✔	
Trouble-Tracking Tools		
Expert Systems		
Documentation Tools	✔	
Modeling Tools		✔
Security Management Tools		

mance management. The following section summarizes the present status of change management processes in most organizations.

2.5.1 Present Change Management Processes

In many organizations, change management is supported manually and is, therefore, a very slow process. In many instances, if organizations took the time to re-engineer their existing procedures, they could eliminate unnecessary steps.

The periodical change management processes in most organizations today do not match the timeliness required by present networks. Furthermore, the typical change management processes in place in most companies do not guarantee integrity between change and fault management.

Often, there exist unnecessary differences between change requests initiated by clients, performance analysts, operators, and vendors. Synchronization of the configuration database is not always supported in a timely manner.

The Change Control group should be the focal point of change management activities. Basically, there are two different types of change requests or service orders:

Preprovisioned requests dealing with minor changes These may be accepted by the Client Contact Point (help desk) without double-checking with other management groups.

Non-preprovisioned requests dealing with major changes These require a coordinated approach between various management groups.

2.5.2 Pre-Provisioned Change Requests

Preprovisioned change requests are depicted in Figure 2.4. Typically, these change requests arrive from one of two sources: the Client Contact Point or the Operations Support group.

In the first case, clients (users) send service orders (in the form of change requests) to the Client Contact Point. Changes may take the form of scheduled network, system or software upgrades, ongoing network and systems evolution, moves, adds, and resetting of certain parameters. Depending on the nature of the change, the Planning and Design group may be involved, although this can be too time-consuming to be effective. The Client Contact Point receives the requests, evaluates their completeness, classifies them, and forwards them to the Change Control group. The Operations Support group sends other types of requests to the Change Control group; these are in most cases fixes or emergency changes required to reassure operations. In any case, the Change Control group evaluates the content of each request before approval for execution or before forwarding them to the Planning and Design group for further evaluation. The use of standard change request forms containing the information listed in Table 2-12 is recommended.

Change request forms are usually provided and updated electronically. If the Change Control group is dissatisfied with the completeness of the form, requests

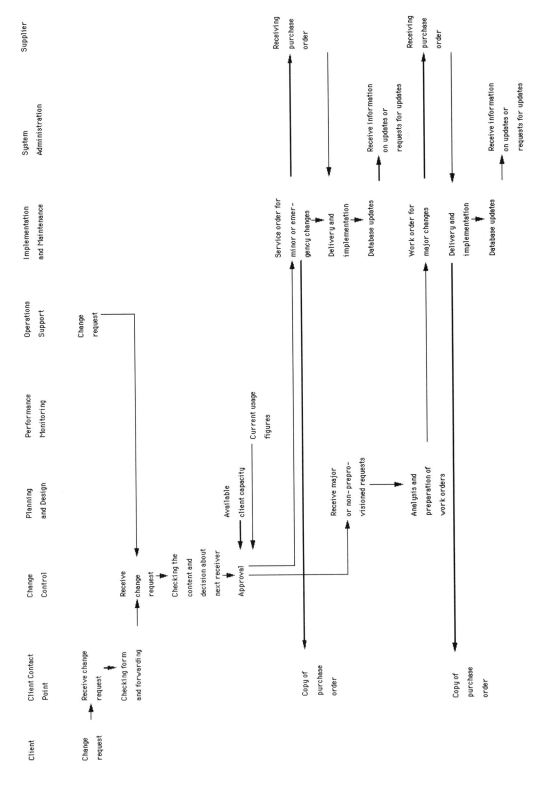

Figure 2.4 Preprovisioned change management process

TABLE 2-12 Information Contained in Standard Change Request Forms

Segment	Information
Change coordinator	Identification of the change Change number Date of request

Requester	Requester name and affiliation
	Location
	Change description
	Network components involved by inventory identification
	Network components affected by change:
	    minor impact = change nondisruptive
	    regular impact = change may be disruptive
	    major impact = change disruptive
	Due date
	Priority
	Reason for change
	Personnel involved in executing the change
	Fallback procedure when change fails

Approval	Date of approval Signature
Evaluation	Result of change Downtime due to change Date of actual implementation Cancellation or postponement

must be sent back to their originators for improvement. End users must typically be taught to use change request forms: after the second or third refusal, persons making change requests learn how to fill in the forms. Occasional consultation is necessary with the Planning and Design group to ensure that the client still has adequate capacity (e.g., bandwidth or ports in multiplexers) to handle the change. Also the Performance Monitoring group may be asked to provide usage statistics on the resource involved in the change. In minor changes, these dialogs are usually unnecessary.

The approval form contains accurate scheduling and responsibilities for other management groups. Frequently, single changes may invoke a chain of additional change requests. The Change Control group may have to use automated project management tools to supervise changes. Approval is granted for minor changes (or emergency changes) to the Implementation and Maintenance group. In case of major changes, the Planning and Design group issues the work orders. In either case (but with different urgency) purchase orders are issued to the suppliers. After delivery of parts and components, changes can be implemented, followed by tests and the necessary database updates. Documentation of the change control process includes:

- Approval reports
- Change summaries

- Components affected by changes
- Implementation schedules

Finally, the System Administration group and the Client Contact Point are provided with the documentation for executed purchase orders and changes.

2.5.3   Non-Preprovisioned Change Requests

Figure 2.5 shows the flow of non-preprovisioned change requests or service orders. The provisioning of such orders requires a complete specification of the order, to design and implement the modifications necessary to the existing network. The Client Contact Point forwards the order after logging it to the Change Control group. Change requests are assigned when the content of the request is complete. The same form may be used as with preprovisioned change orders. The Planning and Design group must become much more involved in handling non-preprovisioned change requests than with preprovisioned change requests. Using an accurate representation of the current inventory, configuration, and spare capacity on facilities and equipment, the modifications and extensions can be designed. The design has to be evaluated in terms of technological and financial feasibility. The Finance and Billing department must also issue their approval. Upon receiving the approval, detailed designs and plans are produced. Modeling tools may be used to evaluate disaster scenarios and validate the design. The Change Control group bases approval of the change request on these designs and plans. The Planning and Design group then produces a detailed implementation plan which details all activities that must be completed to execute the order. It defines work order packages, dependencies, and time scales. After the approval, Client Control Point confirms the order to the client.

The Change Control group tracks the execution of the implementation plan. The Planning and Design group must immediately report any deadline violations to the Change Control group. After receiving the approved change request, the Planning and Design group allocates equipment and bandwidth and informs Finance and Billing of ordered assets. Purchase orders are then sent to the suppliers and progress is tracked by the Planning and Design group.

After the Implementation and Maintenance group carries out the work orders, it will begin testing. The group must report all major milestones to the Planning and Design group. The Change Control group receives supervisory information from the Planning and Design group

After printing the final provisioning report, an "order completed" message may be sent to the Client. After approval, the service order maybe closed, inventory and configuration databases will be updated, and billing will be started.

Typical applications that support the change management processes are listed in Table 2.13.

2.6   THE FAULT HANDLING PROCESS

By necessity, fault management is a realtime activity. As a result, the functions of fault management must address various phases of problem determination.

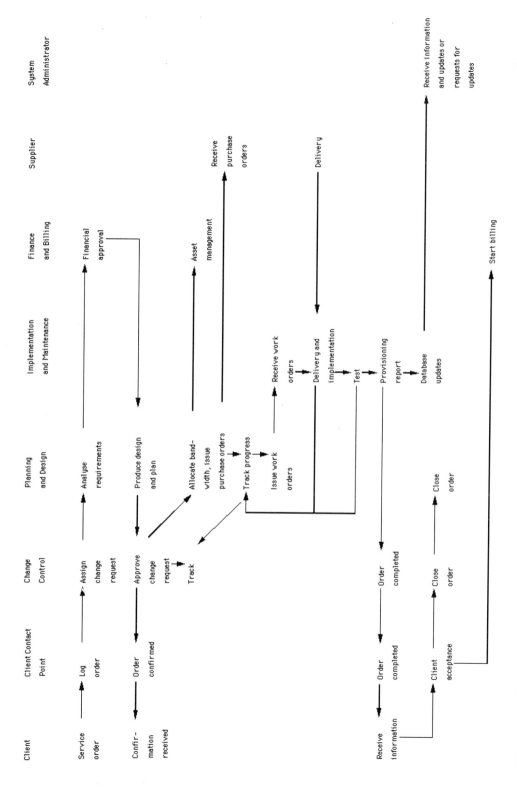

Figure 2.5 Non-preprovisioned change management process

TABLE 2-13   Typical Tools for Change Management

Tools	Primary Use	Secondary Use
Management Integrators	✔	
WAN EMS	✔	
LAN EMS	✔	
WAN Monitors		
LAN Monitors		
WAN Analyzers		
LAN Analyzers		
Network Monitors		
Software Monitors		
Console Emulators		✔
Presentation Tools		✔
Administration Tools	✔	
Databases	✔	
MIB Tools		
Trouble-Tracking Tools	✔	
Expert Systems		
Documentation Tools	✔	
Modeling Tools		
Security Management Tools		

The following section summarizes the present status of fault management in many end user organizations.

2.6.1   Status of Fault Management

It is extremely difficult, if not impossible, for most businesses to carry on with daily operations if important network and systems elements have failed and appropriate backup components and procedures do not exist. Unfortunately, backup is becoming increasingly expensive, driving customers to consider outsourcing network and systems management.

In many organizations, the speed with which problems are detected, isolated, and diagnosed is simply inadequate. The result is that downtime increases, causing financial losses—especially to larger organizations.

Technology is still immature with respect to supporting expert decision making during the problem determination process. As a result, the need for more staff increases uncontrollably. Because present management platforms and applications are unable to correlate events between the physical and logical segments of the network, automated bypass and restoration of failed network elements is very difficult.

To compound this problem, most network control centers have to work with too many consoles, including single monitors of network elements, network element management systems, or integrators.

It is very difficult to limit the number of operators and customer support desk personnel and to distribute the workload among these persons over the course of a shift, a day, or a week. It is often easier to build a fault management team than to keep one.

2.6.2   Aspects of Fault Handling

There are two aspects of the fault handling process:

- Handling faults reported by end users (client reported faults)
- Handling faults detected by network and system management applications

In both cases, many of the same functions and applications are affected. The following section addresses client-reported faults.

2.6.3   Handling Faults Reported by End Users

The client reports a problem to the Client Contact Point electronically or by telephone or fax. The client is automatically identified and the appropriate site details, and recent faults associated with the site are displayed to the Network Management Systems user. If no associated calls on this problem have been received, a problem report is automatically created. Otherwise, the problem report is opened. This assumes that users are notified when problems affecting service have been reported. In other words, a trouble ticket is opened only when the system has determined that the call is reporting a new fault. For a new fault, the client is requested to give fault details in order to diagnose the fault and to determine appropriate action. Support text should be provided to assist the help desk or other first level support personnel diagnose the fault and to suggest possible causes. The user may want to interrogate the trouble ticketing database for similar problems. All dialogue between the client and user is logged in order to maintain a complete fault history, which should be included in the trouble ticket when it is passed to Operations Support. To enable Client Contact Points to assign the problem to the appropriate personnel, supporting information (such as contacts, escalation procedures, and equipment and facility attributes) is absolutely necessary.

When a problem is reported, the Client Control Point should be able to use the service reference number to interpret, analyze, diagnose, and correlate the problem report with other client or network/systems-reported problems. After service has been restored by other management groups, the Client Control Point must notify the client so that the client can test the service and confirm that the problem has been resolved. If the fault is traced to equipment maintained by third-party maintenance organizations, the trouble ticket should be sent to the third-party, as shown in Figure 2.6. The progress of the resolution process is tracked

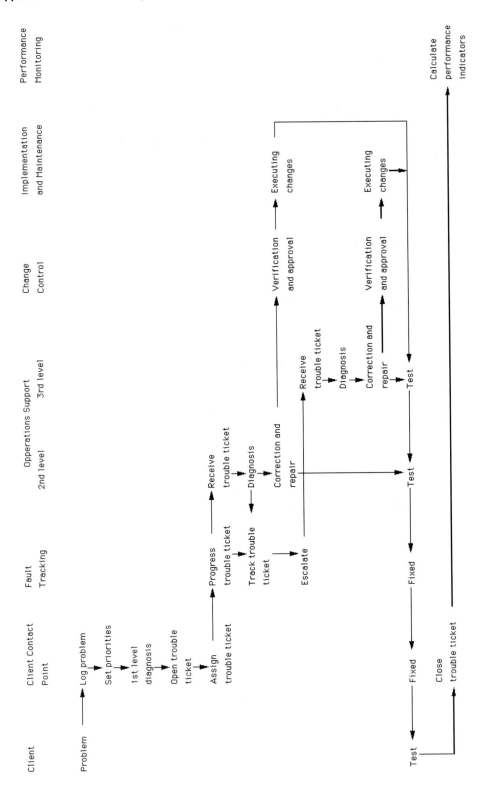

Figure 2.6 Handling of client-reported faults

by the Fault Tracking group. The trouble ticket should be referred to the new owner according to problem type, time of day, severity, and maintainer of the resource. If actions are to be taken by different parties, the trouble ticket should be sent to both. The client must be notified of any significant action on the trouble ticket, such as changing the ownership of the problem. Expected time to repair should also be given to the client.

The Fault Tracking group forwards trouble tickets to new owners (including third-party maintenance organizations) for action. In certain cases, trouble ticket information must be split into smaller units to generate actions by different owners. If possible, related trouble tickets should be associated, collapsed, and sent together to the new owner. Progress is monitored against critical milestones or time scales defined by service level agreements (SLAs). Escalation reminders notify users about deadline violations. Shared fault knowledge is extremely important to anybody taking actions on a problem. The whole fault history is expected to be available to the old and new owners of the fault. Significant events must be reported back to the client. SLAs include escalation guidelines defining the time a problem is allowed to stay in any one state. A problem may remain in a pending state without escalation when progress depends on another event.

The Operation Support group provides both second and third level support for problems. They handle calls from clients that require a technical expert to handle and help identify the course of action. Complex problems are usually handled by the secondary level and very sophisticated and/or subtle problems by the third level. Third level may also include actions for remote sites. The Operations Support group must have access to a complete fault history and details of the site and location where the fault occurred. Dialogue with the client should be kept to a minimum.

Problem diagnosis includes a number of testing procedures which may have to be invoked remotely. Both disruptive and non-disruptive tests must be considered. Support managers must also be able to turn on performance monitoring functions on facilities and equipment for specified periods. Diagnostics tools differ greatly by wide and local area networks. Second and third level support personnel may need to activate predefined diagnostic and testing procedures for the purpose of determining or verifying the location of faults. Support personnel must be able to select the right problem isolation procedure from a set of predefined procedures. Support personnel may want to use other network information (e.g., test and measurement data) to speed fault isolation and to identify possible causes. State-of-the-art trouble tickets allow support personnel to enter the results of diagnostic tests and analysis. Support personnel may want to execute testing procedures on-line or off-line. They may also want additional support data, such as dumps, status information, statistics, etc.

Support personnel may execute corrective actions and repairs. They may change and reset systems parameters, or attribute values, deactivate, activate, and restart components. As corrective actions in response to faults, they may be required to reconfigure portions of (or even the whole) network. Change requests—excluding minor fixes—are communicated to the Change Control group for verification and approval. The actual execution of changes and repairs is performed by the Implementation and Maintenance group. In any case, the Operations Support group must insure that the problems have been resolved. If so, the Fault Tracking group notifies the Client Control Point to advise clients about performing client-initiated tests. If tests are successful and no new problems are introduced, trouble-tickets may be closed and stored in the trouble-ticketing database. Performance calculations maybe completed in near-realtime or in batch mode.

2.6.3.1 Handling Faults Detected by Management Applications

The second alternative is to use advanced fault monitoring features to detect problems in the network. If a fault occurs in the network or in its systems, redundancy or fallback mechanisms designed into the network or systems may be automatically invoked to ensure that the effect on services is minimized. This automated correction may be temporary or permanent in nature. There maybe, however, some interruption of service or degradation of performance despite the fallback. Outages and degradation should be recorded for performance evaluation and reporting. The Fault Tracking group receives the fault, and in order to set priorities, evaluates its client impact. After setting priorities, trouble tickets are opened or extended on the basis of the fault's nature. Trouble tickets are only opened for new faults.

When faults are detected automatically via software, fault detection includes the results of first level diagnosis. As part of the notification, trouble tickets are sent to Client Contact Point. They may be then be correlated with similar or other client problems. Trouble tickets are referred to Operations Support with the complete fault history. If the fault is traced to equipment maintained by a third party, the trouble ticket should be sent directly to the maintainers, as shown in Figure 2.7. The progress of the resolution process is tracked by the Fault Tracking group. The trouble ticket should be referred to the new owner according to problem type, time of day, severity, and maintainer of the resource. If actions are to be taken by different parties, trouble tickets should be sent to both. The client must be notified of any significant action on the trouble ticket, such as changing the ownership of the problem. Expected time to repair should also be given to the client.

The Finance and Billing department may be involved with this process by updating the asset list and occasionally calculating the refund to clients due to service outages.

Typical applications and products assisting fault management processes are listed in Table 2.14.

2.7   THE TUNING PROCESS

Performance management involves optimizing existing resources and notifying the Planning and Design group if existing resources are exhausted and tuning is no longer applicable. The status of performance tuning in most organizations today is summarized below.

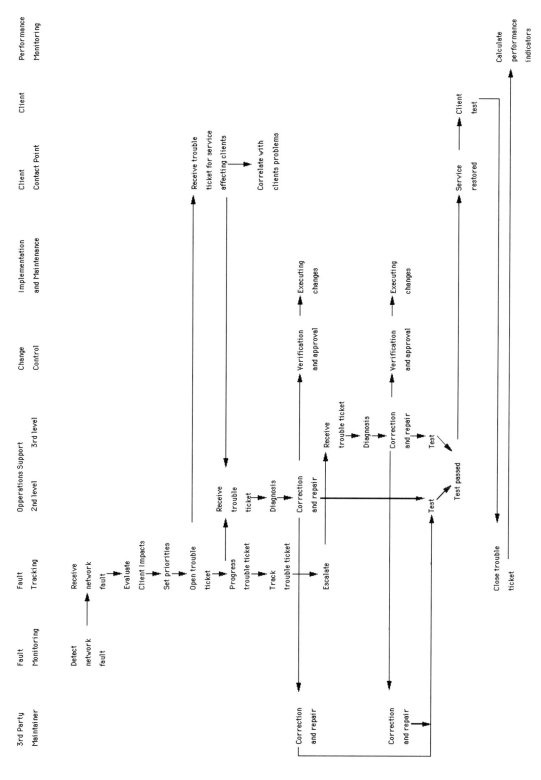

Figure 2.7 Handling of network/system-reported faults

TABLE 2-14   Typical Tools for the Fault Management Process

Tools	Primary Use	Secondary Use
Management Integrators	✔	
WAN EMS	✔	
LAN EMS	✔	
WAN Monitors	✔	
LAN Monitors	✔	
WAN Analyzers	✔	
LAN Analyzers	✔	
Network Monitors	✔	
Software Monitors	✔	
Console Emulators		✔
Presentation Tools		✔
Administration Tools	✔	
Databases	✔	
MIB Tools	✔	
Trouble-Tracking Tools	✔	
Expert Systems		✔
Documentation Tools		
Modeling Tools		
Security Management Tools	✔	

2.7.1   Present Status of Performance Tuning

Performance management is not yet a realtime activity in most organizations. As a result, administrators cannot yet make ad hoc performance improvements on the basis of realtime or near-realtime measurement data.

No standard procedures exist for analyzing performance data for voice and data networks. Unfortunately, this often results in redundant work.

Very few organizations maintain "experience files" that capture the human element of managing systems and networks. This makes development and implementation of expert systems extremely difficult.

While performance statistics and historical data are automatically or semiautomatically saved in databases or files, most of these files have vendor-specific formats for further analysis. Too many reports are often generated and there is too little use of so-called display databases with on-line, realtime enquiry capabilities.

The analysis of an end user service level requires the use of multiple applications and products in combination, covering LAN-, MAN-, and WAN-related performance indicators. There is still a shortage of powerful techniques for correlating information from various sources. Educating and cross-educating staff to conduct performance-related work is very time-consuming and, therefore, expensive.

In summary, the lack of realtime or near-realtime performance analysis and a good combination of tools are the principal obstacles to improving performance management efficiency.

2.7.2   Input to Performance Tuning

Tuning occupies a central role in performance management. Input to the tuning process comes from various sources, including the following:

Data generated during continuous monitoring of the whole network
End user complaints about performance
Violation of Service Level Agreements based on evaluation of measurement
    results
Requests from the Planning and Design group for performance assessment and
    organization

The tuning process is shown in Figure 2.8. The Performance Monitoring group is the focal point for accepting client-driven and device-driven tuning requests. When Service Level Agreement violations are reported to Finance and Billing; repayment or discounts may be initiated for the user organization.

When an organization seeks to improve its tuning processes, existing available data is usually insufficient. The Performance Monitoring group may query the Performance Database, which is usually maintained by the System Administration group. If available, data records can be ported to the local database on the analyst's workstation. In most cases, however, the level of detail does not satisfy the information need. On rare occasions, the experience file of history tuning data may help managers quickly recognize similarities to past problems. However, few organizations maintain adequate experience files.

Once a hypothesis has been formulated, cost efficiency and technical feasibility should be tested step-by-step in order to avoid uneconomical and nonfeasible alternatives. Frequently, technical and economical performance evaluation can be supported by modeling tools.

After receiving financial approval, the Implementation and Maintenance group implements and tests the solution. If successful, the requesters will be provided with measurement logs. In case of nonfeasibility or insufficient improvements, an additional hypothesis should be worked out. If the results are still unsatisfactory, capacity planning actions are required.

Table 2-15 lists typical applications that support the system and network tuning process.

2.8   THE SECURITY CONTROL PROCESS

Companies must establish policies and guidelines for the use of computer and telecommunications resources and for safeguarding information while it is

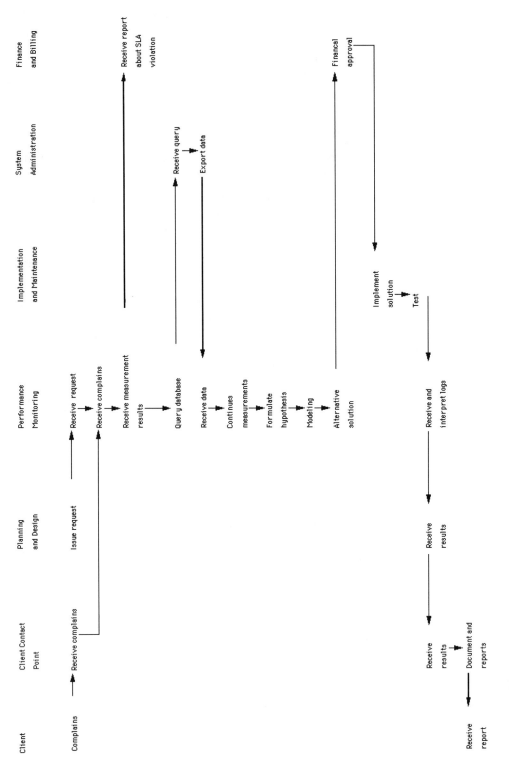

Figure 2.8 The tuning process

TABLE 2-15   Typical Tools for the Performance Tuning Process

Tools	Primary Use	Secondary Use
Management Integrators		✔
WAN EMS		✔
LAN EMS		✔
WAN Monitors	✔	
LAN Monitors	✔	
WAN Analyzers	✔	
LAN Analyzers	✔	
Network Monitors	✔	
Software Monitors		✔
Console Emulators	✔	
Presentation Tools		✔
Administration Tools		
Databases	✔	
MIB Tools		✔
Trouble-Tracking Tools		
Expert Systems		
Documentation Tools		
Modeling Tools	✔	
Security Management Tools		

stored or processed by a system. The policy must also address misuse or theft of company telecommunications and computing equipment and the software, data, and/or documentation associated with it. Major security management activities help to accomplish the following goals:

- Minimizing the possibility of intrusion by using a layered defense system (i.e., a combination of policies and hardware and software solutions that build a uniform barrier to unauthorized users).
- Providing a means of quickly detecting unauthorized use and determining the original violation entry point. This should provide an audit trail of the violator's activity.
- Allowing the network manager to manually reconstruct any damaged files or applications and restoring the system to the state just prior to the violation. This reconstruction feature helps to minimize damage and allows system recovery.
- Ultimately, allowing the violators to be manually monitored and trapped by a network operations group, ending with a reprimand or prosecution.

The following section summarizes the status of most security implementations in organizations today.

2.8.1   Present Status of Security

For most people involved in voice or data communication, security is an unknown area. There are no violation indicators, techniques are considered complicated, and responsibilities are not clearly assigned. Often, there are no clear guidelines regarding what should be protected in a complex networking environment or whether applications, databases, files, nodes, communication links, end user devices, or a combination of all these need to be protected. Without an adequate sensitivity analysis, budgets cannot be properly assigned to any of these areas. Typically, there is little awareness of who commits security violations and why. No or very few reports and records are available from organizations on this topic. The reasons for this include:

- Violations are not detected by the network operations group.
- Violations may be detected but not reported because admitting to a violation may cause the public to have a lack of confidence in the company that owns and operates the network.
- Violations are committed by legitimate users of the network that have found ways to access applications and data that they should not have the authority to access. In many instances, the organization may not consider or be aware that this is a problem. Indeed, the users may not believe they are committing a security violation—they are simply using a password and log-on code that belongs to a co-worker or manager because it is convenient. Company employees commit far more violations of computer systems security (approximately 75 percent) than outsiders (approximately 25 percent).

There is currently little acceptance of upcoming new techniques such as biometrics. To compound this problem, the instrumentation of even traditional security mechanisms is lacking in physical facilities, LANs, and end-user devices. The majority of available solutions protecting mainframe hosts and applications.

In many organizations, security management is considered overhead and treated with low priority, with a resulting insufficient budget.

2.8.2   The Security Management Process

The Security Management group is primarily responsible for the security management process within an organization (Figure 2.9). This group is in charge of defining security indicators and monitoring guidelines that are sent—and periodically updated—to the Fault and Performance Monitoring groups. Continuous monitoring helps to detect violations in realtime. Violation detection includes capturing or accessing information about changes of client profiles, modifications of the hardware/software configuration, changes in access authorization, turnover in currently active users, increase of file numbers, saturated systems, password violations, etc. In addition to monitoring information, client's calls are received by the security offices. The Fault and Performance Monitoring groups may invoke automated procedures against the penetrator if severity thresholds have been exceeded. If the violations are not severe, the security officer analyses them; occasional help may come from the System Administration group about user profiles (internal), client profiles (external), special habits, history of viola-

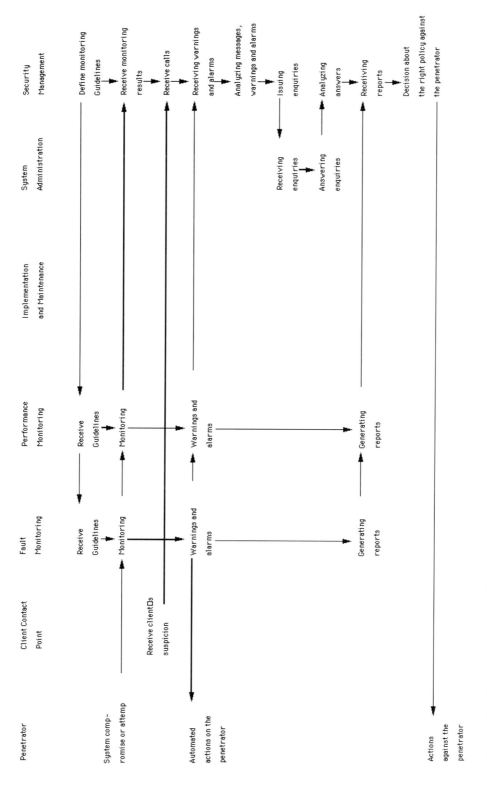

Figure 2.9 The security control process

tions, reassignment of responsibilities for employees, moves and changes in scope of control, and other statistics. Also, reports are generated by the Fault and Performance Monitoring groups—including the security of the Network Management System—and sent to the Security Management group. The final output of the process is the decision about the right policy against the penetrator.

Typical applications assisting in the security control process are listed in Table 2.16. Currently, Open*V SecureMax from OpenVision is one of the only security applications available for open management platforms such as HP OpenView.

2.9   THE COSTING AND BILLING PROCESS

In general, the corporation's accounting policy defines the financial strategy and procedures that will best meet overall corporate objectives. Collecting information, analyzing cost elements, and processing and verifying vendor bills are absolutely necessary. However, establishing charge-back policies, defining charge-back procedures, and integrating network accounting management into corporate accounting depends on corporate management. These functions are optional, but most corporations have some solution in place.

TABLE 2-16   Typical Tools for the Security Management Process

Tools	Primary Use	Secondary Use
Management Integrators		✔
WAN EMS		✔
LAN EMS		✔
WAN Monitors		✔
LAN Monitors		
WAN Analyzers		✔
LAN Analyzers		
Network Monitors		
Software Monitors		
Console Emulators		✔
Presentation Tools	✔	
Administration Tools	✔	
Databases		
MIB Tools		
Trouble-Tracking Tools	✔	
Expert Systems		
Documentation Tools	✔	
Modeling Tools		
Security Management Tools	✔	

The next section summarizes the status of costing and billing activities in organizations today.

2.9.1   Present Status of Costing and Billing

The most difficult problem in accounting management is accurately determining telecommunications costs and then equitably charging these costs back to the user. It is difficult to determine costs accurately because many direct and indirect factors make up true costs of a device, service, product, or system. Additionally, modern accounting practices and tax issues further complicate the correct calculation of costs. When numerous elements such as hardware, software, systems, personnel, and overhead costs are included, as is true in all large telecom networks, completely accurate cost determination is simply not possible.

Similarly, it is difficult to accurately and fairly charge back those costs to end users who are provided with network services. In most if not all cases, only charge-back approximations are possible. It is difficult if not impossible to equitably allocate switching and transmission costs to voice information and data information carried over the same physical network. This is especially true when voice is digitized at 64 kbps or digitized and compressed to 32 kbps or 16 kbps. When assessing costs, one must consider multiple factors such as quality of service, bandwidth, message contents, gateways, technology options, off-net tariff requirements, and unit costs of support hardware and software.

Accurate accounting requires continuous and detailed monitoring, which often carries unnecessarily high overhead. Even bill verification is very difficult due to frequent tariff changes and differences between carriers, countries, and even by states.

The present life cycle of processing accounting released information is too long; realtime or near realtime processing results are expected by most users. Accounting in LANs is virtually nonexistent today; most corporations consider LANs as another element of the infrastructure. Only a few applications introduce the concepts of resource accounting and usage accounting to interconnected LANs.

2.9.2   Elements of the Costing and Billing Process

The Costing and Billing process has a number of prerequisites. These include deciding up front whether the corporation runs the telecommunication division as a profit or cost center, and whether costing and billing are going to be incorporated into the corporate accounting policy. As shown in Figure 2.10, this process unifies three major inputs:

- Service orders from clients
- Service and network usage from ongoing use of the network
- Supplier bills

Service orders or change requests are generated by clients, as described in sections 2.2 and 2.5. After the entire change request process is complete, the client's approval is the prerequisite of client billing.

The Finance and Billing department plays the central role in the Costing and Billing process. Besides approving changes and service orders, several other functions must be supported. These functions include:

- Defining costing categories (hardware, software, infrastructure, communications, and personnel)
- Calculating depreciation
- Maintaining asset inventories

The Finance and Billing department must also verify incoming bills from suppliers. This activity is supported by Performance Monitoring group, which determines potential Service Level Agreement (SLA) violations on behalf of the suppliers. The Performance Monitoring group is also responsible for providing information on service and network usage on ongoing basis. This is a prerequisite for calculating variable costs. If Service Level Agreements have been violated—as monitored by Performance and Fault Monitoring—rebates must be calculated by Finance and Billing.

Finally, client bills are generated and sent to clients. Bill justification follows eventual billing enquires on behalf of the client. Applications which assist costing and billing are listed in Table 2.17.

TABLE 2-17 Typical Tools for the Costing and Billing Process

Tools	Primary Use	Secondary Use
Management Integrators		✔
WAN EMS		
LAN EMS		
WAN Monitors	✔	
LAN Monitors		
WAN Analyzers	✔	
LAN Analyzers		
Network Monitors	✔	
Software Monitors		
Console Emulators		
Presentation Tools		✔
Administration Tools	✔	
Databases		
MIB Tools		
Trouble-Tracking Tools		
Expert Systems		
Documentation Tools	✔	
Modeling Tools		
Security Management Tools		

2.10 SUMMARY

The right combination of management processes and tools is critical to successful management of systems and networks. The starting point for reengineering each processes is the consolidation of the management database. To maximize efficiency and levels of automation of management functions, multiple configuration databases should be merged into an integrated database. In the future, object-oriented technology will support integration of these segments into one logical database. Eventually, as organizations transition to the platform/applications model of management, familiar stand-alone products will take the form of applications.

3

Typical Management Problems and How to Solve Them

3.1 INTRODUCTION

The principal management processes referenced in Chapter 2 may encompass many functions. A typical Fortune 500 company defines and implements approximately 80 to 120 different network and systems management functions. Prioritizing these diverse functions is not an easy job. This chapter addresses the management functions and processes considered high-priority by users, vendors, and industry consultants. In particular, remote configuration of routers, electronic software distribution, software licensing, fault isolation, expert systems, and security using Kerberos are discussed. Commercially available management applications and products are referenced throughout this chapter.

3.2 REMOTE CONFIGURATION OF ROUTERS

Internetworking of local area networks (LANs) and metropolitan area networks (MANs) is now an integral part of today's enterprise networks. Routers are the foundation of internetworking. (Faulkner, 1993).

Routers are sophisticated devices with traffic filtering and decision-making capabilities. Their built-in intelligence requires that a number of parameters and performance indicators be set-up, customized, supervised, and changed if necessary. But routers can be difficult to configure and maintain, particularly in large, complex networks. This is due both to the number of routers involved and to the large geographical distances they must span. Management applications are absolutely necessary to simplify, synchronize, and accelerate the configuration process.

3.2.1 SNMP and SNMPv2

Most router manufacturers are taking advantage of SNMP capabilities to maintain and configure local and remote routers. Even the first version of SNMP helped automate router management to some degree by providing standard mechanisms for periodically obtaining status information. SNMPv1 was an adequate solution to receive and interpret MIB entries. There are, however, three major limitations of SNMP version 1 with respect to maintaining and to configuring routers:

- Insecure SETs commands due to the simplicity of community name
- Lack of bulk data retrieval capabilities
- Requirement of using TCP/IP as transmission protocol.

SNMPv2, defined in RFCs 1445 and 1448, addresses all three limitations. Security specifications for SNMPv2 now define methods of assuring both the authentication and privacy of communications. Authentication provides a means of reliably identifying the originator of the message, while privacy indicates a means for the message to be protected from disclosure. The basis of the implementation is the "party" concept. This is a unique set of security parameters, which could include the network location, plus privacy and authentication protocols that are going to be used between communicating entities. An SNMPv2 entity may define multiple parties depending upon the communication partner. SNMP managers may use different keys for different agents. For the communication process, all the "party-parameters," encryption keys, and other parameters must be validated. When implemented, the security parameters are placed before the SNMPv2-PDU (Figure 3.1). Vendors who implement the security features will use two protocols:

- The Digest Authentication Protocol. Verifies message integrity and origin
- The Symmetric Privacy Protocol. Assures message privacy using secret keys that are only known to the originator and recipient.

In addition, the authentication of encrypted messages may be required. In summary, the security of configuration commands can be enhanced by using all or some of SNMPv2's new features.

Distributing configuration files and changes requires the transmission of large files, such as routing and bridge-forwarding tables. Using the new Get Bulk Request in SNMPv2, large quantities of information may be moved by a single request. This type of request should help reduce network bandwidth demands by eliminating many polling messages.

As an application layer protocol, SNMP relies upon underlaying layers for transmitting messages. Originally, SNMP was designed to run over TCP/IP networks. SNMPv2 changes and expands this by adding support for AppleTalk, OSI, and Novell Internetwork Packet Exchange (IPX). Expanded transport support will help users to incorporate many non-TCP/IP and UDP/IP devices into the SNMP management domain.

Now that SNMP's problems have been addressed, router manufacturers are beginning to write new SNMPv2-based applications to configure and maintain

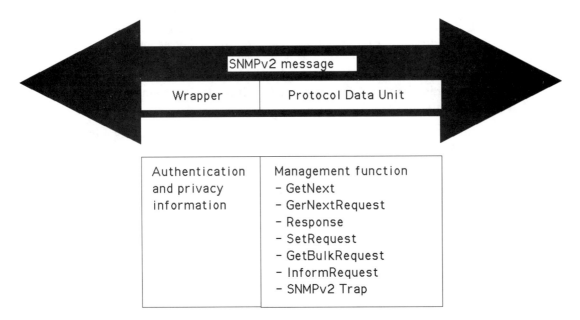

SNMPv2 message format

SNMPv2 message

Wrapper	Protocol Data Unit

Authentication and privacy information	Management function – GetNext – GerNextRequest – Response – SetRequest – GetBulkRequest – InformRequest – SNMPv2 Trap

Figure 3.1 SNMPv2 message format with security wrapper

their devices. Cisco was one of the first vendors to implement SNMPv2 security. CiscoWorks, Cisco's router management application, is discussed in some detail (Figure 3.2) in the following section. This implementation currently uses SNMPv1, however.

3.2.2   CiscoWorks

CiscoWorks provides a series of applications for day-to-day router monitoring and troubleshooting. In addition, Cisco offers a management series for off-line analysis of network traffic and trends. Together, these utilities help satisfy both realtime immediate concerns of network managers, and requirements for long-term planning and trend analysis.

CiscoWorks' operations series includes six major components:

- Configuration File Management
- Path Tool
- Health Monitor
- Environmental Monitor
- Device Management Database
- Security Management

Configuration File Management organizes and manages router configuration files, storing them in a Sybase relational database management system (RDBMS) which is integrated with CiscoWorks. The RDBMS is critical, particu-

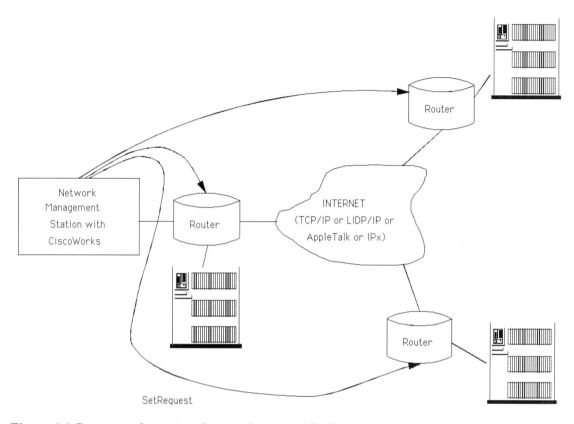

Figure 3.2 Remote configuration of routers by secured SetRequests

larly in larger networks, where it is impractical to query individual routers each time a user requires configuration or status information.

Configuration File Management allows network managers to perform automatic comparisons for detecting changes. CiscoWorks compares the configuration file in the database to the file running on the device. It can then alert network managers to routers that are configured differently than specified. The database also provides an audit trail—the comments field is automated to record what was changed and when, and by whom.

The Path Tool provides a graphical, end-to-end logical view of a path between any two IP nodes on the internetwork. This includes realtime information about the amount of traffic on each interface or link error rates. This capability allows the network manager to pinpoint the location where a path is blocked. At that point, the network manager can employ the Health Monitor to obtain diagnostic information such as a breakdown of the protocols currently being routed or utilization percentage of each interface.

Environmental Monitor is a simple but useful tool that can check the temperature, voltage, and airflow of local or remote routers. (The Cisco router must support an environment monitor card, available as an option from Cisco.) The Device Management Database allows network managers to keep an inventory of equipment, including hardware and software versions, serial numbers, network addresses, and vendor contact information.

Security Manager allows network managers to segment users into groups for granting security privileges. These privileges range from read only (of data and/ or passwords), to modify (data and/or passwords) and to execute management applications. By giving managers the flexibility to allow selected operators to view router configurations but not change them, Configuration File Management is protected by the Security Manager.

The Management Series portion of CiscoWorks assists managers in achieving long-term goals of network management, such as historical trend analysis for determining the cost-effectiveness of transmission options, determining usage, identifying potential problem areas, and isolating chronic problems. Its Data WorkBench feature is actually a Sybase tool that allows administrators to create reports. These reports can display traffic through every router interface, including throughput and error rates, traffic peaks, and percentage of broadcast traffic versus total traffic.

CiscoWorks also includes an AutoInstall feature that supports a protocol that lets remote routers obtain their own IP addresses from neighboring routers. This enables remote routers to obtain configuration files from the central site. Since routers need to obtain their address before they can be installed, AutoInstall circumvents the need to take the router to the central site to get the IP address.

Another feature is a global command facility, which allows users to apply one command to a group of routers. This can save time in enabling passwords on all routers. Also, a new software manager feature will manage upgrades easier and add protection against human error, such as preventing accidental erasure of old version of configuration files during backups.

3.3   SOFTWARE VERSION CONTROL IN CLIENT/ SERVER ENVIRONMENTS

Version control is part of electronic software distribution services. This service allows network administrators to distribute, install, and maintain software throughout an internetwork, using either a distributed or a centralized method. It supports both the push and pull models of software distribution. The push model requires the server to load the software to the workstation; the pull model requires the workstation to request the software from the server (Figure 3.3). Software distribution and updating is one of the major reasons for the high operating costs of managing client/server-structures. Manufacturers that offer distribution services estimate that approximately 20 percent of the real cost of software lies in distribution and installation. Basically, desktops with software are much more difficult to manage than legacy-type terminals.

Electronic software distribution can reduce labor costs substantially by eliminating site visits, reducing the cost and length of time for a software change, enforcing version control, synchronizing software changes, helping vendors prevent unauthorized copying, and simplifying software installation by automation.

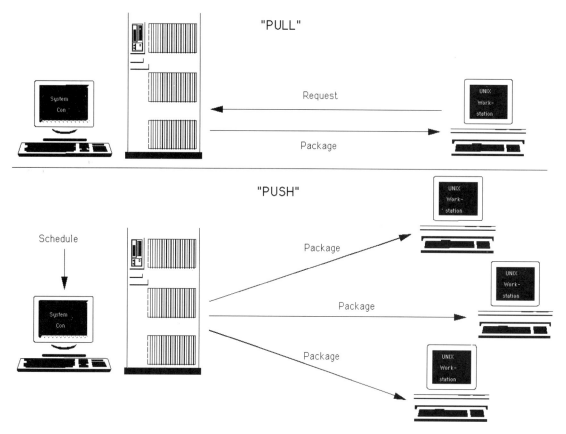

Figure 3.3 Push versus pull distributions

Electronic software distribution is also helpful in managing vendor license agreements.

There are, however, still many unresolved issues regarding electronic software distribution. Some vendors resist changing their distribution mechanisms; some products are still immature.

The majority of users must control versions of software running on multiple servers and clients. Consequently, distribution services must be able to communicate with different servers and clients installed by different vendors running under various operating systems, such as UNIX, OS/2, DOS, etc. Finally, distribution over WANs may cost a lot due to high bandwidth requirements.

3.3.1   Components of Electronic Software Distribution

The electronic software distribution process is broken down into fundamental functions that are treated as individual modules. These modules include package creation, distribution scheduling, package transfer, and package installation: (Viat, 1993)

Package Creation The first step in distributing software is to create a software package. Each software package is a set of programs or data files with installation and backout methods that are assembled for distribution into one file (Package). The package moves around the network as one unit and is not "unpacked" until it reaches its destination (the target machine). Packages are the smallest unit of distribution.

Distribution Scheduling Distributing a package involves moving it from its source location to one or more target machines. Similar to scheduling a package for delivery using a parcel carrier, "distribution scheduling" allows the system administrator to specify "shipping" information for the software package. The shipping information includes the source and target machines (i.e., TO: and FROM: addresses) as well as the dates and times (i.e., when to pick up and deliver the package) for distribution and installation.

Package Transfer The package transfer object functions as the shipper in the above example. It picks up software packages and delivers them to their proper destination. Some electronic software distribution packages, such as Xfer from ViaTech, can specify multiple destinations. In this case, a Package Transfer object handles duplication to minimize network traffic. It also determines the proper network path to take when delivering the software, which may include dropping off the package at an intermediate location.

Package Installation Once the package is delivered, it must be unpacked and installed using its embedded installation methods. By embedding the installation methods in the package, an administrator is guaranteed that a package built today will install years from now, even if the target machine's base software has changed. The package installation object unpacks the package after its installation time is reached. It verifies the contents of the package, installs it, and notifies one or more administration machines of its progress.

These processes do not occur in isolation. Rather, they are usually seamlessly coupled to other management functions, such as inventory management, managing the installed software, and license management.

Prior to distributing software, maintaining an accurate software configuration inventory is essential. The control software is expected to locate all targeted servers and clients on LANs, MANs, and WANs and configures them so they will report their inventory each time a distribution is intended. Agents will report any changes in memory, disk space, versions, applications supported, and other systems conditions.

In the future, most software running at the desktop level will support the Desktop Management Interface (DMI) specifications, and will store management data in Management Information Files (MIFs), as defined by the Desktop Management Task Force (DMTF). The MIF is an ASCII file that contains a wide range of useful management information about workstation resources. Vendors are expected to provide MIFs for system components, operating systems, expansion cards, and application software. Prior to distribution, MIFs are interrogated and imported by the control software. Menus from Microsoft supports this type of a inventory control phase.

During the software distribution process "backouts" may be required if things do not go as planned. If the administrators distribute a package and it cannot be received and installed on the target machine due to turned-off power or insufficient disk space, distribution will be automatically backed out. An alarm, which may be customized, notifies the control software of the backout. Not only does the control software automatically blackout distribution, but the administrator also has the option to manually backout the distribution.

After successful distribution, systems management functions are executed continuously. These functions are supported by other protocols.

Important suppliers of electronic software distribution applications include Hewlett-Packard (Software Distribution Utilities), IBM (NetView Distribution Manager), Microsoft (Menus), Novell (Navigator), ViaTech (Xfer), Siemens/Nixdorf (DSM-SAX), and AT&T (Software Manager).

Figure 3.4 shows a simplified structure for the distribution process. The management system may be a stand-alone system, but the preferred alternative is to implement the distribution control software on the same platform used for other management applications. The Software Depots are implemented by relational or object-oriented databases. In complex networks, additional depots can be installed serving various LANs. The workstation of the manager is equipped

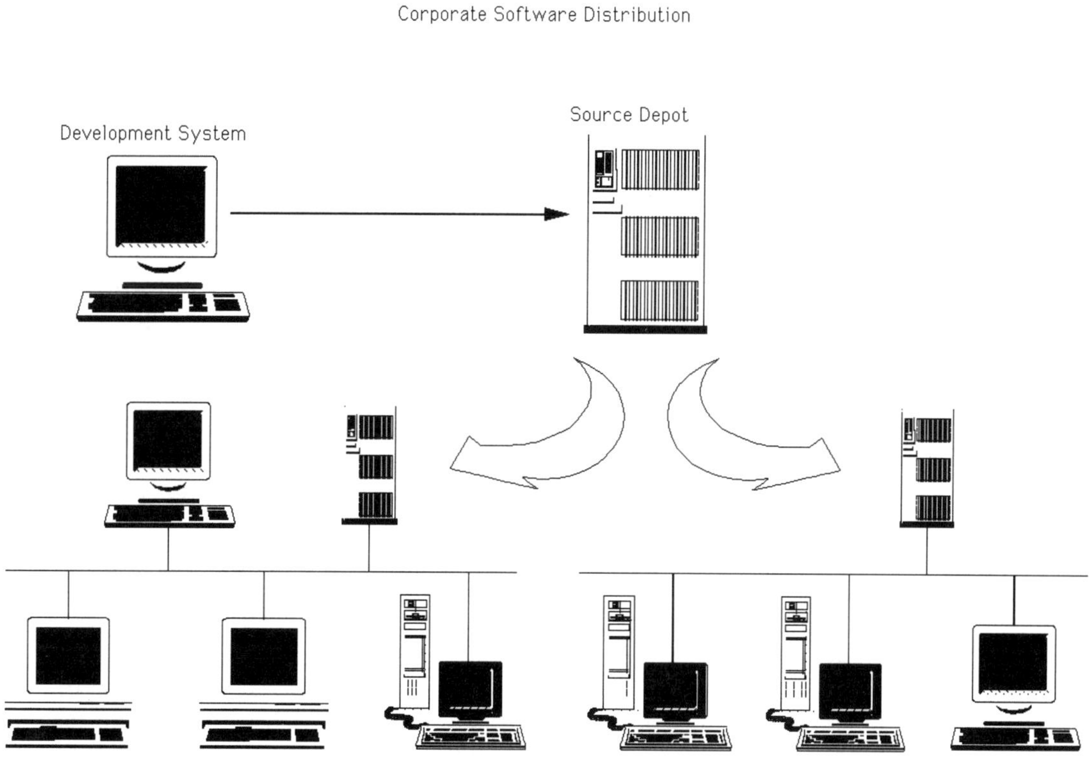

Figure 3.4 Distribution process by using multiple depots

with standard systems software and GUIs such as Motif, Openlook, and XWindows.

3.4   ISOLATING FAULTS USING SMART HUBS

Fault management is a classic realtime activity. Any delay in determining, isolating, and resolving a problem may cause serious impacts on users' productivity. Various techniques for accelerating the fault resolution process include:

- Display of detailed topological information
- Proactive detection of deteriorating quality
- Efficient trouble-ticketing products to register and to track faults quickly
- Optimal staffing of client service points
- Use of experience files and expert systems
- Optimal combination of traffic monitors, protocol analyzers, and test devices to diagnose problems
- Use of extremely user-friendly graphics to show the status of managed objects continuously.

The goal of all this is rapid and accurate detection and isolation of faults. In present enterprise networks, wiring hubs allow users to segment networks and greatly accelerate the fault isolation process. Hubs also serve as a focal point for housing other critical managed objects including routers, bridges, FDDI nodes, and ATM nodes. In collapsed backbones, the degree of integration around the hub is even higher. Management applications in the hub—or for the hub help to isolate fault at the port level—assists managers in advising and dispatching engineers to the right place. Hub management applications collect vital management data that can be transported, via protocols such as SNMP, to other management applications. These other applications can interpret data and launch scripts or other actions, or alert networks and systems operators of failures.

The following example shows port-level fault isolation using SynOptics products and the Optivity family of applications. SynOptics is a leading smart hub manufacturer, and Optivity is the vendor's management application for its hub product line.

3.4.1   SynOptics Optivity

Using traditional SNMP implementations, the number of agents polled in the network must be increased if an organization wants to obtain more SNMP-based data. However, this additional polling may increase overhead traffic to unacceptable levels.

To relieve the problem of polling-induced overhead, Optivity supports distributed hierarchical polling. Optivity supports network control engines (NCEs) that can support either master and slave or sub-agents—facilitating localized polling between the NCE (agent) and the sub-agent. (See Figure 3.5.) NCE performs certain management functions such as polling, data filtering, local interpretation, and compression. NCEs are basically screen-less Sun workstations co-located with a hub.

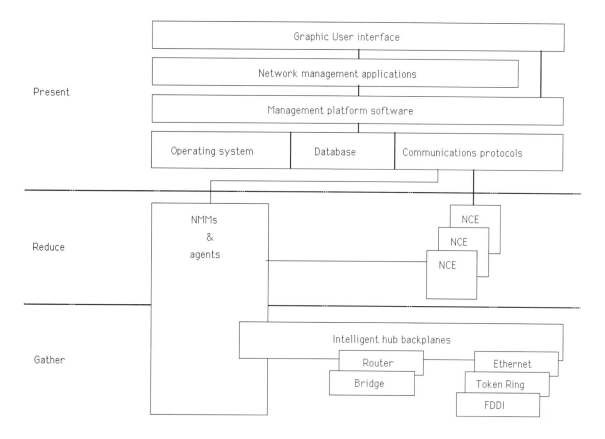

Figure 3.5 SynOptics management, network management, and internetworking connectivity

Optivity supports a number of applications to provide users with a more complete solution. These applications include the following:

- TRENDman: uses existing performance data to predict future performance.
- POLICYman: evaluates thresholds and dynamically enables and disables ports of wiring hubs.
- FAULTman: administers trouble-tickets for tracking and resolving network problems.
- PATHman: allows a manager to trace the physical transmission path of a packet from one MAC or IP address to another. This tracing assists the user in pinpointing client/server problems.
- ROUTERman: provides real-time status of routers on the network.
- BRIDGEman: automatically identifies and shows the status of all bridges on the net.
- DESIGNman: provides network design and optimization information.

SynOptics Optivity works with various platforms including SunConnect Sun-Net Manager, Hewlett-Packard HP OpenView, IBM AIX NetView/6000, and Novell's NetWare Management System (NMS). The following example shows how Optivity, running on Novell's NMS, can help isolate faults to the port level.

3.4.2   Isolating Faults using Optivity

Seamlessly integrated with Novell's NMS and working with other "snap-in" applications, Optivity contributes key network fabric management capabilities to the overall Novell system. The application, bundled with the core NMS platform, can also serve as a stand-alone hub management solution for NetWare environments.

The system includes a number of dynamic network views that provide visibility into the network infrastructure. All IP and IPX routers and subnetworks are automatically discovered and displayed in a comprehensive map of the network topology, giving the user a detailed overview of the internetwork.

SynOptics IPX hubs, NetWare servers, IPX client stations, and all other IPX devices are also automatically discovered and displayed, further refining the map. By manually adding traditional SynOptics IP devices to the map, users can create a complete and accurate blueprint of the overall network topology. Hierarchical maps of specific network segments or subnetworks can also be created to provide further visibility into the system. As new devices are added to the network, the dynamic maps are automatically updated to reflect the change, and color-coded displays report network status at a glance for rapid fault detection and resolution.

SynOptics applications such as Expanded View and Ring View are launched directly from the platform map. These SynOptics views provide a real-time window into the network, allowing managers to monitor and control performance from a central management station.

Expanded View supports port-level-fault-isolation. It provides a real-time display of any selected LattisHub, LattisRing or System 3000/5000 concentrator, including active LEDs and configuration status. From the Expanded View image, network managers may obtain information to monitor performance and review status down to the port level.

Information is acquired via Fault, Configuration, and Performance pull-down menus on the Expanded View display. From the Fault menu, network managers can selectively enable specific nodes, obtain diagnostic data, and wrap (Token Ring) or partition (Ethernet) individual ports. The Configuration menu offers Show Profile, Show Nodes, and Validate options for the concentrator or individual ports, while the Performance menu allows users to display charts that graphically report specific activities over time to monitor network performance.

Out-of-band connections can also be established through Expanded View. The out-of-band feature enables network management to continue over the telephone system if in-band communications fail.

Figure 3.6 shows an Optivity display of port status for SynOptic's LattisHub. This display has been embedded into NMS running under Windows. Utilizing this option, fault isolation may be fully supported from the enterprise network to the hub-port level. Similar management applications supporting port-level fault isolation are available from Cabletron, Bytex, Ungermann Bass, IBM, and Digital Equipment.

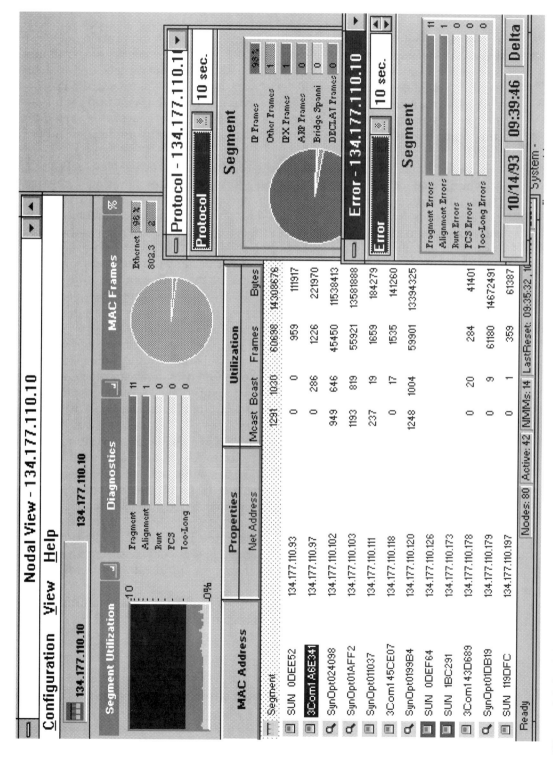

Figure 3.6 Optivity screen shot showing port status

3.5   ARE EXPERT SYSTEMS WORTH THE COST?

The requirement for adequate service level in complex communication networks drives the demand for fast, consistent, expert quality response to operational problems. Effective, flexible automation of both routine operations and problem handling and determination would satisfy this demand by improving the productivity. However, the fault management environment is characterized by high—and usually increasing—complexity, making the automatic operator very difficult to implement. There is no doubt that procedural software does not afford sufficient flexibility.

Network administrators perform many routine tasks, such as data collecting, activating and deactivating components, answering user questions, starting tests, and alternating routes. In addition, network administrators watch a number of consoles for applications, processors, operating systems, communication software, and network monitor-related messages. Problem determination and resolution usually involves requesting more information about network status, service status, consulting system and network documentation, and experience files, and submitting corrective actions or calling for on-line and/or off-line technical support. Information message rates are very high and supporting documentation is not easy to handle. In certain cases, there is no opportunity to consult references or outside assistance.

Due to these complex and dynamic responsibilities, a long training period is necessary for educating help desk and network operators and technical support staff. Even the training of newly-hired experienced personnel can represent substantial costs to the installation, since responsibilities vary across networks with management policy, with particular nodes and links installed, and with workload characteristics.

The dynamic nature of this environment is also a challenge. Operational procedures must evolve with the changing technical environment as well as with changes in staffing. The shortage of skilled personnel, increased network complexity, and growing demands to solve problems faster all create a need for more powerful network and systems management applications. In particular, applications are needed to ease the load of operators, to provide fast, consistent reactions to networking problems, to decrease the installation's dependence on specific personnel, to provide a basis for enforcing operational control methodology, and to provide a facility for integrating new procedural alternatives with old ones.

In summary, the following problems create a need for expert-system facilities in the network and systems management arena:

- Human expertise is rare.
- Educating new technicians ("human experts") is difficult.
- This expertise is in high demand.
- The activities of problem determination and resolution can be well defined, and solutions do exist.
- Problems are complex, and usually no time is available to consult references or outside help.

- Mistakes and delays may impair the service level of the enterprise's networks and, consequently, the operation of the entire business is affected.

3.5.1   Expert System Architecture

Figure 3.7 depicts the general architecture of an expert system. Two principal information sources trigger the expert system:

- Monitored input with or without filtering, representing a gateway to various monitors, analyzers, and element management systems.
- Manual input generated by user calls at the client contact point.

The expert system "fires" rules (pre-specified actions) once the application is triggered by special events, alarms, program calls, or status changes of attributes in the Configuration database. Depending on the rule's execution, further status information may be requested.

The expert system provides output in the following forms:

Interpretation Measurement values are combined and correlated; alerts may be issued.

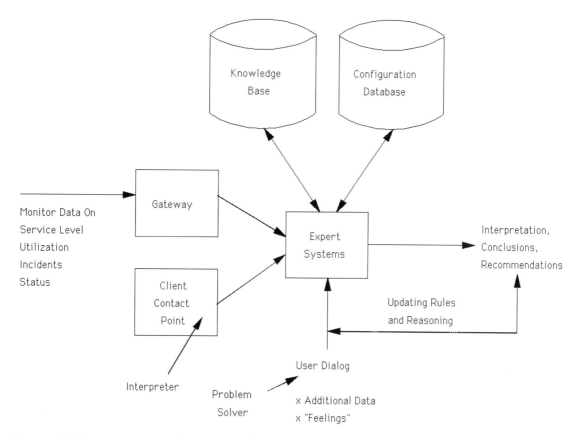

Figure 3.7 Expert system architecture for fault management

Recommendations Further data and/or operator actions are required while the expert system execution is pending and waiting for additional input.

Conclusions Problem diagnosis either has been concluded or additional actions are required. In more advanced systems, problem restoration can be solved automatically, and messages are displayed about successful execution.

Suppliers of expert-like systems are working to enhance their products to support more comprehensive management solutions. Some vendors are merely providing shells; others start with an off-line system and migrate slowly to on-line systems.

Currently, the most effective expert-system prototypes are implemented as either off-line or on-line systems. With off-line implementations, the network operator specifies the tasks for the expert system. The expert system responds with the most likely fault reason and displays recommended actions. The operator accepts or rejects these recommendations.

In on-line implementations, the expert system is part of the automated monitoring and control system, and works without specified tasks defined by the network operator. Results of fault diagnosis and conclusions are displayed while control actions are automatically taken. In most cases, however, the network operator can overrule the conclusions.

The majority of expert systems in the field of network management are off-line; therefore, overreactions or false conclusions do not risk the system's—and the network's—health. Off-line solutions are typical of WAN and LAN diagnostic tools, such as Network Advisor from Hewlett-Packard and Expert Sniffer from Network General. On the other hand, few expert systems are offered for large-scale network management. One exception is NetExpert from Objective Systems Integrators (OSI, 1993). The following section describes NetExpert in detail.

3.5.2   OSI NetExpert

The NetExpert is a series of software modules, each of which performs a specific network management function. NetExpert tools provide the ability to generate system interfaces to heterogeneous systems, databases and network elements (NEs). Because NetExpert was designed for use in a multi-vendor environment it does not care what these heterogeneous devices are or the protocols they use. NetExpert was written using object-oriented tools and design principals.

The heart of the expert system implementation is in the generic gateways and in the intelligent dynamic event analysis subsystem (IDEAS). (See Figure 3.8a.)

The Generic Gateway toolkit is responsible for message interchange between the managed objects and IDEAS. It accepts raw messages from managed objects, filters them, and reformats the returned message into a CMIP event message. It then parses out attributes and passes the event message to IDEAS.

There is an instance of Generic Gateway for each managed object. Generic Gateway is class-specific. Generic Gateway can communicate with managed objects in two ways; direct connection or dial-in/out (polling). Direct connect includes protocols such as X.25, 3270, or Ethernet/internet. Dial-in/out uses asynchronous ASCII.

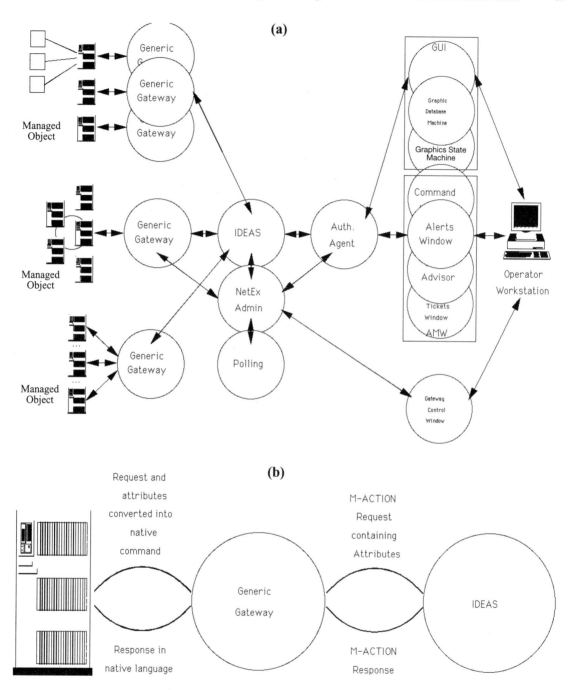

Figure 3.8 (a) NetExpert architecture and (b) Expert-heart of NetExpert

Generic Gateway's runtime analysis is defined through different kinds of rules which the network expert specifies for a class of managed object. The rules are loaded from the NetExpert Database when a Generic Gateway is started. There are separate toolkits for each of NetExpert's editors.

Four kinds of rules are downloaded to and compiled by Generic Gateway; message identification rules, message parse rules, dialog command state rules, and dialog response state rules. These rules are composed of operators, operands, and attributes for the class of managed object which is being analyzed.

Message identification rules are used by Generic Gateway to analyze messages received from the managed objects. These identification rules must test true in order for the message parse rules to be invoked. These identification rules are organized in an event hierarchy tree, starting with the most common, and working out to the most specific.

When each rule leading from the root to the leaf tests true, message parse rules are used to parse information from the message stream. The parse rules extract values from the message stream and assign them to attribute names.

Attributes are specific to that instance of the managed object. Suppose the network had three PBXs of the same class, each generating a separate message stream. Attributes parsed from each message stream would be specific to the PBX generating the messages. Attributes are encapsulated in an M-EVENT-REPORT and passed to IDEAS for further analysis.

Dialog command and response rules can be invoked several ways, i.e., by the Generic Gateway or by an M-ACTION, M-SET, or M-GET request from IDEAS. If Generic Gateway receives an M-ACTION request, Generic Gateway translates the action ID from the dialog command table to native MO (managed object) commands and substitutes the values of the attributes passed in the M-ACTION request into the attributes of this native command. Generic Gateway sends this command to the MO and waits until a response is received from the MO. Generic Gateway then identifies this response using the dialog response identification and parse rules. The result of the dialog ID and parse is passed back to IDEAS in an M-ACTION response. Generic Gateway handles M-GET and M-SET similarly.

IDEAS analysis is defined by the network expert using the Rule Editor and the Dialog Editor, and is stored in the NetExpert Database. This declarative analysis logic is downloaded from the NetExpert Database when IDEAS is started. The IDEAS toolkit supports many different types of operations, including the following:

- attribute assignment
- arithmetic operations
- boolean operations
- conditional logic
- dialoguing
- event correlation
- user-defined functions
- threshold objects
- timers

IDEAS interacts with Generic Gateway, Authorization Agent, and the Graphics module. (See Figure 3.8b.) IDEAS analyzes M-EVENT-REPORTS from Generic Gateway and creates and maintains internal events. These events are analyzed to determine further action. Possible actions include the creation of an alert for display in the operator's window, incrementing a frequency or threshold counter, or deletion of the event due to subsequent information.

Events are internal objects in IDEAS, while alerts represent information of interest which will be presented to the NetExpert operator.

Alerts are represented by text and graphics in the Alert Management and Graphics Windows. IDEAS also analyzes M-GET, M-SET, and M-ACTION responses from Generic Gateway. M-ACTION, M-GET, and M-SET requests can be sent to IDEAS via the Authorization Agent. The operator can communicate directly with an MO via a Cut Through Window or use the command and response capability set up in the Dialog Editor. IDEAS stores event and alert records in the NetExpert Database. These records can be accessed further in the Alert Management Window.

The inference machine with the rules base and configuration should be continuously maintained. For updating rules, source information, reasoning, and expert system output should be logged and evaluated. In certain circumstances, additional data and even "feelings" of the master operator may be required. In other words, problem solving is interrupted for human guidance about further rules execution. These statements justify the applicability of fault management functions for successful expert-systems implementation.

3.5.3   Benefits of Using Expert Systems

The principal benefits of using expert systems for network operational control may be summarized as follows (Terp, 1992):

- Faster problem determination: Actions not requiring manual intervention are executed at computer processor speed.
- Knowledge-intensive decision making: The best available knowledge is available in the knowledge base. This knowledge level is probably higher than that of an average network operator.
- Data-intensive decision making: Problem determination may be based on large amounts of network-related information not easily organized or comprehended by a human operator.
- Reliability: Expert systems execute repetitive tasks without taking breaks.
- Decreased worker requirements: Experts systems help to avoid an explosion of human resource demand because network operational control personnel are needed only to handle exceptional incidents and to operate the expert system.
- Stability: Reactions to incidents are consistent and follow network-management strategy.
- Decreased dependence on specific personnel: Knowledge and operational rules are encoded in the knowledge base rather than in the private "non-visible files of the most experienced operators.

- Flexibility: Knowledge-based and operational rules may easily be updated as a function of network evolution, tools, and changing operational conditions.
- Avoidance of human interpretation of operational rules: The knowledge base is applied directly; thus the effects of operational-control policy changes can be better isolated, observed, and evaluated.
- Tool integration: Expert systems may interface with various information extraction tools but require one information type for a certain command. Operating in this manner, information-extraction redundancy may be avoided. Expert systems help decide what is the right source and activate tools automatically.

Despite these benefits, caveats are involved in network operational control-oriented expert systems. An expert system is truly effective only if it can determine problems faster than the human operator. Also, maintaining an expert system is not a trivial task. The sheer volume of devices and systems in a network may require thousands of rules, unless rules may be symbolically formulated. Also, dynamic network changes may require frequent updates in the knowledge base.

Often, the interpretation and synthesis of message groups is more complex than initially estimated due to the difficulty of determining the start and end of events relevant to a certain symptom. A fairly large number of additional management applications may be required for identifying the actual network status, and the expert system should interface to all of them. Despite these potential limitations, expert systems are worth the money if they are well designed and well maintained.

3.6   TURNING REAMS OF DATA INTO CONCISE, USEFUL INFORMATION

The activity of performance management demands far more measurement data than does the activity of fault management. Performance management processes cannot be satisfied by typical SNMP-MIB-entries providing managed object status in pre-defined intervals. Rather, in-depth measurements are required at various levels of systems and network architectures. State-of-the-art monitoring technology offers a number of measurement options, but unfortunately few measurement strategies are offered.

3.6.1   Barriers to Effective Performance Monitoring

Network managers are confronted with a number of problems when facing the task of measuring performance across the enterprise network. While many LAN and WAN monitors can provide a rich set of data, the information is localized to the link or segment on which the monitor is installed. Transmitting the large volumes of management data over LANs and WANs requires considerable in-band or out-band bandwidth. This can become very expensive very quickly. In addition, costs of special master platforms must not be underestimated.

Standard or de-facto protocols, such as SNMP or CMIP, introduce higher overhead than proprietary protocols, reducing the efficiency of transmission. In some cases, this may persuade managers to use proprietary protocols.

Once data is transmitted, is must be interpreted, filtered, analyzed, processed, databased, and displayed in realtime or near-realtime. With the exception of legacy solutions, support for performance databases is almost non-existent in today's management systems.

Efforts have been made to standardize aspects of performance monitoring. In particular, the Internet Engineering Task Force (IETF) has defined a Remote Network Monitoring (RMON) MIB that defines certain types of performance indicators. While RMON represents a step forward, but it is also a "least common denominator" that is limited in comparison to the rich functionality of the proprietary monitors. (See Table 3-1 and Table 3-2.)

Cost is another barrier to effective performance monitoring. High-end monitors and analyzers that support expert-like analysis capabilities are too expensive to deploy at multiple remote sites. Costs can be reduced by putting monitoring and analysis capabilities into hub modules. At that point, however, remote reconfiguration by the central site requires a very powerful hub management system, which may become expensive.

TABLE 3-1   RMON MIB Groups

Statistics Group	Features a table that tracks about 20 different characteristics of traffic on the Ethernet LAN segment, including total octets and packets, over-sized packets and errors.
History Group	Allows a manager to establish the frequency and duration of traffic-observation intervals, called "buckets." The agent can then record the characteristics of traffic according to these bucket intervals.
Alarm Group	Permits the user to establish the criteria and thresholds that will prompt the agent to issue alarms.
Host Group	Organizes traffic statistics by each LAN node, based on time intervals set by the manager.
HostTopN Group	Allows the user to set up ordered lists and reports based on the highest statistics generated via the Host Group.
Matrix Group	Maintains two tables of traffic statistics based on pairs of communicating nodes: one is organized by sending node addresses, the other by receiving node addresses.
Filter Group	Allows a manager to define, by channel, particular characteristics of packets. A filter might instruct the agent, for example, to record packets with a value that indicates they contain DECnet messages.
Packet Capture Group	This group works with the Filter Group and lets the manager specify the memory resources to be used for recording packets that meet the filter criteria.
Event Group	Allows the manager to specify a set of parameters or conditions to be observed by the agent. Whenever these parameters or conditions occur, the agent will record an event into a log (Mier, 1993).

TABLE 3-2 Token Ring RMON MIB Groups

Statistics Group	This group includes packets, octets, broadcasts, dropped packets, soft errors and packet distribution statistics. Statistics are at two levels: MAC for the protocol level and LLC statistics to measure traffic flow.
History Group	Long-term historical data for segment trend analysis. Histories include both MAC and LLC statistics.
Host Group	Collects information on each host discovered on the segment.
HostTopN Group	Provides sorted statistics that allow reduction of network overhead by looking only at the most active hosts on each segment.
Matrix Group	Reports on traffic errors between any host pair for correlating conversations on the most active nodes.
Ring Station Group	Collects general ring information and specific information for each station. General information includes: ring state (normal, beacon, claim token, purge); active monitor; number of active stations. Ring Station information includes a variety of error counters, station status, insertion time, and last enter/exit time.
Ring Station Order	Maps station MAC addresses to their order in the ring.
Source Routing Statistics	In source-routing bridges, information is provided on the number frames and octets transmitted to and from the local ring. Other data includes broadcasts per route and frame counter per hop.
Alarm Group	Reports changes in network characteristics based on thresholds for any or all MIBs. This allows RMON to be used as a proactive tool.
Event Group	Logging of events on the basis of thresholds. Events may be used to initiate functions such as data capture or instance counts to isolate specific segments of the network.
Filter Group	Definitions of packet matches for selective information capture. These include logical operations (AND, OR, NOT) so network events can be specified for data capture, alarms, and statistics.
Packet Capture Group	Stores packets that match filtering specifications.

To overcome these problems, network managers can implement the following strategies:

- Share the master console between the SNMP manager and the monitor ensuring high correlation between fault and performance management functions
- Purchase products that support the RMON specification
- Build a distributed and networked structure of the monitors using lower-priced on-site tools

- Implement various applications at the platform level that help to analyze data, interpret load, generate load, database data, and display results.

3.6.2 HP NetMetrix

The following example shows how organizations can overcome the problems described previously by using a product called NetMetrix from Hewlett-Packard. The purpose of selecting this example is twofold:

- The product supports both standard MIBs (RMON, MIB-II) as well as private MIBs extensions
- The product architecture limits the use of SNMP and X-Windows to remote analysis, reducing bandwidth demand.

Figure 3.9 depicts the HP NetMetrix architecture, showing the server, agents and the Remote X-Windows system.

NetMetrix is a client-server package consisting of two basic components. The server component includes the GUI and the applications that correlate the information gathered by the clients (agents) at remote sites. Because it supports the RMON MIB, the server can simultaneously gather and consolidate information

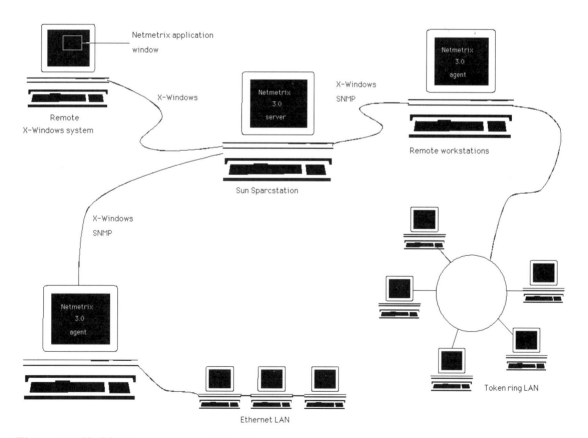

Figure 3.9 NetMetrix measurement structure

about multiple LAN segments. The client component runs on any remote UNIX workstation. It collects information about its network segment and either displays it remotely using X Windows or sends it back to the server using SNMP.

The NetMetrix agent software is available in several versions, each with varying levels of support for the RMON MIB. The Basic Agent includes Groups 1, 2, 3, and 9 of the RMON MIB for Ethernet LANs. The Load Monitor Power Agent adds Groups 4, 5, and 6, as well as HP NetMetrix's proprietary RMON MIB extensions for Ethernet, token ring, and FDDI. Finally, the Protocol Analysis Power Agent supports all RMON groups and decodes data at all seven layers of the OSI stack.

Compliance with the RMON MIB allows NetMetrix to collect traffic information from those third-party monitors that also implement this MIB. However, even with the benefits of using RMON MIBs, a central management facility is required to poll remote sites.

The amount of data for a complex, distributed internet could quickly overwhelm a LAN. To get the benefits of RMON without polling, NetMetrix uses X-Windows, which processes remote segment information on the segment itself, via commands generated at a central display station. Employing a combination of RMON and X-Windows, NetMetrix users can zoom in on specific segments and switch into local mode to run applications on those segments.

The NetMetrix server can run as a stand-alone application on workstations under SunOS from Sun Microsystems Inc. It also can be remotely accessed by any net management system that supports X-Windows. NetMetrix also supports integration with HP Openview Network Node Manager from Hewlett-Packard Co., IBM AIX Netview/6000, SunConnect SunNet Manager, and other platforms. This allows the network monitor to be activated through an icon from the system's main menu. The server software can handle information from an unlimited number of agents.

In addition to basic measurement capabilities, NetMetrix offers a number of applications. The most important ones include:

Internetwork Monitor Allows users to view segment, MAC, and network levels of an internetwork. True end-to-end visibility and performance monitoring is achieved via multi-segment network level statistics correlation. Thresholding allows any user to get information fast.

Load Monitor Flexible user controlled ZOOM feature allows users to correlate network statistics into meaningful information. Users can ZOOM in to see who talks to whom, when, and with what protocols at different OSI layers. The Load Monitor can be used in real time or in historical mode to recreate problem events.

Protocol Analyzer NetMetrix supports the display of packets during capture and automatic match of Request/Reply packets and high level filters. Seven-layer protocol decodes for all major protocol families is also supported.

NFS Monitor This application measures load and response time by server, client, NFS procedure, or time interval. NFS Monitor assists users in load balancing NFS traffic. The ZOOM feature allows users to optimize traffic and effectively distribute servers across the network. By using Load Monitor, operators can see which clients access what servers and when.

Traffic Generator This application can simulate load for capacity planning or edit and replay captured traces for development tests. It can recalculate checksums on edited frames and allow users to produce conditional responses to captured frames on the fly. The Traffic Generator works simultaneously with other NetMetrix applications to display the results of tests in realtime.

All NetMetrix applications run remotely in background mode on each segment monitor. By using X-Windows to display the results of network monitoring and analysis, users save system resources and bandwidth.

In addition to HP NetMetrix, other excellent solutions are available from Network General (Distributed and Expert Sniffer), from Concord (Trakker), and from Novell (LANAnalyzer). In the future, traffic monitoring and analysis applications may be enhanced to include remote switchover capability for the agents. For example, the Bytex Division of Network Systems is currently developing an enhancement to its ProSentry application based on remote switchover, which can make these remote site monitoring tool sets even more affordable.

RMON-based monitoring supports both LANs and WANs. Frontier Software Development, Inc.'s NETScout monitors WAN links and LAN internetwork domains. Similar solutions are expected from the DA-30 family of WAN and LAN monitors from Wandel and Goltermann.

3.7   APPLYING KERBEROS TO INCREASE SECURITY

Kerberos is an authentication process developed at the Massachusetts Institute of Technology (MIT) that is designed improve security in a distributed computing environment. Kerberos technology has been incorporated into the Open Software Foundation's (OSF's) Distributed Computing Environment (DCE). Digital Equipment Corp. has implemented Kerberos on its UNIX-based Ultrix operating system.

The Kerberos authentication system that uses a private key system to produce self-authenticating messages known as tickets and authenticators. These messages are sent from the clients to any server the clients need. Tickets contain different information fields. Included is a session key that is unique to the communication between a client and a server. The session key can also be used to encrypt communication between the client and server. The Kerberos server distributes tickets and authenticators to the clients. Kerberos servers generate session keys and maintain a database of private keys which are used only between a particular client and server.

3.7.1   Authentication Using Kerberos

During implementation, the responsibilities of the Kerberos server maybe split into authentication and ticket generating as shown in Figure 3.10. Authentication using Kerberos consists of the following steps:

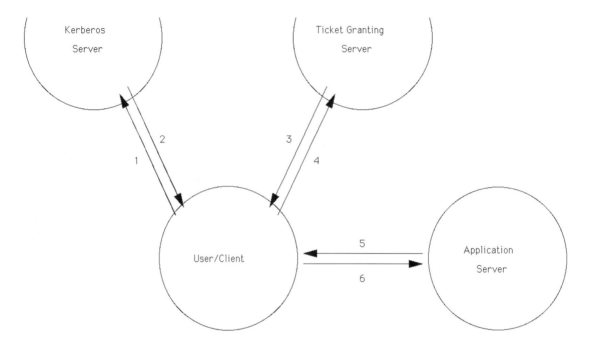

Figure 3.10 Authentication process by Kerberos

Step 1: Client sends a ticket request to the Kerberos server. The request contains the user's name and the name of the service being accessed.

Step 2: The Kerberos server responds by sending back a ticket request. The Kerberos server authenticates the identity of the user indirectly, by sending the response encrypted in the private key of the user. Thus, only the real user can decode this message.

Step 3: The user sends the request to the Ticket Granting Service without any major changes or additions.

Step 4: The ticket granting service provides the ticket including the session key. The ticket is encrypted in the private key of the application server, and it cannot be interpreted by the user. The client decodes the response using a key derived from the password typed by the user. The ticket conveys the session key to the application server. The ticket is valid for a limited period.

Step 5: The user sends a request for a service message, containing the ticket and the authenticator to the server. The authenticator is encrypted with the session key. The server decodes everything without contacting the Kerberos server.

Step 6: Acknowledgment is being sent back to the user from server, encrypted again in the session key.

In summary, use of Kerberos ensures that no secret information is passed over the network unencrypted. The client needs only to interact with the Kerberos server, and then only once per network service requested within a certain time period. By using session keys that timeout, exposure can be minimized. The system can be used to authenticate either people or systems. Maintenance is central in the Kerberos server, and it is flexible in terms of changing rights and allocations. The Kerberos server may be partitioned allowing multiple user groups to share the same platform for various application servers.

On the down side, Kerberos' use of the DES encryption algorithm may cause problems when implementing systems outside the United States, since the U.S. government regulates the exportation of DES technology.

3.7.2   Obtaining Kerberos Systems

The core of Kerberos is available from MIT and has been adopted by OSF for its Distributed Computing Environment (DCE) security services. A number of vendors—including Digital Equipment, IBM, Hewlett-Packard, and SunSoft—are incorporating OSF's DCE into their UNIX-based operating systems. Compatibility problems will not occur until Kerberos is implemented in specific flavors of UNIX. In this area, Tivoli Systems and Cygnus have been working on commercially available products.

Once OSF's DCE gets moved to other operating systems, however, or if Kerberos itself becomes more widely used outside OSF DCE, there might be problems in heterogeneous environments. In particular, problems may arise involving the following issues:

- Portability of the original Kerberos code to new UNIX systems
- Database migration to the non-UNIX environment
- Customizing data communication between the servers, users, and applications.
- Version control of Kerberos may be with different vendors in addition to OSF, who is actually responsible.

The wide acceptance of Kerberos technology is a positive sign for implementing an industry-wide standard.

3.7.3   UNIX Systems Security

Related to Kerberos is the question of UNIX security in general. State-of-the-art management platforms are based on UNIX. The vulnerability of this operating system means high rates of security violation at the most sensitive level. How realistic are the threats? UNIX does not contain an overwhelming number of features to guarantee absolutely the security of all data and applications on the system. The primary gaps in UNIX security are not due to a lack of measurements, but rather to a lack of awareness of security issues in the UNIX environment and the role each user plays in securing the system. The bottom line is that UNIX systems may be protected by following these steps:

- changing passwords frequently
- preventing the implementation of untested or unsafe software
- refusing to grant public access to files and directories
- equally securing the management servers and management workstations
- not declaring any processors of the management structure as trusted hosts

Of course, a combination of the above with more powerful hardware- and software-based security measures would give the necessary protection to the management system.

3.8 LICENSE MANAGEMENT IN THE DISTRIBUTED SYSTEMS ENVIRONMENT

Software license management is closely related to software distribution and maintenance. Businesses have a legal responsibility for their licensed software. Network and system administrators are at risk if they do not control the application packages loaded on and available from the network. License management improves quantification in two respects:

- Accounting and chargeback within the company based on actual use of applications and resources.
- Controlling the licensing agreement with the vendor.

In most organizations today, license management is made difficult because of many factors. First, pricing structures offered by software vendors are obsolete and no longer accepted by users. Often, organizations exercise practically no control over who is using what types of software. Typically, internal chargeback is based upon resource categories rather than actual use of applications and systems resources.

As with electronic software distribution, practically no standards and no recommendations exist for license management application programming interfaces.

3.8.1 Solutions from the Open Software Foundation (OSF)

The Open Software Foundation (OSF) has selected Network License (NetLS) Server from Gradient Technologies (in cooperation with Hewlett-Packard and Digital Equipment Corp.) as the basis for the licensing management position of its Distributed Management Environment (DME). Many vendors are expected to support NetLS.

NetLS consists of the license server software, which issues "permissions to run" to applications over the network. At the same time, the usage counter is increased for the user who has requested the permission. NetLS may be also utilized as the basis of the inventory software and track program versions, user identification, and usage. This would allow businesses to eliminate applications that are not being used or to buy additional licenses for high-demand applications. In addition to NetLS, there is another defacto standard, called Licensing Service API (LSAPI) that defines how applications talk to the licensing server. The two defacto standards do not conflict because they address different areas (Figure 3.11).

The Network License Server may be extended by a Software Application Depot. In such cases, licensing means that users may use the whole library, but they will be charged for the actual use—as controlled by the Network License

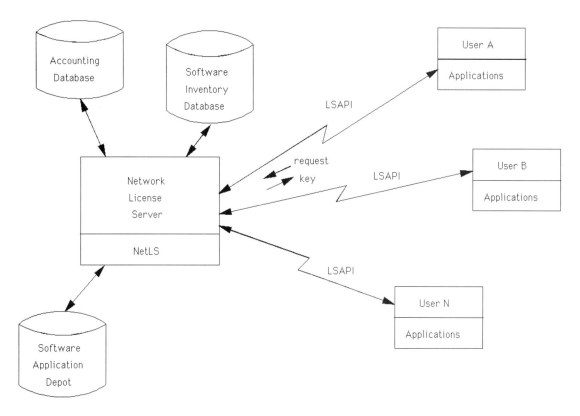

Figure 3.11 License management using NetLS and LSAPI

Server. Such a library will typically be sent to the user on a CD-ROM disk, which is the preferred delivery solution for suppliers with a large number of software products and a large installed base.

Suppliers are expected to incorporate license calls into their applications using LSAPI. Each call will generate a request to a license manager, which will distribute a license key giving information about the license. Additional control opportunities may be incorporated in the license server. In order to control the usage of certain applications and to optimize systems and networks load, permissions may only be granted for certain periods of time. If permitted, the server returns a key and the application is allowed to run, provided the user has the valid security clearance. If the system is overloaded, user requests may be put into a temporary queue.

3.8.2   Tally Systems' NetCensus

Tally Systems Corp. of Hanover, New Hampshire, recently introduced a software product called NetCensus that automates the inventory of hardware and software residing on networked PCs. Tally System's NetCensus is aimed at network managers who have large systems to track and software licenses to enforce and at financial professionals who need precise inventories to predict upgrade costs.

The software runs on network operating systems, including Novell, Inc.'s NetWare, Banyan Systems, Inc.'s Vines, and Microsoft Corp.'s LAN Manager. It collects serial numbers for leading software packages such as Lotus Development Corp.'s 1-2-3, Microsoft's Excel, WordPerfect Corp.'s WordPerfect, Aldus Corp.'s PageMaker, and Borland International, Inc.'s dBase IV.

For the major network operating systems, NetCensus includes identification of network shell and driver versions and LAN addresses. The software also inventories hardware components such as type of PC, manufacturer, amount of storage, add-on boards, and monitor types.

3.9   SUMMARY

The accelerated implementation of solutions for high-priority management processes will help increase the effectiveness and efficiency of systems and network management. This section described several products that can assist users in solving high-priority management problems. The following chapters will describe many more products, as well as industry trends. In particular, single stand-alone hardware- or software-based products will give way to a combination of management platforms and applications. While many of these applications are ports of existing stand-alone products onto various management platforms, there are a number of completely new applications now in development by independent software vendors (ISVs) and other startup companies.

4

Management Platforms

In the network management industry, the term "platform" is used to describe a complex software package that forms the basis for an organization's enterprise-wide network and systems management solution. Systems management vendors such as Tivoli also refer to their enterprise-wide, distributed systems management products as "platforms" or "frameworks." Unfortunately, the word "platform" can be initially confusing for those who are accustomed to seeing this term used to denote a specific hardware base, such as Intel X86 for example.

Webster's dictionary defines a platform as a "plan or design" and "a declaration of principles or policies." That is precisely what a management platform is meant to be—a blueprint for managing networked systems. It is not a complete turnkey solution, but a starting point—a "shell" as it were, to which one must add third-party and user-written applications capable of solving specific management problems.

The management platform and the applications it supports adhere to certain principles of openness, including use of published, vendor-neutral protocols and provision of application programming interfaces (APIs.) While most management platforms support the SNMP today, a truly open management platform must also be capable of supporting future and emerging standards such as CMIP, the Desktop Management Task Force (DMTF) specifications, and the Object Management Group's (OMG's) Common Object Request Broker Architecture (CORBA). To be more specific, the platform should be modular in construction, allowing incorporation of new protocols without affecting the management applications it supports.

4.1 NETWORK MANAGEMENT MODELS

The fundamental characteristics of data communications networks are changing rapidly. As mainframe-based, centralized computing has given way to client/ server systems, so have proprietary, monolithic network management solutions been pushed aside for multivendor, standards-based models.

4.1.1 Global Operations Director

In a single-vendor environment, it is theoretically possible to employ one powerful, centralized management system for monitoring and controlling all network devices and systems, or "elements." Central managers of this type, as in Figure 4.1(a), have been referred to as "global operations directors" (GODs) (Her, 1991).

A global operations director uses a proprietary management protocol to transport management data and issue commands directly to network elements. The advantage of a global operations director is that the proprietary management protocol and related mechanisms are optimized for that vendor's devices and are, therefore, very efficient.

The drawback to this approach is, of course, that it is incapable of effectively managing third-party devices or subsystems. While protocol converters, or proxy agents may be employed, the global operations director's knowledge of third-party device behavior and commands is limited. Thus, the end-user who has purchased a global operations director is effectively locked into one vendor's product offerings as well as that one vendor's view of what constitutes "network management."

The most widely used global operations director to date has been IBM's mainframe-based NetView (e.g., the "original" IBM NetView, introduced in 1987). However, IBM is restructuring the entire NetView family to accommodate today's networks (see Chapter 6.)

4.1.2 Manager-of-Managers

The proprietary global operations director is not designed for multivendor distributed networks. While GOD is highly efficient in single-vendor environments, its design runs counter to the whole "plug-and-play" philosophy of open systems and multivendor networking.

Once a network moves away from a single-vendor solution, companies are faced with the temptation to purchase a network management system for each additional manufacturer represented in the network's composition. For example, Codex modems and multiplexers require Codex's 9800 NMS; Ungermann-Bass concentrators require the NetDirector network management system; a Digital LAN would require Ethernim; the SNA network would require mainframe NetView, and so on. The result is a conglomeration of multiple, disparate management consoles, also called "element management systems" (EMSs) in the network operations center.

To reduce "console clutter" and restore order to the network operations center (NOC), two alternative network management models have evolved: the manager-of-managers (MOM), and the platform/applications model.

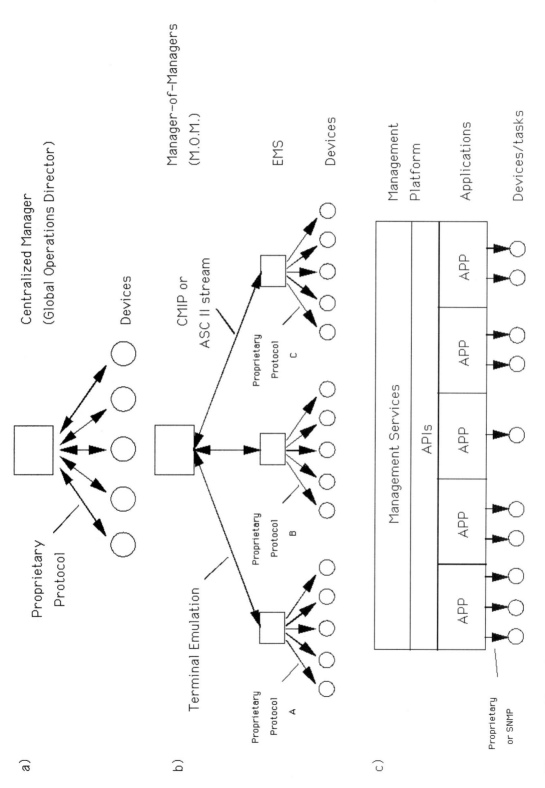

Figure 4.1 Network management models

The MOM depicted in Figure 4.1(b) relies on multiple EMSs, each communicating with its respective devices using either proprietary protocols or an "open" vendor-independent protocol such as the SNMP. Each EMS digests raw management data and forwards only critical alarms and processed data to the manager of managers—usually over a standard management protocol such as SNMP or the CMIP. EMSs may reside at remote locations or in the central NOC. In some cases, the MOM can communicate directly with managed elements via terminal emulation facilities.

The advantage of the MOM is that it can reduce console clutter in the NOC, and provide a somewhat unified view of network status on a single screen. There are several disadvantages to the MOM, however—chiefly, it is typically very expensive up front. The user must still purchase multiple element management consoles which may run from $10,000 to $20,000 or more, as well as the MOM itself, which typically costs from $50,000 to $1 million, depending on how much artificial intelligence is built into it.

Another limitation of the MOM structure is the difficulty of implementing interfaces to element management systems. The MOM vendor has two options: to persuade third-party device vendors to develop interfaces for supporting the MOM management protocol or to intercept third-party device messages from the RS-232 port (ASCII stream) and create a library of alert translation tables for various devices.

IBM's NetView/PC is implemented using the first option, where third-party vendors develop interfaces that translate native alerts into IBM Network Management Vector Transport (NMVT) messages. The AT&T Accumaster Integrator also used option A, however, vendors translated native messages into a CMIP-like format. Most current MOM product offerings use a second option, including Boole and Babbage Command/Post, Maxim's MAXM, Objective Systems Integrator's NetExpert, and Allink's Operations Coordinator.

Ultimately, the MOM has limited value to a majority of end-user corporations unless many vendor interfaces are available on the market. However, the MOM interface is usually much more restrictive in functionality than the third-party vendor's own management software. This dissuades third parties from investing money to develop a MOM interface that does not put the manageability of their equipment in the best light.

Finally, the level of integration afforded by the MOM is typically limited to fault detection and some correlation. Typically, little or no sharing of data occurs between EMS processes and the MOM, other than passing alerts—this makes activities such as configuration management difficult. Reconfiguration and other tasks that require sending commands to the EMS are usually accomplished via terminal emulation. In that case each EMS presents its own user interface on the central MOM console. In many cases, there is no sharing of information between different EMSs; this results in redundant data, redundant polling and reduced efficiency of fault isolation and diagnosis. If the MOM supports an rules-based expert system capability, some redundancies and inefficiencies can be reduced, however.

On the other hand, MOMs are capable of addressing the management of legacy systems, at least to some degree. In particular, complex MOM frameworks and development environments, such as Advanced Computing Device's Network-Knowledge and Teknekron's Objective System Platform (OSP) can be used to create highly effective, integrated management systems. Legacy system management is a weakness of open management platform (see following section). Many organizations reject purchasing a $100,000+ MOM because of the high initial price tag, but they ultimately pay a systems integration firm twice that much to develop applications for legacy system management under an open management platform such as HP OpenView or SunNet Manager.

4.1.3   Open Management Platform

The third network management model, now becoming the most widely implemented in client/server networks, is the platform/applications model as shown in Figure 4.1(c). In this model, element management systems still exist but take on a new form—as software modules integrated into the management platform, rather than as a separate console. Communications between the management platform and the application typically use SNMP or proxy agents.

Management platforms support a "manager-agent" model characteristic of both Open Systems Interconnection (OSI) management frameworks and SNMP specifications. In brief, a manager-agent paradigm dictates that an agent (a passive software process residing on a managed device or system) collects data and reports it to the manager. The manager process is user-initiated. (See Figure 4.2.)

In the SNMP environment, the manager can obtain information from the agent by polling managed objects on a periodic basis. Also, agents can transmit unsolicited event messages, called "traps," to the manager.

The management platform-applications model has several benefits for the user: (1) elimination of multiple consoles, (2) flexibility in mixing and matching applications as required, and (3) better command/control over the third-party devices. The terminal emulation step is eliminated, so the application provides full direct control.

Of course, the effectiveness of the platform/applications model hinges on widespread availability of third-party applications and the degree of harmonious integration between the platform and the applications. So far, the model has been more successful than the MOM's model in attracting third-party support. In particular, the platform/applications model allows third parties to enhance the manageability of their products without the restrictions of a limited command set. Furthermore, it relieves third-party vendors of the financial burden of developing their own GUIs and management consoles. To date, however, most applications are very loosely integrated with the supporting platform, and very little application-to-application integration exists (see section 4.6). Theoretically, applications may also communicate among themselves to reduce polling overhead and database redundancies. This capability has been realized in very few products to date, however.

The widespread acceptance of the platform/applications model has also been enabled by the popularity of SNMP, which has made it possible to easily and inexpensively implement standardized communications between applications and devices, and between applications and platforms.

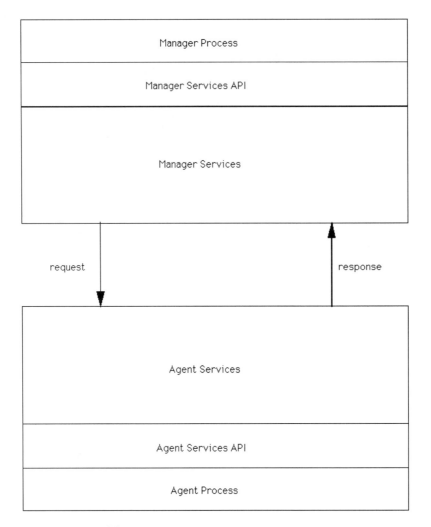

Figure 4.2 Manager-agent model

4.1.4   Evolution of SNMP Platforms

In 1988, the SNMP was developed to monitor routers and gateways across mul-tivendor environments within the Internet. As the first widely-implemented vendor-neutral management protocol, the SNMP quickly gave rise to a new market as network device vendors sought to use "manageability" as a product differentiator.

By late 1990, the U.S. market had become crowded with SNMP-based network management systems, called "stations." SNMP stations were offered by at least 60 different vendors, most of whom were suppliers of bridges, routers, intelligent concentrators, and other internetwork devices.

These early stations were not much more than glorified MIB browsers, capable of displaying raw data or "variables" stored in the standard MIB of any device supporting SNMP agent implementation. By supporting the standard MIBs, SNMP stations could provide rudimentary monitoring of third-party SNMP devices. Typically, each station vendor also added an application for interpreting data stored in the proprietary "private" enterprise MIBs specific to their product line. These device-specific "value-added" applications were of much greater value to the network manager than MIB browser support; but to obtain value-added management features for each device in the network, users were forced to purchase multiple SNMP stations.

The proliferation of these vendor-specific SNMP management stations created two problems:

1. Poor rate of return-on-investment (ROI) for the vendor
2. Continued "console clutter" for the user

Due to increased competitive pressures, network device vendors were forced to continue investing in network management product development to maintain a "leading edge" image. Vendors specializing in connectivity solutions found themselves diverting their R&D to enhancing the GUI, device discovery, MIB browsers, and other network management features of their stations. Marketing SNMP management stations quickly became a sink-hole; internetworking device vendors discovered that R&D money could be more profitably spent on creating a faster router or a more flexible hub.

Manageability was (and still is) a key selling point for networking equipment. But now, organizations are not willing to add another SNMP station to the operations centers each time a new type of device gets plugged into the network. Organizations are demanding management solutions that fit in an overall strategy. Enter the platform—one console capable of supporting multiple applications from various vendors.

4.2   BASIC MANAGEMENT PLATFORM SERVICES

In 1991, the notion of an standards-based, "open" management "platform" began to gain widespread attention in the network management industry. In particular, Sun Microsystems' SunNet Manager and Hewlett-Packard's HP OpenView were the first vendors to incorporate basic platform services into their SNMP stations, and promote the idea of supporting third-party applications as well as their own.

Now, several years later, it is clear that only a handful of both network and systems management products—the open management platforms—will survive as "base products" or frameworks upon which organizations will fashion their network and systems management strategies. The platform/applications model appears to be the only viable method of productizing effective solutions for managing the distributed systems network environment.

4.2.1   Management Platform Services vs. Station Services

A management platform provides the same services as an SNMP station—and more. Typical SNMP stations provide alarm facilities and, of course SNMP support in the form of MIB browsers, compilers, and underlying transport facilities. Platforms are typically designed with a more modular architecture, enabling future support for protocols besides SNMP, without affecting existing applications. Most importantly, management platforms provide published application programming interfaces (APIs), developer's toolkits, partner's programs, and other incentives to encourage third parties to develop applications for the platform. This feature is the most clear distinction between an open management platform and the run-of-the-mill SNMP management station. Moreover, in the current market shakeout, many users are of the opinion that the only platforms with strong third-party support are truly viable product choices.

In addition to these basic platform services, the more advanced platforms also provide features such as the ability to support management domains; manager-to-manager communications; advanced alarm correlation and network modeling; conditional state alarming; polling on classes of objects as well as on individual devices; distributed implementation (whereby polling and data analysis can be processed locally, and only processing information sent back to the central console); and distributed database. Some platforms are also distinguished by their support for additional specifications such as the Open Software Foundation's Distributed Management Environment (OSF/DME) and the Network Management Forum's OMNIPoint.

Many network management functions are now supported by third-party applications rather than by the platform itself (see Chapter 5). Examples include device-specific management (hubs, routers, terminal servers, workstations, etc.), traffic monitoring and analysis, data analysis and reporting, system and network inventory and physical configuration management (wiring), trouble ticketing and internal help desk, and support for managing legacy (non-SNMP) equipment.

4.2.2   Description of Basic Management Platform Services

Management platforms support the following basic services:

- Device discovery and network mapping
- Alarm capabilities
- Management protocol support
- SQL Database links
- APIs and developer's toolkits

Many third-party management applications now rely on management platforms to provide these services. The following sections briefly describe basic management platform services.

4.2.2.1   Device Discovery/Network Mapping

Discovery refers to the network management system's ability to automatically learn the identity and type of devices currently active on the network. At minimum, a management platform should be capable of discovery active IP devices by retrieving data from a router's IP tables and address resolution protocol (ARP) tables.

However, even this capability does not guarantee that all IP devices on a given network will be detected. For example, relying solely on routing tables is inadequate in purely bridged networks where there are no routers. Thus, a more comprehensive discovery facility should also include other mechanisms such as broadcast messages (PING and others) that can reach out to any IP device and retrieve its address and other identifying information.

On the other hand, discovery mechanisms that rely completely on broadcasting will incur a tremendous amount of overhead in finding devices out on the network. Ideally, a management platform should support a combination of ARP data retrieval and broadcasting.

Furthermore, a complete network discovery facility should be capable of detecting legacy system nodes, such as DECnet and SNA. Currently most platforms rely on third-party applications or traffic monitoring applications to supply discovery data on non-TCP/IP devices.

Another desirable feature is the ability to run automatic or scheduled "dynamic discovery" processes after the initial discovery to discern any changes made to the network after the initial discovery took place. In large networks especially, the price (in terms of overhead and consumed bandwidth) for running a dynamic discovery process continually in background mode may be too great; therefore the ability to schedule dynamic discovery updates at off-peak hours is important.

It is also important for the user to have the ability to set limits on the initial network discovery. Many corporate networks are now linked to the Internet, and without pre-defined limits, a discovery application may cross corporate boundaries and begin discovering everything on the global Internet. Some management platforms allow users to run discovery on a segment-by-segment basis. This can help the discovery process from becoming unmanageable.

Many management platforms are capable of automatically producing a topological map from the data collected during device discovery. However, these automatically generated maps rarely result in a graphical representation that is useful for humans. Particularly when there are hundreds of devices, the resulting map can look very cluttered—enough to be of little use.

Even when the discovery process operates on a limited or segment-by-segment basis, eventually a time will come when the operator must edit the automatically generated network map to create a visual picture to which human beings can relate. Therefore, the ability to group objects on the map, and move them around in groups or perform other types of collective actions, can be a real time-saving feature.

4.2.2.2   Alarm Capabilities

Management platforms act as a clearinghouse for critical status messages obtained from various devices and applications across the network. Messages arrive in the form of SNMP traps, alerts, or event reports when polling results indicate that thresholds have been exceeded.

The management platform supports setting of thresholds on any SNMP MIB variable. Typically, management platforms poll for device status by sending

SNMP requests to devices with SNMP agents, or Internet Control Message Protocol (ICMP) echo requests ("pings") to any TCP/IP device.

The process of setting thresholds may be supported by third-party applications or by the management platform. Some platforms (but not all) allow operators to configure polls on classes of devices; most require operators to configure a poll for each device individually. An example of an individual threshold may "errors on incoming packets from Router A > 500."

Most platforms support some degree of alarm filtering. Rudimentary filtering allows operators to assign classifications to individual alarms triggered when thresholds are exceeded: such as "informational," "warning," or "critical." Once classifications are assigned, the user can specify, for example, that only critical alarms are displayed on the screen, while all other alarms are logged.

More sophisticated alarm facilities support conditional alarms. An example of a conditional threshold may be "errors on incoming packets from device A > 500 for more than 3 times in 15 minutes." Conditional alarms can account for periodic spikes in traffic or daily busy periods.

Finally, the platform should support the ability to automatically trigger scripts when specific alarms are received.

4.2.2.3   Management Protocol Support

All leading management platforms today support SNMP. NetLabs/DiMONS and HP OpenView Distributed Manager (DM) Platform also support CMIP. Currently, most end users are only familiar with SNMP support.

The management platform provides SNMP support in several ways. First and foremost is the ability to poll SNMP devices and to receive SNMP TRAPS, as described previously. However, in order to configure polls on MIB variables of various devices, one must first know what those variables are. Management platforms provide MIB "browsers" for this purpose. A MIB browser queries user-selected SNMP network device and displays its MIB values. In addition, most platforms can display line or bar graphs of those MIB values, provided they are in numeric form (counters, etc.).

MIB browsers are crude tools, at best, displaying raw and often cryptic, low-level device information. For this reason, platforms also provide MIB application builders that allow users to quickly create applications for displaying information on MIB objects in a more meaningful way. MIB applications may include graphing realtime information on selected network nodes. However, even MIB applications builders are limited in supporting high-level analysis—that is more often provided by third-party applications.

MIB compilers allow users to bring in third-party, device-specific MIBs (also called "private" MIBs or "extended" MIBs) and register them with the management platform. While most platforms ship with a number of third-party MIBs, they do not include all possible MIBs from all vendors. A MIB compiler is necessary for adding support for third-parties whose MIBs are not shipped as part of the standard platform.

Some MIB compilers are more robust than others. Some MIB compilers will fail or abort processing if there is an error in the MIB being compiled. Unfortunately, errors in third-party MIBs are not rare. Therefore, it is desirable to have a MIB compiler that can flag errors and recover, rather than stop dead.

4.2.2.4 Graphical User Interface (GUI)

Platforms today support user-friendly GUIs. Most platforms today support OSF/ Motif; SunNet Manager supports OpenWindows.

The GUI uses color changes to indicate differences in network status; red is down, for example. Most management operations are available from a menu bar; others are available from contexmenues. Point-and-click operations are standard features, as is context-sensitive help. Most platforms allow some degree of customization of maps and icons.

While most platform GUIs are the same, a few subtle differences can be found. Some GUIs have larger icons than others. While this simplifies reading information on the icon and distinguishing status changes more quickly, a screen can quickly become cluttered with only a few large icons. Icon size is strictly a matter of user preference.

4.2.2.5 SQL Database Links

Most platforms maintain event logs in flat-file ASCII format for performance reasons. However, this format limits the network manager's ability to search for information and manipulate the data. Therefore, links to relational database management systems (RDBMSs) are now important aspects of platform architecture. Example databases supported include Ingres, Sybase, Informix, and Oracle.

An RDBMS is essential for manipulate raw data and turning it into useful information. Users can obtain information from an RDBMS by writing requests, or queries, in Structured Query Language (SQL), a universally standard language for relational database communication. Integral RDBMSs are also appearing in high-end applications, such as Cisco's CiscoWorks and Isicad Command. (For more information on these applications, see Chapter 5.)

While most management platforms also supply report writer facilities, these tools are generally not top-notch. However, most higher quality third-party reporting applications can extract data from an RDBMS using SQL.

4.2.2.6 APIs and Developer's Toolkits

Platform vendors encourage third-party applications by providing published application programming interfaces (APIs), toolkits that include libraries of software routines, and documentation to assist applications developers. Another aspect to this effort is the "partners programs"—the marketing angle of encouraging third-party applications development.

An API shields applications developers from the details of the management platform's underlying data implementation and functional architecture. Management platform vendors generally include in their developer's kits, several coded examples of how APIs can be used, and the APIs themselves.

Unfortunately for applications developers, management APIs have yet to become standardized. The programming interfaces supported by the two largest selling platforms, SunConnect's SunNet Manager and Hewlett-Packard's HP OpenView, are completely different. However, HP has licensed OpenView to several vendors, including IBM, Bull, Data General and Hitachi—and so the products offered by this group of vendors shares the same core set of APIs. However, with the exception of IBM, the installed base of the other OpenView licensees is rather small. Additionally, IBM is differentiating its product, AIX NetView/6000, from HP OpenView, and currently two APIs are unique to IBM. The differences are enough to prevent automatic porting from HP to IBM products. In summary, independent software ventors and other management applications developers are faced with the challenge of using multiple sets of APIs if they choose to develop applications for more than one vendor's platform.

In most cases, when an application takes advantage of platform APIs, the application must be recompiled with the platform code. This results in a tightly integrated end product. Many ISVs and other third-party developers lack the resources necessary to pursue this level of integration. Perhaps a more accurate way of stating this is that ISVs are not convinced that expending the extra effort to fully integrate their applications with all leading management platforms will result in a proportionally larger revenue stream. ISVs and other third-party developers face a choice: to tightly integrate their products with one management platform vendor or to loosely integrate their products with all leading platform providers. Most third-parties have chosen the latter route, as they are unwilling to turn off prospective customers who may have chosen a different platform vendor as their strategic management provider.

As a result, at least 80 percent of the third-party applications available today are only loosely integrated with the underlying management platform—at the menu bar—and completely ignoring APIs and other environment libraries (Faulkner, 1994). This is expected to change as the market matures and as platform vendors begin to offer high-level APIs which make porting applications from one management platform to another into an almost trivial exercise.

In summary, published APIs and libraries make it possible for ISVs and other third-parties to write applications that take advantage of other basic services provided by the management platform. To date, few third-parties have take full advantage of platform APIs, although this is expected to change during the next two years.

4.2.3   Description of Advanced Platform Services

More sophisticated, higher-end management platforms support the following characteristics in addition to basic services described in the previous section:

- Network modeling
- Domain management
- Manager-to-manager communications
- Distributed implementation

As management platforms evolve, support for these advanced services will grow more common among market leaders.

4.2.3.1   Network Modeling

Network modeling is an artificial intelligence capability that can assist in automated fault isolation and diagnosis as well as in performance and configuration management. Modeling allows a management system to infer the status of one object from the status of other objects.

Network modeling is facilitated by object-oriented programming techniques and languages such as C++. The goal of modeling is to simplify the representation of complex systems (such as networks), creating a layer of abstraction that shields management applications from underlying details.

The building block of this technology is the "model" which describes a network element, such as a router. A model consists of data (attributes) describing the element as well as its relationships with other elements. Abstract elements, such as organizations and protocols, can also be modeled, as can non-intelligent devices such as cables. A model may use information from other models to determine its own state; modeling can reduce the complexity of management data and highlight the most important information (Dev, 1992). In this way, fault isolation and diagnosis can be automated. In addition, models can be used to depict traffic patterns, trends, topologies, or distributions to assist in performance and configuration management.

Currently the only leading management platform to support network modeling is Cabletron Spectrum. Network Manager's NMC Vision supports a lightweight object request broker and object models.

4.2.3.2   Domain Management

Domain management refers to the ability to fashion management domains according to an organization's particular business needs, rather than letting management hierarchies be dictated by the limitations of the management platform.

Domain management typically comes into play in larger networks where there is more than one copy of the management platform. For example, the New York central control center may be responsible for overseeing status of the entire network, while regional centers in Paris and Tokyo typically manage elements in their respective geographical regions. However, it may be advantageous for certain events in the Paris domain to be visible to operators in Tokyo, or for all events to be visible to the other domain at certain hours of the day, for example. Events in one domain may signal operators in multiple domains, or events may be delegated from one operator to another. Operators will manage other domains subject to access controls, of course. To obtain this type of flexibility, some type of manager-to-manager communications (see Figure 4.3) is necessary (Sun,1993).

4.2.3.3   Manager-to-Manager Communications

The original version of SNMP does not support manager-to-manager communications. Management information flows strictly from managers to agents, and vice versa. A single copy of an SNMP-based platform is, for all practical pur-

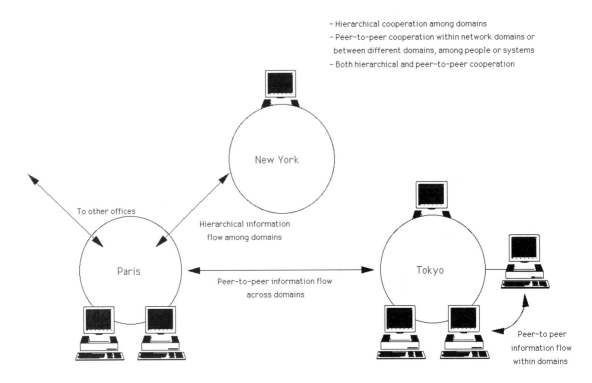

Figure 4.3 Management domains

poses, limited to managing no more than several thousand nodes. This limitation is due both to the hardware processor's inability to handle incoming messages from many thousands of devices, and the speed of execution for background processes such as device discovery and continual device polling.

However, many networks encompass tens or even hundreds of thousands of nodes. Using current technology, these networks must deploy multiple copies of the SNMP manager—each copy with its own database of topology data and event information. Providing an end-to-end view of network status using multiple managers often means sending bit-mapped X displays across the network (which is an incredible waste of bandwidth) and deploying redundant databases which may be out of sync.

A much more preferable solution is to deploy a distributed architecture whereby multiple copies of management software can communicate efficiently and share information with little or no redundancy. Many vendors today claim to support distributed architecture; however, interpretations of the term "distributed" vary.

Manager-to-manager communications is one aspect of distributed management architecture. Current techniques for manager-to-manager communications include:

- proprietary protocols and mechanisms
- SNMPv2
- CMIP

Management platforms and products that currently deploy CMIP to support manager-to-manager communications include NetLabs/DiMONS 3G, AT&T StarSENTRY/3G, Digital Analysis OS/EYE*NODE, and HP OpenView Distributed Management (DM) Platform. HP OpenView and IBM NetView/6000 do not currently support true manager-to-manager communications. However, IBM's Systems Monitor/6000 agent for the RS/6000 uses the SMUX protocol to support multiple agents on a single workstation; these smart agents act as both managers and agents, and they can communicate with other managers or smart agents. AT&T also uses SMUX technology for its StarSENTRY Computer Manager and Agent. Wollongong Management Station uses an implementation of SNMPv2 to support this capability. SunNet Manager supports manager-to-manager communications via a third-party product from DeskTalk Systems that SunConnect labels as its "Cooperative Consoles" feature.

SNMPv2 includes a facility allowing managers to send and acknowledge the receipt of TRAPs. Also, managers can communicate with multiple agents at one IP address using SNMPv2—this is not supported cleanly in the original SNMP (Jander, 1993). Because of these enhancements, platform vendors are expected to provide better support for manager-to-manager communications as demand for SNMPv2 increases.

4.2.3.4   Distributed Architectures

A true distributed architecture supports domain management, manager-to-manager communications, client/server architecture, and distributed database technology. The first product to support all of these features will be the NetLabs/DiMONS 3G management platform, which will also form the basis of SunConnect ENCOMPASS. The combination of these distributed technologies into one product will be interesting but, as yet, its effectiveness and robustness under real world conditions is unproven.

Several products currently support client/server architecture, however. The best example is Wollongong Management Station, in which the GUI is governed by a separate process from the management server. (See section 4.3.7.) Multiple copies of the GUI can be distributed across the network and can communicate with the central server. Cabletron Spectrum also supports this type of architecture (see Figure 4.4).

4.3   EXAMPLES OF UNIX-BASED NETWORK MANAGEMENT PLATFORMS

The leading UNIX-based open management platforms—Hewlett-Packard HP OpenView, SunConnect SunNet Manager, and IBM NetView/6000—represent over 85 percent of the installed base (approximately 25,000 systems as of September 1994). NetLabs/Manager and NCR StarSentry have a combined installed base of approximately 1,500 systems. Cabletron Spectrum, Network Managers,

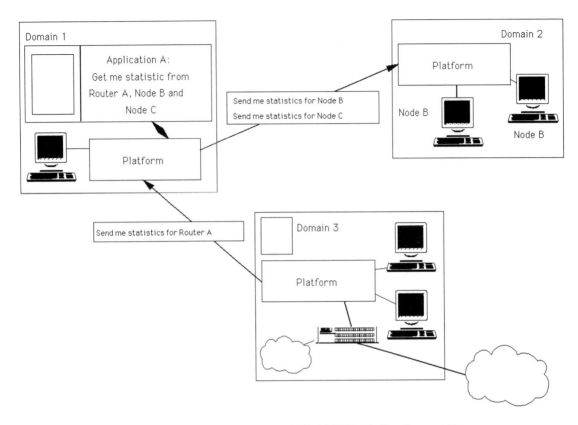

Figure 4.4 Cooperative management under NetLabs/DiMONS 3G–SunConnect Encompass

and Wollongong Management Station represent a combined installed base of about 1,500 systems.

The following section describes features supported by each platform, as well as the product history, market position, third-party support, major strengths/weaknesses, product architecture, expected enhancements and product direction of each product.

4.3.1   SunConnect SunNet Manager

SunNet Manager was first introduced in 1989. The product was the first open management platform on the market to gain a critical mass of third-party support. SunNet Manager is based on a protocol-independent architecture that uses Sun's Open Network Computing Remote Procedure Call (ONC RPC) messaging services. The product supports SNMP via proxy agents. SunNet Manager can also communicate to any proprietary management protocol through a proxy written to its agent services API.

Strengths

SunNet Manager has the largest installed base of any UNIX-based management platform, with over 14,000 copies installed as of September 1994. Its popularity is due to its very affordable price ($3,995), and Sun's vast installed base of UNIX workstations and its early entrance into the market. More than 60 third-party applications were shipping for SunNet Manager as of February 1994. This positions SunNet Manager in the number one spot for third-party support, although Hewlett-Packard and IBM are expected to at least equal that position during 1995.

Limitations

SunNet Manager is a very basic platform. It provides support for integrating SNMP devices, including third-party private MIBs, however, it is very weak in alarm filtering, configuration, and accounting management.

SunNet Manager uses an SNMP proxy implementation rather than native SNMP support. This means that all communications use Sun's Remote Procedure Call/Open Network Computing (RPC/ONC) protocols, and communications with non-Sun devices must go through a proxy agent (protocol converter). (See Figure 4.5.)

In some cases, this proxy-based architecture is a drawback, because it can slow down performance. For this reason, some third-party applications developers including Cisco and SynOptics support their own SNMP stack to improve performance when running with SunNet Manager.

On the other hand, SunNet Manager's ONC/RPC-based architecture does provide a measure of flexibility. For example, proxy agents in Sun workstations can perform a limited amount of polling and processing and forward alarms to the SunNet Manager console. Also, the proxy architecture simplifies development of support for legacy devices, such as X.25 switches.

In upcoming releases, SunConnect plans to add "smart request" polling for enhanced ease-of-use, which would support configuring polls on groups of devices, rather than just on individual devices.

Device Discovery/Network Mapping

Basic Platform Services

Device Discovery/Network Mapping

SunNet Manager's "Discover Tool" supports initial discovery of IP and SNMP-addressable elements. It also supports the ability to segment the network and spin off multiple discoveries, bringing a measure of control over the discovery process. Version 2.0 does not support continual auto-discovery of new nodes added to the network after the initial discovery.

Discovered elements are mapped into a default configuration through a hierarchy of domains, subnets, and local segments. Network mapping facility is supplemented by third-party applications such as Network Layout Assistant from Tom Sawyer Software.

Alarm Capability

Polling/thresholding SunNet Manager can poll MIB variables at user-defined intervals and perform Boolean operations on results to set thresholds and trigger actions such as launching third-party applications for pagers and beeper

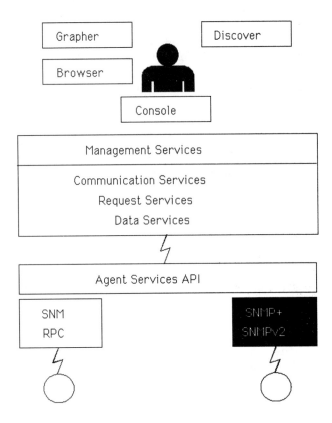

The current SunNet Manager architecture consists of three interfaces for management:
—The user interface
—The management application interface
—The protocol interface

Figure 4.5 SunNet Manager architecture

notifications. Distributed proxy agents monitor types or groups of devices, off-loading polling from the central console. Proxy agents can also be placed in routers, for example. Users must set polls on each individual device; polling on object classes is not supported in Version 2.0.

Event Filtering

Filters are user-defined at the proxy agent; filtering is supported for alarms triggered via polling. Trap filtering is not supported.

Alarm Correlation

SunNet Manager supports suppression of related events, but no cross-correlation of event traffic. Some third-party applications are providing this capability, however.

SQL Database

SunNet Manager currently stores performance data in an indexed sequential file.

SNMP, Other Protocol Support

An SNMP "mib2schemea utility" translates third-party "private" MIBs into schemas used by SunNet Manager. No private MIBs are shipped with the product. However, a number of third-party MIBs are available to SunNet Manager customers from a Sun-supported mail server.

CMIP is not currently supported; support for OSF/DME is contingent upon customer demand.

APIs, Developer's Kits, Partners Program

SunNet Manager 2.0 provides three APIs

— Manager Services API (ONC/RPC-based communications services)
— Agent Services API (allows users to write proxy agents for managing other devices and objects)
— Database/Topology MAP API (lets developers modify the database and customize the topology display)

Other Features

Results Browser tool presents traffic and activity summaries, error counts, and Sun Workstation statistics such as memory and disk utilization. Supports systems-management statistics gathering agents in Sun workstations.

Advanced Features

Network Modeling: not supported.

Distributed Implementation/distributed database: SunNet Manager 2.0 supports a distributed implementation in the sense that it allows use of local proxy agents to localize polling, thereby reducing SNMP traffic overhead. A distributed database capability is not supported

Domain support: not supported.

Manager-to-manager communications: True manager-to-manager communications are not supported, although third-party applications such as Desk-Talk Systems' TrendLink can provide some support. Pseudo support is achieved by allowing multiple copies of SunNet Manager access the same MIB.

4.3.2   Hewlett-Packard HP OpenView for UNIX

HP OpenView is actually the name of a product/service family, and not a particular product. The OpenView family includes both DOS and UNIX products. The UNIX-based OpenView products include Network Node Manager, the HP Open-View SNMP Management Platform, and the Distributed Manager (DM) Platform. The API services differ among these offerings.

The core offering is the HP OpenView SNMP Platform, which provides basic platform services and developer's environment. However, "HP OpenView" is most commonly used to refer to HP's Network Node Manager—this product includes the HP OpenView SNMP Platform (see Figure 4.6) and, in addition, multiple third-party MIBs, a MIB application building, and other application-level functions for end-users. HP OpenView Distributed Management (DM) Platform is actually a different product; while it includes the SNMP Platform, it also has added functions and APIs for supporting OSI CMIP. HP OpenView DM is targeted for telecommunications and OSI environments, and it is not intended to be purchased by end-users for managing TCP/IP internetworks. (See section 4.3.8.) Also, HP offers a DOS-based product called HP OpenView for Windows (see section 4.4).

Strengths

HP OpenView Network Node Manager has a fast-growing installed base of approximately 7,000 systems as of mid-1994. There is a strong perception among end-users that HP OpenView is a "safe" investment because of its "support" for the OSF/DME. HP OpenView also provides a very friendly development environment, and many third-parties are enthusiastic about creating applications for the platform—even though the developer's kit is priced much higher than competing vendor's offerings. There are approximately 50 third-party applications running on HP OpenView for UNIX as of mid-1994. Also, in

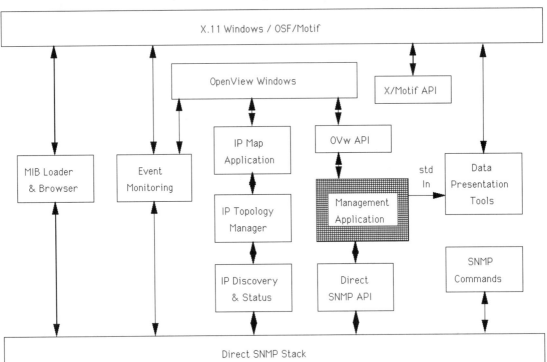

Figure 4.6 HP OpenView SNMP management platform

Version 3.3 of Network Node Manager, event types can be customized on a node-by-node basis. This helps operators distinguish between the critical crash of a mission-critical server and the less critical system crash of a one-user PC.

Limitations

HP OpenView Network Node Manager lacks alarm correlation, multi-user, manager-to-manager communications, and sophisticated polling features necessary for managing complex networks comprising thousands of nodes.

Features

Basic Platform Services

Device Discovery/Network Mapping

Supports autodiscovery of TCP/IP nodes and hierarchical IP mapping, however, no automatic grouping of node types is supported. NNM also updates network map when status of TCP/IP nodes change. Continual autodiscovery supports a backoff mechanism that polls nodes on less and less frequent intervals to detect network changes. The intervals are not user-configurable, however.

Alarm Capability

HP OpenView Network Node Manager includes a Data Collector feature that can be set up to poll on an individual object's MIB variables. HP OpenView does not support the ability to track multiple objects. Distributed polling is not supported. The platform's Event Management Services routes alerts describing component failures, security violations, etc. to the event log or to management applications.

Event Filtering

The Event Sieve Manager compares each incoming event to simple, local filters, screening out unwanted events. In Version 3.3, HP added the capability to prioritize incoming events and filter out less important messages based on those priorities. Also, Version 3.3 includes the capability to prioritize alarms based on user-defined event categories.

Alarm Correlation

Events can be prioritized; however, the platform does not support alarm correlation or probable cause text. HP OpenView Network Node Manager assumes that intelligent agents will perform advanced filtering and alarm correlation.

SQL Database

Uses a flat-file database with options for links to Ingres (SQL RDBMS) in Version 3.0 and higher; Ingres is used for storing topology data only, not events.

SNMP/Other Protocol Support

SNMP MIB I & II; MIB compiler/loader tool simplifies incorporation of private MIBs; CMIS/CMIP and CMOT is supported by the Distributed Management Platform.

APIs, Developer's Kits, Partner's Programs

HP OpenView SNMP Developer's Kit provides these APIs: OpenView Windows API and SNMP API. HP OpenView Distributed Management Developer's kit provides these APIs: OpenView WIndows API, SNMP API, and XMP API. Currently, over 50 third-parties are shipping applications for HP OpenView for UNIX.

Other Features
Security
Controls access to all components associated with the Communications Infrastructure. Provides object-level authorizations. Supervisor-initiated "Cancel, lock & unlock" controls access to components within that supervisor's domain. Also supports security audit trail, authentication schemes, multilevel password protection, and object-level authorizations. Version 3.3 supports definition of different operator (read only) versus administrator (read/write) SNMP community names (passwords.)

GUI
GUI based on HP OpenView Windows (based on OSF Motif-X11). Provides 3-dimensional windows and dialogue boxes for command inputs. Color changes and other visual cues indicate status of network devices. Supports scroll bars to display several views at once. Up to 3 local GUIs (processes) can access the OpenView database simultaneously.

Remote Access is supported via command line interface (CLI), currently limited to about 13 commands.

Hardware Supported
HP 9000 Series (300, 400, 700, or 800) and Sun SPARCstations.

Advanced Features
Network Modeling: Not supported

Distributed Implementation/distributed database: Not supported

Domain support: Pseudo capability allows each operating node to have a specific "workspace" with a customized view of managed resources.

Manager-to-manager communications: Not supported in current version of SNMP Platform.

4.3.3   IBM AIX NetView/6000

The product is an SNMP-based element management system for TCP/IP networks; the system can also act as a service point for an enterprise-wide NetView management system. AIX NetView/6000 uses HP OpenView Network Node Manager core technology, with IBM-provided enhancements.

Digital Equipment Corp. has licensed NetView/6000 and is using it as the basis for its Polycenter Manager on NetView product (see section 4.3.11.)

Strengths
IBM is adding alarm filtering and event management features that are lacking in the HP OpenView core. NetView/6000 is becoming an increasingly important part of IBM's network management strategy, and its importance may one day eclipse mainframe NetView as customers move toward distributed sys-

tems computing. In response to customer demand, IBM is developing SNA management applications for NetView/6000. IBM is putting a lot of muscle behind its support program, both for end-users and third-party vendors who join the NetView Association.

Limitations

It is the authors' opinion that to maximize sales potential of this product, IBM will have to increase its focus on sales and support of its AIX/UNIX products and reduce emphasis on proprietary solutions—and on mainframe NetView in particular. The number of third-party applications shipping for NetView/6000 still trails the tallies for HP OpenView and SunNet Manager, but this gap is expected to narrow substantially during 1995.

Features

Basic Platform Services

Device Discovery/Network Mapping

"Dynamic Network Discovery" automatically discovers IP-addressable nodes and tracks IP network device adds and changes, keeping the network topology map current. In a typical configuration, 1,000 nodes can be "discovered" in about 20 minutes. Automatic map drawing/redrawing (autotopology) is supported to a limited extent. The system continually verifies network device connection. Operators can save current network maps to compare with later maps; no sophisticated change management software provided.

Alarm Capability

Monitors IP network node status; generates events if user-defined thresholds are exceeded; alarms can trigger NetView alerts. Users can configure polls for groups of objects and examine the states of multiple components simultaneously. Traps and events can trigger user-defined shell scripts and NetView alerts; can receive RUNCMD commands from mainframe NetView. TCP/IP "diagnostic" routines include IP PING, TCP connection test, and SNMP agent test.

Distributed polling is supported using System Monitor/6000 agents. Users can install Systems Monitors on RS/6000 workstations throughout the network to offload automation of individual LAN segments and feed that information to a handful of NetView/6000s.

Event Filtering

Filtering rules can span multiple objects (groups) simultaneously; allows users to monitor different states of objects in different groups, and user complete boolean expressions to define thresholds. A Filter Editor and Filter Control Interface allow managers to see graphical representations of selected SNMP events (Jander, 1993). (See Figure 4.7.)

Alarm Correlation

Not supported. However, a problem diagnostic facility allows users to trace a specific data pattern to determine whether a network problem is somehow related to that pattern. Network map can display packet routes for tracing; users can browse MIB to examine values. The SNA Manager/6000 application option of NetView/6000 can automatically trigger shell scripts or NetView/390

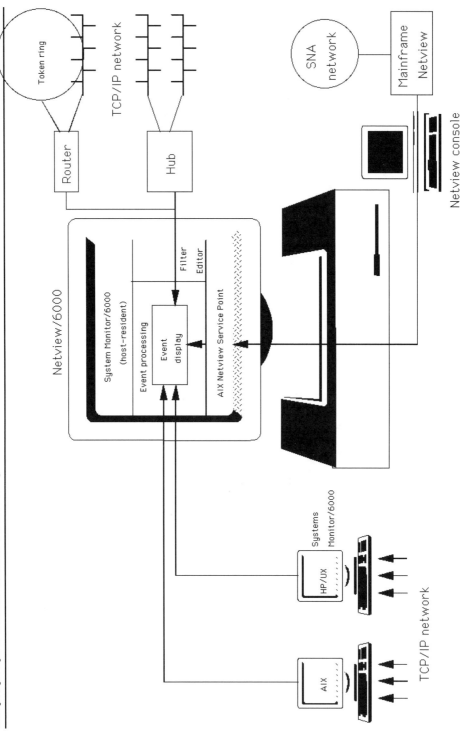

AIX Systemview Netview/6000 accepts alarms and alerts from both SNA and SNMP, filtering out unwanted messages to help net managers get right to the root of a problem without wasting time

Figure 4.7 IBM NewView/6000 event handling. Source: *Data Communications*, January 1994. Copyright © McGraw-Hill, Inc.

RUNCMDs based on alerts to display probable cause or recommended solution text messages.

SQL Database

Flat-file (ASCII) log of events and polled data; interfaces to SQL databases supported.

SNMP/Other Protocol Support

SNMP (MIB I, MIB II) and remote monitoring (RMON) MIB (e.g., SNMP, CMOT, CMOL); private extensions for IBM 6611 router. IBM NMVTs via Service Point (e.g., NMVT, XNS, etc.) Interface.

CMIP support promised, but no delivery date has been set. IBM also supports the XMP API.

Users can browse performance-related MIB variables to examine, chart, or modify values. NetView/6000 maintains historical data based on built-in and user-defined threshold polling; this data can be graphed for analysis in pie/bar charts or line graphs or it can be saved in ASCII files.

Users can customize SNMP thresholds and traps (alert messages). Also, users can dynamically edit maps and set polling intervals determining how often the map is updated. Users can add new devices/device types via SNMP MIB editor.

APIs, Developer's Kits, Partner's Programs

APIs provided for linking to Service Point applications. Version 2 includes an SNMP API and HP OpenView Windows API. Support for OSF/DME Consolidated Management API (CM-API) also supported. NetView/6000 Association provides support for third-party partners

Also NetView/6000 supports the AIX System Management Interface Tool (SMIT), providing command line interface for remotely logged users

Other Features

Access Control

Access control based on AIX security and audit features. GUI; mouse-driven interface; AIX System Management Interface Tool (SMIT) providing a command line interface also supported. GUI based on Motif; users can edit the map with supplied map-editing tools. Menu bar function allows point-and-click access to View, Locate, Test, Edit, and Help functions, etc.

Hardware

IBM RS/6000 POWERstations and POWERservers running AIX Version 3.2 or better.

Advanced Features

Network Modeling: Not supported.

Distributed Implementation/Distributed Database: Supports multiple users through X displays. As a service point product, NetView/6000s can be scattered at sites throughout the SNA network to feed information to central site NetView.

Domain support: NetView/6000 security features provide a pseudo-domain capability.

Manager-to-manager communications

Manager-to-manager communications can be supported using the AIX Systems Monitor/6000 and significant customization effort. Also, NetView/6000 acts as a Service Point, accepting the NetView/6000 SNMP event and issuing an NMVT event to the main NetView console. NetView/6000 accepts mainframe NetView RUNCMDs via the AIX Service Point interface; receipt of RUNCMDs are acknowledged. Information flow between NetView/6000 and mainframe NetView is bidirectional.

Also, the SNA Manager/6000 application can serve as an enterprise management workstation, displaying SNA topology data and alerts. Furthermore, network topology and status can be exchanged with the NetView Multisystem Manager (MSS) for NetView/MVS, allowing graphical display from mainframe NetView Graphic Monitor Facility (GMF) and automation via the Resource Object Data Manager (RODM.)

Native alarms

Converts NetView/6000 SNMP traps to SNA alerts (NMVTs).

4.3.4   NetLabs/DiMONS

NetLabs, Inc. is a very influential player in the SNMP-based management market, even though the installed base of the NetLabs/DiMONS product lags far behind HP OpenView and SunNet Manager. Under the terms of a licensing agreement, AT&T GIS has been using NetLabs/DiMONs as the basis for its AT&T StarSENTRY product for several years—and, indeed, most of NetLabs' revenue has come from OEM agreements with AT&T and several other vendors. However, in July 1994, AT&T GIS announced that it will phase out use of Net-Labs' technology and, instead, license HP OpenView for future versions of the StarSENTRY product line. Also in July 1994, Hewlett-Packard announced that it would license NetLabs' "NerveCenter" technology and incorporate it into future versions of HP OpenView. NetLabs, then, will evolve into a purveyor of network management technology and applications rather than a provider of end-user, open management platforms.

Strengths

The product's chief strength is its configurable polling and "NerveCenter" alarm capability that supports recognition of conditional state alarms. Net-Labs/DiMONS can manage networks up to 10,000 devices; its architecture supports multi-user/multi-domain configurations. NetLabs/DiMONS flexible conditional-state alarm model and polling features can also be very useful in large networks. Upward scaling is achieved by interconnecting the NetLabs/100 entry-level model at remote sites, linking them to a central NetLabs/DiMONS.(See Figure 4.8).

Limitations

NetLabs is a small company whose profitability depends solely on network management. There are few third-party applications shipping for DiMONS as

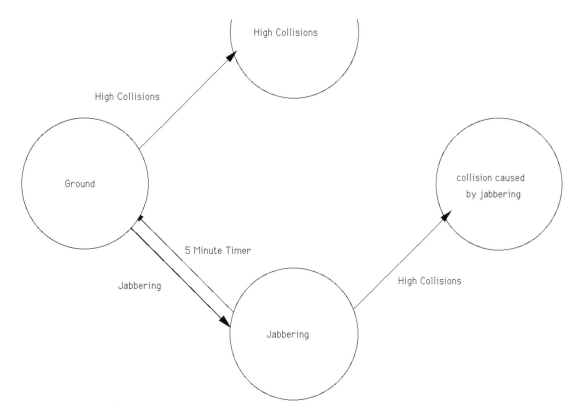

Figure 4.8 NetLabs/DiMONs can recognize complex conditions with its model

of mid-1994. NetLabs does not have the name recognition of the other leading vendors.

Features

Basic Platform Services

Device Discovery/Network Mapping: Supports an optional NetLabs/Discovery application which provides two modes of device discovery. The first, "Complete Discovery," performs a full PING sweep to detect network nodes and physical and logical connection paths. This feature will place icons on a map, and each icon includes the logo of the vendor's device represented. The second mode is a "Fast Discovery" that detects only those nodes active since the last time "Discovery" was executed.

Alarm Capability

Includes a conditional-state model for defining multi-state alarms and a sophisticated polling algorithm for reducing polling traffic; uses both SNMP polling and traps, and CMOT M-Event Report messages for fault detection. Users can set thresholds based on a change in values over time and can map multiple conditions onto a single event. Object-oriented polling facility allows users to configure polls based on object classes instead of just specific devices.

NetLabs/DiMONS ships with some pre-configured alarms and some device-specific alarms; new Alarm Starter Kit includes sample alarms and device-specific alarms for hubs from Cabletron, Chipcom, and SynOptics, and traffic alarms detected by Novell LANtern.

NetLabs/DiMONS can be configured to automatically respond to changes in alarm states, by triggering beepers, e-mail to supervisors, or issuing SNMP SET commands to control and/or reconfigure affected devices (if the device supports SET).

Event Filtering

Alarm filtering is supported

Alarm Correlation

NetLabs/DiMONS can correlate alarms to a single port, however, user must set up the correlation via triggers from traps, events, and polls. Users can attach problem determination and resolution instructions to graphical "Notepads" associated with each device icon on the network map. No expert system is include.

SQL Database

Flat-file configuration database, supporting file export to Informix RDBMS and Informix Wingz spreadsheet.

SNMP/Other Protocol Support

SNMP, (MIB I, MIB II) plus (e.g., SNMP, CMOT, CMOL) SNMP Multiplexer (SMUX) using StarSENTRY Manager Gateway Developer's Toolkit from AT&T; other MIBs include FDDI and the Remote Monitoring (RMON) MIB, and a "Parse MIB" tool for integrating new "private" MIBs. SNMP SET is supported. CMIP support is available.

APIs, Developer's Kits, Partner's Programs

NetLabs/DiMONS supports nine published APIs; a high-level API will be supported in the forthcoming DiMONS/3G release. (See section 4.6). The NetLabs Application eXchange (NAX) program provides third-party developers with a mechanism for marketing and distributing their applications to a variety of vertical markets. NetLabs works with third-party vendors to help create well-integrated solutions for customers.

Other Features

"Action Router" feature of the optional NetLabs' Assist software utility provides some problem resolution assistance; according to user-defined rules (time-of-day, device type, etc.) Action Router will determine the appropriate operator, sending a time/date- stamped alarm and notes regarding problem location, severity, and other pertinent information.

NetLabs Assist option can produce several graphs of performance data, and Discovery visually depicts traffic load (high, medium, and low) traversing selected connections.

Security

Supervisor can manipulate the APIs and other configuration files to selectively restrict users from modifying device attributes or applications.

Hardware

Platforms supported: Sun SPARCstations, IBM RS/6000, IBM PCs (386 or better), MIPS workstations, Intergraph InterPro 2000, Siemens-Nixdorf.

Advanced Features

Network Modeling: Not supported.

Distributed Implementation/distributed database: Supported in forthcoming release

Domain support: Allows users to define management domains (number of nodes/users managed per console) that match the organization's business model. Users can localize a domain, so that alarms will be processed locally—and then define a "shadow" manager that will take over that local management domain if conditions warrant.

Manager-to-manager communications: Collaborative management feature allows multiple DiMONS to communicate with each other and transfer control for added backup.

4.3.5   Cabletron Spectrum

Cabletron is a leading provider of intelligent concentrators ("smart hubs") and networking solutions. Because network management is a key differentiator in the smart hub market, Cabletron has invested heavily in developing leading-edge network management technology to help maintain its leading position as a hub provider. While Cabletron Spectrum is the most advanced open management platform in its class on the market today, the product's installed base still lags behind SunNet Manager and HP OpenView. Cabletron has had difficulty garnering third-party support for Spectrum, although it appears that the vendor started to achieve greater success in that area with the release of Spectrum 3.0 in May 1994.

Strengths

Cabletron Spectrum is capable of managing large, heterogeneous internetworks; it operates at a higher level than other platforms due to its artificial intelligence capabilities. Spectrum uses inductive modeling technology and an object-oriented database; this supports modeling the entire network, forming a relationship between devices. This allows Spectrum to provide useful information and perform proactive functions without human intervention.

Spectrum supports a client/server architecture, supporting multi-user access; in contrast with most other management platforms which are single-user systems relying on X-terminal windows for remote access.

Limitations

Spectrum's primary weakness has been its lack of third-party support. As of mid-1994, third party applications available for Spectrum included Remedy Action Request System, Isicad Command, Calypso MaestroVision, NetTech

BlueVision, and an SAS Gateway. However, third-party support is expected to increase substantially during 1995, with the addition of important ISV applications such as HP NetMetrix and Legent Paradigm.

While a comprehensive Spectrum package can be fairly expensive, modular packaging allows users to start small and scale up to managing the largest interconnected LAN networks.

Features

Basic Platform Services

Device Discovery/Network Mapping

Spectrum includes an autotopology feature which creates a network map automatically, using PING, SNMP, and reading of router tables. Supports the TCP/IP "PING" protocol to discern network changes and revise maps. Mapping capability groups discovered items to make the discovery process more manageable, creating logical topological groupings of devices. Discovery feature can detect logical network changes and revise maps. Automatically maps interconnection of routers, bridges, concentrators, and end-point devices supported by preloaded device models.

Alarm Capability

Generates events if user-defined thresholds are exceeded. Spectrum detects faults and filters alarms using model- based reasoning technique. The efficacy of fault detection depends on how thoroughly each network device is modeled; Cabletron supplies 35 device models.

Spectrum provides alarm notification via beeper or phone through the SpectroPHONE option.

Event Filtering

Supported extensively through Spectrum's network modeling capabilities.

Alarm Correlation

Spectrum suppresses downstream alarms to highlight actual cause of fault. Spectrum distinguishes between down devices and manually disabled or isolated devices.

Database

Object-oriented database plus ISAM files (see Figure 4.9); can export to relational database for reporting purposes via the SAS Gateway.

SNMP/Other Protocol Support

SNMP (MIB I & MIB II) (e.g., SNMP, CMOT, CMOL). The following third party private MIBs are available as extra-cost options: Novell LANtern, Fibronics, cisco, Proteon, Unisys, Vitalink, Wellfleet, BBN, 3Com, ACC, Cayman, Hughes LAN, Alantec, Xyplex, Emulex, SynOptics, David Systems, ODS, Chipcom, Banyan, Rockwell PC card, Sun NFS driver, NCR PC, IBM RS/6000, DEC 5000, Silicon Graphics IRIS, DEC MicroVAX, DG Aviion, HP 900, and Prime 2850 users can browse performance-related MIB variables to examine, chart, or modify values.

Supports IBM Netview NMVTs via Brixton's SNA gateway software; and NetTech BlueVision. CMIP support promised but not yet shipping.

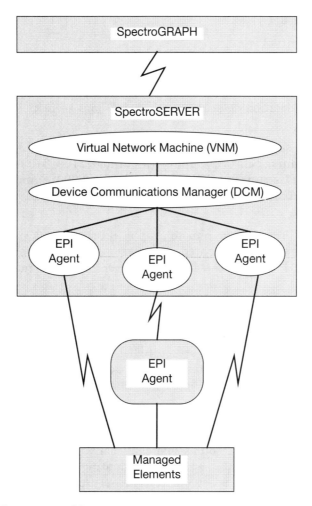

Figure 4.9 Cabletron Spectrum architecture

Users can add support for new devices and device types via Modelling Editor. Spectrum supports a Level I toolkit aimed at SNMP devices—compile in the private MIB and browse it, and select the values you want presented on the screen (strip charts, bar charts, etc.), all without programming.

APIs, Developer's Kits, Partner's Programs

Eight published APIs are provided: X.11/Motif API, SpectroServer API (includes SNMP services), Inference Handler API, Basic Extensions API, Extensive Integration API, Generic Information Block Editor API, Icon Inf. Block API, Model Type Editor API.

Spectrum also supports a command line interface (VT-100) for remote queries/obtaining alarm information. Spectrum provides an RS-232 port for out-of-band management.

Other Features

Access Control

Built-in security access control lets supervisors restrict access according to organization, application or building categories (or any combination thereof). Supports an audit trail for user commands and changes. Spectrum supports security violation detection and lockout—logs security events.

Hardware

Platform supported Sun 3/4 or SPARCstations; Sun SPARC Processors 1, 1+, and 2 running SunOS; Digital DECstations 2100, 3100 running ULTRIX; IBM 386/486 PCs running SCO UNIX; IBM RS/6000 running AIX; Apple Mac IIs running AUX; Silicon Graphics INDIGO, IRIS 4D.

GUI

Up to 10 local and/or remote graphical user interface (processes) can access Spectrum's object-oriented database simultaneously. The GUI (SpectroGRAPH) console can be the same or different from the server (SpectroSERVER).

Advanced Features

Network Modeling: Spectrum uses model-based reasoning to isolate faults by inferring status from structure/behavior of connected devices. Spectrum derives a variety of rates and raw packet counts (rates calculated as part of object models). Also, Spectrum can consolidate statistics from multiple LANs.

Distributed Implementation/distributed database

Distributed management is supported in two ways. 1)Cabletron's hubs can support optional modules that can locally poll and monitor any SNMP or IP device on the LAN segment, eliminating the need to keep polling every device from the Spectrum console. 2) Spectrum supports a client/server implementation. Supports simultaneous access for multiple users with different levels of security. More complete distributed functionality expected in future versions.

Domain support: Spectrum can limit operator access to one or more network views—allowing operators to control and configure only a predetermined set of network aspects.

Manager-to-manager communications: Supported via proprietary mechanisms.

4.3.6   Network Managers' NMC Vision

Network Managers' product strategy is to market third-party applications (called "Product-Specific Modules" or PSMs) rather than to rely solely on outside vendors. These PSMs are tightly integrated into the NMC platform. Network Managers, Ltd. is pouring significant money into enhancing and expanding product functionality.

Network Managers provides some unique technology, including a lightweight object request broker and "adapter" layers that shield third-party applications developers from the differences between various management platforms. For this reason, Network Managers recently entered into several significant strategic partnerships with major vendors including IBM and AT&T.

NMC's "Vision" line of products include NMC Vision 1000 for Windows, NMC Vision 3000 for UNIX systems, and NMC Vision 4000 for Windows NT.

Strengths

The tightly-integrated "product-specific modules" offered by Network Managers provide third-party device management and "one-stop shopping" at the same time. Network Managers is also very active in the Network Management Forum, and its "Open Management Edge" implementation provides a practical and affordable migration path to Forum interoperability and eventual compliance with Forum specifications. This is particularly important in Europe and Asia.

Limitations

While the vendor has several large PTTs as customers, as a recent startup Network Managers is not well known outside of Europe.

Features

Basic Platform Services

Device Discovery/Network Mapping

The NMC Vision products support automatic tracking of connections between maps, and ensures network connection continuity. An IP Autodiscover module is included. NMC Vision supports Upload and Download options. In the Upload operation, the complete current physical subsystem configuration is copied from the physical subsystem to the database. Download allows the database image of the configuration to be downloaded to the physical subsystem; if desired, a different product can be used as the download master.

Alarm Capability

Process-driven system uses polling to detect status; supports user-defined alarm thresholds on five severity levels. Each alarm automatically opens a trouble ticket, which attaches to an historical fault record; performs automatic fill of data on opened trouble tickets; trouble ticketing system is linked with NMS database.

Event Filtering

Limited ability to suppress unnecessary alarms.

Alarm Correlation

Fault "masking" filtering process and optional "fuzzy logic" fault interpretation module aid problem determination.

SQL Database

NSI standard SQL RDBMS, now supporting Ingres and Informix.

SNMP/Other Protocol Support

Supports SNMP (MIB I, MIB II, Hub/Repeater (e.g., SNMP, OSPF, RMON, FDDI) MIB. Calculates rates from raw MIB data. Also supports "Product-Specific" modules for the following vendors: Hubs from SynOptics, David Systems, AEG, Cabletron, Chipcom, Proteon, Herschmann, LANNET; bridges from Retix; routers from Wellfleet, cisco, Proteon ACC; monitors from Novell (LANtern), N.A.T. (EtherMeter), X.25 products from Ascom, EDA; provides MIB integrator; MIB editor available. (See Figure 4.10.)

Open protocols (e.g., CMIP) CMIP, IEEE 802.1b, MAP/TOP. DECnet EMA gateway, NetView (e.g., NMVT, XNS, etc.) gateway optional.

APIs, Developer's Kits, Partner's Programs

Developer's Toolkit includes "class libraries" that provide the basis for developing new applications; APIs define the interface to class libraries and show how objects can be used.

Other Features

Access Control

Two-level access (user and user/group) controlled by password; individual network maps appear for each group. In future release, each application will have restricted access to other processing, depending upon the level of permissions granted to that application. Separately definable user rights govern access to specific applications, maps.

Hardware

Platforms supported—Sun SPARCstation 1+, 2, IPC, or IPX running SunOS 4.1 or higher.

Advanced Features

Network Modeling: Not supported.
Distributed Implementation/distributed database: Not in current release.
Domain support: Not provided
Manager-to-manager communications: Not currently supported

4.3.7   Wollongong Management Station

Wollongong is a provider of communications and open systems software. Its Management Station product is offered as a part of its Pathway family of software products. Management Station was one of the earliest open management platforms on the market. The product is very extensible and provides strong support for open standards. However, Wollongong has not actively sought the endorsements of third-party vendors. The lack of third-party support has deterred some users from purchasing Management Station, although the product provides excellent price-to-performance value.

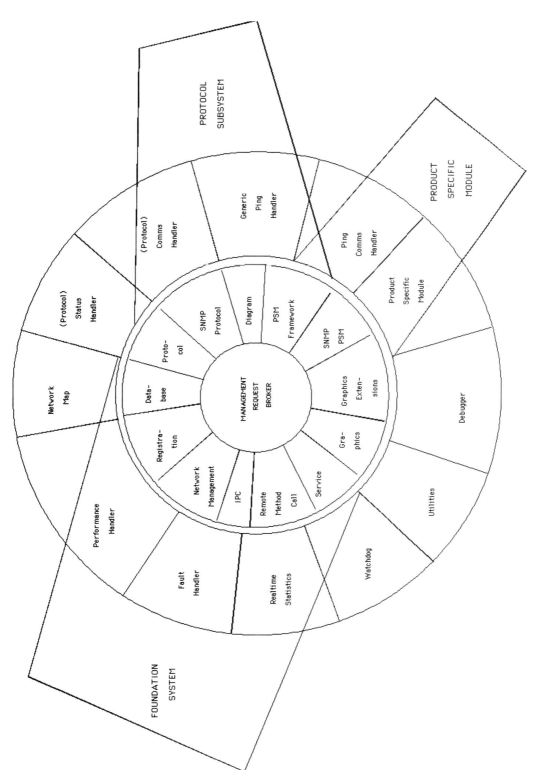

Figure 4.10 The Network Manager's NMC 3000 architecture

Strengths

Wollongong Management Station features a truly distributed architecture that allows other systems on the network to share in management responsibilities. Wollongong Management Station is composed of two processes: the management server (called the Network Management Daemon or NMD) and the GUI process which creates the network map. SNMP over TCP is used between the NMD, and the network map is used to communicate status change events, new devices, SNMP traps, and user-defined alarms. The NMD polls SNMP devices and receives SNMP traps from localized management domains. The NMD also provides device discovery. (See Figure 4.11.)

Wollongong Management Station's architecture allows organizations to obtain distributed management at an affordable price by deploying multiple server processes; currently, charges apply only to the GUI process.

Limitations

Wollongong is a small company that lacks visibility in the network management marketplace. It does not have third-party applications support.

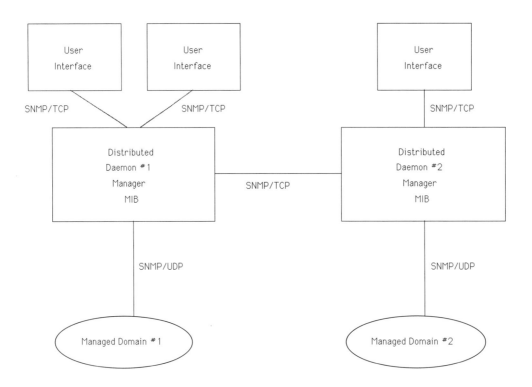

Figure 4.11 Wollongong's distributed network management architecture

Features

Basic Platform Services

Device Discovery/Network Mapping:

The network map is the SNMP Client (or "station") and the primary entry point for the user interface. All other management and system applications can be accessed from the network map.

The Manager server process (NMD) supports device discovery of all devices on the TCP/IP network. Device discovery can be efficiently accomplished in a distributed fashion—carried out by local NMD processes, with information forwarded to the central process. The device discovery algorithm uses a list of user-specified IP network addresses and masks to send an SNMP packet to each possible IP address within these bounds. Timeout and retry parameters are provided to give users an added measure of control over the discovery process. If an SNMP response or an ICMP unreachable port message is not received, then an ICMP echo request is generated to detect the device. The discovery process is capable of searching a 254-node network in under nine minutes. The continual discovery scanning interval is user-defined (e.g., once an hour, once a day).

Alarm Capability

The Management Server performs fault monitoring, SNMP trap message processing, and thresholding/alarming. Management Station receives SNMP traps, including vendor-specific traps. Any change in device status that does not generate an actual SNMP trap will cause the NMD to send a generic "device status trap" to the network map. The user can define alarm expressions based upon specific MIB values, changes in values, or arithmetic MIB variable expressions, using any Boolean expression. Alarms can be displayed, logged, trigger UNIX commands, sent to the SQL database, or forwarded to another SNMP station.

Event Filtering

Specific traps can be filtered.

Alarm Correlation

The user can assign a priority to specific alarms to prevent floods of alarms from failure of key devices (e.g., routers). The NMD also learns the routing topology and uses ICMP unreachable network messages to determine that only a router went down—not all of the devices that are dependent upon that router.

SQL Database

The Management Server can forward all data to either Ingres or Oracle relational database.

SNMP/Other Protocol Support

Management Station provides a MIB Compiler, MIB Form, MIB Browser Tool, and MIB Chart to support SNMP management. The MIB Compiler is an ASN.1 compiler that accepts properly formatted SNMP MIBs. The MIB Form allows users to GET and SET MIB variables from one or more SNMP agents. MIB variables can be aliased, and their values can be automatically interpreted. The MIB Browser Tool supports browsing (or walking) the MIB; the MIB Chart provides for the simultaneous charting of individual or multiple MIB variables and/or MIB variable expressions from single or multiple agents.

Wollongong Management Station supports SNMPv2—including a GUI for the SNMPv2 administration, authentication, and support for the GetBulk Protocol Data Unit (PDU).

APIs, Developer's Kits, Partner's Programs

Wollongong publishes a set of APIs for access routines used in Management Station applications. The APIs provide access to the NMD and the ability to develop SNMP applications. Wollongong also supplies sample source to support applications development.

Wollongong also offers an optional tool for building new applications. This allows a user, through use of a GUI, to design and build SNMP-based Motif applications. A similar feature is available for charts.

Other Features

Security

Management Station supports two levels of user access: (1) Users authorized to issue Set-Requests and (2) Users not authorized to issue Set-Requests. Also, the product supports authentication with SNMPv2.

Advanced Features

Network Modeling: Not supported.

Distributed Implementation/distributed database: Supports a distributed implementation through Management Server (NMD) and GUI processes. Wollongong Management Station's NMD is capable of generating reports, providing a distributed reporting mechanism.

Domain support: Supported.

Manager-to-manager communications: Supported via Wollongong's private Manager MIB that includes device discovery parameters and information describing what devices are a part of each domain. NMDs exchange management information between each other and among any configured GUI processes. These paths of information flow are user-configurable into distributed and/or hierarchical topologies. Wollongong plans to support the SNMPv2 Manager MIB in a future release of the product.

4.3.8   HP OpenView Distributed Management (DM) Platform

HP OpenView DM Platform is targeted at high-end customers in the telecommunications industry and also at international organizations seeking an OSI-based solution. It is designed to support development of OSI-based systems and network management applications, and it will appeal primarily to developers with a WAN focus seeking security and support for OSI CMIP.

Strengths

Support for manager-to-manager communications and distributed event manager services, Generic Definition of Managed Object (GDMO) metadata services, and object registration services (these are OSI-based services); conformance to NM/Forum OMNIpoint specifications.

Limitations

The product is complex and requires significant understanding of OSI technology. It is applicable only if OSI elements are prevalent in the network.

Features

Basic Platform Services

Device Discovery/Network Mapping: Not supported

Alarm Capability

Supports ISO alarms.

Event Filtering

Filters alarms according to ISO criteria.

Alarm Correlation

Supports alarm correlation according to ISO criteria.

SQL Database

HP DM supports an option that allows users to store event routing configuration information in an Ingres SQL database. If Ingres is not used, this data can be stored in a separate file.

SNMP/Other Protocol Support

Supports OSI CMIP as well as SNMP.

APIs, Developer's Kits, Partner's Programs

The X/Open Management Protocol API (XMP), also called CM-API (developed by Groupe Bull) is the fundamental API of HP OpenView DM. The product also includes an X11/Motif API (OvW API), direct SNMP API, SQL API (to Ingres RDBMS), and an XOM management API. (See Figure 4.12.)

In addition, the product development environment includes an XMP package generator and an XOM code generator to increase developer productivity. Specifically, developers can run object definitions through these generators and automatically build code. HP also provides sample applications (e.g., /etc/passwd file manager) and a built-in hyptertext help system to simplify XMP programming.

Other Features

Security

Security features are supported differently than HP OpenView for UNIX due to ISO requirements.

GUI

GUI based on HP OpenView Windows (based on OSF Motif-X11). Provides 3-dimensional windows and dialogue boxes for command inputs. Color changes and other visual cues indicate status of network devices. Supports scroll bars to display several views at once. Up to 3 local GUIs (processes) can access the OpenView database simultaneously.

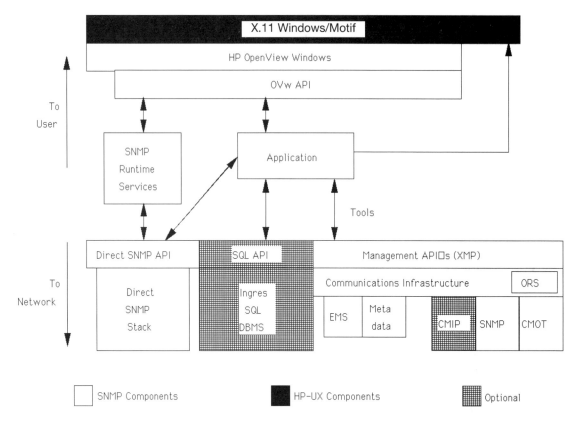

Figure 4.12 HP OpenView Distributed Management (DM) platform architecture

Remote Access is supported via command line interface (CLI), currently limited to about 13 commands.

Hardware Supported

HP 9000 Series (300, 400, 700, or 800), Sun SPARCstations and IBM RS/6000.

Advanced Features

Network Modeling: Not supported

Distributed Implementation/Distributed Database: Supports distributed and scalable services for event handling, and a communications infrastructure for integrating and distributing multiple applications

Domain support: Supported using ISO criteria.

Manager-to-Manager Communications: Supported via CMIP.

4.3.9   NetLabs/DiMONS 3G, and SunConnect ENCOMPASS

NetLabs is a leading provider of network management technology. DiMONS 3G is a "third-generation" network management platform, providing distributed database management capabilities and manager-to-manager communications. SunConnect has licensed DiMONS 3G from NetLabs and markets it under the label "ENCOMPASS." ENCOMPASS is essentially a replacement for SunConnect's popular SunNet Manager product.

Strengths

Supports a fully distributed architecture with distributed data model overlaying existing RDBMS. Supports message passing between consoles, enabling multiple platforms to keep updated on network status without redundant polling. This helps minimize overhead associated with polling as well as with maintaining redundant databases. Cooperating "kernels" allows communications with other DiMONS 3G systems or other vendors platforms. Multiple users can edit the same network map concurrently, facilitating cooperation for quicker problem resolution.

Limitations: The technology is very new and, so far, unproven in real networks. Uses complex GDMO templates.

Features

Device Discovery/Network Mapping

Support is similar to that of NetLabs/DiMONS. Supports an optional NetLabs/Discovery application which provides two modes of device discovery. The first, "Complete Discovery," performs a full PING sweep to detect network nodes and physical and logical connection paths. This feature will place icons on a map, and each icon includes the logo of the vendor's device represented. The second mode is a "Fast Discovery" that detects only those nodes active since the last time "Discovery" was executed.

Alarm Capability

Support similar to NetLabs/DiMONS. NerveCenter application includes a conditional-state model for defining multi-state alarms and a sophisticated polling algorithm for reducing polling traffic. The product uses both CMOT M-Event Report messages and SNMP polling and traps for fault detection. Users can set thresholds based on a change in values over time, and they can map multiple conditions onto a single event. Object-oriented polling facility allows users to configure polls based on object classes instead of specific devices only.

NerveCenter can be configured to automatically respond to changes in alarm states, by triggering beepers, e-mail to supervisors, or issuing SNMP SET commands to control and/or reconfigure affected devices (if the device supports SET.)

In addition, a fully distributed implementation in DiMONS 3G minimizes overhead of polling and data redundancy.

Event Filtering

Alarm filtering is supported.

Alarm Correlation

Support similar to NetLabs/DiMONS. DiMONS 3G can correlate alarms to a single port. However, user must set up the correlation via triggers from traps, events, and polls. Users can attach problem determination and resolution instructions to graphical "Notepads" associated with each device icon on the network map. No expert system is included.

SQL Database

DiMONS/3G overlays a distributed data model across the existing user's RDBMS architecture. This common network model ensures data integrity when multiple users write to the network map simultaneously. A "backing store" API allows applications developers to choose SQL, ASCII flat file, or checking memory to store transient objects such as TCP connections.

SNMP/Other Protocol Support

CMIP; SNMP MIB I & II; MIB compiler/loader tool simplifies incorporation of private MIBs.

APIs, Developer's Kits, Partner's Programs

DiMONS 3G supports a high-level, protocol-independent API as well as the XMP API, low-level CMIS/CMIP API, Directory Service API, Security Service API, GUI API, Object Method API, Naming Services API, Backing Store API, and Management Protocol API (see Figure 4.13).

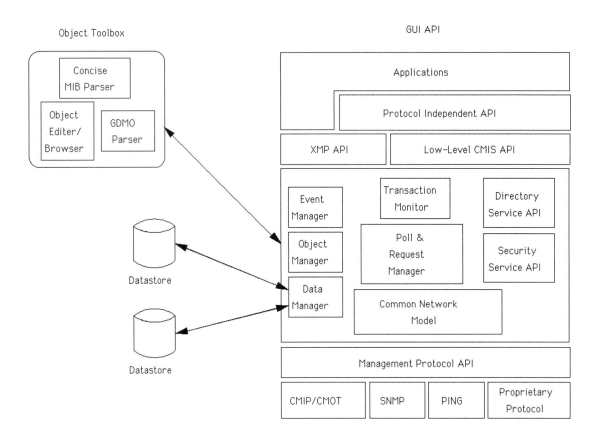

Figure 4.13 NetLabs/DiMONS 3G architecture

Object toolkit includes object editor/browser, concise MIB parse, and GDMO parser to accelerate applications development. Other Features: Security: Security Services API provides access to external security service

GUI
OS/F Motif.

Hardware
Sun SPARCstations, IBM RS/6000, IBM PCs (386 or better), MIPS workstations, Intergraph InterPro 2000, Siemens-Nixdorf.

Advanced Features
Network Modeling: Not supported.

Distributed Implementation/distributed database: Supported via CMIP, distributed message passing capabilities, and distributed data model. Applications can be installed remotely from the platform. Distributed message passing between consoles allows multiple copies of DiMONS 3G to be kept up to date without redundant polling; ensures data integrity when multiple users write to the network map simultaneously.

Domain support: Allows users to define management domains (number of nodes/users managed per console) that match the organization's business model. Users can localize a domain, so that alarms will be processed locally—and then define a "shadow" manager that will take over that local management domain if conditions warrant.

Manager-to-manager communications: Supported via CMIP

4.3.10   Bull Integrated Systems Management (ISM)

ISM is the management component of Bull's Distributed Computing Model (DCM). ISM supports both systems and network management in UNIX and in heterogeneous environments. ISM supports modules for managing Novell NetWare LANs, Microsoft LAN Manager, and Bull's Open Team LANs, as well as for UNIX systems. Bull's Consolidated Management API (CM-API) was adopted by both X-Open and the OSF, and it was renamed XMP.

Because ISM provides comprehensive support for both network and systems management, the following evaluation will include both network and systems management criteria.

Strengths
ISM provides comprehensive support for both systems and network management. The product includes integrated modules for UNIX file system monitoring, UNIX operating system monitoring, backup/restore capabilities, software distribution, and user administration as well as a network alarm facility and SNMP support.

Limitations
The product is not yet well known in the United States. To date, there are only a handful of third-party applications supporting ISM.

Features

Basic Platform Services

Device Discovery/Network Mapping

The ISM Discovery module supports automatic discovery of IP and IPX routers, gateways, and other SNMP nodes. The module will dynamically draw network topology.

Alarm Capability

The ISM Alarm module supports acknowledgment of incoming alarms as well as filtering and alarm logging. Integrated trouble ticketing facilities are supported by integrating Remedy ARS.

Event filtering

Filters are based on priority levels (severity scales)

Alarm correlation

Not supported.

SQL Database

SQL links to Oracle RDMS as well as Bull DPX/2, DPX/20, and GCOS7 systems are supported.

SNMP/Other Protocol Support

Can manage both SNMP and CMIP agents as well as proprietary agents. The ISM Framework communicates with the managed system via agent integrators—either SNMP or Bull DSAC NAD. Alarm formats conform to NM-Forum definitions.

APIs, developers kits, partners program

ISM's Consolidated Management API Library (CM-LIB) supports access to the CM-API (also know as XMP). Third-party developers can build extensions to the management system without impacting the base product. ISM supports a set of tools and languages for developing specific management applications. The ISM Management Language Interpreter and Object Definition Compiler expedites applications development.

Other Features

ISM uses an object-oriented approach to resource management. Extensive support for monitoring of 3Com LinkBuilder hubs and NETBuilder bridge/routers is supported.

Hardware

Bull ISM Server/090 through 490 running GCOS, UNIX (DPX)

GUI

OSF/MOTIF.

ISM also supports comprehensive monitoring of Oracle Database applications across hosts, servers, and SQL*rbt gateways. DBA Expert produces consolidated reports of database performance.

Advanced Features

Network Modeling: Not supported.

Distributed Implementation/distributed database: ISM supports a distributed implementation via CMIP, distributing management functions across the enterprise. Management services are supported on a series of ISM servers.

Domain Support: The user management feature supports a high degree of customization to reflect and enforce an organization's security policies.

Manager-to-Manager Communications: Supported via CMIP

Systems Management Features

Fault and Status Monitoring

The ISM-MN gives the distributed system administrator visibility of all manageable objects. For example, it will provide color-coded notification if a UNIX file system is almost full or if available memory reaches a threshold. The ISM OS Monitor provides a more detailed view of UNIX systems including User ID, Group ID, Login time, and UNIX processes associated with resources in use.

The ISM Peripheral Monitor displays names and status of devices, as well as disk-level utilization. Bar charts, graphs, and gauges depict device status—for disk controllers, channel adapters, and other components. A Performance Monitor supports realtime monitoring of TCP/IP LANs.

Inventory and Configuration Management

ISM Peripheral Monitor can automatically draw the current peripheral configuration and display. The discovery feature discovers network components and creates a network topology display including IP nodes and nodes on Novell NetWare LANs. The Distributed Printing Facility (DPF) supports remote printer configuration and administration.

Software Distribution and Licensing

ISM enables the delivery of BOS/2 and BOS/X applications on UNIX and PC environments. ISM supports software distribution to Novell NetWare and LAN Manager target environments as well. ISM includes tools for packaging, installation, distribution, listing, and removal.

Backup and Archival Storage

ISM automates backup/restore for UNIX networks allowing one tape drive to perform backup and restores for any number of machines. Requests are kept in order by priority. Events are logged indicating backup status.

Resource Accounting and Chargeback

Not supported.

Security

ISM User Management can create a depository of users, services, and site organization information and relationships between them. ISM assists in identifying and registering users and their privileges in a consistent fashion across the distributed environment. ISM supports a security audit trail.

Other

ISM supports a collection of terminal emulators to support remote operations of distributed systems. ISM also features an integrated trouble ticket facility.

4.3.11   Digital Polycenter Manager on NetView

In September 1993, Digital entered into an agreement with IBM to license NetView/6000 technology. Polycenter Manager on NetView is one result of that agreement. The product is a port of NetView/6000 to Digital's Alpha AXP hardware. Polycenter Manager on NetView supports all of IBM's APIs as well as the NetView/6000 GUI. An optional DECnet Manager applications supports management of Digital DECnet networks.

Strengths

Polycenter Manager provides the same depth of TCP/IP management functionality as IBM NetView/6000, including an Open Topology manager and advanced alarm filtering and event handling. Polycenter Manager offers attractive 64-bit price/performance advantage of Digital's Alpha AXP chip technology, and added applications for managing legacy DECnet environments. Also, Polycenter Manager is available on Windows NT systems.

Weaknesses

As a management platform vendor, Digital has lost ground because of its failed effort to create third-party support for its previous enterprise management offering, DECmcc. As of September 1994, only a handful of third-party applications were shipping for Polycenter Manager on NetView. However, as a primary partner in the NetView Association, Digital should benefit from access to IBM's business partners and third-party support should increase during 1995.

Features
Basic Platform Services
Device Discovery/Network Mapping

"Dynamic Network Discovery" feature automatically discovers IP-addressable nodes and tracks IP network device adds and changes, keeping the network topology map current. In a typical configuration, 1,000 nodes can be "discovered" in about 20 minutes. Automatic map drawing/redrawing (autotopology) is supported to a limited extent. The system continually verifies network device connection. Operators can save current network maps to compare with later maps; no sophisticated change management software provided. There is support for multiple protocols, including correlation of IP and non-IP devices. The optional DECnet Manager application provides management of DECnet and Digital terminal servers and bridges.

Alarm Capability

Monitors status of IP network nodes; generates events if user-defined thresholds are exceeded. Users can configure polls for groups of objects and examine the states of multiple components simultaneously. TCP/IP "diagnostic" routines include IP PING, TCP connection test, and SNMP agent test.

Event Filtering

Filtering rules can span multiple objects (groups) simultaneously; allows users to monitor different states of objects in different groups, and user complete boolean expressions to define thresholds. A Filter Editor and Filter Control Interface allow managers to see graphical representations of selected SNMP events. (See Figure 4.7.) Users can easily identify traps, and throttle redundant traps, eliminating excessive events by displaying notification only when the same trap occurs a user-specified number of times within a given time period.

Alarm Correlation

Not supported. However, a problem diagnostic facility allows users to trace a specific data pattern to determine whether or not a network problem is somehow related to that pattern. Network map can display packet routes for tracing; users can browse MIB to examine values.

SQL Database

Flat-file (ASCII) log of events and polled data; interfaces to SQL databases supported.

SNMP/Other Protocol Support

SNMP (MIB I, MIB II) and remote monitoring (RMON) MIB (e.g., SNMP, CMOT, CMOL); private extensions for DECnet and other Digital devices. A MIB loader allows point-and-click loading and unloading of RFC 121-compliant private MIBs.

CMIP support promised, but no delivery date has been set. IBM also supports the XMP API.

Users can browse performance- related MIB variables to examine, chart, or modify values. The product maintains historical data based on built-in and user-defined threshold polling; this data can be graphed for analysis in pie/bar charts or line graphs or saved in ASCII files.

Users can customize SNMP thresholds and traps (alert messages). Also, users can dynamically edit maps and set polling intervals determining how often the map is updated.

APIs, Developer's Kits, Partner's Programs

APIs provided for linking to Service Point applications. Version 2 includes an SNMP API and HP OpenView Windows API. Support for OSF/DME Consolidated Management API (CM-API) is also supported. The NetView Association provides support for third-party partners.

Other Features

Reporting

Includes five sample shell scripts for creating custom reports. A "xnmgraph" utility allows placing of custom graphs into reports.

Control Desk

This features allows users to run multiple applications in a single window.

Access Control

Access control based on Ultrix security and audit features. GUI based on Motif; users can edit the map with supplied map-editing tools. Menu bar function allows point-and-click access to View, Locate, Test, Edit, and Help functions, etc.

Hardware
Digital Alpha AXP (OSF/1, OpenVMS, and Microsoft Windows NT operating systems) and Intel hardware (Microsoft Windows NT operating systems).

Advanced Features
Network Modeling: Not supported

Distributed Implementation/distributed database: Supports multiple users through X displays.

Domain support: Polycenter Manager on NetView security features provide a pseudo-domain capability.

Manager-to-manager communications: Manager-to-manager communications are not yet supported.

4.4   EXAMPLES OF DOS/WINDOWS-BASED NETWORK MANAGEMENT PLATFORMS

Today, many organizations employ a two-tiered structure for enterprise management. DOS/Windows-based utilities and tools are used for monitoring the local LAN, and UNIX-based platforms such as those just discussed, manage the interconnections between local LAN segments.

Increasingly, LAN administrators are seeking integrated toolsets for local LAN management. The two leading DOS/Windows-based SNMP management platforms for LAN management are Novell NMS and HP OpenView for Windows.

4.4.1   Novell NMS

Novell NetWare Management System (NMS) is a DOS-PC based system that runs under Microsoft Windows. While it supports Novell and third-party applications for managing routers and hubs, it is primarily used in the local LAN environment for managing NetWare servers. Novell NMS supports monitoring of NetWare servers and management through access to NetWare's RCONSOLE and FCONSOLE utilities but requires additional applications for full management of PC workstations (see Figure 4.14).

Given an adequate hardware base with additional hard drives and lots of memory, NMS can scale upward to manage larger LANs and at least a dozen routers.

Strengths
NMS is affordably priced at $4995 per NMS console and up to $495 per server agent. The product is excellent for managing distributed NetWare servers—including monitoring status and performing administrative tasks such as software distribution and backups. The product is well suited for Windows environments.

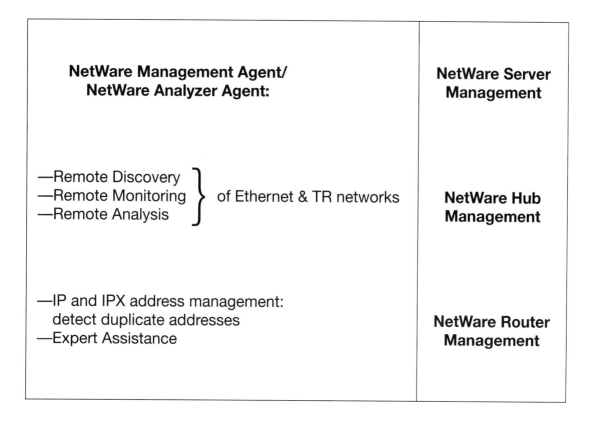

Figure 4.14 Novell's NetWare Management System (NMS)

Limitations
Lack of multi-user support, limited alarm filtering, and inflexible polling and map editing makes NMS a better choice for smaller networks.

Features

Basic Platform Services

Device Discovery/Network Mapping
"NetExplorer" (NXPPLUS) process discovers IP devices, DOS and OS/2 workstations (if they have an NXPPLUS agent), and IPX devices (servers, routers, bridges). Discovery starts from the server and propagates to neighboring servers; it takes several hours to discover a 250-node network. Novell documentation suggests running initial NetExplorer discovery overnight.

Supports continual autodiscovery of new nodes; users report no performance degradation if proper hardware is installed and polling is set at 15-second intervals. Provides logical mapping; users can edit maps to make physical views, but each object on the map must be moved individually—moving of grouped objects is not supported.

Alarm Capability

User must set thresholds on each server individually; no facility to replicate thresholds from one server to another or configure polls on other groups of objects. All information is collected at the NetWare servers scattered throughout the network.

Event Filtering

Coarse filtering capability based on several categories of traps (critical, major, minor, warning). User can specify only that all or none of the traps in that category should be displayed. NMS filtering does not support the notion of dependencies; no ability to set filters on groups of traps (each trap filter must be set individually).

Alarm Correlation

Not supported.

SQL Database

Logs polls, alarms into Btrieve database. Database resides on NMS console incurrent release; database will reside on server in future releases.

SNMP/Other Protocol Support

Can monitor any SNMP device.

APIs, Developer's Kits, Partner's Programs

Provides published APIs and a software developer's kit (SDK).

Advanced Features

Network modeling: Not supported.

Distributed implementation/distributed database: Not supported.

Domain support: Single password to console does not allow "scoping" of authority or configuring different views for specific operators.

Manager-to-manager communications: Not supported.

4.4.2   HP OpenView Windows

HP OpenView for Windows is designed to manage PC LAN networks from 50 to 1,000 nodes. The product currently supports a MIB compiler for monitoring any SNMP-based device. Tighter integration with HP OpenView for Unix is expected in the future.

Until 1994, Hewlett-Packard marketed HP OpenView for Windows strictly on an OEM basis; vendors such as Cabletron used HP OpenView for Windows as a basis for their own entry-level management products. Hewlett-Packard is now retooling HP OpenView for Windows as a general purpose management platform, capable of supporting multiple third-party applications

Strengths

HP OpenView for Windows is an extremely affordable, low-end platform. Its support for Visual Basic should encourage a flood of third-party applications by 1995 (see Figure 4.15).

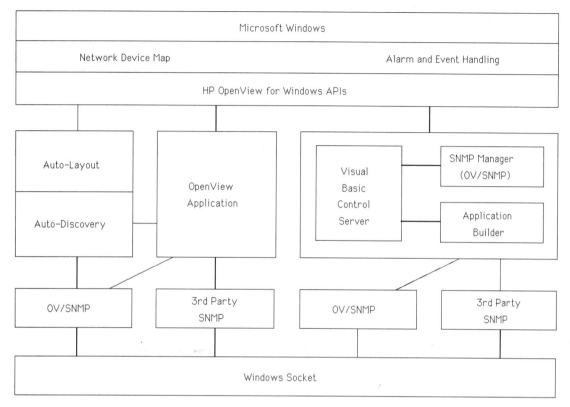

Figure 4.15 HP OpenView for Windows architecture

Limitations

HP OpenView for Windows provides only the basic management "shell" functions (alarm management, device discovery, and SNMP interface). Functionality is supplemented by Hewlett-Packard's Workgroup Node Manager application and third-party applications.

Features
Basic Platform Services
Device Discovery/Network Mapping

Concurrent autodiscovery of IP and IPX nodes; routers are discovered first; then routing tables are used to discover additional network devices (ARP cache, etc. NetWare diagnostic services are used to find IPX devices; the server bindery or SPX facilities are used to identify the device. Users can configure time intervals for continual, automatic discovery. However, the product does not support broadcast for discovering nodes in non-routed (e.g., purely bridged) networks. HP OpenView Windows supports hierarchical mapping of discovered nodes.

Alarm Capability

Can forward alarms and status information to HP OpenView for UNIX.

Event Filtering

Filtering is based on alarm levels and device type; can configure alarms to allow only certain classes to forward to pagers, beepers, e-mail.

Alarm Correlation

Not supported.

SQL Database

Alarms are stored in a Paradox database.

SNMP/Other Protocol Support

Supports SNMP GET and SET for compiled MIB variables; network administrator must configure polls for each variable individually; once a GET has been defined it can be saved for later execution; "block SET" feature is supported to help minimize network traffic.

APIs, Developer's Kits, Partner's Programs

HP OpenView for Windows supports applications developed in Visual Basic.

Advanced Features

Network Modeling: Not supported.

Distributed Implementation/distributed database: Distributed polling is not supported.

Domain support: Not supported.

Manager-to-manager communications: Not supported.

4.5   EXAMPLES OF UNIX SYSTEMS MANAGEMENT PLATFORMS

Systems management software is responsible for monitoring computers, servers, workstations, and other end-user devices (printers, plotters, etc.). The primary functions of systems management include:

- Fault and status monitoring of hardware (disks, CPU, memory) and software (applications, files, operating system components, network operating systems, database applications, drivers)
- Inventory and configuration monitoring of hardware (disks, CPU, memory) and software (versions of applications, files, operating system components, network operating systems, database applications, drivers)
- Software distribution and licensing
- Backup and archival storage
- Performance monitoring of hardware and software components
- Resource accounting and chargeback
- User administration
- Security

Major systems management vendors, including Computer Associates and Tivoli, are working on packaging aspects of their products as applications that can run under network management platforms. However, many of these vendors are also positioning their product offerings as platforms or "frameworks" themselves, capable of supporting third-party applications (both network and systems management applications) under a single graphical user interface, and providing all applications with access to common data (see Figure 4.16).

Currently, most network management platforms do not provide third-party applications (including systems management applications) with full access to common data (Jander, 1994). Likewise, systems management platforms, including those described in the following sections, are still largely self-contained products with no network management application support. However, as distributed computing becomes the norm rather than the exception, the convergence of network and systems management will take hold and systems management platforms will be capable of supporting many network management functions, primarily through third-party applications. The following platforms already support APIs and some development tools, as well as fledgling third-party partners programs aimed at getting this type of applications development off the ground. (Because of the immaturity of these products, strengths and limitations are not provided.)

4.5.1   Tivoli Management Environment

The Tivoli Management Environment (TME) is a suite of products designed for managing distributed UNIX computers. Tivoli differs from its competitors in that it employs strictly an object-oriented approach, and supports an distributed object database (see Figure 4.17).

TME consists of Deployment Management Products and Operations Management Products residing on the object-oriented Tivoli Management Platform. The Deployment Management Products include the following:

- Tivoli/Admin, supporting system administration, user/group management, configuration management
- Tivoli/Courier, supporting software distribution management
- Tivoli/Print supporting distributed printer management
- Tivoli/Partners, supporting database administration

The Operations Management Products include the following:

- Tivoli/Enterprise Console
- Tivoli/Workload
- Tivoli/EpochBackup
- Tivoli/Sentry

Fault and Status Monitoring

Tivoli/Sentry is a remote resource monitoring application that allows users to set thresholds for monitoring file systems, printing services, memory/paging status, disk utilization, common daemons (processes) and network traffic remote UNIX computers. Users can customize Sentry to monitor the status of additional resources as well. When thresholds are crossed, Sentry follows preset instructions to notify staff of the event (notification messages, e-mail, flash

A management framework gathers information from all devices and systems on a network and shares it across a wide range of applications. As common data models emerge, frameworks from different vendors will be able to work together.

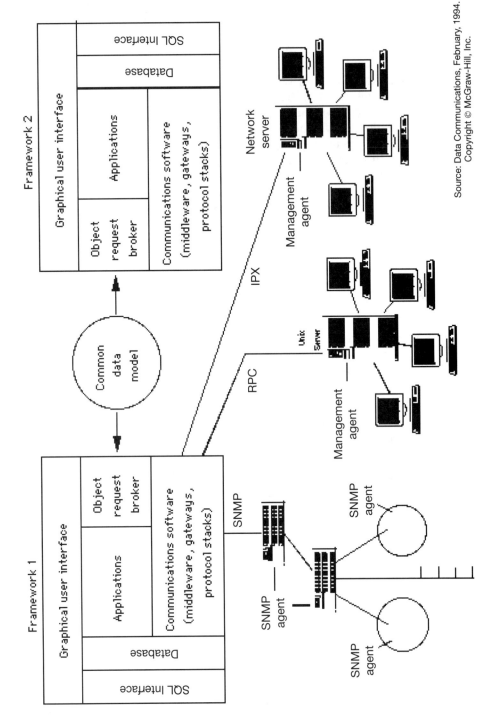

Figure 4.16 A management framework

Figure 4.17 Components of Tivoli Management Environment

an icon or alarm pop-up window, or execute a user-written program to call a beeper).

Tivoli/Enterprise Console supports event management and automated operations.

Inventory and Configuration Management

The Tivoli platform discovers all managed resources during the software installation process, providing systems managers with a fully distributed object database that reflects the actual configuration of all managed systems. Managed/modeled resources include user account profiles, authorization groups, host configuration (for each network node), Network Information Service (NIS) domain and map information, and Kerberos realms. Resources modeled and tracked include: hosts (IP address/name, aliases, NIS tokens, netgroup membership, and other characteristics), NIS domains (ethers map, hosts map, networks map, netmsak map, protocols map, RPC map, services map, netwgroups map, NIS overrides), user accounts (name/uid/gid/, password, and other characteristics), and Kerberos realms (realms, service principals, user principals, authentication services, service passwords).

Software Distribution and Licensing

Tivoli/Courier allows administrators to define software packs and automatically distributes them to any number of machines on the network

Courier allows system managers to build templates and indicate which target machines will subscribe to the software. Tivoli Courier supports "push" paradigm on demand or on a scheduled basis.

Workload Management

Tivoli/Workload supports scheduling and workload management.

Backup and Archival Storage

Tivoli/EpochBackup supports an intelligent mechanism for reducing overhead. It can scale up to hundreds of nodes. EpochBackup includes a self-service recovery feature allowing end-users to recover lost data without administrator intervention. A coverage monitor scans networks to detect new file systems, and automatically adds them to the backup plan. Tivoli/EpochBackup includes an application for automatic, baseline backups, supporting disaster recovery.

Performance Monitoring of Hardware and Software Components

Tivoli/Sentry monitors the following UNIX parameters: number of page faults, percentage and amount of available swap space, number of free/used "i" nodes, percentage of used/available disk space, root logins on "tty," subscriber host status, printer queue size/active, printer daemons active, percentage of disk space used/available for spooling directory, system load average number of network file system (NFS) write failures, remote procedure call (RPC) calls rejected/timed out, number of ingoing/outgoing packets, errors, and packet collisions. All events are logged to audit files for later trend analysis.

Resource Accounting and Chargeback

Not supported.

User Administration

Tivoli/Admin allows administrators to group resources into "policy regions" with administrator-specified policy guidelines for all resources in each region. The Policy mechanism goes beyond the access-approved/access denied mechanism of UNIX permissions. Tivoli/Admin provides delegation of time-consuming tasks to junior staff without compromising security.

Security

Tivoli/Admin provides comprehensive access control through managing Kerberos Authentication Services and the Network Information Service (NIS). Tivoli/Admin puts a "front-end" on these services and updates them transparently for the system administrator as managed resources are created, modified, or deleted.

Application Interfaces and Customization

The Tivoli/ADE toolkit provides a complete development environment for those wishing to develop new management applications for the Tivoli framework. In addition, Tivoli/Works supports a traditional command line interface, allowing operations to be performed from shell scripts, programs, or scheduled through the UNIX command "cron." Also, Tivoli/AEF allows customers to extend and enhance the operations of any Tivoli application—without complex programming—by attaching existing scripts writing new scripts. Tivoli/AEF supports extensions through PERL scripts, Shell scripts, and binary (UNIX) executables. Tivoli/AEF provides complete documentation and several extension examples.

4.5.2 Computer Associates' CA-Unicenter

CA-Unicenter for Unix is a systems management product for HP 9000 processors running HP-UX; an optional package called CA-Unicenter/Star can also gather information from MVS hosts. Support for Sun workstations is forthcoming.

CA-Unicenter's architecture centers around a relational database structure (see Figure 4.18). Support for "wildcards" to select data based on user-defined criteria assists systems administrators in obtaining information based on demands of specific users, groups, or departments without having to reorganize

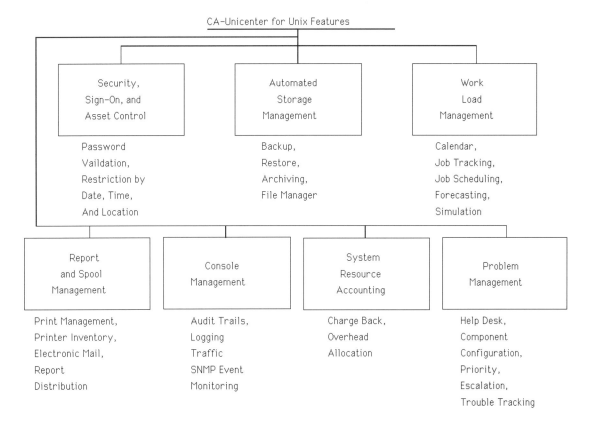

Figure 4.18 CA-Unicenter features

stored data into separate files. CA-Unicenter also supports a central calendar system for scheduling all operations.

Fault and Status Monitoring

The CA Event Notification Facility (CA ENF) intercepts systems events and notifies specific UniCenter modules, according to user-defined rules. A "Monitor dialog" feature allows operators to monitor only those messages that are relevant. CA-Unicenter will automatically open a trouble ticket when a system job fails to run. Also, the product automatically escalates notification to systems administrators if a problem is not resolved. Users can set custom status codes and categories for problem management.

CA-Unicenter can determine which devices are inoperable due to faults in "parent" devices. CA-Unicenter also supports console automation, including automated console interaction, allowing users to automatically trigger actions in response to specific console messages. The product provides restart/rerun instructions for guiding users in recovery, in the event of abnormal completion of scheduled jobs.

Inventory and Configuration Management

CA-Unicenter maintains an inventory and hierarchy of hardware and software components. This data is maintained in a "configuration" schema which includes component ID, serial number, tag number, description, manufacturer, installation data, primary user, service department, warranty, maintenance, internal/external address, and other vital information. CA-Unicenter accounts for the dependencies or relationships between components, such as monitors and printers that are connected to a specific CPU. CA-Unicenter's relational database structure allows systems administrators to establish parent/child relationships between components. Complex one-to-many and many-to-one relationships can be represented.

Software Distribution and Licensing

Not supported

Backup and Archival Storage

Automates archiving and backup as well as tape management and print spooling. A variety of media types are supported including tape, storage disks, and high-capacity optical disks. Backup and archive management can be triggered through the GUI—including copying, moving, deleting, and viewing files. Automated storage management protects files from being overwritten accidentally.

Archive provides the ability to remove backed up files from the active file system, freeing valuable space for new work. CA-Unicenter supports threshold archiving, which prevents potential UNIX system outages caused by the file system becoming exhausted. Also, the product supports intelligent transparent restore (IXR) which prevents the failure of processes due to missing files. CA-Unicenter supports IXR by restoring files to the active file system upon request by a user or a process. CA-Unicenter also provides for report distribution.

Performance Monitoring of Hardware and Software Components

Monitors process activity, device performance, memory utilization, UNIX file system directories, print queues. A workload management feature supports automated job scheduling—both calendar- and event-based scheduling.

A modeling and simulation facility helps users analyze the impact of changes to the UNIX system.

Resource Accounting and Chargeback

Includes a sophisticated chargeback and accounting module, supporting account structure specification, rate specification, budgeting, and charge inquiry. Information is available in multiple formats.

The CA-Unicenter accounting structure can identify up to five levels of accounting hierarchy within an organization. Chargeback provides containment policies used to determine which charges are to be assessed against the various levels and entities defined in the accounting profile. Chargeback profiles are comprised of charge elements, rate adjustments, split charges, and overhead allocation. All accounting and chargeback reports are preformatted.

User Administration

Supports policy-based security management by groups.

Security: Includes a security module that enables organizations to restrict superusers (systems administrator) privileges. This feature goes beyond the normal UNIX permissions scheme to support policy-based security of groups of users and assets. Supports single-point sign-on for a network of UNIX computers, with global enforcement of both user access controls and asset access controls.

Application interfaces and customization

CA-Unicenter (all versions) will support a common communications interface, allowing users to manage systems across multiple platforms and networks. However, this interface is not yet available.

To customize CA-Unicenter, users can define actions to be performed automatically when system messages are intercepted. Users can create console automation scripts

4.5.3   HP OperationsCenter

HP OperationsCenter is primarily a fault management tool for centralizing the operations and problem management of distributed UNIX systems, including HP 3000, HP 9000, IBM RS/6000, and Sun SPARCstations. OperationsCenter runs on top of the HP OpenView SNMP platform.

OperationsCenter is a distributed, client/server program that operates from a central management station and interacts with intelligent software agents installed on the managed systems.

HP PerfView and the new PerfRX applications can run under Operations-Center. HP PerfView tracks recent performance data for HP-UX and SunOS systems; PerfRX is a performance analysis tool for evaluating historical trends, load balancing, and problem diagnosis. HP PerfView includes two components: (1) Central analysis software (incorporating HP Network Node Manager) and (2) Intelligent agents that reside on the managed systems.

Fault and Status Monitoring

Users can define thresholds on systems parameters. Configuration of thresholds values and polling intervals is done at the central management system and automatically downloaded to the managed nodes. Polling ("monitoring service") is done locally at managed nodes to minimize network traffic overhead. Filter conditions can be specified at the managed nodes to further minimize traffic. In some cases, OperationsCenter provides event-specific instructions to guide users during problem resolution. OperationsCenter can also be configured to trigger corrective actions to user-specified problems.

Inventory and Configuration Management

No meaningful automatic systems inventory control features (for example, cannot produce a report listing what processes or software applications are currently running on the network).

Software Distribution and Licensing

An optional HP OpenView Software Distributor application can verify installed software on remote target systems. Using Software Distributor, administrators can build processes that monitor the integrity of software in remote locations. The product supports comprehensive packing, configuration, and removal of software throughout the network.

Backup and Archival Storage

The optional OmniBack application supports networked backup and restore. The optional Hierarchical Storage Manager application manages online storage for servers and client disks, supporting automatic and transparent migration of files between magnetic disks and optical disk libraries.

Performance Monitoring of Hardware and Software Components

PerfView provides an umbrella for the HP GlancePlus stand-alone systems management utilities. It monitors the following performance factors across the network: CPU utilization; CPU queue depth and process wait information; number of processes; disk utilization (percentage peak activity); disk queue depth and process wait data; physical and logical I/O rates; memory utilization; disk activity due to virtual memory management; swap utilization; Network packet rate data; application utilization of CPU; disk I/O, and resources that are blocking processes.

The optional OpenSpool application allows users to centrally monitor and control print spooling of remote printers

PerfRX provides historical trend analysis on transaction rates and response time, as well as parameters monitored by PerfView. This information can assist in workload balancing and capacity planning. PerfRX can display collected data in line, pie, or stacked graphs

Resource Accounting and Chargeback
The HP PerfRX application has the capability to identify the actual applications or processes using system resources, however, no accounting or chargeback utilities are included.

User Administration
Not supported.

Security
Password protection is supported. User profiles control the activities of each user on the management system and managed nodes.

The Workspace Manager feature allows administrators to specify the managed nodes and message groups for which each operator is responsible. The Workspace Manager creates a specific task-oriented work environment for each operator.

Application interfaces and customization
Collected data can be used to create and enhance problem resolution guidance. From OperationsCenters "Applications Window," users can launch custom scripts. OperationsCenter can be configured to collect messages and SNMP traps from any source.

4.5.4 AT&T StarSENTRY Systems Manager/ OperationsAdvantage

AT&T positions StarSENTRY as a platform for integrated network and systems management. The product is essentially a port of NetLabs/DiMONS to NCR 3300 (single processor) or NCR 3550 (multiprocessor) system hardware.

StarSENTRY supports the following integrated applications:

Systems Manager—the basic SNMP management platform (NetLabs)
Software Manager—software distribution for DOS, OS/2, and UNIX systems
Client Manager—fault/configuration management and control of DOS and OS/2 desktop systems
Computers Manager—monitoring/administration of multiple remotely located UNIX systems (support for NCR, IBM, HP, Sun, and others)

Applications for managing AT&T Frame Relay service and AT&T StarGroup hubs are also supported.

Fault and Status Monitoring
StarSENTRY Systems Manager employs localized polling to reduce overhead from monitoring activities (see Figure 4.19). Management of resources on

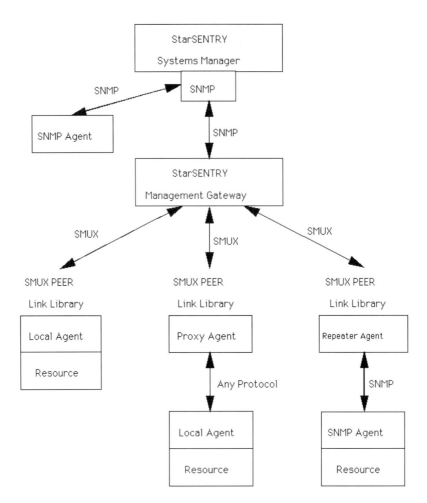

Figure 4.19 AT&T StarSENTRY configuration

remote LANs is accomplished through a management gateway residing on a remote workgroup processor. A lower-level protocol switch in the management gateway allows the use of any transport protocol providing a basic datagram service, such as TCP/IP, LU6.2, NetBEUI, and OSI. Multiple smart agents (also called "mid-level managers" or "management entities") attached to a management gateway can be grouped together in a SMUX peer arrangement. (SMUX is the SNMP multiplexor protocol, that is basically SNMP with the addition of a "join SMUX" function, allowing an agent to act as both an agent and a manager.) The management gateway (SMUX) and each SMUX peer are all separate UNIX processes.

Users can define polls based on object classes. Like NetLabs/DiMONS, AT&T StarSENTRY supports a flexible alarm configuration capability based on a conditional-state model. In addition, StarSENTRY's Computer Manager and Systems Manager applications allow administrators to set alarm thresholds on key system parameters such as disk space, memory, and usage. Specifically, Computer Manager forwards UNIX system alarms to the Systems Manager, which then displays them graphically on the screen.

Network and systems administrators can create messages to suggest corrective actions when a particular network event occurs. Administrators can create scripts that will automatically execute commands or reset MIB objects when a particular network event occurs. Systems Manager includes over 20 automated actions, such as dialing a beeper, resetting a devices, or forwarding an alarm to another management system.

Inventory and Configuration Management

Like NetLabs/DiMONS, AT&T StarSENTRY supports "fast discovery" alerting operators to active nodes and "full ping sweep" for discovering all nodes according to user-defined IP boundaries. An automatic mapping facility shows what is connected, and what has been changed. Also supported is a "non-polling" map that allows users to perform administrative tasks without adding network traffic overhead from polling.

In addition, the Client Manager application searches for newly-installed workstations and records client configuration data on all nodes equipped with agents. Inventory data includes memory, disk space, ports, machine type, PC bus types, DOS versions, and other component data for DOS and OS/2 systems.

Software Distribution and Licensing

The Software Manager supports centralized control of software distribution of applications to UNIX, OS/2, and DOS systems on remote LANs. This automates the retrieval, distribution, and installation of software at remote sites. Support for software distribution on Novell NetWare LANs is also provided.

The Client Manager supports transfer of files such as CONFIG.SYS and WIN.INI to and from remote computers, allowing administrators to replicate optimal configurations as needed.

Backup and Archival Storage

This is supported by the OperationsAdvantage option. An archival storage facility provides concurrent, parallel backup and restore of Teradata; provides a single-source solution to tape archiving and management; and eliminates the need for mainframe attachment. The Lifekeeper Fault Resilient System also supports automated recovery within minutes of failure. REELibrarian provides full capability tape library management, including security and audit facilities.

Performance Monitoring of Hardware and Software Components

The Systems Manager can poll any IP device at user-defined intervals. The Computer Manager tracks UNIX file system activity, user disk space, response time, CPU usage, memory usage, process count, and other parameters on remote UNIX systems. The Client Manager tracks similar parameters (disk space, memory, etc.) for DOS and OS/2 systems.

The Systems Manager Traffic Summary displays six levels of traffic for each of 12 different line speeds. The Computer Manager can produce tabular reports or performance graphs on key system parameters.

Resource Accounting and Chargeback
Computer Manager and Client Manager track system usage.

User Administration
Supported by the optional OperationsAdvantage ADMIN application; provides password synchronization for all hosts via a user ID database; simplifies complex administration tasks by allowing managers to categorize users/hosts.
Security: Allows managers to create management domains, protecting against unexpected failure of any management stations, while allowing supervisors to manage specific portions of the network.

Application interfaces and customization
StarSENTRY includes four C program interfaces for adding resource management applications: a Map-level API for applications affecting many managed resources; a host-level API for applications applying to a single host, an object-level API for applications applying to an object within a host, and an alarm transition API for taking actions such as activating beepers via shell scripts.

AT&T offers an SMUX Peer API toolkit for building an SMUX Peer. This toolkit hides the details of the SMUX protocol interface from the developer.

4.6 INTEGRATING APPLICATIONS ONTO MANAGEMENT PLATFORMS

Platforms provide a starting point for the management of distributed computing networks, but they are an incomplete solution without the addition of special-purpose third-party applications. In one sense, a management platform is little more than a fancy MIB browser, capable of retrieving raw data—and not capable of doing much with it. Applications are essential to filling the functional gap in the platform/applications model. Applications are required to process, manipulate, and transform the raw data into useful information that managers can use to make quick and effective decisions about what is best for the network.

In short, applications (and in particular, third-party applications) are a key component to the viability of the open management platform as a solution for client/server, distributed computing.

The availability of integrated applications still lags behind customer demand. This is because there are still technological and economic barriers to meeting market demand. The largest technological barrier is the multiplicity of APIs supported by various management platforms. Each platform has at least several APIs, affording varying levels of integration. Furthermore, each platform supports a completely different set of APIs (with different coding conventions, libraries, etc.) than the next. The one exception is IBM NetView/6000, which shares the same core technology and basic APIs with HP OpenView. Third-party developers have neither the economic resources nor the expertise to create software that takes advantage of all available APIs; and few vendors are willing to choose one platform vendor over another to begin the effort, for fear of alienating other platform vendors and their customers. Figure 4.20 depicts the various types APIs provided by the leading management platforms, arranging them according to the levels of integration they support.

Chapter 5 discusses the various types of applications available today, including their functions and use in network operations. The following sections describe how the platform supports integration of those applications. The methods can be roughly categorized as loose integration (menu-bar launching and simple command-line), moderate integration (enhanced command-line and map integration), and tight integration (use of APIs, compiled code and database integration.)

These integration methods are described briefly below, ranging from very loosely integrated to tightly integrated:

1. Drop-in or "menu-bar" integration—an application is "launched" from the platform menu, and no contextual information is passed from the platform to the application, or vice versa.

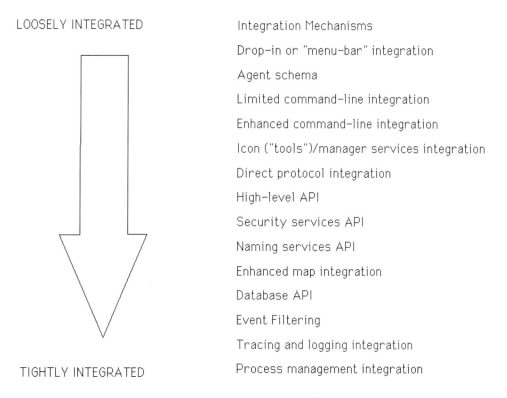

LOOSELY INTEGRATED

Integration Mechanisms

Drop-in or "menu-bar" integration

Agent schema

Limited command-line integration

Enhanced command-line integration

Icon ("tools")/manager services integration

Direct protocol integration

High-level API

Security services API

Naming services API

Enhanced map integration

Database API

Event Filtering

Tracing and logging integration

TIGHTLY INTEGRATED   Process management integration

Figure 4.20 APIs and levels of integration supported (note: applications may use APIs but not to full advantage, resulting in less than optimal degree of integration)

Drop-in or "menu-bar" integration is simple to implement and requires virtually no programming. Applications that use menu-bar integration typically register their actions with the platform user interface—little or no context is passed from the platform to the application when the user clicks on the menu-bar item symbolizing the application.

2. Agent schema integration—an agent schema is a file describing the management data available from an agent. Knowing an agent schema can assist an application in performing tasks more intelligently.

3. Limited command-line integration—an application obtains limited context of network state from parameters passed via the platform's command-line interface rather than from the GUI.

4. Enhanced command-line integration—an application is passed within the context of network state and key parameters.

5. Icon ("tools")/manager services integration—an application is launched from the platform menu with limited context of network state, such as the meaning of an icon on a map.

6. Direct protocol integration (SNMP. CMIP, etc.)—this involves more than merely accessing the MIB of an SNMP device; it provides more high-level support including blocking and non-blocking function calls, support for manual and automatic retransmission, memory management, location transparency for proxy agents, and the ability to both send and receive traps. CMIP APIs support distributed messaging passing and CMIS-like messages.

7. High-level API—a high-level API allows developers to write applications without having to know where and how data objects are stored, and hides the differences between underlying platforms. However, a high-level API cannot be used in cases where an application requires extensions to a platform.

8. Common functions API—facilitates rapid applications development with common queuing, scheduling, and event dispatching mechanisms as well as hashing, network addressing, exception handling, and ASN.1 support.

9. Enhanced map/topology integration—an application can react to map modifications and to status changes in map objects and their attributes; multiple applications can have access to a given attribute field of a map object. Shared maps allow multiple applications to work together to create a total picture of network status.

10. Database API—the application can access the platform's event database and modify the data if necessary.

11. Event Filtering— allows applications to filter out unnecessary events; filters remain persistent in the event database.

12. Tracing and Logging API—used for debugging of unexpected problems in production networks.

13. Process Management API—used to coordinate the activities of various manager and agent processes in a complex management environment.

14. Inference Handling API—allows development of applications which can infer status of network components from knowledge of attributes and behavior of other network components; an artificial intelligence capability.

Table 4-1 lists all major platforms and the APIs they support. The following sections describe these APIs in detail.

4.6.1   SunConnect SunNet Manager APIs

SunNet Manager supports three classes of APIs, described as follows:

1. Manager Services API, for building management applications
2. The Agent Services API, for creating new agents
3. The Database/Topology Map API, for modifying the SunNet Manager database and customizing the topology display

Applications may be tightly integrated with SunNet Manager using the Manager Services API and access the database through the Database/Topology MAP API. However, applications may be only minimally integrated via SunNet Manager's console menu or through knowledge of agent schemas or specific icons on the map.

4.6.1.1   Manager Services API

Developers use the Manager Services API and libraries for creating applications that obtain information from remote network agents. This API allows an application to send requests to agents and collect responses and other data. The Manager Services API does not currently support its own database of network elements and requests.

Before a SunNet Manager management application can obtain information from an agent, it must register for data and event reports (such as SNMP Traps). Since SunNet Manager supports an RPC-based architecture, applications must have an RPC program version number in order to register as an RPC service with the local SunOS portmapper. The RPC program number is the basis for all SunNet Manager communications. Likewise, all agents must have permanent RPC program numbers compiled in to communicate with SunNet Manager. It is possible to register with more than one function per process by using callback mechanisms.

A management application can receive traps (asynchronous events) from agents or from other applications that use the SunNet Manager Database/Topology API to modify database elements (see Figure 4.21). Applications can also specify to receive traps exclusively from the database.

The Manager Services library has an SNMP proxy agent option that an application may use when sending an SNMP request to target devices. The Manager Services library also supports SNMP SETs through the proxy option.

A management application may use *agent schemas* to find out what types of information an agent can furnish. An agent schema is a file describing the types and names of an agent's possible object attributes. In a sense, the agent schema "publishes" information about a particular device or device type's available management data.

TABLE 4-1 Application Programming Interfaces (APIs) on Leading Management Platforms

Platform	APIs
SunNet Manager	Manager services Agent services Database/topology map
HP OpenView	GUI (OVwAPI) Direct SNMP (snmpAPI) XMP_API (DM platform only) Database API (OVwDbAPI) Tracing and logging (OVTlAPI) Process management (OVpmdAPI)
IBM NetView/6000	End-user API (OVwAPI) Direct SNMP (snmpAPI) XMP_API Database API (OVwDbAPI) Tracing and logging (OVTlAPI) Process management (OVpmdAPI)
NetLabs/DiMONS	High-level API (3G and Sun Encompass only) Low-level CMIS-like API Management protocol API Object method API XMP API Backing store API GUI API Topology API Common functions API
Cabletron Spectrum	SpectroServer and View API (GUI) External Protocol Interface API Inference Handler API
Network Managers APIs	Database class library Diagram class library Graphics class library Graphics Extensions class library Network Management class library SNMP Protocol class library Product Specific Module (PSM) Framework class library SNMP Product Specific Module class library
Wollongong Management Station	Network map Network management daemon Configuration manager MIB chart MIB chart editor MIB form MIB form editor MIB compiler MIB tool Log viewer SNMP agent Trap test Verbose

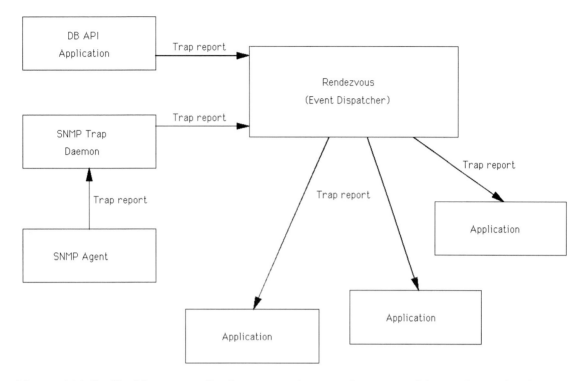

Figure 4.21 SunNet Manager applications can receive traps from agents (via trap daemon) or from other applications that use the Database API

4.6.1.2   Agent Services API

SunNet Manager comes pre-packaged with a number of agents for managing Sun workstations (see Table 4-2). These agents are already integrated with Sun-Net Manager via the Agent Services API.

Many organizations require information that is not provided by the prepackaged agents. For example, it may be desirable to have an agent for a different protocol subsystem. The Agent Services API allows developers to write agent software that can communicate with the SunNet Manager console.

Table 4-3 outlines the steps involved in writing an agent. Once the agent is written, it must be incorporated into SunNet Manager via an agent schema (Sun, 1992).

Agents interact with SunNet Manager using RPC mechanisms. An agent identifies itself by its RPC service name, RPC program, and version number parameters. Callback routines, supplied by the agent, are called by the Agent Services library to validate a request from a manager, dispatch the request, communicate with "child" processes, or shutdown agent processes.

Once an agent is written and compiled, it must be integrated with SunNet Manager. Each agent source code file must include a SunNet Manager header file, and the agent object modules must be linked with the SunNet Manager

TABLE 4-2 Agents Included in SunNet Manager

diskinfo	provides disk information
etherif	provides Ethernet interface statistics
hostif	provides interface statistics
hostmem	provides memory utilization statistics
hostperf	provides host performance data
iostat	provides disk i/o, CPU, and tty statistics
ippath	provides IP packet route trace information
iproutes	provides IP route table and statistics
layers	provides protocol layer statistics
lpstat	indicates printer status
ping	provides IP connectivity information
rpcnfs	provides RPC and NFS statistics
snmp	supports MIB I, II, and private MIBs
snmpd	an SNMP agent for Sun SPARCsystems
sync	provides synchronous interface statistics
traffic	provides Ethernet traffic data

TABLE 4-3 Steps for Writing an Agent for SunNet Manager

1. Facilitate access to the managed object (e.g., write code that provides management data).

2. Assign a name (attribute) to each discrete management data item. For example, let ipkts denote the input packet count.

3. Determine the data type for each attribute (e.g., ipkts is an integer).

4. Use the attribute information to form the agent schema definitions.

5. Expand the original code (from step 1) to incorporate agent schema definitions.

6. Write code for initializing the agent, handling requests, and reporting errors using the SunNet Manager Agent Services library.

7. Incorporate any agent-specific error messages into the agent schema file.

8. Test and integrate the completed agent code and schema file with SunNet Manager.

library. The agent schema must also be copied to the user/snm/agents directory of the SunNet Manager Console.

In addition to writing new agents, SunNet Manager's Agent Services API also supports the conversion of existing applications to SunNet Manager agents.

4.6.1.3   Database/Topology API

The Database/Topology API allows developers to perform the following tasks:

- open the database
- lock and unlock the database

- retrieve information about database elements
- add a new element to the database
- delete an element from the database
- modify database elements
- load an ASCII file into the SunNet Manager Console
- save an element or save the Console's runtime database into an ASCII file

The API functions are used in conjunction with a header file supplied with SunNet Manager. The header file defines the data structures for a cluster record buffer that is used with database operations.

Retrieving information from the database requires use of a simple read operation (snmdb_read). The read command will return an element's type, property, color, agent(s), view(s) or connections, depending upon the parameters passed. Developers can also retrieve elements of a specific type in a particular view by using library routines.

4.6.1.4   Forthcoming APIs

Future versions of SunNet Manager (e.g., the Encompass products) will support an entirely new set of APIs, including a high-level API. Section 4.6.7. describes the Encompass development environment.

4.6.2   HP OpenView APIs

As discussed in section 4.3.2, HP OpenView actually encompasses three primary products: the SNMP Platform, the Distributed Management Platform, and the Network Node Manager. The Distributed Management Platform includes all of the APIs provided by the SNMP Platform, as well as additional APIs for OSI support. The Network Node Manager includes the SNMP Platform and additional end-user functions, but no added APIs.

The HP OpenView SNMP Platform supports these APIs:

- OpenView Windows API (OVwAPI)
- Direct SNMP API
- Database API (OVwDbAPI)
- Event Filtering API
- Tracing and Logging API (OVwTlAPI)
- Process Management API (OVpmdAPI)

In addition, the Distributed Management Platform also supports the XMP API which provides both OSI and SNMP support.

The clear separation, and the definition of multiple application programming interfaces allows third-parties to integrate their applications into the platform (see Figure 4.22).

The distinction between a management platform and a management application is sometimes blurred by the fact that applications can also define their own "integration points" where other applications can share functionality and services. For example the HP OpenView products, Network Node Manager, and

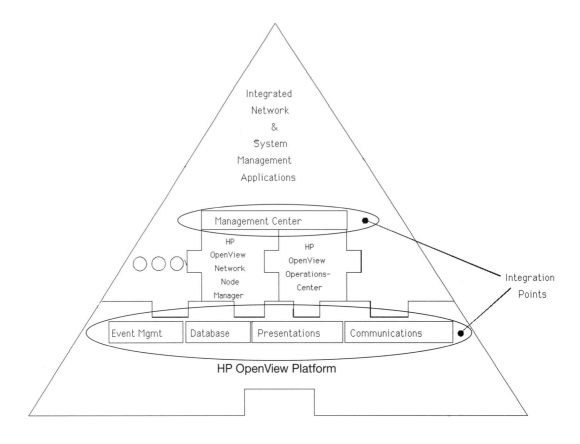

Figure 4.22 Integration points of HP OpenView

OperationsCenter provide functionality which is not available to only the application end-user, but also to other applications.

Hewlett-Packard categorizes the integration supported by HP OpenView as follows:

1. User Interface—supported by OVwAP
2. Data—supported by OVwDbAPI
3. Protocol Access—supported by SNMP API and XMP API
4. Event—supported by OVeEventSieve
5. Product Support—supported by OVuTL API, OVsPMD API, file placement guidelines, and package and installation routines

4.6.2.1 Application Integration for the User Interface—HP OpenView Windows API (OVwAPI)

The user's first exposure to any integrated facility is through the user interface. A common look and feel means that the individual tools will operate in a similar fashion, and information will be presented in a common format. This can improve operator efficiency.

HP OpenView Windows (OVW) is the GUI, and a primary integration point for third-party and user-developed applications. While use of the OVwAPI can facilitate a more integrated network management solution, Hewlett-Packard does not consider OVW integration "mandatory."

Applications integrated under HP OpenView Windows can be grouped into three broad categories: drop-in applications, tool applications, and map applications. The application developer chooses which category is best for a particular application.

Drop-in applications are those applications that are minimally integrated with HP OpenView Windows. These menu-integrated applications register their actions with HP OpenView Windows to provide convenient menu access to the application. An example of a drop-in application is one that provides access to a terminal window from an HP OpenView Windows menu item.

A tool application is one that presents its functionality through tools and subtools accessible from HP OpenView Windows menu items or as executable symbols. A tool application may also allow users to perform actions on objects that already exist in the graphical map. HP OpenView Windows defines the concept of tools and subtools to organize the functionality of an application. A tool is an integration point for a narrowly focused and related set of functionality. Each of the specific tasks carried out from the tool is a subtool.

A map application interprets a scheme of collected objects and their interrelationships and directs HP OpenView Windows on how to present the information to the user. Such an application uses the HP OpenView Windows API to create submaps, add symbols to a submap, and add connections between symbols. The HP OpenView IP Map application is an example of an HP OpenView Windows map application.

The HP OpenView GUI encourages multiple applications to coexist and manage data in the same map, in the same submap and for the same objects. Capability fields enable menu item overloading, allowing multiple applications to register and be invoked for the same menu item. The HP OpenView Windows object database stores field values for global objects. Applications can create new fields of their choosing in the database and relate the fields to a particular object, in effect combining their object attributes with the object attributes defined by other applications. HP OpenView Windows' submap sharing ability enables data from multiple applications to be presented in the same submap. This feature allows users to get a combined view of their management information. Users can configure the applications to create a map that most closely approximates their management environment.

The HP OpenView Windows Application Programming Interface (OVw API) contains library routines enabling applications to integrate with HP OpenView Windows. Based on X-Windows programming concepts, the OVw API interface and programming model are event-driven.

The HP OpenView Windows library includes routines for manipulating map and presenting network and system management information. The routines range from changing the label of a symbol on the map, to creating a submap and populating it with symbols in particular coordinates, to verifying user modifications to the map.

A variety of HP OpenView Windows API convenience routines are available; these routines ease programming tasks by incorporating actions of multiple calls into a single call, or by reducing the number of data structures the application developer must see.

In order for an application to use the HP OpenView Windows API, it must be registered with HP OpenView Windows in an application registration file. The file provides the necessary information for HP OpenView Windows to invoke and manage the application process.

HP OpenView Windows supports events associated with map modification, user editing, status change, select list change, and others. Applications may define callback routines to be invoked when specific events have occurred.

Applications may also engage in a handshaking mechanism with HP OpenView Windows that allows the application to control whether map editing changes are allowed. This handshake, known as the Query-Verify-Confirm sequence, allows HP OpenView Windows to notify an application that map editing is occurring (Query). Once notified, the application can verify the user input or changes (Verify). If verified, HP OpenView Windows can then notify the application that the operation was completed (Confirm).

The HP OpenView Windows API calls are grouped into several categories. These categories are process management, event processing, object access, symbol type, map integration, user editing verification, help integration, application registration, and miscellaneous.

4.6.2.2   Data Integration

Sharing data between applications and platforms provides users with a more complete view of the managed environment. Sharing data requires both a common repository and a common method for accessing the data within it.

The OpenView Windows (OVW) Object database manages all object and field information for OVW. All OVW maps on a particular management station use the same object database. OVW objects persist across all OVW sessions, so these objects and fields can be used by multiple applications concurrently. Developer access to the object database is limited to the supplied OVwDb API routines since they shield the developer from the underlying database implementation.

An OVW Object is a representation of a logical or physical entity or resource that exists on a computer network. An OVW object consists of a unique object identification and a set of fields or attributes which specify the characteristics of an object. The OVW API provides routines to create and delete objects, as well as change the object fields.

Fields are identified by a field ID and a data type. They can either contain a single element or list of multiple elements. Since fields are essentially global and shared across all applications of the OVW environment, it is preferable to define them by using the Field Registration at OVW startup. The OVW API routine, OVwDbCreateField(3), can be used by an application to define a field, but to do so would create a dependency on that particular application. If for some reason the application was not present, any other application expecting the existence of that field would fail.

In a highly integrated OVW application environment, both objects and fields would be shared between many applications concurrently. For instance, a network discovery application might find a new object on the network which represents a type of a computer system, and has fields that represent certain characteristics about the object. Another independent "hardware inventory application" might use that information for tracking the new system as an instance of an asset that needs to be accounted for on the network. This sharing of information is possible if the fields used by both applications are documented and made sharable by the developers of the management applications.

There are a set of fields defined by the OpenView platform products that can be used by OVW applications. Applications may define new fields that other applications can use, but only if the Field Definition entry in the Field Definition File is made available to all applications. Application products may have their fields registered as part of HP OpenView certification to prevent interoperability problems with other applications, and optionally to "share" information with other network management products.

4.6.2.3   Relational Database Support

HP OpenView SNMP and DM runtime products include support for Ingres relational databases and an SQL interface. SQL is a widely understood model, and it provides a mechanism to transform the high volume of management data into useful information. Map topology information and Event Sieves can be configured to use the relational database instead of the default proprietary methods. The same OVwDb APIs are used by applications as before, but the data is now available to other applications through the standardized SQL interface. Applications may also use the relational database to store and share their information with other applications. While these capabilities previously existed with the OVwDb facility, the flexibility of the relational model allows a higher level of data integration within the network and system management environment.

4.6.2.4   Protocol Access Integration

The HP OpenView products provide the ability to manage network objects which use SNMP and OSI management protocols. The direct SNMP API and the XMP API enable applications to talk to the protocol stacks at a high level. Other services are available to translate raw data into useful management information. By integrating with these facilities, the developer can provide additional application functionality with reduced effort. The two major directions for this level of integration are SNMP and XMP.

SNMP-API   The HP OpenView SNMP API is based on revision 1.1 of the Carnegie Mellon University (CMU) SNMP Library. The CMU SNMP Library introduces a connection-oriented model from the application perspective. The HP SNMP API extends this model by introducing the concept of a session, or a logical binding, between the SNMP manager and agent.

Data is exchanged between SNMP processes using the Basic Encoding Rules defined for the Abstract Syntax Notation (ASN.1). An application developer does not need deal directly with ASN.1 nor the Basic Encoding Rules. The HP Open-View SNMP API takes care of the ASN.1 encoding and decoding. ASN.1 data types supported by the HP OpenView SNMP API include integer, octet string object identifier, counter, gauge, time ticks, and IP address.

Both blocking and event-driven applications are supported by the HP Open-View SNMP API. Models exist for both X-based applications and other event-driven applications. In both cases, the application developer provides a callback function to handle the non-blocking arrival of responses.

The HP OpenView SNMP API library includes extended support for event-driven X-based applications. Such applications will use the X environment to manage calls to read or receive responses and retransmit messages; they need not manage these calls themselves.

Applications may issue SNMP requests in either blocking or non-blocking mode. If a request is used in blocking mode, the application is suspended until the response arrives or a timeout occurs. Issuing an SNMP request in non-blocking mode allows the application to continue processing while the request completes.

The mode in which a request is sent affects an applications's need for managing retransmission, SNMP's usage of the unreliable User Datagram Protocol (UDP) at the transport layer may result in lost messages and require that some messages be retransmitted.

The HP OpenView SNMP API will handle retransmission for applications using blocking requests. Applications issuing non-blocking requests may manually manage retransmissions using the system select(2) function. Alternatively, these applications may manage retransmissions automatically using the X extensions to the HP OpenView SNMP API.

The HP OpenView SNMP Management Platform provides special support for applications communicating via an agent through a proxy. These applications can address a message directly to the true agent; HP's underlying SNMP implementation determines which host is the proxy and routes the message accordingly. An SNMP configuration application and file exist to provide proxy information. While it allows the generation of traps, the HP OpenView SNMP API does not support the development of SNMP agents.

The HP OpenView SNMP API has four categories of functions; these include the session management, message setup and management, communication, and manual retransmission categories.

Session Management: The Session Management functions setup, manage, and terminate the logical "session" between the SNMP manager and agent. SNMP sessions can be set up for any request/reply SNMP operation or for trap receipt.

Message Setup and Management: Message Setup and Management functions facilitate the creation of SNMP data structures. The HP OpenView SNMP API provides functions to create and free SNMP protocol data units, and create, delete, and set elements of an SNMP variable bind list. Other Message Management functions include converting an SNMP error value to a text string.

Communication: The Communication functions are used to send and receive SNMP messages. Different variations of the calls are provided for blocking and non-blocking (X-based and other event-driven) modes.

Manual Retransmission: Manual Retransmission functions are provided to get retransmission information on pending SNMP requests and to actually retransmit a pending SNMP request.

XMP and XMP-Based APIs   The HP OpenView Distributed Management (DM) Platform supports the current preliminary version of the X/Open Management Protocol Application Programming Interface (XMP API). The XMP API is based on the Consolidated Management API specification, co-authored by HP, Groupe Bull, and IBM, and was selected as the OSF DME "network management option."

The HP OpenView XMP and XMP-based APIs are available for developing SNMP- and CMIS-based network and system management applications. These APIs provide access to SNMP, CMOT, and CMIS services, enable OSI fully distinguished name access to objects in the HP OpenView Windows graphical map, and provide simplified access to the HP OpenView Event Sieve and Event Log Agents.

XMP employs another standard interface, the X/Open OSI-Abstract-Data Manipulation API, known as XOM. XMP uses XOM to manage the information objects, or arguments, to XMP functions.

Writing applications that interface to XMP/API is relatively difficult. However, HP OpenView Distributed Manager 4.0 contains a number of new programmer tools to make writing to XMP a bit easier.

XMP supports seven CMIS services and four SNMP services. XMP uses the XOM API to create, examine, modify, and destroy the arguments to these XMP functions.

The XMP API provides all the required functionality to implement various types of agents and managers. While the XMP API supports both the synchronous and asynchronous modes of operations for managers, all agent (response) functions are supported in synchronous mode only.

XMP provides a variety of ways to identify the source or destination of a message. By specifying either the OSI fully distinguished name, network address, or title, the message is sent to the appropriate agent or manager. If neither the network address nor the title is specified for a CMOT or CMIS request, HP OpenView Object Registration Services is used to map the OSI fully distinguished name to the destination.

4.6.2.5   Event Integration

Both OSI and SNMP environments communicate system and network exceptions through events. By configuring the event subsystem to forward specific events to a management application, the user has the ability to take immediate action on problems regardless of their location in the network. HP OpenView includes tools for distributing these events to the appropriate management application, then filtering and interpreting them to allow the manager to decide what action should be taken.

The three different alternatives for this type of integration—SNMP events, ISO events, and Event Sieves—can be differentiated.

SNMP Events   SNMP events are messages sent in the form of SNMP traps by applications. SNMP events are used to inform applications that have registered for those events that something significant has happened, such as when the status of a node on the network has changed or a threshold has been exceeded.

Because events are really SNMP traps, the content of the events needs to be described as to how they fit into the SNMP trap format. SNMP traps are composed of enterprise, agent address, a generic trap number, a specific trap number, a time stamp, and the "variable binding" (information related to the trap). The specific trap number identifies the "sub type" or reason the trap was generated. Applications that create or use their own events should provide help documentation that includes detail on the event, possible causes of it, and how the application user should handle it.

In Version 3.3 of Network Node Manager, event types can be customized on a node-by-node basis. This helps operators distinguish between the critical crash of a mission-critical server and the less critical system crash of a one-user PC.

Because HP uses "enterprise specific traps" to provide this functionality, the trap "sub types" may change in future releases.

ISO Events   The Distributed Management Platform provides HP OpenView event management services and supports registration for distribution of events with the Event Sieve Agent (ovesmd). The agent does this with eventForwardingDiscriminator objects as described in ISO/IEC 10164-5 (Event Report Management) and as specified in the MIB definitions in ISO/IEC 10165-2 (Definition of Management Information). For backwards compatibility with older releases of HP OpenView, the agent also supports the Hp proprietary OVeEventSieve object as described in /usr/OV/hpsmi_mibs/ovesmd.mib.

An event manager system is one that receives events from other systems, either because it has an event log agent (ovelmd) on it or because it has applications that want to receive events from other systems. An event agent system is one that has agents on it that generate events which are of interest to managers on other systems.

Event Sieves   Event sieves are objects managed by the event sieve agent. Like most objects managed by agents, the sieve objects will be persistent from the time they are created until they are deleted, even if the agent should be stopped and restarted. To accomplish this, the event sieve agent stores information about the event sieve objects in a database when creating them and reads that information whenever it is restarted.

By default, the sieve information is stored in an ASCII flatfile. Each sieve is stored in six lines of information: a text comment, the name or address of the system the sieve is on, an integer sieveID, the destination address of the sieve, the length of the sieve filter string, and a binary encoded event filter string.

The only sieves stored persistently are those that have been programmed to send events to remote systems.

4.6.2.6   Product Support Integration

HP OpenView is a very complex set of tools and databases. Unless special precautions are taken within the design and implementation of such a system, the administration of the management station itself may become difficult. For this reason, the applications integrated into the HP OpenView platform products should be common administrative tools and procedures for both initial installation and ongoing support.

HP OpenView supplies functionality for installing applications, performing tracing and logging, managing system components and processes, and validating database consistency.

Over time, as more management applications are integrated into the platforms there is a possibility that the various applications may interfere with each other. The most obvious area of contention is file naming and usage.

HP offers integration help to avoid these contentions and to incorporate all kinds of applications into the platform by the following services:

*   File usage and placement
*   Application software distribution
*   Installation and configuration of the application products
*   Tracing and logging
*   Process management
*   Security and access control

File usage and placement: Hewlett-Packard provides recommended guidelines for file placement. It is particularly important for applications that share files to place them according to these guidelines. To help ensure that certified applications do not interfere with each other under normal circumstances, HP registers the use of application directory names and files as part of the HP OpenView certification process.

Application software distribution: The HP OpenView tools "ovpkg" and "ovinstall" utility assist developers in installing application product packages.

Installing and configuring application products: HP supplies a set of installation tools that detect missing dependencies and versions of prerequisite software, among other things.

Tracing and logging: HP OpenView includes the OVuTL API for supporting a tracing and logging facility to enable troubleshooting and debugging.

Process management: HP OpenView requires multiple UNIX processes to support basic platform services; the OVsPMD management facility assists users in managing the processes required by HP OpenView; the OVsPMD API allows applications or agents to communicate with this process management facility.

Security access and control: HP OpenView does not provide integrated facilities for restricting access by specific users; however, the platform does support a command for viewing and modifying UNIX permissions associated with OpenView Windows maps.

4.6.3   IBM AIX NetView/6000 APIs

IBM AIX NetView/6000 shares core technology with HP OpenView. This includes all critical APIs. While the programmatic names of these APIs are identical between the two products, IBM has chosen to group the APIs under different functional categories in its documentation (see Figure 4.23). These categories include:

1. End-User API—for manipulating the GUI and the object database. This includes application integration, callback routines (which notify the application that the operator has selected a particular action through the console's GUI), object database access (including over 40 routines), symbol routines, map and submap routines, user action verification (five routines to verify user-specified changes to maps and map objects), and dynamic registration routines for configuring the NetView/6000 menu structure. (End-User API includes OVwAPI and OVwDbAPI.)

2. SNMP API—providing extensions to the basic SNMP command set

3. XMP API—for SNMP and CMOT application support

4. OVuTL API—comparable to the HP OpenView tracing and logging facility, for debugging

5. OVsPMD API—comparable to the HP OpenView process management facility API

6. Event Filtering API—comparable to the HP OpenView Event Sieve facility

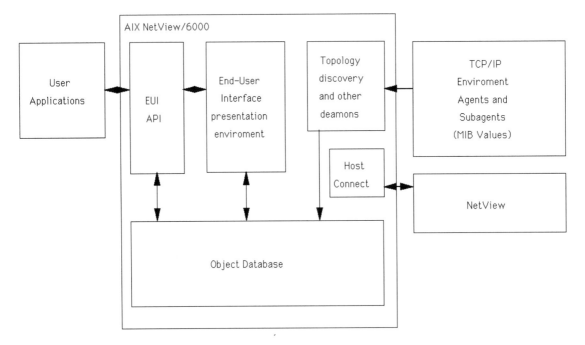

Figure 4.23 Overview of IBM NetView/6000

As with HP, IBM distinguishes between minimally integrated drop-in applications, moderately integrated tool applications, and tightly integrated map applications.

The End-User API is the most commonly used integration point. Figure 4.24 provides a general outline of a NetView/6000 End-User API program. As indicated in this figure, the End-User API can be divided into four segments:

1. Initialization—The application is connected to the NetView/6000 program by using the OVsInit() routine or, if the application is merely accessing the object database, then the OVwDbInit() routine is used. These routines initialize internal API data structures and establish a connection from the user application to the NetView/6000 GUI.

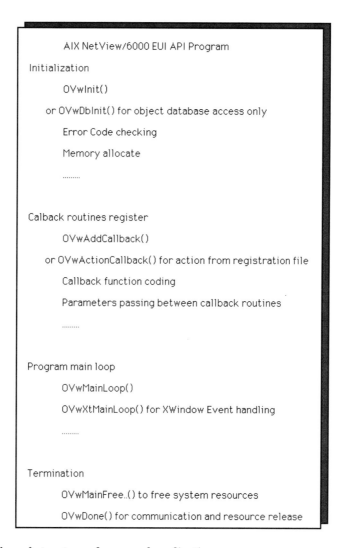

Figure 4.24 API calls and structure of a general application

2. Define callback routines for events—Applications must register for the call-back for specific events; otherwise, they will not receive notification of these events.

3. Main processing loop—This is used to process events.

4. Termination—The application calls OVwDone() to termination communications with AIX NetView/6000.

AIX NetView/6000 applications can modify the object database according to events registered through the End User API. Events may be generated from Net-View/6000 or from commands received via a driver program (either at the AIX IPC message queue or the TCP/IP socket). Commands received via driver programs may originate from the local command line, from a remote machine, from an external program, from a configured event (poll), or from a NetView/390 RUNCMD.

4.6.4   NetLabs/DiMONS, DiMONS 3G, and SunConnect Encompass APIs

Eight different APIs are defined within the NetLabs/DiMONS development environment. DiMONS 3G and SunConnect Encompass will also support a ninth API, the High-Level API, which will allow applications developed for one platform to be ported to another (see Figure 4.25).

With the exception of the High-level API and GUI API, effective use of Net-Labs APIs require C++ experience; however, NetLabs plans to offer C as well as C++ bindings in the future.

4.6.4.1   GUI API

The GUI API is based on XLIB and the Solbourne Object Interface (OI) facility developed by ParcPlace. The look of the interface is generated using the Parc-Place GUI prototype tool. The developer provides the actions (the "feel") of the interface using Perl scripts or C++ code.

4.6.4.2   Object Method API

The Object Method API lets developers treat all managed objects within the platform as C++ objects. When an application needs to support new resources or new kinds of resources, the API provides ways to generate the appropriate C++ classes. The API can also provides ways for extending the object classes when an application needs to elicit some new kind of behavior from a managed object. Developers can use shell scripts, PERL or C++ with the Object Method API.

4.6.4.3   Backing Store API

This API allows applications to store data in an external repository that is independent from the platform (e.g., independent of the platform's dynamic memory). The Backing Store API is an abstraction of the methods that the platform uses to store persistent data. It provides a simple configuration policy for determining which repository is to be accessed for each data element. In the future, NetLabs

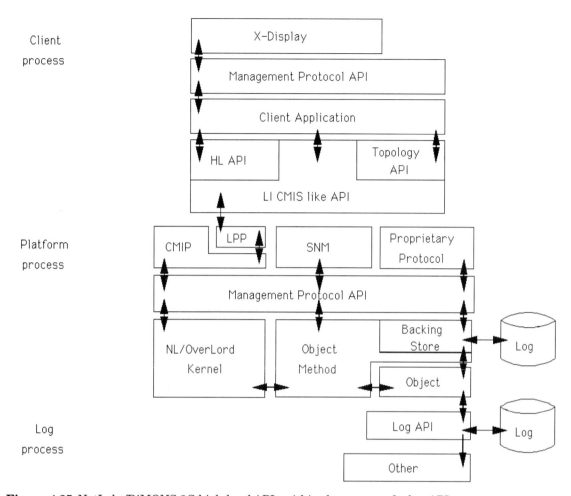

Figure 4.25 NetLabs/DiMONS 3G high-level APIs within the context of other APIs

plans to support a relational database (RDBMS) repository providing access to all industry leading RDBMS products.

4.6.4.4 Low-Level CMIS API

This API allows applications developers to formulate Common Management Information Services (CMIS) messages that DIMONS 3G kernel components use to communicate. Most applications developers will not need to use this API, as the high-level API maps its message formats into low-level CMIS messages automatically.

4.6.4.5 Log API

The Log API provides classes and functions for access to either NetLabs or OSI format logs. Each log object in NetLabs/DiMONS includes a filter which is used to test whether or not specific events should be recorded.

4.6.4.6   Management Protocol API

This API allows additional management protocols to be added to NetLabs/ DiMONS (in addition to the SNMP and CMIP/CMOT protocol driver modules already included). The Management Protocol API uses a pair of Kernel Message Service Access Points to provide communications between a protocol driver module and the DiMONS message routing module. These access points use a procedure call interface as a transport mechanism to pass messages.

4.6.4.7   Common Functions API

The Common Functions API provides a number of commonly used object classes, functions, and types to facilitate rapid applications development. These functions include queuing, scheduling, and dispatching events; hashing; ASN.1 support; network addressing; and exception handling. NetLabs also provides debugging and tracing facilities.

4.6.4.8   Topology API

DiMONS/3G maintains a common network model, which tabulates information about the connections between network components and network topology. Network components and their relationships are represented as objects within the Common Network Model; the Topology Database is the instantiation of those objects. Applications can access information in the Common Network Model by using the Topology API. This information includes a set of interrelated graphs, as well as groups of objects called "collections."

4.6.4.9   High-Level API

Most developers writing NetLabs/DiMONS 3G applications will choose to use the High-Level API, which provides a protocol-independent, object-oriented interface into the platform. The High-Level API allows vendors and end-users to develop applications without specific protocol knowledge. However, developers wishing to define new object classes or new object methods must have knowledge of the OSI General Definition of Managed Objects (GDMO) specifications, as well as Abstract Syntax Notation.1 (ASN.1). Netlabs has submitted this High-Level API to X/Open, Ltd. for consideration as a contribution to the object-oriented services that will be layered on top of the X/Open Management Protocol (XMP).

When using the High-Level API, the applications developer does not need to know where and how objects are stored. This is called locational transparency. The High-Level API makes all objects appear to be local. To do this, the High-Level API must be platform independent—capable of translating generic data (text strings and numbers) and requests from the application into the format expected by a particular platform. The API does this by providing a common representation for the identical features of different platforms. When features are similar but not identical, the API hides the differences as best it can. When it's impossible to hide differences, the API should present these differences as differences in the data rather than in the flow of control. When it is impossible to hide differences in flow of control between platforms, the API adopts a canonical order, or allows access to the data by name rather than just position.

The API permits all data values to be represented in a textual form, without regard to the internal representation. At the same time, the API allows the application to pass raw, platform-specific, binary-encoded data around the program without encoding/decoding every step of the way.

The API also automatically propagates event sieves from the application to the platform, and automatically caches various sorts of data in the application process.

Shielding the developer from details about object storage is desirable but, at the same time, the application itself needs to know where and how its objects are stored. This is called locational flexibility. This means that the application needs to have access to some of the low-level primitives upon which the High-Level API is built.

Scheduling services support both asynchronous and synchronous function calls. Synchronous calls must wait until an operation is complete before performing any other action; asynchronous calls will start the operation and return immediately, indicating completion of the operation by issuing a callback. The use of synchronous calls is discouraged if a user is developing an application that is to be purely event-driven. The API allows developers to rule out the use of synchronous calls by setting a timeout parameter to 0.

4.6.5   Cabletron Spectrum APIs

Cabletron Spectrum supports three types of APIs and several additional interfaces for adding support for third-party devices and customizing the display of management information. Cabletron groups these capabilities into two categories: Level I Developer Tools and Level II Developer Tools.

4.6.5.1   Level I Developers Tools

Level I provides basic tools and documentation to model new devices and edit the map/icon display. Since Spectrum is built around an artificial intelligence engine called the Virtual Network Machine (VNM) which can model network behavior, including connections and relationships between devices. The network model is a composite of individual device models. The Level I toolkit includes five products: Basic Extension Toolkit, Model Type Editor, Generic Information Block Editor, Icon Information Block Editor, and Extension Integration Toolkit.

Basic Extension Toolkit Includes the Management Module Build Program, used to create the files and directories needed for new types of models. It also provides the fundamental knowledge required for all development work in Spectrum

Model Type Editor Provides access to templates (model types) used to create and modify objects in Spectrum's object-oriented database (see Figure 4.26). To help developers, Spectrum includes pre-defined several model types called "derivation points;" examples include routers, bridges, and other common SNMP devices. Developers can create a new model type by inheriting attributes, intelligence

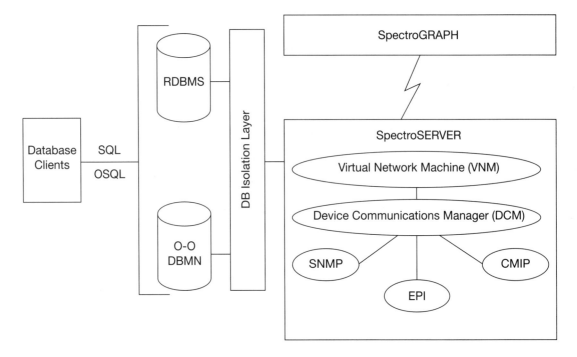

Figure 4.26 Spectrum's open database architecture

and rules from existing model types, such as the derivation types. Once a new model type is defined, the developer can use Spectrum's MIB Import feature to add new attributes to that model type. The MIB Import feature allows information from ASN-1 MIBs to be converted into Spectrum attributes.

Generic Information Block Editor Provides a GUI to modify the way the device model information is presented on the screen. For example, device model information can be displayed in pie charts, tables, or graphs. The user can see the effect of edits immediately on the screen because editing occurs on-line.

Icon Information Block Editor Allows the user to manipulate the base icon that represents a device model. One or more sub-icons are layered on top of the base icon; these sub-icons may represent functions of the device or device status.

Extension Integration toolkit Packages changes onto an installable cartridge tape; this facilitates propagating changes among several Spectrum systems in an organization, exporting or importing changes to a new version of Spectrum, or creating a product for sale.

4.6.5.2   Level II Tools Level II

Developers' Tools include the actual APIs—External Protocol Interface (EPI) API, SpectroSERVER API, and VIEW API, and Inference Handler API. Each API includes programming libraries (C++), documentation, and sample programs.

External Protocol Interface API This API allows programmers to write applications which can communicate with other devices through non-SNMP protocols or directly through the device's SNMP agent. (See Figure 4.27). This API shields developers from Spectrum internals, while allowing use of existing protocol/agent software. This API acts as a protocol converter (proxy). Also, it allows developers to create one protocol module capable of handling information from many devices, preprocessing the information before it reaches Spectrum. Non-networking devices, such as building automation or manufacturing systems, can be managed with the appropriate software/hardware interfaces using applications called from this API. The External Protocol Interface API requires TCP/IP for its lower-level communications.

SpectroSERVER and VIEW APIs These collectively provide access to the data stored in Spectrum's object-oriented database. They include the Asynchronous SpectroSERVER API, the Synchronous SpectroSERVER API, and the View API. These APIs are used to develop C++ applications that act as clients to SpectroSERVER. The View API allows an application to be a client to the SpectroGRAPH process as well as to the SpectroSERVER process. Applications written to these APIs are provided the same access to Spectrum data as has SpectroGRAPH.

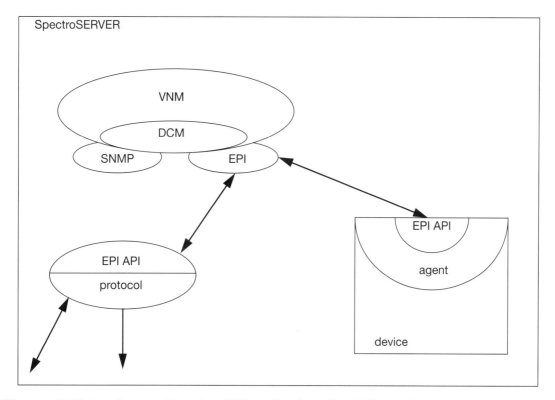

Figure 4.27 External protocol interface (EPI) applications allow Cabletron Spectrum to communicate with non-SNMP protocols and devices.

The SpectroSERVER APIs both provide access to SpectroSERVER, they have different request/response mechanisms. The Ansychronous SpectroSERVER API uses a callback paradigm—when a request is made, the client can perform other processing while "waiting" for a response. This is useful for X Windows applications and others designed as a series of separate subtasks. In contrast, the Synchronous SpectroSERVER API must wait for the response from each request before performing any other processing. This API is most appropriate for batch applications.

These APIs provide the applications developer with an object-base architecture. The client application creates "handle" objects representing items in the Spectrum database. The Asynchronous and Synchronous API interfaces can pass parameters (or "parameter objects") bidirectionally, to and from Spectrum. A third type of object, called the "service object," provides access to device models and model types, attributes, relations/rules and associations, statistical and event logs, and alarm information.

With these APIs, Cabletron provides header files, object libraries, global libraries, sample source code, and extensive documentation.

Inference Handler API The Inference Handler API supports development of compact C++ routines that have access to the network modeling engine or Virtual Network Machine (VNM). These routines are invoked through sets of triggers which reflect changes in the VNM environment. Changes may include creating or deleting device models, changing attribute values or relations, invoking actions, or generating events. Inference handler applications must be designed to operate in the VNM's multi-threaded environment. Cabletron supplies sample source code, debugging macros, header files, object libraries, global libraries, and extensive documentation with the Inference Handler API.

4.6.6   Network Manager's APIs

Network Managers supplies a Developer's Toolkit which includes eight Class Libraries and Application Program Interface manuals. These API manuals define the interface to the Class, and show how the objects can be used. The Class Libraries are written in C++ and provide the basis for the development of new applications. The seven libraries include:

- Database Class Library
- Diagram Class Library
- Graphics Class Library
- Graphics Extensions Class Library
- Network Management Class Library
- SNMP Protocol Class Library
- Product Specific Module (PSM) Framework Class Library
- SNMP Product Specific Module Class Library

The Developer's Toolkit includes example PSM source code, including how to create, modify, delete, and configure PSM objects. A diagram editor, debugger, and dialog box file conversion utility are also included in the toolkit.

Developers use object-oriented coding techniques to create NMC applications. The Toolkit provides all the necessary libraries and header files for application writers to develop PSM. Much of the functionality required for SNMP applications—such as establishing the internet address at Create time—is already included in the SNMP PSM Class Library. Other common functionality required for creating PSMs is provided in the PSM Framework Class Library.

4.6.7   Wollongong Management Station APIs

All Wollongong Management Station applications have APIs to support customization. For access to the APIs, examples written in C are provided to help programmers develop their own applications. This includes an API to the extensible agent included in Wollongong Management Station.

The Wollongong Management Station applications supporting APIs include the following:

- Network Map (provides graphical representation of the network)
- Network Management Daemon (responsible for fault monitoring, device discovery, and trap/alarm management)
- Configuration Manager (for site-specific customization)
- MIB Chart (user-configurable tool supporting simultaneous charting of individual or multiple MIB variables and/or MIB variable expressions from single or multiple agents)
- MIB Chart Editor (provides for chart editing and definition, including 3-D bar graphs and line and strip charts)
- MIB Form (user-configurable tool for GET/SET of MIB variables)
- MIB Form Editor (configuration application for MIB Form)
- MIB Compiler (ANS.1 compiler)
- MIB Tool (a generic application for walking the MIB)
- Log Viewer (provides X-windows based viewing of log files, with sort and filter options)
- SNMP Agent (an extensible SNMP agent that supports MIB II)
- Trap Test (an application for building and sending traps for testing purposes)
- Verbose (provides textual output of SNMP PDUs for troubleshooting purposes)

4.6.8   Bull ISM APIs

ISM's Consolidated Management API Library (CM-LIB) supports access to the CM-API (also known as XMP). Third-party developers can build extensions to the management system without impacting the base product. ISM supports a set of tools and languages for developing specific management applications. The ISM Management Language Interpreter and Object Definition Compiler expedites applications development.

4.6.9   Digital Polycenter Manager for NetView APIs

The APIs supported by Polycenter Manager for NetView are identical to those supported by IBM NetView/6000. (For more information, see section 4.6.4.)

4.7 SUMMARY

A "platform" is a complex software package that forms the basis for an organization's enterprise-wide network and systems management solution. Platforms provide a starting point for the management of distributed computing networks, but they are an incomplete solution without the addition of special-purpose third-party applications. The availability of integrated applications still lags behind customer demand. This is because technological and economic barriers to meeting market demand still exist. The largest technological barrier is the multiplicity of APIs supported by various management platforms. This chapter describes how the platform supports integration of applications via APIs; Chapter 5 discusses the various types of applications available today, including their functions and use in network operations.

5

Network and Systems Management Applications

5.1 OVERVIEW OF THE STATUS OF MANAGEMENT APPLICATIONS MARKET

Open management platforms are designed primarily to support basic management services, as described in Chapter 4. While SunConnect, Hewlett-Packard, IBM, NetLabs, and other management platform vendors offer a selection of their own value-added management applications, crafting a comprehensive management solution for a multivendor distributed computing network from only one vendor's offerings is impossible. Table 5-1 describes the many components and processes that must be managed effectively to build a comprehensive management solution.

5.1.1 Application Categories

Most management applications can be classified broadly as device-specific, process-specific, or platform enhancing applications. Systems management applications may include both device-specific and process-specific elements; while traffic monitoring and analysis applications typically capture data going across the wire—this data originates from many devices. Toolkits and development environments do not perform management tasks per se, however, they can make it easier for applications developers and users to create valuable, customized management software. Figure 5.1 shows the breakdown of the types of applications that are currently being shipped (Faulkner, 1994).

Device-specific applications typically focus on improving the manageability of one particular vendor's device (hub, router, etc.). When broadly defined, device-

TABLE 5-1 Applications Solution Set

Third party applications are typically required to create a comprehensive solution set that addresses these following key areas:

Device-Specific	Intelligent concentrators (hubs) and terminal servers
	Bridges/routers/repeaters/network interface cards
	WAN devices (multiplexers, modems, ATM switches)
Systems Management	UNIX systems management (servers and workstations)
	UNIX systems security
	Software distribution
	PC LAN and PC systems management (NetWare LANs; DOS/Windows workstations)
Traffic Monitoring and Analysis	LAN monitors
	WAN monitors
	LAN/WAN monitors
Process-Specific	Data analysis and report generation (performance management)
	Help desk/trouble ticket (problem management)
	Service level agreement reporting (performance management)
	Physical asset/cable management (configuration management)
	Usage and chargeback (accounting management)
Platform Extensions	Alert notification to pagers, wireless systems; log managers
	Console management
	Legacy systems monitoring and gateways (IBM SNA, DECnet, other non-SNMP)
	Mapping applications
Service-Specific Applications	Frame relay, SMDS, private line
	Mobile data services
Toolkits and Development Environments	

specific applications also include software for monitoring and controlling carrier-provided services such as a frame relay or private line service. They may also include traffic monitoring applications, which interpret data from network monitoring devices called probes.

Device-specific applications are rarely an important source of income for the device vendor. Rather, they are offered as an adjunct to the main (and more profitable) device product lines. These devices are put forth as "value-added" which may help differentiate the product, particularly in competitive market niches.

Systems management applications focus primarily on the performance and fault monitoring of a computer system—such as a UNIX or DOS workstation or server. Systems management applications vary widely in terms of the scope of functions covered. Some applications merely monitor the status of a few key

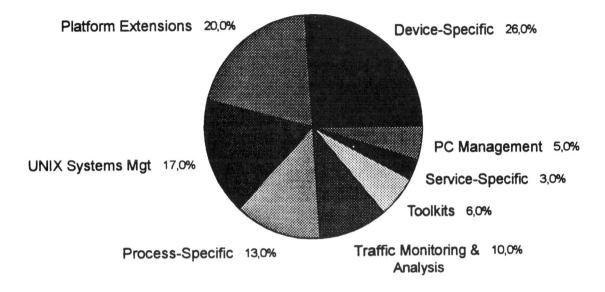

Figure 5.1 Percentage breakdown of applications by category

parameters, such as CPU usage and disk space, while others provide comprehensive security management and configuration management; still others focus strictly on database applications status monitoring. A fair number of UNIX systems management applications are available for use with SNMP management platforms. However, there is a lack of similar applications for DOS PC and NetWare LAN management. The outlook is expected to improve with more widespread implementation of new interfaces developed by the Desktop Management Task Force (DMTF) consortium, which is led by Intel, Microsoft, and SunConnect.

In proprietary environments, performance indicators are often embedded in communications protocols. Due to the lack of such embedded support in TCP/IP, users must rely heavily on external monitoring tools such as traffic monitors, probes, and protocol analyzers. Users are discovering the value of integrating traffic monitors into the enterprise management framework; hence, the number of SNMP-based traffic monitoring and analysis applications is quite adequate.

Process-specific applications are not associated with any specific network device or service. Rather, these applications focus on improving the workflow or processes of network and systems management, including problem management, configuration management, data analysis and reporting, security, and accounting. Process-specific applications are provided by ISVs who may have no other major hardware or software product line, or who offer software in a related product area, such as communications or systems security.

Platform enhancements extend the platform's existing capabilities or enhance its ease of use. Platform enhancements are also often provided by ISVs. Gateways to legacy systems and applications for managing legacy networks (IBM

SNA, Digital DECnet) are becoming increasingly important as user organizations seek to deploy SNMP management platforms to manage the entire enterprise network.

Finally, toolkits and development environments are increasingly important as organizations extend the functionality of platforms to meet specific network needs.

5.1.2   Managing SNMP and Non-SNMP Components

Today's networks include both SNMP and non-SNMP components. The platform is capable of addressing SNMP components, at least in a limited sense. Third-party applications are absolutely necessary for addressing non-SNMP components including many WAN devices and legacy systems.

For SNMP components, the management platform itself provides the capability to inspect or "browse" the MIB variables (device parameters and status indicators) of any device or host on the network supporting an SNMP agent. However, third-party applications are necessary to interpret the meaning of parameter values and to analyze or manipulate the data using higher-level mathematical expressions. For example, a platform can obtain a raw data MIB value of packet errors per second, however, an application is required to calculate a number indicating errors as a percentage of total traffic. Currently, more applications are available for managing SNMP-components than for managing non-SNMP components.

5.1.2.1   The Need for Third-Party Applications

Widespread availability of a variety of quality third-party management applications is vitally important to the success of the platform/applications model and to the platform vendors themselves. The number and types of third-party applications shipping have been doubling every six months since March 1993. Currently about 100 third-party network and systems management applications are being shipped for open, SNMP-based management platforms. However, there is still a lack of available applications, particularly for critical areas such as DOS/PC and Novell NetWare server monitoring, non-SNMP device monitoring (multiplexer/modems), as well as for processes such as network security, LAN and internetwork accounting and chargeback, and data analysis and reporting tools. Also, the number of applications shipping from vendors outside of the U.S. (including Germany, the U.K., France, Italy, Spain, Israel, Japan, Australia) is still small but growing rapidly (Faulkner, 1994).

While the number of applications is steadily increasing, the degree of integration between applications and the underlying platforms is still woefully inadequate. A tremendous opportunity exists to automate, simplify, and enhance management of distributed systems and networks by forging integrated links between various third-party applications. A few, but not many, applications vendors are now working on this problem.

5.2   LEVELS OF INTEGRATION

Most applications today are typically very loosely integrated with the underlying platform; a few are moderately integrated, and even fewer are tightly integrated. While in general, tighter integration supports a higher degree of automation, a moderate degree of integration is perfectly adequate for supporting process automation in many cases. One example of this is the very effective command-line integration between Remedy's Action Request System and a number of platforms and other applications.

Examples of applications that are tightly integrated with the underlying management platform include Gandalf's Passport, Remedy's Health Profiler, and SNA-Expert from Alcatel Bell. In each case, the application is taking full advantage of underlying platform APIs.

The primary integration methods are listed below, ranging from very loosely integrated to tightly integrated:

1. Drop-in or "menu-bar" integration—an application is "launched" from the platform menu, and no contextual information is passed from the platform to the application, or vice versa;

2. Limited icon ("tools") or map integration—an application is launched from the platform menu with limited context of network state, such as the meaning of an icon on a map, and perhaps the connections between icons;

3. Enhanced map integration—an application can react to map modifications and to status changes in map objects and their attributes;

4. Limited command-line integration—an application obtains limited context of network state from parameters passed via the platform's command-line interface rather than from the GUI;

5. Enhanced command-line integration—more context of network state and key parameters are passed to an application, perhaps including a pointer to a file containing device settings;

6. SQL Database API—the application can access the platform's event database and modify the data, if necessary;

7. Protocol integration (SNMP. CMIP, etc.)—in addition to making a device's MIB data available to the platform, the application can access SNMP services of the platform;

8. Event Filtering—supports correlation of event filtering across multiple applications;

9. Broad product support—coordinates file usage, placement, tracing, and logging functions, and process management between different third-party applications; and

10. High-level API—application can access the platform using protocol-independent, object-oriented interfaces that shield the application from details of the platform.

Chapter 4 discusses the APIs and levels of integration supported by all major SNMP-based management platforms and the APIs supported.

5.3   APPLICATION SHIPMENTS

There are currently about 100 third-party management applications shipping today, and approximately 24 applications shipping from the platform vendors. Faulkner provides a listing of these applications according to platforms supported (Faulkner, 1994).

Third-party applications support is vital to the successful deployment of management platforms. Management platforms support basic features (IP node discovery, network mapping, protocol support, alarm management, graphic user interfaces, and applications development tools) while the third-party applications provide the "value-added" functions targeting specific areas of equipment monitoring, systems management, and management processes.

5.3.1   Third-Party Support for Market Leaders

As Figure 5.2 shows, the number of third-party applications shipping for the three leading vendors—SunConnect, Hewlett-Packard, and IBM—is expected to be very close by early 1995. IBM will remain slightly behind, due to its later entrance into the SNMP-based management platform market. However, the

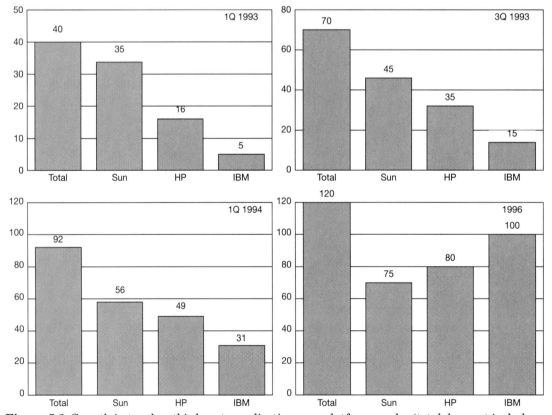

Figure 5.2 Growth in turnkey third-party applications per platform vendor (total does not include overlap for multi-platform product)

number of third-party vendors supporting each of these platforms is sizable enough to create the market pressure needed to draw customers and persuade the platform vendors to continue enhancing and investing in their products.

5.3.2 Third-Party Support for NetLabs and AT&T

Third-party support is also important for NetLabs and AT&T StarSENTRY. However, NetLabs is in the process of revising its third-party strategy. Previously, third-party applications were available exclusively from OEM vendors who bundled their applications in with the platform. Now, through its NetLabs/Vision partners, NetLabs is enabling third-parties to market NetLabs/Vision applications (usually device-specific management applications) unbundled from the platform. Within the framework of this new strategy, third-party applications support for NetLabs/DiMONS is still in the early stages.

Likewise, AT&T StarSENTRY (which is a port of NetLabs software to a different hardware base) is also nurturing a fledgling third-party applications program. While only one third-party application was shipping as of early 1994, over a half-dozen more are expected to be released later in 1994. As a product offering, StarSENTRY should be successful in AT&T Global Information Solutions' (formerly NCR) traditional vertical markets, retail and banking. However, AT&T has a formidable marketing challenge in convincing non-AT&T customers to consider StarSENTRY as a player and stayer, even though the product has some very impressive client/server management and software distribution capabilities built into it.

5.3.3 Third-Party Support for Cabletron and Network Managers

Cabletron Spectrum and Network Managers are less dependent upon third-party application support than are the other platform vendors. Both Cabletron and Network Managers produce their own applications for a variety of computer systems and network equipment. In the case of Cabletron Spectrum, these applications, called "device models," provide integrated views of device behavior and status, produced using network modeling technology that is part of Spectrum's object-oriented core. Network Managers also developed several "product-specific modules" that display device status and behavior using a rules-based technology. One advantage of the Cabletron and Network Managers approach is that users can obtain more comprehensive management capabilities in one-stop shopping. Customer support issues are also simplified with this approach. However, the start up costs tend to be a bit steeper, and some customers are put off by this initially (though in the long run, this option is no more expensive than buying multiple applications from several third-party vendors). Another advantage is that Cabletron and Network Managers are in a better position to ensure more seamless integration of their models and modules with the underlying platforms.

In terms of installed base, Cabletron Spectrum trailed both SunNet Manager and HP OpenView as of mid-1994, with installations numbering in the hundreds for Spectrum and in the thousands for SunNet Manager and HP OpenView. The difference in installed base between Spectrum and other players, including IBM NetView/6000, is not as pronounced. More significant is the fact that Spectrum has been deployed in some very large and complex networks, and it appears to be shouldering the load more effectively than HP OpenView or SunNet Manager in complex environments. The product's unique technology has proven itself under rather strenuous conditions in large production networks, although the previously-mentioned high initial cost and installation has been a barrier for some organizations.

While still relatively unknown in the U.S., Network Managers is gaining a strong presence in Europe, as evidenced both by recent large sales of the product and by growing third-party support. About 15 percent of the total third-party applications for all management platforms verified as shipping as of early 1994 were from non-North American suppliers—many of whom indicated that Network Managers' NMC is a very important product in their geographical target market (Faulkner, 1994).

5.4 APPLICATION EXAMPLES

The following section lists all management applications shipping to date. In addition to briefly describing each application, the following section also provides an in-depth examination of one or two of the leading applications in each category.

5.4.1 Device-Specific Applications

5.4.1.1 Smart Hubs

The following applications for managing intelligent concentrators (hubs) and terminal servers were shipping as of mid-1994:

- 3Com LinkBuilder Vision
- 3Com Transcend
- Atlanta David System Hub Views
- AT&T/NCR StarLAN 10 Smart Hub Manager
- Bytex 7700 Series NMS
- Cabletron Spectrum for Open Systems
- Chipcom ONdemand NCS
- Cisco Crescendo Manager
- Dornier FNS 7090 Network Manager
- FiberMux LightWatch Open
- Hirschmann StarCoupler Manager
- IBM Hub Management Program/6000
- LANNET Data Comm. MultiMan
- Network Solutions Cabletron MMAC Hub Views
- Optical Data Systems LANVision
- Raylan Network Manager
- Sestel HubMan

- Synernetics ViewPlex
- SynOptics Optivity
- Ungermann-Bass NetDirector for UNIX
- Xyplex ControlPoint

The characteristic that distinguishes the smart hub from a repeater is its ability to be managed—its "intelligence." One can construct a LAN without using smart hubs; however, the morass of cabling and the complexity of accommodating moves, adds, and changes to a hub-less network makes that approach infeasible. Because manageability is such a key selling point for hubs in general, hub vendors direct a lot of effort into enhancing the quality and integration of their management applications. Consequently, more applications are available for managing hubs than for managing any other type of network device.

The following section briefly describes key characteristics of each application.

3Com LinkBuilder Vision

Function: Graphical display of hub status using look-and-feel of NetLabs/ Vision.

Platforms supported: NetLabs/DiMONS.

Integration methods: Via NetLabs/Vision application.

3Com Transcend

Function: Integrated management for 3Com adapters, hubs, and routers.

Platforms supported: SunNet Manager; support for HP OpenView and IBM NetView/6000 forthcoming.

Integration methods: Menu bar.

Transcend software obtains information from SmartAgent intelligent device agents embedded in 3Com adapters, hubs, and routers. 3Com SmartAgents localize polling and organize collected data to reduce bandwidth overhead of management data. SmartAgents are capable of correlating information from multiple 3Com devices to provide a more integrated view of network status and to assist in the creation of baselines for performance management.

Atlanta David System Hub Views

Function: Graphical, realtime displays of David System hubs for monitoring purposes.

Platforms supported: NetLabs Vision.

Integration methods: Menu bar.

AT&T StarLAN 10 Smart Hub Manager

Function: Configuration and fault management of remote or local AT&T StarLAN 10 Network SmartHubs.

Platforms supported: AT&T StarSENTRY.

Integration methods: Menu bar; traffic and performance statistics are gathered through the application and alarms are forwarded to the StarSENTRY alarm panel.

Bytex 7700 Series NMS

Function: Software-controlled configuration management for LANs operating through Bytex Series 7700 intelligent switching hubs.

Platforms supported: HP OpenView.

Integration methods: Intercepts SNMP Traps.

Cabletron Spectrum for Open Systems

Function: Management of Cabletron MMAC hubs, desktop network interface (DNI) cards, and bridge/router modules. Supports alarm management and device configuration upload/download.

Platforms supported: SunNet Manager, HP OpenView, IBM NetView/6000, and Novell NMS (Windows).

Integration methods: Menu bar.

Spectrum for Open Systems allows Cabletron's line of products to be managed under other vendors' platforms. In addition to this application, Cabletron also provides management of its devices from its Spectrum management platform.

Chipcom ONdemand NCS

Function: Management of Chipcom's ONline System Concentrators, including expanded graphical views of component status and security modules, graphical displays of various components, portraying status and supporting device configuration.

Platforms supported: SunNet Manager, HP OpenView, and IBM NetView/6000

Integration methods: Menu bar.

Cisco Crescendo Manager

Function: Monitoring and control of Crescendo's FDDI wiring concentrators; displays graphical image of concentrators including current status of all panel indicators.

Platforms supported: SunNet Manager, HP OpenView, IBM NetView/6000.

Integration methods: Menu bar.

Dornier FNS 7090 Network Manager

Function: Management of FNS 7090 FDDI concentrators.

Platforms supported: SunNet Manager.

Integration methods: Menu bar; SNMP MIB

FiberMux LightWatch Open

Function: Management of Crossbow Multi LAN hubs, including remote control of any-port-to-any-port redundancy.

Platforms supported: SunNet Manager, HP OpenView, IBM NEtView/6000.

Integration methods: Menu bar.

Hirschmann StarCoupler Manager

Function: Management of Hirschmann Ethernet StarCoupler ASGE XX hubs.

Platforms supported: SunNet Manager (shipped by Network Managers), HP OpenView, Cabletron Spectrum; support for IBM NetView/6000 forthcoming.
Integration methods: Menu bar; also device modeling for Cabletron Spectrum.

IBM Hub Management Program/6000
Function: Management of IBM 8250 Multiprotocol Intelligent Hubs, including expanded graphical views of component status, and security modules.
Platforms supported: IBM NetView/6000.
Integration methods: Menu bar.

IBM 8250 hubs are OEM'd from Chipcom; therefore, the Hub Management Program/6000 is essentially equivalent to Chipcom's ONline NCS.

LANNET Data Comm. MultiMan
Function: Management of LANNET intelligent hubs via graphical displays; supports configuration of hub elements at multiple levels and establishing security policies on a port-by-port basis.
Platforms supported: HP OpenView; support for SunNet Manager and IBM NetView/6000 forthcoming.
Integration methods: Menu bar, database integration with HP OpenView.

Network Solutions Cabletron MMAC Hub Views
Function: Graphical views of Cabletron hubs, including device status.
Platforms supported: NetLabs/DiMONS.
Integration methods: Via NetLabs' Vision application

Optical Data Systems LanVision
Function: Monitoring and control of ODS Ethernet, token ring, and FDDI network modules of ODS chassis; provides status and configuration of hub elements.
Platforms supported: SunNet Manager, HP OpenView, IBM NetView/6000.
Integration methods: Accesses the SunNet Manager database; also access HP OpenView and NetView/6000 files and graphing tools.

The LanVision Database Update (DBI) feature on the SunNet Manager version allows users to update the SunNet Manager database with ODS-specific information. All file loading and configuration is done automatically during installation.

Raylan Network Manager
Function: Monitoring and control of Raylan Network Series fiber-optic, Ethernet, and token ring concentrators.
Platforms supported: NetLabs/DiMONS.
Integration methods: Via NetLabs' Vision application.

Sestel HubMan
Function: Management of Sestel hubs.
Platforms supported: SunNet Manager; HP OpenView.
Integration methods: Menu bar; also uses SunNet Manager APIs.

Synernetics ViewPlex
Function: Management of FDDI LANplex 5000 switching hubs.

Platforms supported: SunNet Manager.

Integration methods: Menu bar and SunNet Manager Event Services API

SynOptics Optivity
Function: Network "fabric" management for SynOptics' smart hubs and routing/bridging modules.

Platforms supported: SunNet Manager; HP OpenView, and NetView/6000.

Integration Methods: Icon launching, "SuperAgent," Global Enterprise Management (GEM) applications.

Optivity collects hub, board, and port-level data such as MAC-layer diagnostics, errors, and utilization information. Optivity also provides detailed Ring and Segment Views, as well as realtime views of SynOptics' LattisHub, LattisRing, or System 3000 concentrators, including active LEDs and configuration status. Optivity also includes an Autotopology Plus feature, which employs a heuristic, recurring algorithm for dynamically creating and updating a hierarchical network map.

In addition to these features, there are several other aspects which make Optivity a unique product offering. On the UNIX platforms (SunNet Manager, IBM NetView/6000, and HP OpenView UNIX), it supports distributed domain management by employing what SynOptics calls "SuperAgent" software residing in critical hubs throughout the network. Each SuperAgent uses polling to collect a wealth of data in a given domain (such as a single Ethernet segment) and processes that data locally, forwarding on concise packages of information to the central Optivity application. By distributing intelligence to the SuperAgents scattered throughout the network helps to reduce traffic overhead and speed up the management process (see Figure 5.3).

Network "intelligence" requires processing power, and SynOptics supplies this in the form of "Network Control Engines" or NCEs (Faulkner 1993). An NCE is essentially a Sun SPARCstation residing on a SynOptics concentrator module. Since the NCE comes pre-loaded with UNIX, many customers use NCEs to distribute SunNet Manager functions—such as collecting and processing data locally to avoid traffic overhead—as well. NCEs also support HP NetMetrix traffic monitoring and analysis applications from Metrix Systems. While customers may choose to run Optivity in centralized mode without NCEs, NCEs are required to support Optivity's distributed domain management capabilities.

Optivity and the SuperAgents form a foundation for SynOptics' value-added "LattisWare" applications such as RouterMan, PathMan, MeterMan, and BridgeMan. For example, RouterMan displays all protocols and interfaces supported by routers on the network, including performance statistics. PathMan can determine and display the path between any two stations in the network, to assist in troubleshooting.

Optivity also supports another class of applications, called Global Enterprise Management (GEM), developed by third parties. The first GEM applications available are NetLabs' Vision Desktop and Asset Manager. Both Vision Desktop

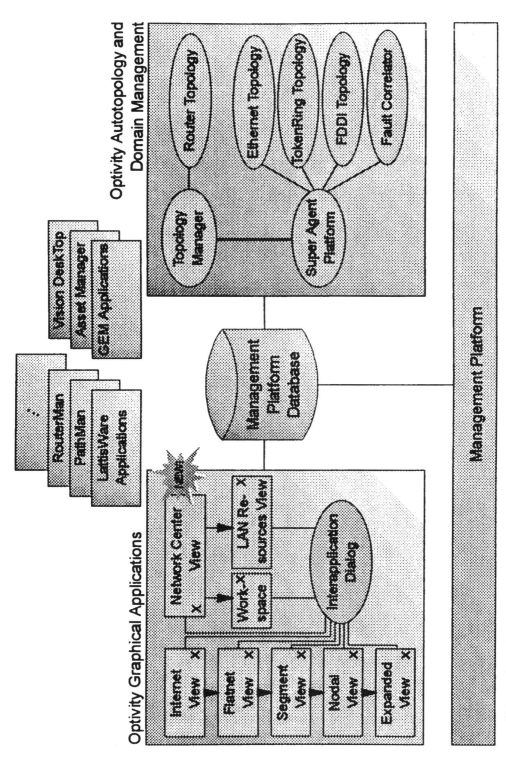

Figure 5.3 SynOp

and Asset Manager support the IETF Host Resources MIB and emerging Desktop Management Task Force (DMTF) specifications. Asset Manager supports automatic collection of PC component data; Vision Desktop provides a graphical interface and can assist in monitoring software licensing violations.

Ungermann-Bass NetDirector for UNIX

Function: Management of Ungermann-Bass Access/One hubs including graphical displays; supports modules for automating IP address administration.

Platforms supported: HP OpenView.

Integration methods: Menu bar.

Xyplex ControlPoint

Function: Management of Xyplex chassis and DECserver terminal servers; provides graphical status, configuration, and performance data.

Platforms supported: SunNet Manager; NetLabs/DiMONS; support for HP OpenView forthcoming.

Integration methods: Menu bar.

5.4.1.2   Router and Bridge/Router Management

The following applications for managing bridges, routers, and repeaters were shipping as of mid-1994:

3Com Transcend
Cisco CiscoWorks
ConWare Computer Consulting NEMA
Gandalf Passport
HP OpenView Interconnect Manager
RAD Network Devices MultiVu
Siemens-Nixdorf Bridge Management
Wellfleet Site Manager

Router management applications help simplify the task of configuring routers. (See Chapter 3 for more information.) Despite the inroads made by SNMP, the router configuration process is anything but "standardized." Each vendor has its own unique approach to setting up its routers; some vendors put a lot of configuration and control information in SNMP format, others do not. Most support the TCP/IP "TELNET" virtual terminal emulation mode for configuration and control, as well as the Trivial File Transfer Protocol (TFTP) for downloading configuration data to the router. Beyond that, however, the methods of configuring differ widely.

Right now, most leading vendors have simplified the user interface for configuring an individual router. The use of graphical point-and-click interfaces has helped speed up the time required to configure a router. Many vendors provide management applications with improved editing capabilities, helping to simplify the task even further. Router vendors have also added safeguards in their management applications to minimize the impact of human error in the configuration process.

More and more network managers would like to see the router management application supported on the platform of their choice. That way, they can manage multiple types from one console—rather than employ a separate console just for the routers. Ideally, a router management application should be tightly integrated with the underlying platform as well. This is not the case today; all router management applications are launched primarily from the platform menu, with little or no integration in event management and platform database.

The following section briefly describes key characteristics of router management applications.

3Com Transcend

Function: Integrated management for 3Com adapters, hubs, and routers.

Platforms supported: SunNet Manager; support for HP OpenView and IBM NetView/6000 forthcoming.

Integration methods: Menu bar.

In an effort to simplify the router configuration process even further, 3Com has introduced an architecture called "boundary routing," which takes standard routing software for n-way local routing and extends the LAN interface portion over the wide area. The goal of this is to simplify routing software functions for remote routers—which are often located at branch offices where there are no technical support staff. 3Com Transcend takes advantage of boundary routing to simplify router management.

Transcend software obtains information from SmartAgent intelligent device agents embedded in 3Com adapters, hubs, and routers. 3Com SmartAgents localize polling and organize collected data to reduce bandwidth overhead of management data. SmartAgents are capable of correlating information from multiple 3Com devices to provide a more integrated view of network status and to assist in the creation of baselines for performance management. (See Figure 5.4.)

Cisco CiscoWorks

Function: Configuration, performance, fault, and security management for Cisco's routers.

Platforms supported: SunNet Manager; HP OpenView and NetView/6000 will be supported by year end.

Integration methods: Icon launching from SunNet Manager map; command line integration possible with HP NetMetrix (traffic monitoring) and Remedy ARS (trouble ticketing).

CiscoWorks is a suite of SNMP-based operations and management applications for users of Cisco's routers. CiscoWorks has been installed at customer sites since early 1993. Version 2.0, which was shipped at the end of 1993, includes significant enhancements for easing remote installation and router software management. In particular, Version 2.0 of CiscoWorks provides a group editing feature. The CiscoWorks global command capability allows managers to specify a group of routers and apply common configuration changes or software updates to the entire group. In addition, the CiscoWorks menu specifically calls out frequently

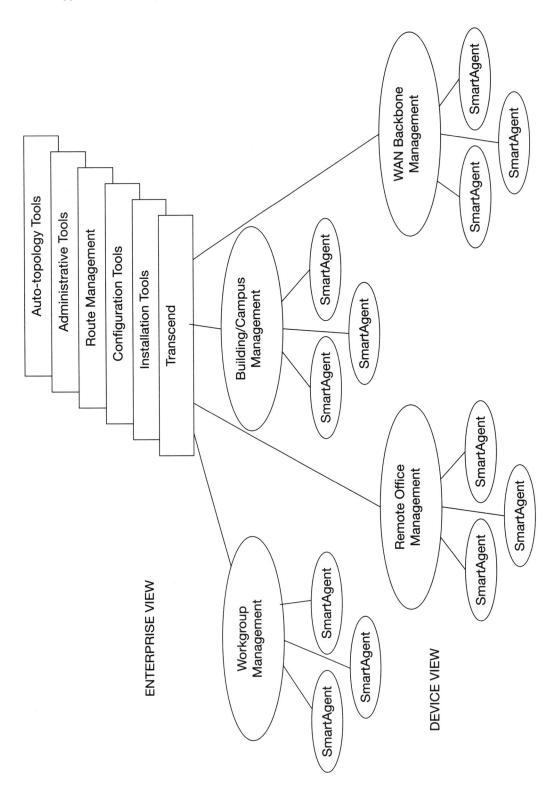

Figure 5.4 3Com Transcend Architecture

used commands, such as enable passwords, SNMP community strings, and access lists. CiscoWorks includes a feature for checking a router's configuration against information stored in an SQL database.

CiscoWorks provides an operations series of applications for day-to-day router monitoring and troubleshooting. In addition, Cisco offers a "management series" for off-line analysis of network traffic and trends. Together, these utilities help satisfy both realtime immediate concerns of network managers and requirements for long-term planning and trend analysis. (See Figure 5.5.)

CiscoWorks' operations series includes five major aspects:

- Configuration File Management
- Path Tool
- Health Monitor
- Environmental Monitor Device Management Database
- Security Management

In particular, CiscoWork's Path Tool provides visualization of the actual path taken by the data; it detects interface changes much more efficiently than SNMP monitoring alone.

```
#Compare Devices Summary
#Started: Wed Jul 17 10:15:09 1991
debris            //Result: identical
dent          //Result: different
dross             //Result: identical
gorky             //Result: identical
gregs-gw          //Result: identical
mira          //Result: identical
pebbles           //Result: different
scrap             //Other problems (see log file)
```

```
#Compare Result File
#Started: Wed Jul 10 15:09 1991

***Database  Wed Jul 10 19:27:32 1991
---debris     Wed Jul 17 10:15:35 1991
* * * * * * * * * * * * * * * * * * * * * * * * * * * * * * *
***15,21***
    ip forward-protocol udp 77
    ip forward-protocol udp 111
    !
! decnet routing 13.5
    decnet node-type area
    !
    xns routing aa00.0400.7bcc
---15,21---
    ip forward-protocol udp 77
    ip forward-protocol udp 111
    !
! decnet routing 2.101
    decnet node-type area
    !
    xns routing aa00.0400.7bcc
```

Figure 5.5 CiscoWork's compare configuration determines if a router's configuration has been changed. The sample report shown provides a detailed listing of inconsistencies.

The Management Series portion of CiscoWorks assists managers in achieving long-term goals of network management, such as historical trend analysis for determining the cost-effectiveness of transmission options, determining usage, identifying potential problem areas, and isolating chronic problems. A Data WorkBench feature is actually a Sybase report writer tool that allows administrators to create reports. These reports can display traffic through every router interface, including throughput and error rates, traffic peaks, and percentage of broadcast traffic versus total traffic (Faulkner, 1993).

Conware Computer Consulting NEMA

Function: Management of all Conware network interconnection systems, including TP repeaters, bridges, routers, and high-performance modular carrier systems for hubs, bridges, and multi-protocol routers.

Platforms supported: HP OpenView, Network Managers.

Integration methods: Menu bar, map integration.

Gandalf Passport

Function: Integrated LAN and WAN management of Gandalf 2000/2050 and 2300 multiplexers as well as Gandalf Access hubs, bridges, and routers (see also section 5.4.1.3).

Platforms supported: HP OpenView.

Integration methods: Full use of all HP OpenView APIs; proxy agent on communicate with Passport using SNMP.

HP OpenView Interconnect Manager/UX

Function: Management and control of hubs, bridges, and routers; graphics-based router configuration facility for HP and Wellfleet FN, LN, and CN routers.

Platforms supported: HP OpenView.

Integration methods: Menu bar.

RAD Network Devices MultiVu

Function: Monitoring, device configuration, and display of dynamic routing data for RND OpenGate routers and other internetworking products; displays graphic representations of router and bridge status (LED indicators) and modules.

Platforms supported: HP OpenView.

Integration methods: Menu bar.

Siemens-Nixdorf Bridge Management

Function: Management of bridge configuration parameters from centralized console.

Platforms supported: NetLabs/DiMONS; support for other management platforms forthcoming.

Integration methods: Uses NetLabs/APIs.

WellFleet Site Manager

Function: Fault and configuration management of Wellfleet routers.

Platforms supported: SunNet Manager, HP OpenView, IBM NetView/6000, NetLabs/DiMONS, Cabletron Spectrum, Network Managers NMC.

Integration methods: Menu bar.

Wellfleet provides default factory settings which can eliminate up to 80 percent of the redundant data entry when configuring groups of routers. Prior to this improvement, users had to enter lots of common information over and over again for each router. Soon, Wellfleet plans to enhance this feature by allowing users to edit this template of "common" configuration data before replicating it on other routers. Wellfleet Site Manager provides range checking of parameter values as well as validation of the uniqueness of IP addresses.

5.4.1.3   WAN Devices (Multiplexers, Switches—ATM, X.25)

The following applications for WAN device management were shipping as of mid-1994:

AT&T Frame Relay
Fore Systems ForeView
Gandalf Systems Passport

Currently WAN device management lacks enough applications. Major vendors such as N.E.T., Ascom Timeplex, T3Plus, and Newbridge Networks have indicated possible plans to port existing proprietary management systems to SNMP-based schemes; however presently, most of the vendors are providing SNMP support in the form of device management information bases (MIBs) only. Applications that can interpret device MIB data will be forthcoming only if customer demand warrants development efforts.

The following section briefly describes key characteristics of WAN device management applications.

AT&T Frame Relay

Function: Management of AT&T Network System frame relay switches.

Platforms supported: AT&T StarSENTRY.

Integration methods: SNMP MIB; alarm interface; menu bar.

Fore Systems ForeView

Function: Management of Fore Systems ATM switches.

Platforms supported: HP OpenView; support for SunNet Manager and IBM NetView/6000 forthcoming.

Integration methods: Menu bar.

Gandalf Systems Passport

Function: Integrated LAN and WAN management of Gandalf 2000/2050 and 2300 multiplexers, as well as Gandalf Access hubs, bridges, and routers.

Platforms supported: HP OpenView.

Integration methods: Full use of all HP OpenView APIs; proxy agent on communicate with Passport using SNMP.

Passport automatically discovers both LAN and WAN devices; LAN devices appear in the Passport LAN map, and WAN devices appear in the WAN map. Operators have the option of viewing an integrated map of both LAN and WAN devices.

Passport automatically identifies router and bridge interfaces as either LAN interfaces or serial (WAN) interfaces, and shows segments attached to serial interfaces as serial segments. Passport displays panel views for all Access Series and 2XXX Series products. Passport also supports multiple users.

The product triggers alarms for Gandalf devices based on default parameters and trap, supporting basic fault management and network-level performance monitoring. The product supports an integrated relational database for storage and retrieval of LAN/WAN configuration, channel, link and card logic status, statistics, alarms, and events. Passport can generate reports based on default parameters.

Passport is designed to handle as many as 1,500 nodes. Passport is a distributed-weighted system that relies on some network device intelligence for management, allowing fast response to changing network conditions.

5.4.2   Systems Management

5.4.2.1   UNIX Systems Management

This section includes systems administration and monitoring of client/server applications and monitoring. The following applications for UNIX systems management were shipping as of mid-1994:

AT&T Computer Manager
Breakaway Software PICUS
Calypso Software MaestroVision
CompuWare EcoTools
Digital Analysis OS/EYE*NODE
HP OmniBack Link
HP OperationsCenter
HP PerfView
HP Systems Manager
IBM AIX Systems Monitor/6000
Independence Technologies DB Analyzer
Independence Technologies iVIEW Event Manager
Independence Technologies Log Manager
Independence Technologies TM Analyzer
Independence Technologies System Manager
Landmark Systems Probe/Net
Network Partners, Inc. Trapper
Open Network Enterprises M.O.O.N.
Patrol Software DDS/Patrol Link

Unison Tymlabs Maestro
UNIX Integration Services HeartBeat

The growing number of UNIX systems management applications now being developed for or ported to SNMP-based management systems indicates the convergence of network and systems management. While many of the existing applications are currently less than comprehensive, the large potential revenues from a rapidly growing deployment of distributed UNIX client/server environments are tempting these and other vendors to develop and enhance these products and the levels of integration they support.

AT&T StarSENTRY Computer Manager

Function: Monitoring of individual UNIX System V and OSX 5.1 computers; forwards UNIX system alarms. Responds to administrative requests (such as changing parameter settings or adding new users).

Platforms supported: AT&T StarSENTRY.

Integration methods: Agents on UNIX systems forward data to Computer Manager via SNMP or SMUX protocols.

Breakaway Software PICUS

Function: Monitors multiple clients and servers in distributed UNIX computing environments.

Platforms supported: NetLabs/DiMONS; support for SunNet Manager, HP OpenView, and IBM NetView/6000 forthcoming.

Integration methods: PICUS is integrated at the menu-bar level; it intercepts alarms from the management platform and feeds that information into the PICUS graphical user interface.

PICUS is designed to help systems administrators monitor complex networks of multiple clients and servers. The product itself has a client/server architecture. PICUS is available in two versions: a server-based version, which supports system monitoring and configuration of a single UNIX server, and a networked version, which allows administrators to monitor and configure a series of networked hosts and workstations. (See Figure 5.6.)

PICUS is capable of monitoring UNIX file systems, printers, TTY ports, users, and user groups. File system monitoring includes tracking disk usage by file system, username, and group name; alarms are triggered when user-defined thresholds are exceeded. PICUS also provides reports such as disk usage summaries, disk utilization, and disk usage by user and group.

PICUS can make it easier for users to perform incremental or full backup on all disk partitions or on selected file systems. Because PICUS prompts operators for all necessary information to create the backup, operators do not need to know specific UNIX backup commands. PICUS also includes a security module that includes native executables for checking security loopholes and logging threats in a file for later viewing. The product also allows operators to configure users, groups of users, TTY ports, or create custom printer modules.

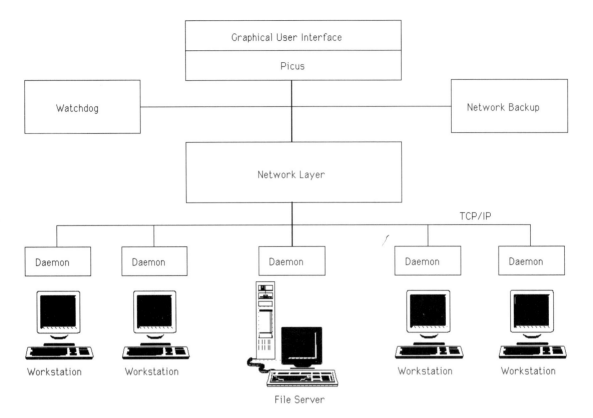

Figure 5.6 Breakaway PICUS—network version

Calypso Software MaestroVision

Function: Monitors UNIX (SunOS, SGI IRIX, IBM AIX, DEC Ultrix, HP-UX) and Windows NT workstations.

Platforms supported: Cabletron Spectrum.

Integration methods: MaestroVision takes advantage of Spectrum APIs and inductive modeling technology to suppress secondary alarms and infer status of network components.

MaestroVision works in conjunction with Cabletron Spectrum to provide a highly graphic display of UNIX and Windows NT system resources. MaestroVision automatically creates a model for each file system, CPU, and disk subsystem in the distributed computing network. Operators do not need to know primitive commands or manipulate text to monitor or configure computing system resources.

MaestroVision monitors and controls all processes running on the network. It graphically depicts CPU usage, RAM, applications, swap space, and local and remote file systems. MaestroVision allows operators to apply user-defined thresholds on activity levels and other metrics. Operators can also create administration groups to enforce organizational policies on groups of workstations.

MaestroVision's "process views" list all processes present on a system; operators can also obtain details on any single process by selecting that process from the list. Operators can also add, modify, or remove users from groups or workstations using MaestroVision.

Operators can set thresholds on system components and applications. Version 2 of MaestroVision allows users to initiate actions off an alarm by triggering scripts, as well as set an alarm based on more than one condition—such as CPU utilization >90 percent for over two minutes.

CompuWare EcoTools

Function: Systems management for client/server networks; monitors Oracle database applications and client/server activity; alerts operators to potential database performance bottlenecks and can trigger scripts to counteract those conditions.

Platforms supported: HP OpenView; support for IBM NetView/6000 and NetLabs/DiMONS forthcoming.

Integration methods: Menu bar.

Digital Analysis OS/EYE*NODE

Function: A management framework that allows distribution of management functionality across network node using CMIP, SNMP, and proxy agents.

Platforms supported: IBM NetView/6000; support for HP OpenView forthcoming.

Integration methods: GUI APIs (OVw_APIs) and Events; database integration is forthcoming.

Digital Analysis Corp. has repackaged its CMIP/SNMP-based OS/Eye*Node management platform (which previously ran only on Data General Aviion hardware) into several components that can run as applications for IBM NetView/6000 and other market leaders. The key OS/EYE*Node applications include the Network State Machine, a fault management facility that includes a configurable polling model for each managed object. The Network State Machine enables organizations to set up separate fault management domains according to how they wish to manage their resources. Each domain can have its own unique rules (polling frequencies, event thresholds, scripts to trigger, etc.) governing fault management. Each console in a management domain can communicate with other consoles outside the domain without using X technology, which incurs high bandwidth overhead. Essentially, Network State Machines can support a degree of distributed management that is necessary for scaling upwards to managing thousands of nodes. (See Figure 5.7.)

OS/Eye*Node also supports UNIX systems management through two proxy agents, OS*Proxy and ACCT* Proxy. OS*Proxy is an SNMP instrumentation of the UNIX operating system for monitoring disk, memory, swap space, and CPU utilization. It reports on over 20 key system parameters and generates traps when thresholds are exceeded. ACCT*Proxy is similar to OS*Proxy except that it focuses on monitoring system utilization by user, which can support chargeback activities.

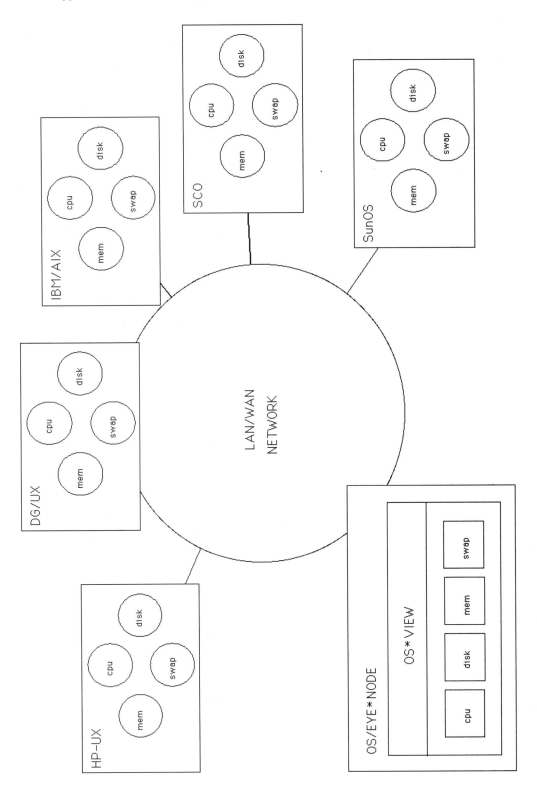

Figure 5.7 Digital Analysis' OS/Eye*Node systems management capabilities

HP OmniBack Link

Function: Centralized backup/recovery management for HP-UX and SunOS/NFS systems.

Platforms supported: HP OpenView.

Integration methods: Menu bar; OmniBack/Link module allows HP OmniBack to send error notifications directly to HP OpenView.

HP OpenSpool Link´

Function: Centralized administration and monitoring of distributed printers/plotters (HP JetDirect cards, LM/Xxxx and NetWare/9000 PCs).

Platforms supported: HP OpenView.

Integration methods: Menu bar; OpenSpool/Link module allows HP OpenSpool to send error notifications and configuration data directly to HP OpenView.

HP OperationsCenter

Function: Monitors UNIX (HP-UX, HP-MPE, SunOS, and IBM AIX) workstations.

Platforms supported: HP OpenView.

Integration methods: Menu bar; alarms from OperationsCenter are displayed on the HP OpenView map.

OperationsCenter is a distributed, client/server program that operates from a central management station and interacts with intelligent software agents installed on the managed UNIX systems. The intelligent agents perform localized polling, collect information, and process it before forwarding pertinent information onto the central OperationsCenter or HP OpenView console. Agents use remote procedure calls (RPCs) to communicate processed information.

Operators define thresholds on systems parameters and set polling intervals at the central management console; this is automatically downloaded to the managed nodes. Polling ("monitoring service") is done locally at managed nodes to minimize network traffic overhead. Filter conditions can be specified at the managed nodes to further minimize traffic. (See Figure 5.8.)

OperationsCenter includes a Workspace Manager feature allowing administrators to specify the managed nodes and message groups for which each operator is responsible. The Workspace Manager creates a specific task-oriented work environment for each operator.

The optional OmniBack application supports networked backup and restore. The optional Hierarchical Storage Manager application manages online storage for servers and client disks, supporting automatic and transparent migration of files between magnetic disks and optical disk libraries.

An optional HP OpenView Software Distributor application can verify installed software on remote target systems. Using Software Distributor, administrators can build processes that monitor the integrity of software in remote locations. The product supports comprehensive packing, configuration, and removal of software throughout the network.

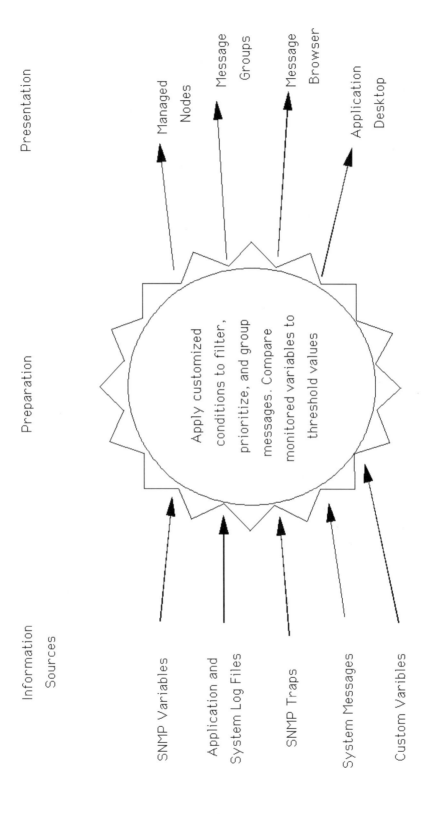

Figure 5.8 HP OperationsCenter processes and consolidates systems messages and SNMP traps.

HP PerfView

Function: Performance tracking on UNIX systems (HP-UX, SunOS).

Platforms supported: HP OpenView (through OperationsCenter).

Integration methods: Menu-bar; alarms from Perfview appear on the HP OpenView screen.

HP PerfView tracks recent performance data for HP-UX and SunOS systems; PerfRX is a performance analysis tool for evaluating historical trends, load balancing, and problem diagnosis. HP PerfView includes two components: (1) Central analysis software (incorporating HP Network Node Manager), and (2) Intelligent agents that reside on the managed systems.

PerfView provides an umbrella for the HP GlancePlus stand-alone systems management utilities. It monitors the following performance factors across the network: CPU utilization, CPU queue depth and process wait information, number of processes; Disk utilization (percentage peak activity), disk queue depth and process wait data; physical and logical I/O rates; Memory utilization, disk activity due to virtual memory management, swap utilization; Network packet rate data; Application utilization of CPU, disk I/O, and resources that processes are blocked on.

PerfRX provides historical trend analysis on transaction rates and response time, as well as parameters monitored by PerfView. This information can assist in workload balancing and capacity planning. PerfRX can display collected data in line, pie, or stacked graphs.

IBM AIX Systems Monitor/6000

Function: Localized polling and monitoring of IBM RS/6000 workstations; parameters tracked include CPU utilization, disk usage, virtual memory, product inventory data, and system activities. Data is processed locally and reduced before it is forwarded to the management console.

Platforms supported: IBM NetView/6000.

Integration methods: Uses SNMP and SNMP SMUX protocols to collect information and forward it to the NetView/6000 console.

Independence Technologies DB Analyzer

Function: Monitors status, configuration, and performance of relational databases; supports trend analysis of database performance over time.

Platforms supported: SunNet Manager, HP OpenView, IBM NetView/6000, NetLabs/DiMONS.

Integration methods: Menu bar; SNMP agents.

Independence Technologies TM Analyzer

Function: Transaction monitoring for UNIX systems; triggers an alarm when a transaction server is down, performs poorly, or if the number of queued jobs exceeds user-defined thresholds, etc. supports paging as well as screen or e-mail notification of alerts.

Platforms supported: SunNet Manager, HP OpenView, IBM NetView/6000, NetLabs/DiMONS.

Integration methods: Menu bar; SNMP agents.

Independence Technologies iVIEW Event Manager

Function: Monitors UNIX systems and application software to verify software revision levels; supports event notification between applications.

Platforms supported: SunNet Manager, HP OpenView, IBM NetView/6000, NetLabs/DiMONS.

Integration methods: Menu bar; SNMP agents.

Independence Technologies System Manager

Function: Monitoring, control, and automatic restart of UNIX hardware, relational databases, transaction monitors, and applications.

Platforms supported: SunNet Manager, HP OpenView, IBM NetView/6000, NetLabs/DiMONS.

Integration methods: Menu bar; SNMP agents.

Landmark Systems Probe/Net

Function: Monitors status and performance of UNIX systems (SunOS and Solaris, AIX and HP-UX) including processes, programs, users, groups, devices file systems, I/O, CPU, memory, swap space, and NFS statistics.

Platforms supported: SunNet Manager; support for HP OpenView and IBM NetView/6000 forthcoming.

Integration methods: Menu bar.

Probe/Net is a client/server application for monitoring remote UNIX systems, providing immediate online system tuning. Probe/Net runs as an application under SunNet Manager. Probe/Net allows systems administrators to set specific performance thresholds and polling intervals. Agent software graphically notifies the central console when thresholds have been met or exceeded. Supports integrated exception reporting of bottlenecks on monitored nodes.

Using Probe/Net, operators can invoke quick dumps, data requests, and event requests for debugging purposes. When used on the SunNet Manager platform, the SunNet Manager API allows information to be filtered and collected. Using the SET command, users can alter job priorities directly from Probe/Net to address or prevent problems.

Probe/Net collects the following statistics at each managed node:

- System level: user response time, resources consumed per transaction, per-file system and per-process breakdown, and over 100 other metrics.
- Per process level: local and remote file system service statistics, socket service statistics, CPU/memory/ utilization and I/O statistics.
- NFS level: client and server statistics, service characteristics per-client load.
- I/O level: per file breakdown, I/O device access methods, disk metrics, access data.

Probe/Net presents bottleneck analysis and system-wide utilization including rates, peaks, overflows, etc. on each monitored station. Probe/Net organizes and presents data in logical groupings at global and process-specific levels, and presents data in graphic format where applicable.

Performance statistics are logged at user-defined intervals on each node in the network. A browser tool can be used to format custom reports or to regenerate graphical data. A snapshot tool captures or prints portions of the console display for reporting purposes. Users can change performance characteristics of managed nodes across local and wide-area networks from the central SunNet Manager console.

Network Partners, Inc. Trapper

Function: UNIX systems management; event-driven monitoring for alarm and data collection for UNIX files, file queries, file systems, printer queues, virtual memory, physical memory, critical processes, kernel parameters, network statistics, and hardware inventory.

Platforms supported: SunNet Manager; support for HP OpenView forthcoming.

Integration methods: Menu bar; SNMP and SMUX agent runs on each monitored system.

Open Network Enterprises M.O.O.N.

Function: UNIX system management; monitoring and administration of workstations and servers (SunOS, AIX, HP-UX); comprehensive spooling, disk, user, and applications monitoring is supported; users can define rules governing activation and reporting of events and thresholds for those events.

Platforms supported: HP OpenView, IBM NetView/6000.

Integration methods: Menu bar integration, icon-level map integration, database integration.

Patrol Software DDS/Patrol Link

Function: Monitoring and control of Oracle databases and applications; as well as UNIX systems, database module monitors space, users, statistics (hit ration, latches, caches, redo, i/o), errors, archive log space, SQL*Net, and applications such as financials, mail, etc. UNIX system module monitors NFS, net load, collisions, swap space, user logins, file system, and process table for SunOS, HP-UX, AIX, Sequent, 88 Open, DG Aviion, Motorola and SGI.

Platforms supported: SunNet Manager; support for HP OpenView and IBM NetView/6000 forthcoming.

Integration methods: SNMP traps.

Unison Tymlabs Maestro

Function: Centralized workload management for distributed systems (AIX, HP-UX and HP MPE), including job scheduling, job tracking, automated recovery, audit trail of job execution, and logging statistics for reporting and analysis.

Platforms supported: IBM NetView/6000.

Integration methods: Menu bar.

UNIX Integration Services HeartBeat

Function: Monitors the following UNIX system performance indicators: CPU load, CPU utilization, disk utilization, message queues, semaphores, shared memory, defunct processes; separate optional tool called "Software Distribution Facility" (SDF) manages the storage, version levels, user profiles, and program executables in use on a LAN or WAN network of processors.

Platforms supported: HP OpenView; support for SunNet Manager, IBM NetView/6000 forthcoming.

Integration methods: Menu bar.

5.4.2.2   UNIX Systems Security

As of mid-1994, OpenVision OpenV*SecureMax was the only applications supporting open management platform technology and dedicated solely to security management. In addition to SecureMax, the XRSA application from Elegant Communications, Inc., a service-level agreement monitor, also supports security secondarily. (See section 5.4.4.3.)

OpenVision OpenV*SecureMax

Function: Centralized security management for distributed UNIX systems (SunOS, HP-UX, AIX, Ultrix, and OpenVMS).

Platforms supported: SunNet Manager.

Integration methods: Menu bar.

OpenV*SecureMax allows an operator to access the security status of multiple workstations and servers from a central console and perform a detailed security audit, if necessary, and correct any security problems. The GUI leads the operator through a complete four-phase security management process. This process includes an audit of overall security level, analysis of specific security risks, correction of identified security exposures, and monitoring of security-specific changes over time (SecureMax for UNIX 3.1, Demax Software, Inc. 1992). OpenV*SecureMax can also generate reports for auditors or managers who may not be familiar with UNIX technology. The product is also capable of producing a consolidated network report providing a single-line summary status for each monitored system.

OpenV*SecureMax assesses security for five major security categories: system files, networks, accounts, passwords, and file systems. An Audit Facility allows users to generate reports explaining security risks on specific systems as well as recommendations for correction. An Analyze Facility produces detailed reports on specific files and accounts with security exposures. By using the Correct Facility, operators can create customized shell script files to address security problems.

Users can create baselines using OpenV*SecureMax and compare them to future security reports. Baselines are stored in encoded, data checked models. Additionally, OpenV*SecureMax can monitor SunOS, Ultrix, HP-UX, and AIX systems. It is a read-only product that runs on the UNIX operating system.

5.4.2.3   Software Distribution (Cross Platform)

The following software distribution applications were shipping on open management platforms as of mid-1994:

AT&T StarSENTRY Software Manager
ViaTech Development Xfer

At present, few cross-platform software distribution applications are shipping on open management platforms. IBM's offering, NetView DM/6000, is currently in beta test. Both Hewlett-Packard and SunConnect have stand-alone products that are not yet integrated into the network management platforms. The following section briefly describes two software distribution applications that are currently shipping.

AT&T StarSENTRY Software Manager

Function: Centralized software distribution for distributed UNIX System V, DOS, and OS/2 computers and Novell NetWare servers; enables the collection, storage, distribution, and management of software packages and data files from a central management station.

Platforms supported: AT&T StarSENTRY Manager.

Integration methods: Menu bar and alarm integration; uses a software management gateway supporting a "protocol switch" permitting use of TCP/IP, LU6.2 and OSI protocols over AT&T Ethernet StarLAN10 and token ring networks.

ViaTech Development Xfer

Function: Electronic software distribution for networked UNIX systems (SunOS, Solaris, AIX, HP-UX; support for OS/2 and DOS workstations forthcoming).

Platforms supported: SunNet Manager, IBM NetView/6000, HP OpenView.

Integration methods: Menu bar; Xfer uses the SunNet Manager database APIs on the Solaris operating system.

ViaTech Development, Inc. Xfer is an electronic software distribution package designed for UNIX systems in a distributed computing environment. Xfer uses SNMP to communicate with several open management platforms including SunNet Manager, IBM NetView/6000, and HP OpenView. The advantage of this integration is the ability to share configuration information and operational alarms (Faulkner, 1993).

Xfer is designed to simplify and automate software distribution among distributed UNIX computers. While the product does not require an underlying management platform to operate, it can be effectively used from a management console. Xfer is designed to take advantage of the auto-discovery and topology information gathered by the management platform—node information stored in the management platform does not need to be re-keyed into Xfer's database. Xfer does, however, allow users to augment platform-generated information by adding additional asset tracking information such as peripheral configuration, serial numbers, and software version levels. Xfer's "augmented" database can be compiled into asset tracking reports, and it may be used for grouping nodes to ensure proper software distribution. Xfer can also generate SNMP traps and forward them to the underlying management platform if user-specified fault conditions occur during a software distribution transfer.

A key benefit of Xfer is that it helps to reduce the complexity associated with systems management in a distributed, client/server environment. Operators can use a Motif-based GUI to schedule software distributions and collections, and view the status of those activities in realtime. The scheduling feature allows users to automate software distribution, so it occurs during off-peak network hours to minimize the effect the procedure might have on ongoing business of the company. Automated processes can, and do, misfire, and Xfer addresses this possibility by providing an automatic backout that will return all computers to the original software versions in the event of failure of the distribution process—where "failure" is defined by user-specified criteria. For example, if Xfer is distributing software to 100 sites, the user can specify in advance that automatic backout should take place at all 100 locations if distribution fails at one or more sites. Xfer supports manual as well as automatic backout. (See Figure 5.9.)

Xfer has components for each phase of the software distribution process: configuration, packaging, scheduling, and monitoring.

The Xfer Configuration Tool tracks distribution server and target machine hardware and software information—it also manages target groups, profiles, and user security. The Package Tool creates software packages that contain distribution files. A "package" is the combination of all files to be distributed to the target machines, plus the installation and backout scripts. Xfer uses the concept of package "streams" to make rollback more efficient. Streams provide a way of separating applications into like groups that can be installed and rolled back independently of others. Rolling back a package from one stream does not affect packages in others (Faulkner, 1993).

Xfer's Transfer Tool manages distribution schedules. Software packages can be scheduled for transfer using one of three frequencies: immediate, one time (in the future), or periodic. Periodic transfers, which allow a package to be transferred more than once, can be used to collect data from target systems. The Data Collection feature allows Xfer to create packages on the remote node rather than the central server. Data collection is useful for synchronizing data files across large networks. The Transfer Tools also support "fan-out" distribution, where a single copy of a package is send to a remote machine, where it is copied and forwarded to other machines.

A Browser utility provides realtime status information on each distribution; the status list can be filtered and sorted according to distribution date, type, or status. Typically, a network administrator is first alerted to a problem by the underlying management platform; the administrator can than use the Xfer Browser to "drill down" into the distribution by obtaining more detail about events that occurred.

Xfer is written chiefly in C++ and was designed using an object-oriented approach. Software packages created using the Package Tool are self-contained objects that include all procedures required for package installation. Because packages are object-oriented, they contain their own installation and backout methods—thus, changing the surrounding software distribution code does not affect the installation process. Therefore, a "package" built today should install successfully two years from now, even if a later version of Xfer is used to initiate the transfer.

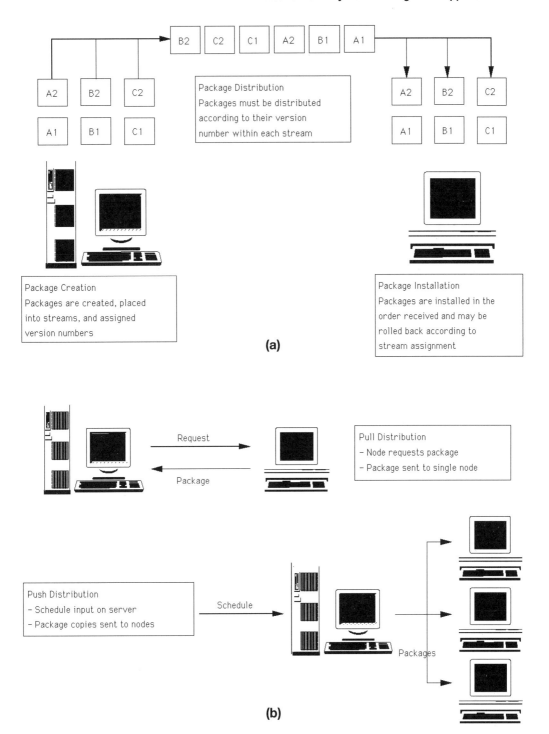

Figure 5.9 ViaTech Xfer supports "streams" technology as well as both "push" and "pull" software distribution: (a) package "streams" to improve rollback efficiency; (b) push versus pull, software distributions

5.4.2.4   PC LAN and PC Systems Management (including Client/Server Applications Monitoring)

The following PC systems and PC LAN management applications supporting open management platforms were shipping as of mid-1994:

AIM Technology Sharpshooter
AT&T/NCR StarSENTRY LAN Manager Monitor
Axlan Administrator
NetLabs Vision/Desktop
Peregrine Systems ServerView
Peregrine Systems StationView
Shany AlertView

Managing small clusters of PCs is relatively straightforward on a local level, maintaining consistency, uptime, and accountability across a vast complex of interconnected PCs LANs is incredibly difficult and time-consuming—and therefore, expensive.

Currently, most organizations employ two separate sets of products and strategies to tackle this problem: DOS/Windows-based utilities such as Novell NMS for managing the local LAN, and UNIX/SNMP-based management systems for managing the internetworking highways that connect those LANs.

However, the need to support a more effective and efficient corporate-wide management structure is driving a new trend toward products that will blur the distinctions between UNIX- and Windows-based management. While there are relatively few UNIX-based applications for PC systems and PC LAN management today, many established PC utilities vendors such as Frye are actively working on porting their existing applications to open management platforms.

AIM Technology Sharpshooter
Function: NFS client/server performance monitor; tracks workload, breaking down NFS read/write activity by file systems and client network services.
Platforms supported: SunNet Manager; support for HP OpenView forthcoming.
Integration methods: Menu bar.

AT&T StarSENTRY LAN Manager Monitor
Function: Monitors AT&T LAN Manager Servers and their clients; generates alarms when server or client session applications are crossed; supports remote login.
Platforms supported: AT&T StarSENTRY.
Integration methods: Not specified.

Axlan Administrator
Function: Centralized monitoring of LAN Manager for UNIX (Solaris/SPARC servers) and OS/2; supports notification of LAN Manager server failures and security breaches.
Platforms supported: SunNet Manager.
Integration methods: Menu bar; SNMP traps.

NetLabs Vision/Desktop

Function: Graphics-based monitoring of desktop systems using the Host Resources MIB; displays status, current values of device parameters; allows operators to monitor configurable parameters and graph performance and error statistics.

Platforms supported: NetLabs/DiMONS.

Integration methods: Menu bar, SNMP traps.

Peregrine Systems ServerView

Function: Centralized monitoring and control of Novell NetWare servers.

Platforms supported: HP OpenView.

Integration methods: Menu bar.

ServerView monitors performance of Netware servers, printer performance, and network connectivity and activity. ServerView allows operators to monitor over 10 key performance indicators on distributed NetWare servers including CPU load, number of connections, number of users attached, disk usage, movable and non-movable memory, permanent memory, short-term allocated memory, and cache buffers. Users can set thresholds; alarms will be triggered when thresholds are exceeded. In addition, ServerView depicts realtime graphs of CPU load, number of users and connections, and disk usage.

ServerView can alert operators to fault conditions and critical server actions such as disk volume dismounts, NLM unloads, and modification of directory rights.

ServerView also supports configuration management by centralizing user administration tasks and server rebooting. ServerView supports editing of server configuration files including autoexec.bat, config.sys, and system login scripts. ServerView can also highlight user and group security privileges and conditions. ServerView can display the top 20 users of server disk space and evaluate each user to determine whether or not accounting limits have been exceeded.

Peregrine Systems StationView

Function: Centralized monitoring of distributed DOS PC workstations.

Platforms supported: HP OpenView.

Integration methods: Menu bar.

One of the first UNIX-based applications for managing PCs is StationView from Peregrine Systems (Carlsbad, CA.). StationView runs as an application on top of HP OpenView Network Node Manager.

StationView allows network management to remotely control system files such as netconfig and autoexec.bat. StationView's ability to retrieve inventory and configuration can save organizations time, particularly when they are upgrading hundreds of PCs to new software environments. StationView can be used to determine quickly if a system has enough memory and disk space to meet the requirements. Performing the same functions using a Windows-based console may be infeasible particularly in flat, bridged network configurations.

StationView provides an accurate picture of workstation components and configuration, including: PC hardware and software inventory, loaded drivers and versions, memory and interrupt mapping, RSFs and AUTOEXEC, CONFIG.SYS, WIN.INI, SYSTEM.INI, and login files. It also displays status and configuration of printer servers and print queues, and shows how each PC is configured for printing. StationView provides realtime status and alerts for all managed components and network connections. StationView can help isolate problems to the workstation, cable, network, or server; and it detects incorrectly loaded drivers and configuration problems. (See Figure 5.10.)

Shany AlertView

Functions: PC applications monitoring.
Platforms supported: IBM NetView/6000.
Integration methods: SNMP traps, menu bar.

AlertView actively monitors interaction between users, applications and system software. The product captures details about events, and can initiate corrective actions, if necessary. For example, if a user attempts to use an unavailable printer, AlertView can report the condition and then redirect the user to an available printer. AlertView actively reports critical application errors, such as when a user's PC freezes because too many Windows files were opened. AlertView can also detect security and access violations, and it can allow administrators to freeze or disconnect the offending PC. AlertView provides detailed reporting on applications, files, servers, print queues, and other resources.

5.4.3   Traffic Monitoring and Analysis

As of mid-1994, the following traffic monitoring and analysis applications were shipping for use with open management platforms:

ARMON Networking ONSITE
Axon Networks LANservant Manager
Concord Communications Trakker
DataStaff Ingeniere NetPerf
Network Application Technologies EtherMeter
Network General Distributed Sniffer
Frontier NetScout Manager
HP Distributed Network Advisor
HP History Analyzer/Traffic Expert/Resource Manager
HP NetMetrix
Wandel & Goltermann IDMS Manager

Despite the industry's progress in fostering growing acceptance of integrated management platforms like SunNet Manager and HP OpenView, the reality is that most network managers still resort to plugging in protocol analyzers when problems occur. Traffic monitors and protocol analyzers are the primary tools for performance management and capacity planning in today's internetworks. The integration of these tools with open management platforms is helping to auto-

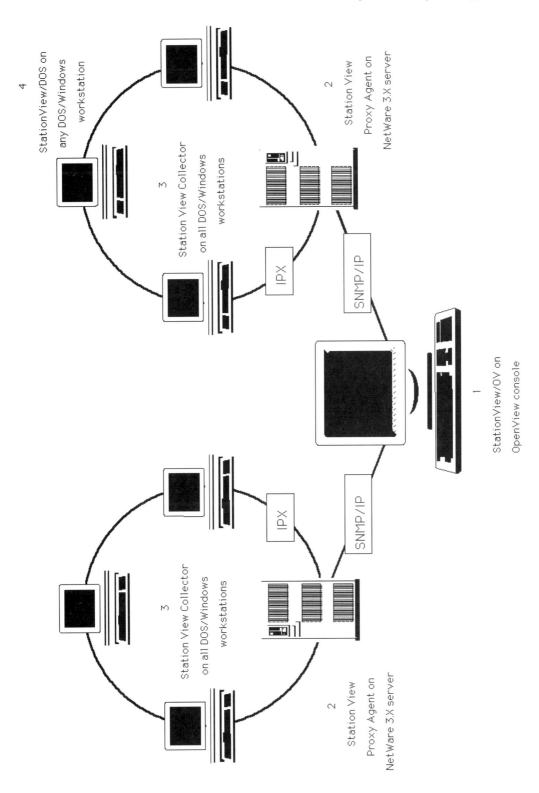

Figure 5.10 Peregrine StationView—sample configuration

mate the fault isolation and diagnosis processes, as well as assisting in proactive performance monitoring.

ARMON Networking ONSITE

Function: Traffic monitoring and analysis for Ethernet and token ring networks using multi-segment agents that collect realtime data using RMON technology; supports analysis of traffic over LAN and WAN links; calculates cost per host based on utilization, time, node, and route costs.

Platforms supported: SunNet Manager, HP OpenView; support for IBM NetView/6000 forthcoming.

Integration methods: Menu bar.

Axon Networks LANservant Manager

Function: Traffic monitoring and analysis.

Platforms supported: SunNet Manager, HP OpenView, IBM NetView/6000.

Integration methods: Menu bar integration and trap handling; also uses data APIs in SunNet Manager.

Concord Communications Trakker

Function: Internetwork traffic monitoring and analysis.

Platforms supported: SunNet Manager, HP OpenView.

Integration methods: Menu bar, some data APIs in SunNet Manager.

DataStaff Ingeniere NetPerf

Function: Continuous measurement of WAN performance and quality of service (now available for IP and X.25 networks).

Platforms supported: SunNet Manager.

Integration methods: Menu bar; database integration forthcoming.

Frontier Netscout Manager

Function: Management of Netscout RMON agents, which run on a variety of systems including Sun SPARCstations, DOS PCs, SynOptics hubs, and Frontier's own hardware. Supports full seven-layer decode of most commonly used network protocols.

Platforms supported: SunNet Manager, HP OpenView; support for IBM NetView/6000 forthcoming.

Integration methods: Menu bar; can also send alerts to SunNet Manager or HP OpenView's Trap Manager.

HP Distributed Network Advisor

Function: Control of multiple HP Network Advisor protocol analyzers; supports network troubleshooting by providing network statistics, protocol decodes, and tests; provides expert system capabilities and commentaries.

Platforms supported: HP OpenView.

Integration methods: Menu bar.

HP History Analyzer/Traffic Expert/Resource Manager

Function: These products are based on HP's Embedded Advanced Sampling Environment (EASE) technology; History Analyzer provides historical data on network traffic to assist in capacity planning; Resource Manager provides realtime network traffic analysis on MAC usage, broadcasts, CRC errors, alignment errors, and other statistics; Traffic Expert provides an adaptive management system that learns network behavior and displays the dynamics of network topology as well as traffic volume, type, usage, and flow directions.

Platforms supported: HP OpenView.

Integration methods: Menu bar.

HP NetMetrix

Function: Workstation-based traffic monitoring and analysis.

Platforms supported: HP OpenView, SunNet Manager, NetView/6000.

Integration methods: SNMP traps, command line interface, enhanced command line interface.

HP NetMetrix incorporates the best features of the traditional traffic monitors and analyzers—such as the ability to simulate network loads, gather statistics, perform traces, and provide seven-layer packet decode—and removes the encumbrances of proprietary hardware probes and clumsy user interfaces. The result is a workstation-based (UNIX/SPARC) segment monitor and an X-windows graphic user interface (GUI) supporting a suite of five very useful NetMetrix applications:

1. Traffic generator—simulates network load, can generate user-defined packet streams, and can respond to decoded packets in realtime.
2. Protocol analyzer—providing seven-layer packet decode on most major protocols.
3. Load monitor—correlates traffic statistics to help users optimize bridge/router placement and answer other critical questions for fine tuning.
4. NFS monitor—measures NFS load and response time (by server, client, NFS procedure, or time interval), client/server distribution analysis, and server performance comparisons.
5. Internetwork monitor—coordinates multiple agents across the network to provide a cohesive picture, such as displaying which groups as well as hosts are talking to each other.

NetMetrix provides a distributed architecture, supporting continuous monitoring, and analysis of all segments in realtime. While several other products provide similar capabilities, NetMetrix is less expensive than these products and more comprehensive particularly in analyzing NFS traffic. However, Metrix's aggressive pursuit of simple, effective methods for platform-application and application-application integration put the company ahead of its competitors in providing automated network management for its customers. NetMetrix has used the enhanced command line approach to integrate NetMetrix with the Remedy Action Request system for automating the problem identification/problem diagnosis/problem tracking process. (See Figure 5.11.)

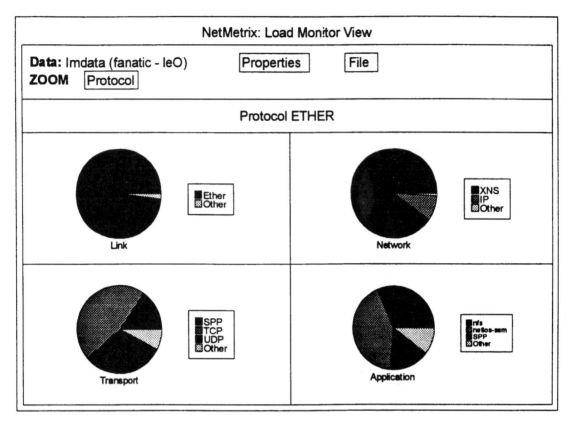

Figure 5.11 HP NetMetrix Load Monitor showing load distribution by protocol

Network Application Technologies EtherMeter

Function: Management of NAT's RMON EtherMeter probes, local and remote Ethernet bridges, and TCP/IP routers.

Platforms supported: SunNet Manager, HP OpenView, IBM NetView/6000; support for AT&T StartSENTRY forthcoming.

Integration methods: Menu bar; also, integrated at icon level with SunNet Manager, and integrated with IBM's trouble ticket facility.

Network General Distributed Sniffer

Function: Traffic monitoring and analysis via management of distributed Sniffer segment monitors.

Platforms supported: SunNet Manager; support for HP OpenView forthcoming.

Integration methods: Menu bar.

Network General's Distributed Sniffer System (DSS) consists of applications, Sniffer Servers (segment monitors), and SniffMaster consoles. Sniffer servers provide continuous monitoring and analysis of ethernet, token ring, and inter-network segments, sending alarms to the SniffMaster console. There are three DSS applications: Expert Analysis, Protocol Interpretation, and Network Monitoring. DSS can run as a loosely-integrated application under SunNet Manager.

DSS can generate alarms when user-defined thresholds are exceeded. Alarms are forwarded to the SniffMaster console. SNMP traps can also be generated for each alarm and sent to an SNMP management station.

Alarms can be generated for intruder alarm (unknown station), rate of error frames threshold, network idle time, network utilization, rate of broadcast frames, oversize frame, broadcast sources address (Ethernet), ring beaconing alarm (token ring), ring poll fail (token ring), network utilization at the station, no response time at a station, and others.

DSS' Network Monitoring Application collects current and historical network statistics for up to 1,024 stations. DSS can monitor TCP/IP, NetWare, NFS, DEC-net, IBM, and X Windows protocol networks.

The Network Monitoring Application can display traffic statistics in numerical format or graphs. History is tracked for user-defined periods of 5 seconds to 24 hours. Statistics may be displayed in realtime or printed. Statistics may also be automatically logged to the server disk in CSV format and transferred to the SniffMaster Console for analysis in spreadsheet programs

Network statistics tracked include number of stations, active stations, network utilization, average network utilization, frames, bytes, average frame size, ring state, errors and error types, ring purges, soft error reports (token ring), inserted stations, network utilization percentage by protocol or frame size, station status, network utilization percentage by route length, route path (token ring), and others

The Expert Analysis application provides "Symptoms, Diagnoses, and Explanations." Symptoms are events that signal potential problems. Diagnoses are problems warranting investigation (typically, when symptoms repeat themselves and exceed a threshold). Explanations are problem-specific explanations of the symptom and diagnosis. DSS provides possible causes of the problem. Examples of problems diagnosed and explained by DSS can include slow servers, broadcast storms, file retransmissions, and duplicate addresses.

Expert Analysis includes a Protocol Interpretation Application, providing a detailed look at the composition of data packets (over 140 protocols in 12 major protocol families can be decoded). The SniffMaster console can display the contents of each frame in English text.

Examples of capture filters supported include: known/unknown station, destination class, station address, protocol, pattern match, good frames, error frames, (CRC, alignment, fragments), DTE/DCE, and RN/RR. Examples of display filters include station address, protocol, pattern match, error frames, address level, and destination class.

The Expert Analysis application automatically learns node names and addresses, connections between the nodes, protocols used on those connections, and the routing paths.

DSS requires that a Sniffer server (monitor) be installed on every segment to be monitored. (See Figure 5.12.)

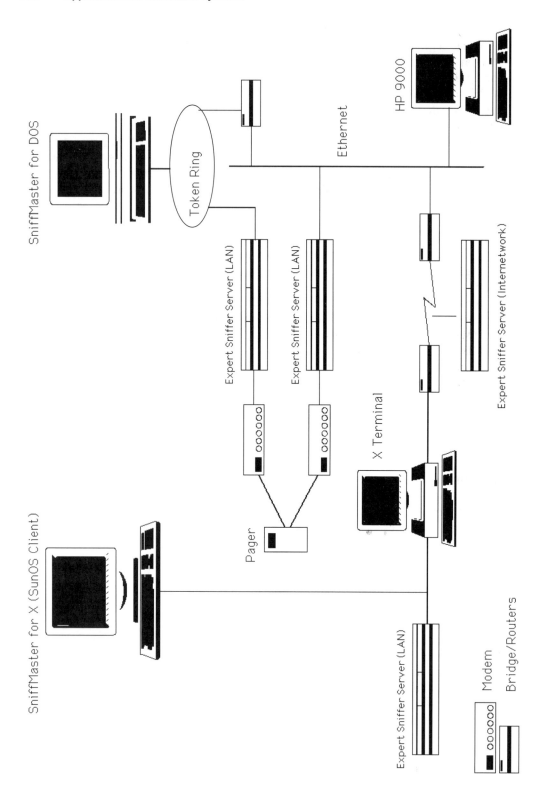

Figure 5.12 Network General Distributed Sniffer—sample configuration

Wandel & Goltermann IDMS Manager

Function: Management of distributed IDMS-30XX segment monitors supporting RMON-based troubleshooting, performance tuning, and network planning.

Platforms supported: SunNet Manager; tightly integrated support for HP OpenView and IBM NetView/6000 forthcoming.

Integration methods: Menu bar.

5.4.4 Process-Specific Applications

5.4.4.1 Data Analysis and Reporting Applications

The following data analysis and reporting applications were shipping as of mid-1994:

DeskTalk TrendAlyzer (Cooperative Reporting)
Remedy Health Profiler RISCmanagement
RISCreporter SAS Institute
SAS/CPE for OpenSystems

DeskTalk Trendalyzer (Cooperative Reporting)

Function: Common viewing and reporting tools for multiple applications and platform; captures performance and event data from various platform and application databases, putting it into a common relational database where it can be viewed by the user; graphically depicts common data.

Platforms supported: SunNet Manager (support for other platforms forthcoming).

Integration methods: Applications communicate DeskTalk's version of SunNet Manager's Manager Services library.

DeskTalk Trendalyzer (also called "Cooperative Reporting" by SunConnect) acts as a common database for platform and application data, providing the user with one access point to all information in the network management system. Trendalyzer goes beyond providing ASCII files and a MIB browser; the product includes graph tools and tabular display tools providing easy-to-read default displays for each table in the Trendalyzer database. Each data column is named and time-stamped.

Trendalyzer captures data that would normally be sent by the platform or applications to the SunNet Manager Services library. Trendalyzer uses both SNMP traps and RPCs as the mechanisms for transferring data. Trendalyzer aggregates the data and converts it into time and value information.

Remedy Health Profiler

Function: Data analysis and reporting of network status and performance using graphical elements. Currently included with the product are libraries for Cabletron IRM2 hubs, Chipcom ONline hubs, Sun workstations, SynOptics 3000 hubs, and Wellfleet routers. Also, Profiler includes an SNMP library, a UNIX library, and an RMON MIB library.

Platforms supported: SunNet Manager; support for HP OpenView and IBM NetView/6000 forthcoming.

Integration methods: SunNet Manager Services API.

Health Profiler is a data analysis and reporting tool that can provide both real time and historical interpretations of SNMP management information base (MIB) data. While other applications are able to provide similar capabilities on a device-specific basis, Health Profiler presents meaningful status and performance information across a range of devices. Health Profiler is tightly integrated with both the underlying SNMP-based network management platform and the various devices from which the application collects raw data.

Remedy's Health Profiler is one of the few management applications capable of graphically presenting meaningful status and performance information about a variety of network devices and systems. (Faulkner 1994) Other "vertical" applications can depict management data from a specific device—however, each application may have its own user interface. In contrast, Health Profiler is a "horizontal" application that processes data from multiple SNMP Management Information Bases (MIBs), providing a common interface for all managed equipment.

SNMP-based management platforms such as SunConnect SunNet Manager typically provide a limited set of reporting capabilities. However, these tools are restricted to displaying raw data—such as the value of a single counter in a device MIB. Health Profiler uses raw data collected by the management platform and greatly improves the presentation of that data by displaying it in user-friendly "dashboard" views (see Figure 5.13). Furthermore, Health Profiler lets the user combine individual MIB variables and apply algebraic expressions to come up with statistics that convey network health in a much more meaningful way. The chief advantage of Health Profiler is that it can help hide the complexity of MIBs and the hundreds of data variables therein and help the user focus on clear, useful "health metrics."

Health Profiler has a client/server implementation in which the clients and servers communicate using remote procedure calls (RPCs). The server communicates with the management platform's application programming interfaces (APIs) to obtain raw MIB data. The client provides the user interface, obtaining the information from any Health Profiler server. A server can support multiple clients, and clients can be distributed anywhere across the network.

From the user's perspective, Health Profiler is made up of two components: the User Tool and the Administration Tool (both of which are part of the client). The User Tool allows the user to select what data to gather, what devices to monitor, and what views and reports to display. The Admin Tool allows users to customize views, reports, expressions, and history models.

Health Profiler simplifies the task of managing a network by supporting arithmetic manipulation of MIB data and by highlighting the key MIB variables in a given device library. Health Profiler's history modules can also assist with baselining and trending analysis.

Health Profiler ships with a number of predefined views and reports for several different types of third-party devices. These libraries were developed under the direction of technical representatives from these third parties—thus, they

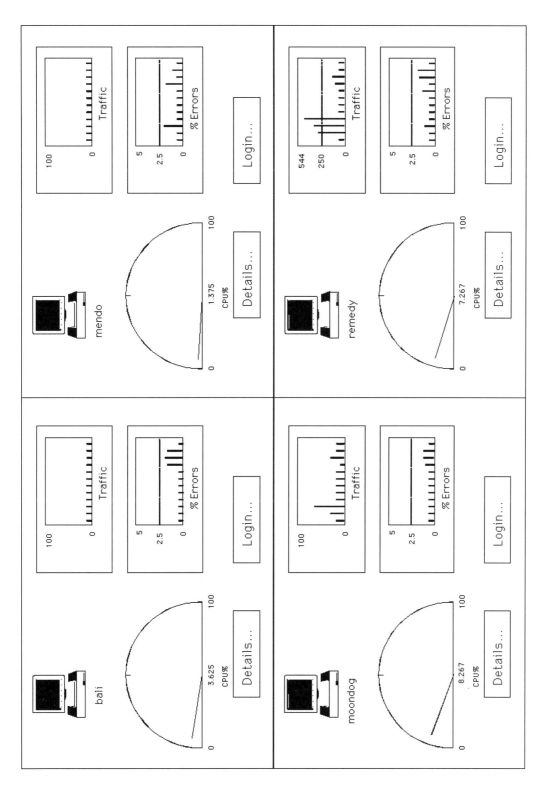

Figure 5.13 Remedy Health Profiler—dashboards and meters

reflect the expertise of each device vendor. In effect, Remedy has sifted through the hundreds of MIB variables supported on a given device and selected the few metrics that provide the best indication of device status and overall network health. The libraries can, therefore, spare the users the time of sifting through arcane MIB variables to determine which are important. Users can, of course, customize these views as they become more experienced with SNMP-based management.

RISCmanagement RISCreporter

Function: Reporting tool for Remedy ARS trouble ticket records.
Platforms supported: HP OpenView, NetLabs/DiMONS.
Integration methods: Menu bar.

SAS Institute SAS/CPE for OpenSystems

Function: Detailed data analysis and reporting.
Platforms supported: SunNet Manager, Cabletron Spectrum; support for HP
    OpenView and IBM NetView/6000 forthcoming.
Integration methods: Menu bar.

SAS/CPE for Open Systems from the SAS Institute, Inc. (Cary, NC). This product is a fully-integrated component of the SAS System for Information Delivery, a family of data analysis and reporting software packages long popular in the mainframe world. SAS is finding a new market for its products as an adjunct to distributed UNIX computing systems and SNMP management platforms (Faulkner, 1993). While most leading SNMP platforms include their own report writers, these tools are notoriously limited and provide few data analysis features. Currently SAS/CPE for Open Systems is one product in the third-party applications market that targets statistical analysis and report writing.

SAS/CPE for Open Systems is designed to make it easier for network administrators to analyze large quantities of management data to accomplish performance management and capacity planning. Network administrators can use SAS/CPE to establish performance baselines and then compare ongoing measurements to detect bottlenecks, hardware problems, and other anomalies. Measurements can include utilization or error rates, for example. Those comfortable with SAS find it extremely useful in staying on top of network conditions, thereby avoiding downtime and performance degradation.

The product can help network administrators read and validate raw data. Once validated, the data is fed into a Performance Data Base (PDB) which is a collection of SAS data sets. The SAS PDB is currently proprietary technology and non-SQL, although SAS may soon also support standard SQL databases in response to customer requests.

SAS/CPE continually performs "data reduction" by replacing multiple data values in with log with collective values such as the mean, range, or standard deviation, summarized over larger and larger time intervals. Management data is stored in nine SAS data libraries, including DAY, WEEK, MONTH, YEAR, DETAIL, DICTLIB, and three additional work libraries. The DETAIL library contains raw performance data with only minor transformations, such as converting continuously ascending counters into rates per second. In general, network administrators find it best to store only a few days worth of data in the DETAIL library before converting it to the more summarized and reduced formats found in DAY, WEEK, MONTH, and YEAR libraries.

SAS/CPE provides menu screens that assist network administrators in using the PDB for the following purposes:

problem determination for common network problems

establishing performance baselines for various network topologies

service level reporting; this includes using measurements such as network and system response time, application throughput, and hardware/software component availability to report on service levels

network performance analysis; this includes analyzing network traffic patterns including setting thresholds for certain measurements, detecting congestion, examining utilization rates for various network topologies, and analyzing error rates

workstation performance analysis; this includes analyzing CPU utilization (queue lengths and percent utilization), memory utilization (paging and swapping rates), disk usage (queue lengths, I/O rates, and the file system), network interface (queue lengths and I/O rates)

SAS/CPE for Open Systems provides a number of canned reports as well as an excellent facility for defining customized reports. Pre-defined reports include baseline, trend, and exception analysis reports. Reports are in either tabular or graphic format. Programmers with SAS experience find SAS/CPE extremely flexible, as the product allows users to code SAS macros outside of the menu interface. Macros may be created to build, manage, and analyze the PDB in numerous ways, to run batch jobs.

5.4.4.2 Help Desk/Problem Management/Trouble Ticket

The following Help Desk/Problem Management/Trouble Ticket applications supporting open management platforms were shipping as of mid-1994:

Answer Computer Apriori
Legent Paradigm
NetLabs ServiceDesk
Peregrine Systems Cover/PNMS
Prolin Automation Pro/HelpDesk
Remedy Action Request System (ARS)

Answer Computer Apriori

Function: Automation of help desk and customer support departments for improving quality of response and providing metrics on help desk performance.

Platforms supported: HP OpenView.

Integration methods: Alarm interfaces (command line).

Legent Paradigm

Function: Trouble ticketing/help desk/problem management.

Platforms supported: SunNet Manager, HP OpenView, IBM NetView/6000.

Integration methods: Filtering of event streams.

Paradigm is a comprehensive problem management system. Paradigm models each critical phase of the problem management process; it supports a database capable of cross-referencing information on devices, trouble codes, status codes, priority classifications, and other key references. Using this database, Paradigm can associate several problems with a single device, correlating multiple events with a single trouble ticket, dispatch multiple actions through a single trouble ticket; relate multiple fields to a single reference on a form, associate service levels to a piece of equipment, and associate trouble codes with a type of problem.

Paradigm filters raw events to detect suspicious patterns. Paradigm includes default filters or users can customize or create their own filters to capture suspicious events before they cause major failures.

Paradigm immediately sends a message to appropriate personnel when a problem is recorded; it can also notify affected users to minimize phone inquiries, or automatically dispatch customized e-mail messages (this requires an SMTP gateway). Audible alarms and pop-up applications are standard; users can add scripts to trigger pages, fax machines, and other notification methods.

Paradigm escalates unresolved problems based on user-defined priority levels and elapsed time. Paradigm maintains status until the trouble ticket is closed. It allows users to record successful repair strategies in "action templates" that operators can reuse to solve similar problems in the future

Paradigm works with the underlying management platform to compile and maintain an inventory of network components, including MAC addresses, manufacturer names, service vendor names, phone numbers, and other device characteristics. The application maintains an accurate record of problems reported, actions taken, actual repair times, service staff performance, and other indicators that help users to identify chronic problems and to better evaluate how different brands of equipment meet specifications. (See Figure 5.14.)

Paradigm allows users to track assignments and analyze help desk workload distribution. It can also track individual or third-party vendor performance. The product provides a full set of analytical reports for improving problem management, including resource failure and repair rates (MTBF/MTTR), vendor response time, and vendor loading.

Paradigm supports a turnkey installation including canned reports and sample trouble ticket layouts. In comparison with competing products, Paradigm is less flexible than Remedy AR System, however, Paradigm's predefined templates are preferred by some organizations that need a preconfigured trouble ticket application. Paradigm was developed by key technical staff formerly with the Boeing Network Management Systems and Services Group.

NetLabs ServiceDesk

Function: Automatic, rule-based creation of trouble tickets based on events reported by NetLabs/DiMONS NerveCenter fault management application.

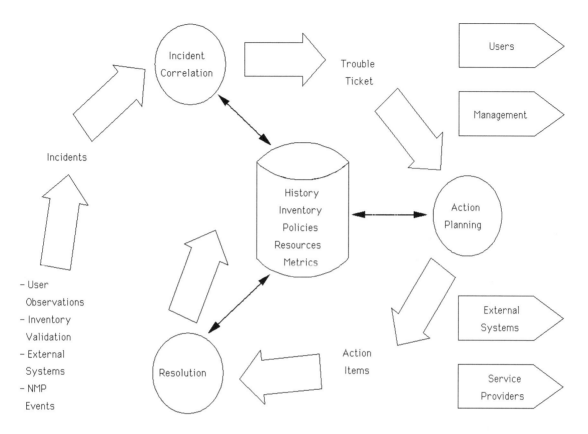

Figure 5.14 Problem management cycle supported by Legent Paradigm

Platforms supported: NetLabs/DiMONS.
Integration methods: NetLabs APIs.

Peregrine Systems Cover/PNMS

Function: Comprehensive problem management/change management/inventory and configuration management/financial management using a 4GL and an integrated SQL relational database.

Platforms supported: HP OpenView.

Integration methods: Via Peregrine's COVER product, which supports menu bar integration with HP OpenView.

Prolin Automation Pro/HelpDesk

Function: Client/server help desk and trouble ticketing; supports configuration management, problem management, and change management; supports Oracle RDBMS.

Platforms supported: SunNet Manager, HP OpenView, IBM NetView/6000; support for Cabletron Spectrum and ICL framework forthcoming.

Integration methods: Menu bar; also, integration through an extensible agent.

Remedy Action Request System (AR System)

Function: Client/server help desk, trouble ticketing and problem management.
Platforms supported: SunNet Manager, HP OpenView, IBM NetView/6000.
Integration methods: SunNet Manager, HP OpenView, IBM NetView/6000,
Cabletron Spectrum, NetLabs/DiMONS, AT&T StarSENTRY.

AR System is a combination trouble ticket/helpdesk/workflow management application that runs on several major open management platforms. The product's modular, flexible design sets it apart from other trouble ticket applications that employ a more static, turnkey approach to problem management. AR System includes a "group engine" allowing it to be used as a workflow tool—making it act like a trouble ticket "spreadsheet."

AR System can be configured to automatically open up a trouble ticket once an SNMP trap is received from the management platform. AR System sends e-mail or a notification (such as a flashing icon) when an operator resolves an open problem. Users can browse through the AR System database to understand the status of requests submitted and potentially look up solutions, depending upon the information that was previously logged. Users can generate a Query By Example to display similar problems and their resolutions, and can add constraints to filter the results.

The customer can control the appearance and content of all AR System trouble ticket forms and reports. AR System also supports creation of macros to automate responses to events. AR System includes a programmer's guide and an API. AR System has been integrated with several other third party applications via command line interface and Remedy's own APIs.

AR System creates a historical audit trail of logged problems. Users can make inquiries to the AR System database for problem analysis. No other trending or data analysis is supported, although data can be exported to other packages for that purpose. AR System includes a flat file database and also supports hooks into several SQL databases including Ingres, Informix, and Sybase. Administrators can assign security privileges to each field on the AR System trouble ticket.

Remedy has integrated AR System with several other important applications including Isicad's COMMAND, Metrix Systems (HP) NetMetrix. AR System employs a distributed client/server implementation. AR System modules can be distributed; they communicate using remote procedure calls (RPCs).

5.4.4.3   Service Level Agreement Reporting

As of mid-1994, there were currently only two Service Level Agreement Reporting applications shipping on open management platforms:

Elegant Communications XRSA
Metrix OpenUpTime

Elegant Communications XRSA

Function: Service level agreement reporting for distributed UNI systems.
Platforms supported: IBM NetView/6000.
Integration methods: Event APIs.

Metrix OpenUpTime
Function: Call management, service call reporting, invoicing, and inventory management.
Platforms supported: HP OpenView.
Integration methods: Menu bar.

5.4.4.4 Physical Asset/Cable Management/Configuration Management

The following physical asset/cable management/configuration management applications were shipping as of mid-1994:

Accugraph MountainView
Autotrol Konfig
ComConsult Kommunikations CCM
Isicad COMMAND

Accugraph MountainView
Function: Cable management, physical asset management, and node-to-node connectivity analysis.
Platforms supported: SunNet Manager, HP OpenView, IBM NetView/6000; support for Cabletron Spectrum and NetLabs/DiMONS forthcoming.
Integration methods: Menu-bar and event handling; also command-line integration with Remedy AR System and Legent Paradigm (trouble ticketing).

MountainView is a configuration management tool which integrates logical and physical network management with trouble ticketing facilities to help automate management processes. MountainView integrates an advanced graphic modeler with a relational database management system (RDBMS-SQL), allowing users to create a complete model of the network's physical infrastructure.

Key components of MountainView include an advanced graphics modeler, integrated spreadsheet, RDBMS (SQL) link, integrated text editor, and expert system cable analyst module, and core MountainView application code.

MountainView relies on the underlying management platform (HP OpenView, IBM NetView/6000) to perform device discovery. Optional MountainView modules can read information directly from SNMP MIBs and can use the "LINK/TRANS" function to load it into the relational database tables linked with the MountainView application.

Users can develop sophisticated hierarchies of physical drawings of network topology from existing CAD files or scanned documents. MountainView supports automatic attachment of any combination of drawings, audio files, raster images, or UNIX programs. The Expert Cable Analysis module supports cable routing and optimization analysis, and network traversal for cable tracing. It supports automatic grouping of path definition for trace correlation and report generation

MountainView can be used to create dynamic models of the physical infrastructure and to automate much of the input involved in tracking network asset data. Network inventory information tracked includes computer equipment, network protocol data, SNMP profiles, network TRAP data, maintenance information, connectivity data, software revision levels and registration, and all aspects of cable plant including validation on common cable types, management pairing assignments, and cable tracing with alpha data.

Using MountainView's LINK/TRANS function, users can automatically updated equipment location changes and contact changes from the underlying network management software. MountainView supports automatic port assignments of cable connections, and it also supports report and work order generation for monitoring moves/adds/changes.

Autotrol Konfig

Function: Cable management and physical network and asset management.
Platforms supported: SunNet Manager, HP OpenView, IBM NetView/6000.
Integration methods: Menu bar; remote procedure calls (RPCs), some APIs; also command-line integration with Remedy AR System.

Konfig tracks physical/wire/asset network configuration by documenting and displaying a detailed view of the voice, data, video, and environmental network. Using a relational database, Konfig builds intelligent relationships between active and/or passive network components, and describes their association with the network.

Konfig uses menus and APIs to interface with SunNet Manager, HP OpenView, and IBM NetView/6000. The API is used to issue SNMP requests and to receive SNMP responses. SNMP responses are stored in Konfig's SQL database.

Konfig includes a relational database for documenting network devices, their arrangement, connectivity, descriptions, and other attributes. A graphic engine depicts logical, physical, facility, and device views of the network on the screen. Advanced cable management functions allow users to represent and manipulate network connections at the circuit level. Konfig can trace circuit paths through bridges and cross-connects. Konfig supports a unique unambiguous identifier (UUI) for each object in the database; database integration with the underlying platform reduces the need to input data twice.

ComConsult Kommunikations CCM

Function: Documentation of network component and terminating equipment configuration. Cables and components are shown in CAD drawings, and parameters are stored in an SQL database.
Platforms supported: HP OpenView.
Integration methods: Menu bar.

Isicad COMMAND

Function: Cable management, physical asset tracking, connectivity tracking.
Platforms supported: SunNet Manager, HP OpenView, Cabletron Spectrum, NetLabs/DiMONS, Network Managers NMC.
Integration methods: Menu bar; SNMP traps, command-line interface with Remedy AR System (trouble ticketing).

COMMAND allows users to view everything from the entire network infrastructure down to the connectivity links between the smallest devices. COMMAND displays physical relationships between all elements on voice, video, LAN/WAN data, and security networks.

COMMAND tracks the inventory of physical network components, including workstations, cable layout, bridges, routers, and telecommunications equipment. Inventory data can include product descriptions, serial numbers, location, port numbers, and cable type. COMMAND can link CAD-based building layouts, floor plans, cable runs, trays, equipment layouts, etc. with database information such as circuit records, tray capacity, inventory data, and connectivity information.

Users can click on icons to obtain closer views or text from pop-up windows; by clicking on an inventory icon, user can call up database records on the displayed device. COMMAND tracks the cable pair, pathway, jack port, patch panel, multiplexer, and every other device connected and how they are connected.

Users can also initiate moves/adds/changes in near real time by making the changes directly on the graphical map—the database will be automatically updated upon the user's approval. COMMAND can automatically generate reports, schedules, work orders, audit histories, and bills-of-materials during moves/adds/changes. COMMAND can now automatically determine the best cabling configuration to support a new LAN station, and automatically create a workorder to accomplish the job.

The COMMANDHelpDesk option, which is actually the Remedy AR System, can help automate troubleshooting operations, by tracking problem histories and building an experience database for ongoing helpdesk management. (See Figure 5.15.)

5.4.5   Platform Extensions

5.4.5.1   Alert Notification (Pagers, Wireless, Voice) and Log Managers

The following alert notification and log management applications were shipping as of mid-1994:

Cabletron SpectroPhone
Cabletron SpectroWatch
Independence Technologies iVIEW Log Mgr
Matrix Technology Mobile Driver
Software Consulting Distributed Error Log Notification (DELN)
Telemon TelAlert

In the effort to decrease network operations staff while increasing network availability and quality of service, organizations are very interested in applications that can reduce the time that operators and technicians spend just watching alerts and messages scroll by on various screens. Alert notification tools can pass alerts to technicians who are away from the console—via pagers, voice response, or wireless communications. Log managers can consolidate logged alerts from multiple management systems into a central repository for viewing and reporting.

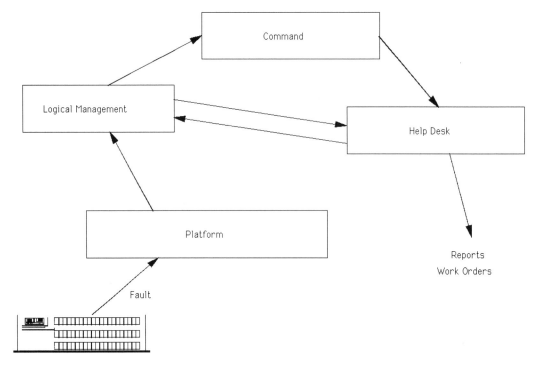

Figure 5.15 Resource and process tool integration using ISICAD Command

Cabletron SpectroPhone
> Function: Directs Cabletron Spectrum alarms to a phone notification system capable of dialing beepers, pagers, etc.; provides a digitized voice describing the alarm and its source, and allows operator to clear the alarms or trigger actions through the touchtone phone.
> Platforms supported: Cabletron Spectrum.
> Integration methods: Cabletron Spectrum alarm interface.

Cabletron SpectroWatch
> Function: Alarm filtering and prioritizing; allows user to put a "watch" on a specific MIB attribute (either entire device types or instances of device models).
> Platforms supported: Cabletron Spectrum.
> Integration methods: Cabletron Spectrum alarm interface.

Independence Technologies iVIEW Log Mgr
> Function: Logs errors and activity data from multiple UNIX workstations and servers into a central system management workstation; data can then be stored in a relational database for browsing, sorting, and reporting.
> Platforms supported: SunNet Manager, HP OpenView, IBM NetView/6000, NetLabs/DiMONS.
> Integration methods: Proxy agent.

Matrix Technology Mobile Driver

Function: A messaging engine supporting wireless communication of alerts; transmits detailed alarm messages to alphanumeric pagers; supports a command line interface for easy messaging and a graphical front-end to directly send keyed messages to pagers and manage the spooler.

Platforms supported: SunNet Manager; support for other management platforms forthcoming.

Integration methods: Menu bar and SNMP traps; ability to read directly from the SunNet Manager data stream is forthcoming.

Software Consulting Distributed Error Log Notification (DELN)

Function: Generates SNMP traps from system error logs of IBM RS/6000s and can send them to any management platform.

Platforms supported: SunNet Manager, HP OpenView, IBM NetView/6000.

Integration methods: SNMP Traps.

Telemon TelAlert

Function: Voice paging/voice synthesis application that can transmit descriptions of events via pagers, voice announcement via speaker, voice announcement via autodialed phone call, visual/audio alarm activation; actions can be initiated for any type of event via the UNIX command line also.

Platforms supported: HP OpenView; support for SunNet manager and IBM NetView/6000 forthcoming.

Integration methods: Command-line integration; can also work with Remedy AR System and Legent Paradigm.

5.4.5.2   Console Management

The following management system console management applications were shipping for open management platforms as of mid-1994:

DeskTalk Systems TrendSystem (Cooperative Consoles)
Hummingbird Communications PC Terminal Emulation
SunSolutions ShowMe

DeskTalk Systems TrendSystem (Cooperative Consoles)

Function: Facilitates communication between multiple management consoles, permitting delegation of operational management responsibilities.

Platforms supported: SunNet Manager.

Integration methods: Managers services API.

Hummingbird Communications PC Terminal Emulation

Function: Terminal emulation, allowing DOS or Windows NT PC users to view IBM NetView/6000 applications on their screens.

Platforms supported: IBM NetView/6000.

Integration methods: Terminal emulation.

SunSolutions ShowMe

Function: Data analysis and reporting; supports interactive videoconferencing, enabling SunNet Manager users to interactively collaborate with remote managers over information displayed from SunNet Manager.

Platforms supported: SunNet Manager.

Integration methods: Menu bar.

5.4.5.3   Legacy System Monitoring and Gateways:

The following legacy system monitoring and gateway applications were shipping for open management platforms as of mid-1994:

Alcatel Bell ITS SNA-Expert
Boole & Babbage CommandPost
Bridgeway EventIX
Brixton Systems BrxOV, BrxSNM
Diederich & Associates NetScript/6000
HP HARMONi
HP OpenView Distributed Novell Manager
IBM NetView Service Point
Ki Research OpenDNM
Miror Systems RARS/2
NetLabs Assist
NetTech BlueVision
MicroMuse LegacyWatch
NYNEX Allink Operations Coordinator
Oscom International Pty OSGATE-700
Peregrine Systems OpenSNA
Perform SAGE/X

As organizations deploy SNMP-based management platforms on a wide scale, the problem of managing non-SNMP (e.g., "legacy" systems) becomes critical. While many organizations use separate tools for managing older legacy systems, a number of new applications are emerging that can bring legacy system management into an SNMP framework. Of particular interest are applications that address management of IBM Systems Network Architecture (SNA) networks—with or without IBM's mainframe NetView product.

Alcatel Bell ITS SNA-Expert

Function: Discovery and topology mapping of IBM SNA networks; also configuration management and high-level correlation of alarms for fault management.

Platforms supported: SunNet Manager (also works with Alcatel Bell NM-Expert, an integrated network management platform with expert system capabilities).

Integration methods: Tightly integrated with SunNet Manager APIs.

SNA-Expert integrates the functions of SunNet Manager with management functions for SNA networks. The principal features of SNA-Expert are automatic discovery of SNA network configuration and incorporation of that data into the SunNet Manager map; the product also supports fault and alarm reporting based on high-level filtering and correlation mechanisms.

SNA-Expert components include the NM-Bridge, the NM-Expert, and the SNM-Bridge. The NM-Bridge is software installed on every IBM SNA host that collects configuration and event data from VTAM and/or mainframe NetView. The NM-Bridge can issue VTAM or NetView commands from the SunNet Manager console. The NM-Expert module is an expert system that filters and correlates information from SNA and other networks, including TCP/IP, X.25, V.24, and SNMP. The SNM-Bridge feeds this information to SunNet Manager. SNA-Expert can communicate to mainframe NetView using LU6.2, and it can send commands directly to VTAM and/or NetView. The product provides realtime, automated fault correlation, analyzing the impact that equipment failure has on active SNA sessions.

Boole & Babbage CommandPost

Function: Message parsing and collection of alerts from multiple device types; alerts are intercepted at the RS-232 port.

Platforms supported: SunNet Manager, HP OpenView, IBM NetView/6000.

Integration methods: Menu bar.

Command/Post supports management of multiple types of SNMP and non-SNMP (legacy) systems through alert consolidation.

Product features include:

Message filtering
Alert prioritization
Message translation
Alert databasing

Command/Post also supports Service Point connection to NetView/390 and an SQL database. The operator interface is OSF/MOTIF.

Command/Post intercepts alerts from printer ports (RS-232) or ASCII streams of multiple element management systems or devices, consolidating, processing, and displaying the messages on a single console. Message processing, or parsing, takes place in Command Post's Alert Logic Filter Editor (ALFE). ALFE removes control characters, translates tool-specific codes into meaningful information, and adds connectivity information. By knowing connectivity, ALFE can perform alarm correlation by analyzing multiple alarms and suppressing secondary alarms to highlight root causes.

A transformer routine scans device and EMs message streams, looking for specific messages. Detection of these messages will trigger user-defined actions. Users can also specify Alert filtering rules to suppress low-priority messages.

Command/Post supports a simplified menu-driven GUI and selective routing of alerts to operators and supervisors. Command/Posts' ALFE component can automatically close outstanding alerts when restoral messages are detected.

Operators can also issue commands to element management systems via Command/Post's terminal emulation facilities. Each individual terminal emulator appears as a window on the Command/Post screen. Command/Post supports VT100, 3270, and many other forms of terminal emulation.

Command/Post comprises a UNIX-based server and one or more client workstations. X-terminals are supported for display only. Also included is a communications server, a programmable interface device manufactured by 3Com, supporting conversion of RS-232 connections to Ethernet.

Bridgeway EventIX

Function: Alarm consolidation and rules-based filtering for managing legacy systems under SNMP management platforms; users can customize EventIX to trigger scripts that take corrective actions based on incoming alarms.

Platforms supported: SunNet Manager, HP OpenView, IBM NetView/6000, NetLabs/DiMONS, AT&T StarSENTRY.

Integration methods: Menu bar; SNMP traps.

The EventIX product family includes several packages, chief of which is the EventIX Extensible Proxy Agent (EPA). EventIX EPA includes applications that allow an SNMP management system, such as HP OpenView, IBM NetView/6000, or NetLabs/DiMONs to manage non-SNMP devices. EventIX is sold both to end-users and to OEM customers who integrate the software into their own products for resale. EventIX has been implemented to extend the reach of SNMP management platforms to "legacy" devices such as PBXs, multiplexers, modems, and X.25 switching systems.

The purpose of EventIX is similar to other products designed to consolidate alarms from various devices onto a central screen. However, EventIX differs from "message parsers" such as Boole & Babbage Command/Post in that it is modular, SNMP-based, and highly affordable. EventIX does not include a sophisticated artificial intelligence engine as does higher-priced alarm consolidators from NYNEX Allink and Objective Systems Integrator's NetExpert; however, applications built using EventIX comprise a set of rules that correlate system and network event conditions with responses or actions, such as triggering scripts for rerouting traffic or automated service restoral.

Because EventIX includes rules-based technology as well as an application monitor, it is actually more than just a proxy agent. The biggest challenge for the 90s is to manage distributed applications—EventIX is a product that helps bridge the gap between old systems and newer generation systems that use SNMP. SNMP systems can generate a lot of traps, and EventIX can act as an intermediate filter. SNMP platforms such as HP OpenView or SunNet Manager can't solve the entire management problem unless you have a very well-defined network. EventIX extends the capabilities of these platforms into environments with mixed technologies.

The EventIX Extensible Proxy Agent (EPA) is designed to allow customers to monitor and control legacy equipment using an SNMP platform, thereby reducing dependency on multiple proprietary element management systems.

EventIX EPA accomplishes this in three ways:

translates alarm messages from non-SNMP "legacy" systems into SNMP trap
allows SNMP platform to query the legacy system for configuration and status
   information
allows the SNMP platform to control the legacy system by setting its operational
   parameters

In addition, the product builds the topology map for the legacy systems, just as
SNMP management platforms discover and map IP devices. EventIX integrates
both the IP and the non-IP maps in the platform database. To support these
functions, EventIX EPA includes the following standard modules:

Trap generator application
MibMaster utility
SNMP command handler
Polling/data collection application
Support applications, including installation scripts, application controls scripts,
   and example applications

The EventIX EPA processes SNMP "Get" and "Get/Next" commands, issued
from the SNMP platform, against a customized MIB definition for the legacy system. Legacy system MIBs can be built by the customer using EventIX's Mib-
Builder utility, which is an optional feature.

EventIX EPA is designed to enable users and applications developers to convert legacy system alarm messages into SNMP traps. A Motif-based graphical
user interface (GUI) displays panels to help users map alarm data into SNMP
Trap components. A menu-driven process guides the user in defining how alarm
messages should be parsed and filtered. In particular, messages can be parsed,
"tokenized," and manipulated in a variety of ways. EventIX EPA provides full
support for UNIX regular expression syntax as well as the use of multiple token
delimiters. Users also set alarm thresholds using the GUI.

Once alarms are converted into SNMP traps, the user can choose to store them
in the legacy MIB—using EventIX, it is not necessary to explicitly issue SNMP
commands in order to accomplish this. The MIB can reside locally on the EventIX
EPA or on any other computer on the IP network.

Another feature of EventIX EPA is that is can process messages arriving from
multiple sources. EventIX EPA supports a DataManager repository for storing
alarm messages before they are processed. Also, multiple EPAs can be "cascaded"
to handle complex integration of alarms from multiple sources. For example, one
EPA may perform initial alarm processing and filtering before forwarding the
alarms to another EPA which converts the alarms into SNMP traps.

The EventIX EPA allows an SNMP platform to obtain device status and config-
uration data from the legacy system by issuing standard SNMP "Get" or "Get-
Next" commands that query the legacy system's MIB, which was built using the
MibBuilder utility. A Polling Data Collection application then issues "native"
commands to the legacy system and parses the responses to those commands.
Responses are stored in the legacy MIB. Users must develop the Polling Data
Collection application themselves, however, Bridgeway provides customization
services that can make this process easier.

To change parameters on a non-SNMP device, the EventIX EPA can issue SNMP "Set" commands to the legacy system MIB. At that point, the MibMaster utility detects the Set command and sends a message to the Legacy System Control application to take action. This application issues native commands, understood by the legacy system, to modify the device's operational parameters. Users must develop Legacy System Control applications, however, Bridgeway provides customization services that can assist users in this task.

EventIX EPA can be distributed among multiple hardware platforms, allowing Trap generator to reside in a different system than the SNMP handler and the polling/data collection applications. The polling/data collection application may reside in one or more systems. These distributed capabilities increase the product's flexibility and effectiveness. In addition, Bridgeway offers an IBM NetView Interface module, supporting bidirectional exchange of NetView Alerts, Class-of-Service (COS) commands, and unsolicited messages.

Brixton Systems BrxOV, BrxSNM

Function: Transfers alarms captured by SNMP platform into mainframe NetView by converting SNMP traps into NMVT (SNA alerts); also, the product accepts RUNCMD requests issued from mainframe NetView consoles.

Platforms supported: SunNet Manager, HP OpenView.

Integration methods: Platform APIs.

Diederich & Associates NetScript/6000

Function: Translates legacy system alarms into SNMP traps; supports higher level and cross-submap visibility of problems and alarms; supports the ability to filter, correlate, time-relate, and threshold incoming alarms; can communicate with mainframe NetView and IBM's Graphic Monitor Facility (GMF).

Platforms supported: IBM NetView/6000.

Integration methods: IBM NetView/6000 APIs.

HP HARMONi

Function: Facilitates telecommunications applications by supporting centralized data and relationship management, and object-oriented inventory application, and object class translator and metadata store.

Platforms supported: HP OpenView.

Integration methods: HP OpenView DM APIs.

HP OpenView Distributed Novell Manager

Function: Management of Novell and TCP/IP networks over X.25 networks using X.25 Eicon PC gateways.

Platforms supported: HP OpenView.

Integration methods: Integrated by HP upon request.

IBM AIX NetView Service Point

Function: Exchange of management information between IBM NetView/6000 and IBM mainframe NetView (NetView/390); uses LU6.2 to communicate management information to NetView/390; enables centralized management of non-SNA devices from NetView/390.

Platforms supported: IBM NetView/6000.

Integration methods: APIs.

Ki Research OpenDNM

Function: Management of the Digital DECnet Phase IV and LAT networks from SNMP-based platforms.

Platforms supported: HP OpenView, IBM NetView/6000.

Integration methods: Proxy agents, command-line interface.

NetTech BlueVision

Function: Management of IBM SNA environments from Cabletron Spectrum; provides topology of SNA and TCP/IP networks on one map.

Platforms supported: Cabletron Spectrum; support for other management platforms forthcoming under the E*View product family.

Integration methods: Communication with NetView/390 using LU6.2; currently requires NetView/390, however, forthcoming versions will communicate directly to VTAM.

MicroMuse LegacyWatch

Function: Client/server management system supporting SNMP-based management of non-SNMP (legacy) equipment; scans messages from the character stream, notes events, and passing them to the management platform.

Platforms supported: SunNet Manager; support for HP OpenView and IBM NetView/6000 forthcoming.

Integration methods: SNMP traps.

Miror Systems RARS/2

Function: Remote alert reporting system for automatically managing major computer center facilities, WANs, and LANs. Platform supported: IBM NetView/6000.

Integration methods: SNMP API and IBM Service Point gateway.

The Remote Alert Reporting System/2 (RARS/2) from Miror Systems, Ltd. is a family of products for managing non-SNMP systems—including remote computers, IBM hosts, PBXs, and environmental controls—from an SNMP management system such as IBM Netview/6000, or from NetView/390.

RARS/2 can improve the fault management process by integrating alerts from a variety of sources onto a single screen. These alert sources include environmental devices, IBM SNA host applications, security systems, video cameras, autodial workstations, and various SNA and TCP/IP network components. RARS/2 provides visibility into these various network and system components as well as physical facilities. This can help organizations increase the availability of complex computer networks and systems. RARS/2 is capable of supporting information exchange between IBM NetView/390 or Sterling Solve: Automation and non-SNA components; also between SNMP management systems such as IBM NetView/6000 and non-SNMP devices.

RARS/2 has also been used to centralize after-hours monitoring of PBXs, multiplexers, and X.25 systems. Another RARS/2 feature is the ability to monitor the status of unmanned computer centers and disaster recovery facilities. RARS/2 can automatically control the status and power supply of remote systems, and alert key personnel of any problems.

Host components of RARS include 1) Host/SNA, displaying panels and applications within IBM NetView/390 or Sterling Solve: Automation, and 2) Host/SNMP, providing MIB information for RARS/2 systems and applications.

Components of the RARS/2 product family include:

RARS Base: supports multitasking and queuing
RARS Gateway: interfaces systems to data port
RARS Paging Management System (PMS): supports automatic paging
RARS Digital Input Digital Output (DIDO): interface to digital input; and
RARS-VIDEO: captures, transmits, and stores video information

Also, RARS-TCP connection to TCP/IP networks, RARS-3270 supports full 3270 terminal emulation, RARS-NET supports application linkage to NetView/390; RARS-DIAL is an auto dial facility. RARS-PMS can improve problem response time by automatically paging the right support personnel, supply them with detailed fault information.

NetLabs Assist

Function: Displays/prints graphs or tables from data in NetLabs/DiMONS log files; includes pre-configured enterprise-specific alarms for Cabletron hubs, Chipcom hubs, SynOptics hubs, and RMON devices.
Platforms supported: NetLabs/DiMONS.
Integration methods: NetLabs/DiMONS APIs.

NYNEX Allink Operations Coordinator

Function: Artificial intelligence engine which monitors, consolidates, filters, and prioritizes alarms using intelligent interfaces to over 50 different element management systems.
Platforms supported: SunNet Manager.
Integration methods: Manager services/event services/database APIs.

Oscom International Pty OSGATE-700

Function: Gateway between proprietary devices (UPS, PBXs, etc.) and other non-SNMP systems (X.25, OSI, etc.).
Platforms supported: SunNet Manager, HP OpenView; support for IBM NetView/6000 forthcoming.
Integration methods: Menu bar.

Peregrine Systems OpenSNA

Function: Management of IBM SNA networks from SNMP-based management platforms; graphically depicts and manages SNA Network Control Processors (NCPs), physical units (PUs), applications, and logical units (LUs);

allows operators to issue VTAM or NetView commands. For more information about Peregrine OpenSNA, see Chapter 7.

Platforms supported: HP OpenView.

Integration methods: Menu bar.

Perform SAGE/X

Function: Management of WAN and other non-SNMP devices by automating TTY and TELNET commands.

Platforms supported: HP OpenView, IBM NetView/6000, Cabletron Spectrum, Bull ISM.

Integration methods: Menu bar.

5.4.5.4   Mapping Applications

As of mid-1994, there was only one third-party mapping application currently shipping for use with open management platforms:

Tom Sawyer Software Network Layout Assistant

Function: Interactive graph editing application supporting automated mapping of large computer networks; supports hierarchical, circular, and symmetric layout libraries (see Figure 5.16).

Platforms supported: SunNet Manager; support for HP OpenView and IBM NetView/6000 forthcoming.

Integration methods: Menu bar; SunNet Manager APIs.

5.4.6   Service-Specific Applications

5.4.6.1   Frame Relay, SMDS, and Private Line

The following applications assist users in managing the customer-allocated portions of their frame relay, SMDS, and private line networks:

AT&T Frame Relay Customer Premises Application
MCI Communications HyperScope
WilTel WilView/X

New SNMP-based applications are expected in the near-term from major carriers including Sprint and Alcatel Network Systems, as well as competitive access providers such as MFS Datanet and Intermedia Communications of Florida.

AT&T Frame Relay Customer Premises Application

Function: Monitoring of AT&T frame relay virtual networks into an SNMP-based management framework; monitors PVS and incorporates their configuration into the AT&T StarSENTRY map; provides PVC and port statistics.

Platforms supported: AT&T StarSENTRY.

Integration methods: StarSENTRY management gateway, frame relay proxy agent.

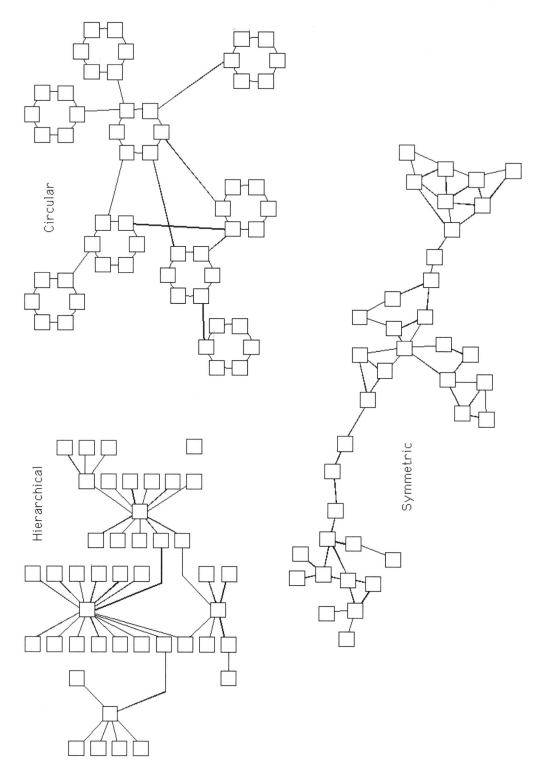

Figure 5.16 Network Layout Assistant supports hierarchical, circular, and symmetric layout libraries

MCI Communications HyperScope

Function: Management of MCI's frame relay and SMDS networks; forwards alarms and performance information to the customer premise workstation.

Platforms supported: SunNet Manager, HP OpenView, IBM NetView/6000.

Integration methods: Menu bar.

WilTel WilView/X

Function: Management of WilTel's WilPak frame relay, Wilband dynamic bandwidth, and private line services; provides interactive management including order tracking, realtime monitoring, and trouble ticket initiation and tracking.

Platforms supported: SunNet Manager, HP OpenView; support for IBM NetView/6000 forthcoming.

Integration methods: Icon launching/topology map integration; also, command line integration with Remedy ARS trouble ticketing.

5.4.6.2   Mobile Data Services

As of mid-1994, there was only one application shipping for the management of mobile data services using an open management platform:

Motorola Mobile Data NMC 5000

Function: Management of alarms and diagnostics for mobile radio networks.

Platforms supported: SunNet Manager.

Integration methods: SunNet Manager APIs, extensive use of proxy agents.

5.4.7   Third-Party Toolkits and Development Environments

The following third-party toolkits and development environments were shipping as of mid-1994 for use in supporting open management platform applications development:

Evolving Systems ESI Environment
Gensym G2
Independence Technologies iVIEW P Agent Kit
NetManSys NMS/FastBench
Peer Networks Programmable Agent and Development Environment
Template Software SNAP
V.I. Corp. DataViews, X-Designer

Evolving Systems ESI Environment and Voice and Data Integration System (VDIS)

Function: ESI Environment is an advanced set of programs and routines which simplify development of robust transaction processing environments for distributed systems. VDIS is a set of APIs and software allowing for rapid development of integrated voice and data applications; these applications facilitate control of multiple telephony and computer components.

Platforms supported: IBM NetView/6000.

Integration methods: SNMP agents; agents allow monitoring from NetView/6000; VDIS agents link Callpath with NetView/6000.

Gensym G2

Function: Expert system shell, including neural network-based tools (graphical programming style), diagnostic assistant; facilitates development of real-time analysis and control applications; includes a built-in simulator.

Platforms supported: HP OpenView.

Integration methods: SNMP APIs.

Independence Technologies iVIEW SNMP Agent Kit

Function: Allows customer to define a set of managed objects (status, number, size of queues) and automatically generates C code for an SNMP agent, permitting seamless management of network equipment and client/server applications by and SNMP-based management platform.

Platforms supported: NetLabs/DiMONS, any SNMP system.

Integration methods: SNMP APIs.

NetManSys NMS/FastBench

Function: Integrated tool suite for developing network management applications; includes a GDMO modeling toolset, a GDMO RDB schema generator, and a GDMO C++ class generator and runtime environment for Agent and Manager.

Platforms supported: HP OpenView DM.

Integration methods: XMP APIs.

Peer Networks Programmable Agent & Development Environment:

Function: Toolset for developing customized SNMP MIBs, for devices or applications; allows developers to extend device code or application using a Sub-Agent, which dynamically registers the MIB variables with the NetView/6000 agent "snmpd"; includes a MIB compiler, runtime libraries, high-level APIs, and MIB extensions.

Platforms supported: IBM NetView/6000.

Integration methods: IBM NetView/6000 "snmpd" agent.

Talarian RT Works

Function: Toolset for developing time-critical monitoring and control systems; provides separate processes for data acquisition, data recording and playback, data distribution, inferencing, and GUI; client/server based architecture.

Platforms supported: HP OpenView.

Integration methods: RT Works C Callable Library.

Template Software SNAP

Function: Application development environment for implementing mission-critical, distributed applications; templates promote large-scale code reuse; uses an object model enabling common data representation; provides knowl-

edge-based inferencing and links to multiple relational databases and facilities for integrating legacy systems.
Platforms supported: HP OpenView.
Integration methods: Supports HP-UX environments

V.I. Corp. DataViews, X-Designer
Function: Supports development of Motif GUIs; provides a point-and-click interactive editor allowing developers to layout Motif widgets to construct the interface, and prevents building of "illegal" Motif widgets.
Platforms supported: HP OpenView.
Integration methods: Supports HP-UX.

5.5   SUMMARY

As of June 1994 there were more than 100 management applications available that support one or more of the leading UNIX-based SNMP management platforms. This number is expect to increase steadily for the next few years. In addition, new third-party applications for DOS/Windows-based platforms, such as Novell NMS and HP OpenView Windows, are starting to emerge. These DOS applications, although not discussed here, represent a broadening of the market for management applications. As of mid-1994 only a handful of DOS-based SNMP applications were shipping, although this number is expected to increase dramatically during 1995.

6

Management Solutions from IBM

For over a decade, IBM's product offerings and statements of direction have greatly influenced both industry directions and the network and systems management strategies of end-user organizations. IBM has long been the leader in logical network management, and it is an important contributor in physical network management technologies as well. The company has offered architectures, products, options for automation, and alternatives for integration. Key questions and issues facing IBM customers today include the following:

- Does IBM intend to maintain all four principal product families: mainframe NetView, AIX NetView/6000, LAN Network Manager, and LAN NetView?
- If not, what product is supposed to become the focal point to manage IBM and non-IBM components?
- What applications are supported and by what products?
- What products are going to manage the "new-SNA," based on APPN?
- What role will the new IBM SNA Manager/6000 application play in facilitating management of SNA networks from SNMP-based systems (e.g., AIX NetView/6000)?
- Where is management positioned under the blueprints of SAA and SystemView?

Customers can not plan effective network and systems management strategies without satisfactory answers to these questions. While IBM has yet to provide complete answers, the information in the following pages will help limit the customer's risk by describing the status of existing products and clarifying IBM's statements of direction thus far.

6.1   IBM PRODUCT FAMILIES

This section addresses the four existing IBM product families—mainframe Net-View, AIX NetView/6000, LAN Network Manager, and LAN NetView. Figure 6.1 shows from IBM's perspective the three major directions with respect to these product families.

IBM's SystemView architecture is intended as a framework for the development of IBM management products, which are aimed at managing large SNA and multiprotocol networks. Through published interfaces and architected formats, IBM is also inviting other vendors to implement compatibility with this architecture, in much the same way that most vendors implement at least limited SNA compatibility. Figure 6.2 summarizes the architecture. Under this framework, there are six architected components.

- Focal points—provide centralized network and systems management support. Focal points support the needs of human and programmed operators and provide a central point for collecting, analyzing, and storing network and system management data. The NetView family of products constitute IBM's strategic

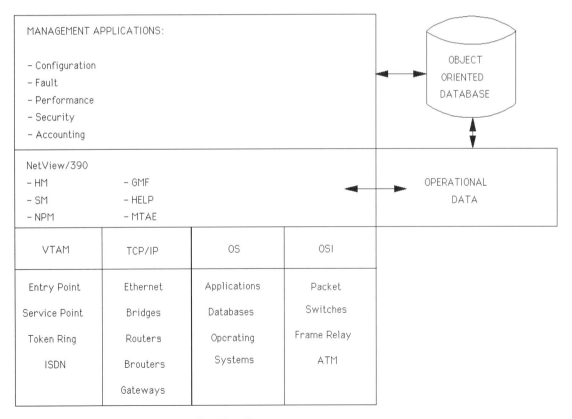

Figure 6.1 Directions for IBM product families

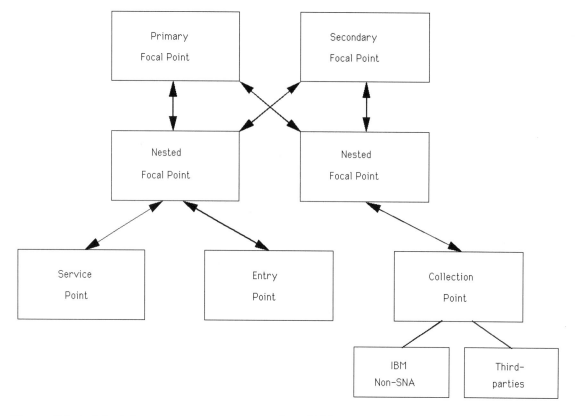

Figure 6.2 Architected management components from IBM

focal point products. NetView is also capable of triggering scripts for automated reactions to network and systems events and alarms.

- Entry points—SNA devices capable of implementing the SNA management services architecture for themselves and other attached products. Most IBM data network products are capable of functioning as entry points.
- Service points—provide SNA management services for themselves and for attached devices and networks that are not capable of being entry points.
- Secondary focal points—redundant focal points that can take over in case the primary focal point fails. Reacting to the need for high availability of the focal point, IBM will be providing increased support for multiple focal points that are able to back each other up.
- Nested focal points—provide distributed management support for segments of large networks, which still forwarding critical information up to more global focal points.
- Collection points—provide a network management relay function from a self-contained SNA subnetwork to a standard focal point. It would appear that the AS/400 or System 88 will act as a collection point for IBM peer-to-peer networks of midrange systems.

The service point is capable of sending network management data about-non-SNA systems to a focal point. It is also capable of receiving commands from a focal point to be executed on the non-SNA systems. The service point is thus a network management gateway, translating between SNA formats and those of non-SNA devices. NetView/PC was the first implementation of a major service point product, although other management packages such as AIX NetView/6000 may contain embedded service point functions.

IBM's intention is to use the focal point to manage all the information resources of the enterprise, even those from other vendors, through the agency of the service point. This is a centric, distributed approach with local automation capabilities at the level of contributing products.

6.1.1 Mainframe NetView

The primary components of mainframe NetView including the following:

- NetView Command Facility (formerly the Network Communication Control Facility, or NCCF).
- Session Monitor (formerly the Network Logical Data Manager, or NLDM).
- Hardware Monitor (formerly the Network Problem Determination Application, or NPDA).
- Status Monitor (STATMON), which allows network operators to look at the status of network resources and issue commands for any displayed resource.
- NetView Graphic Monitoring Facility (GMF) is an OS/2-based system that displays the status of SNA, and eventually non-SNA, non-IBM elements. With the multitasking features of OS/2, users can access other interfaces such as NetView Performance Monitor, Info/System, MVS-Automated Operations Controller, and NetView/PC.

A host-based Resource Object Data Manager (RODM) provides the Graphic Monitor Facility with object-oriented data about multivendor network devices. RODM is a high-speed, high-performance, in-memory data store designed to keep up with the status of the network in real-time. RODM broadens the existing capabilities of mainframe NetView by recognizing specific management situations and responding without operator intervention. In summary, RODM broadens the scope of data that can drive automation.

In addition, mainframe NetView's online help facility supplies data about NetView commands and many of the NetView display panels. A help desk facility offers an online guide to network problem diagnosis. The browse facility allows operators to look through libraries and the network log.

Another product in the NetView family, the NetView Performance Monitor (NPM) collects, analyzes, displays, and reports NCP-related information as well as data online use, response time, transaction, message, and retransmission counts. NPM also includes TSO measurements, dynamic activation/deactivation of definite response, and collection of session-level and gateway-level accounting records. NPM is growing closer to the NetView nucleus by generating performance alarms, such as PIU traffic, line use, and error counts, and sending them to NetView for further processing, correlation, and display.

In addition, mainframe NetView includes an access facility for connecting to other host-based monitors offering terminal access facility features. IBM added the Distribution Manager (DM) that supports functions comparable with previous HCF and DSX products. The DM supports realtime diagnostics and collects error files from remote locations. The new release also enhanced the NetView File Transfer Program (FTP).

Mainframe NetView's network asset management facility collects vital product data from network elements. NetView also includes support for REXX, the SAA procedural language. System programmers can now customize NetView using REXX instead of the more cumbersome command lists. SAA REXX is the default language of choice for automation.

Third-party systems, PBXs, multiplexers, and LANs may also be integrated using NetView/PC as a service point. Four separate functions are supported in NetView/PC's Application Programming Interface/Communication Services (API/CS) of NetView/PC are: host alert facility, operator communication facility, service point command facility, and host data facility. However, IBM no longer considers NetView/PC as the strategic solution for integrating non-SNA and non-IBM devices with mainframe NetView. Instead, capabilities of the NetView Multisystem Manager are replacing NetView/PC as a preferred integration mechanism. For more information on NetView/PC applications, see section 6.3.1.

Within the mainframe NetView architecture, management data flows throughout SNA sessions, which provide reliable, connection-oriented network transport. The basic SNA message unit-called request/response unit (RU), which supports network management-is called the network management vector transport (NMVT). SNA-MS can flow on either LU 6.2 or SSCP-PU sessions.

Many vendors of network management products are currently supporting mainframe NetView. However, the depth of support varies considerably, ranging from forwarding alerts all the way to giving away complete control of their own device family to IBM. There are several alternatives for exporting and importing information between mainframe NetView, VTAM, and SNMP-based management systems. These alternatives are discussed in section 6.3 of this chapter.

6.1.2   IBM LAN Network Manager

IBM's LAN Network Manager targets physical layer management of multi-segment LANs. The product functions as part of an integrated LAN/WAN management solution when used with mainframe NetView. LAN Network Manager can also be used with AIX NetView/6000—while the management capabilities of these products are complementary, integration may be supported at the AIX NetView/6000 platform. When Token Ring management capabilities must be supported, the presence of LAN Network Manager in the integrated solution is required.

LAN Network Manager communicates with AIX NetView/6000 through a TCP/IP socket, sending SNMP traps to an AIX NetView/6000 application. LAN Network Manager runs under OS/2, so it does not require a dedicated workstation. However, depending on the size of the Token Ring LANs that are managed, it may be preferable from a performance standpoint to use a dedicated workstation. The OS/2 requirement only applies to the workstation on which LAN Network Manager is installed. LAN Network Manager is not affected by operating systems on other workstations on the LAN, nor is it affected by LAN network operating systems—thus it can be used on Novell NetWare LANs as well as LAN Manager or LAN Server LANs.

IBM LAN Network Manager supports fault, performance, and configuration management functions. The product supports fault management by generating events when user-specified conditions. Also, LAN Network Manager's graphical interface uses color-coded icons that visualize the status changes of the Token Rings. The product supports an event log, in both static and dynamic formats, that provides recommendations for problem resolution as well as additional information on any event that occurs. The event log is kept in the configuration database.

The graphical user interface (GUI) supports three view levels providing data on LAN topology. The GUI allows the user to select the most appropriate level of detail, depending upon the nature of the problem. The GUI dynamically displays LAN components and their relationships to enable ease in locating and resolving problems. These components include adapters, wiring connections, fiber optic connection, bridges, hubs, workstations, routers, and gateways.

LAN Network Manager collects performance data from all managed IBM 8209 bridges. However, there are some limitations to this function when Token Ring and Ethernet LANs are interconnected. LAN Network Manager can collect ring utilization and asset information from IBM's LAN Station Manager product when the appropriate agent software is installed on each LAN segment. Ring utilization data is provided without requiring any special hardware probe in the link.

The IBM 8230 Token Ring Network Controlled Access Unit (CAU) is an intelligent wiring hub that allows connection of up to 80 workstations, via pluggable lobe attachment modules (LAMs). This unit can identify and isolate a malfunctioning node, automatically recovering—traffic is rerouted to bypass the failed component, allowing the network to remain functional. Through LAN Network Manager, the 8230 can notify the mainframe NetView operator of the problem. Multiple CAUs may be managed by the same LAN Network Manager including local and remote locations. Remote Program Updates (RPUs) are supported by downline-loading new microcode when the CAU needs a version update.

The 8230's systems management capabilities permit automatic wrap/reconfiguration of failing ring segments, enabling/disabling lobes and LAMs, or the 8230 itself. The unit also supports IBM LAN Network Manager's configuration table providing the adapter address, 8230 number, LAN number, and lobe number, so a particular workstation can easily be located to provide maintenance or attention to a problem area.

IBM's LAN Station Manager provides asset management information for workstations and ring utilization data for each LAN segment. The LAN Station Manager console can be a DOS or an OS/2 workstation. Only one Station Manager is required per segment. LAN Station Manager uses the CMOL protocol to communicate with LAN Network Manager. In this scenario, LAN Station Manager acts as an agent for LAN Network Manager.

By using workstation data provided by LAN Station manager and combining this with attachment information from the 8230 CAU, LAN Network Manager can build a topology map that provides information on active and inactive network stations. IBM's LAN Management Utilities/2 (LMU/2), an application-level manager in the LAN environment—may co-reside with LAN Network Manager on a PC and provide complementary functions. However, the GUI and the databases of LMU/2 and LAN Network Manager are not integrated. LAN Station Manager does not have its own GUI, and the data it provides can only be displayed by the LAN Network Manager or by an MVS application such as NetView Performance Monitor or IBM's LAN Automated Operations (LANAO) that uses the mainframe NetView command/response facility to retrieve this data.

LAN Network Manager's GUI conforms' to IBM SystemView guidelines. LAN Network Manager can be a stand-alone manager for physical LAN management—in this case, it has an upper limit of 256 monitored bridged Token Ring segments. LAN Network Manager can also be managed by mainframe NetView. In this scenario, mainframe network can support over 100 variations of commands that are available with LAN Network Manager Version 1.1 or higher. The user can specify up to 1,000 critical resources to be monitored. If the user defines a resource as critical, then changes in the resource's status will be reported to the event log and displayed dynamically on the GUI at all applicable levels. The product currently manages both Token Ring and IBM PC networks.

LAN Network Manager Entry is a single-segment LAN manager. The need for its own GUI is eliminated because management is provided through mainframe NetView. LAN Network Manager Entry is beneficial for users with many remote single-segment LANs—examples include banks, retail marketing chains, and insurance companies.

Other products contributing to integrated LAN management include the LAN-to-LAN wide area network program, IBM 8309 LAN Bridge, which connects Token Ring and Ethernet, and the LAN asynchronous connection server. LAN Network Manager lets customers manage multi-segment Token Ring LANs, broadband and baseband PC networks, and—through the 8209 LAN Bridge—Ethernet segments. The application runs under OS/2 and uses both the presentation manager graphical user interface and relational database manager. Local management support is provided by LAN Station Managers.

Table 6-1 lists the available Token Ring management functions, their descriptions, and the location of the information source that supports the functions. Fault management plays a key role in managing token rings. Errors may be subdivided into hard and soft errors.

LAN Network Manager is still the best way to manage token ring LANs, 8230 CAUs, token ring adapters, and 8209 bridges. SNMP-based management is a better solution for monitoring routers, hubs, and Ethernet bridges. Since most internetworks require a combination of all those devices, two network manager stations are required. Solution alternatives include writing MIBs for token ring LANs and IBM bridges, redefining the station manager or writing integrative applications for LNM.

TABLE 6-1 Available Token Ring Management Functions

Function	Description	Located	Election
Active monitor	Monitor the local ring for missing tokens, duplicate tokens, streaming, etc.	All adapters	Token claiming
Ring error monitor	Collects and analyzes hard errors and soft errors sent by ring stations on a single ring.	Bridge 3174, 9370, AS/400 LAN Manager, 3270EM Lnmgl Ring diagn.	SW definition Addressing through functional address
Ring parameter server	Sends initialization info to new stations on the ring. Forwards registration info from new stations to the LAN manager.	Bridge	SW definition Addressing through functional address
Ring configuration server	Collects and forwards configuration reports generated by stations on the ring. Accepts commands from LAN manager to get info from stations, set parameters, and remove stations from the ring.	Bridge LAN manager	SW definition Addressing through functional address
LAN bridge server	Keeps statistical information about traffic across the bridge. Forwards this information to LAN manager.	Bridge	
Trace and performance	Traces some or all messages on the local ring and stores. Analyzes the stored trace. Measures performance statistics about traffic.	Specific adapter	Specific software
Station manager	Collects the data from a name server. Sends statistics to manager.	PC or PS/2	Software program
Controlled access unit	Controls access to the ring. Acts as name server to stations. Controls IAU to IAU link.	Access unit	Software defined
LAN manager	Collects the data from different servers. Analyzes it and takes management actions.	PC or PS/2	Software program
NetView (SNA control point)	Collects data being from either LAN manager, some REM stations, or applications (alerts).	SNA host	Software program

Figure 6.3 shows a simplified overview of IBM LAN Network Manager and its managed objects. In most cases, it is more beneficial to connect the management station directly to the CAU instead of to the non-manageable 8228 hub.

IBM's future plans include adding management capabilities that do not rely on proprietary Token Ring-architected management solutions, but rather exploit Heterogeneous LAN Management (HLM) capabilities.

As an alternative, customers may wish to implement Sterling's Solve: Automation product (formerly Systems Center's Net/Master) instead of mainframe NetView as a host product. In terms of integration and management of LANs, however, with the exception of RODM, there are no architectural differences between

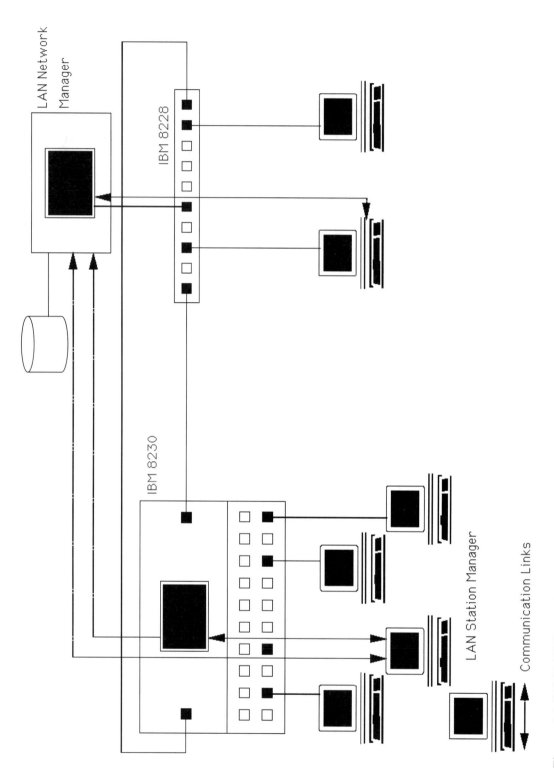

Figure 6.3 IBM LAN Network Manager

IBM's mainframe NetView and Sterling's product. A detailed comparison of mainframe NetView and Net/Master may be found in Terplan. (Terplan 1992)

To support Solve:Automation with LAN-based NMVTs, Sterling offers Solve: LAN for OS/2. This product supports both IBM's and Microsoft's OS/2 operating systems. It is able to monitor a range of LAN alerts and send them to NEWS of Solve: Automation or to mainframe NetView's Hardware Monitor. Also, control commands are supported from the mainframe console. This facility can be used to configure, monitor, add, or delete network adapters from the LAN automatically, if required.

6.1.3   AIX NetView/6000

AIX NetView/6000 is a management tool for heterogeneous devices on Transmission Control Protocol/Internet Protocol (TCP/IP) networks. AIX NetView/6000 provides configuration, fault, and performance management functions, plus many features that make AIX NetView/6000 easy to install and use. For cooperative management of TCP/IP networks, AIX NetView/6000 uses the AIX Service Point program to communicate with mainframe NetView. Digital Equipment Corp. has licensed NetView/6000 and ported it to the Alpha AXP environment. This product is called Polycenter Manager for NetView. (For more information on NetView/6000 and Polycenter Manager for NetView, see Chapter 4.)

AIX NetView/6000 emphasizes the following functions:

- IP Monitoring and SNMP Management: AIX NetView/6000 monitors all IP addressable devices and manages TCP/IP devices that include a Simple Network Management Protocol (SNMP) agent.
- NetView Connectivity: For cooperative management of TCP/IP networks, AIX NetView/6000 uses the AIX Service Point program to exchange information with mainframe NetView. To communicate with mainframe NetView, AIX NetView/6000 filters the SNMP traps received from TCP/IP networks and converts them, on a user-selectable basis, to SNA alerts and sends them to mainframe NetView. This connection also allows to use mainframe NetView automation facilities to invoke shell scripts or to send SNMP network management commands for monitoring and managing the internet environment. NetView Multi System Manager (MSS) also supports TCP/IP connectivity.
- Dynamic Device Discovery: AIX NetView/6000 supports dynamic discovery of the TCP/IP network. In addition, AIX NetView/6000 allows users to choose how much of the network will be managed. To dynamically discover and display changes in the network, the automatic layout feature discovers nodes which are added or removed from the network, automatically changes the topology database, and it updates the network map.
- Graphical User Interface: The graphical user interface, based on OSF/Motif standards, enables the user to monitor the dynamic views of the internet networks. If more information about a particular element is needed, additional windows can be brought up to show specific information about that network element. The map contains color-coded icons that show the status of the various network elements. AIX NetView/6000 updates the status of these icons at

intervals selected by the user. In order to add, move, change, and delete objects from the appropriate views of the map, powerful editing features are supported.

- Network Configuration, Fault, and Performance Management: AIX NetView/ 6000's configuration, fault, and performance management functions can be accessed through the menu bar or by the mouse. Configuration management functions include editing the map and specifying how often the map will be updated. Fault management functions include running protocol tests to diagnose problems with remote devices and customizing the actions taken when an SNMP trap is received. Performance management functions include setting and checking thresholds, monitoring network statistics, and displaying the statistics in line graph format.

- Management Information Base (MIB) Management Tools: AIX NetView/6000 provides a set of MIB management tools to help manage the network. Both standard and vendor-specific MIB objects are supported, and applications can be developed to manage the MIB information.

- Online Information: The graphical user interface provides access to AIX Net-View/6000's online information. The AIX NetView/6000 Administration Reference and the AIX Operating System library can be accessed through InfoExplorer, the online library feature of the RISC System/6000. The hypertext format enables the user to quickly find information in the AIX NetView/ 6000 library, the AIX Operating System library, and any other library that is available on the system. An online help facility provides information about using the product. Reference information about AIX NetView/6000 commands, daemons, and files is also provided as managers.

- Easy Installation and Maintenance: The RISC System/6000 System Management Interface Tool (SMIT) may be used to install, configure, control, and maintain AIX NetView/6000. SMIT prompts for the required information. AIX NetView/6000 may be installed in approximately 15 minutes by using SMIT.

Figure 6.4 shows the types of resources typically managed by AIX NetView/ 6000.

6.1.4   LAN NetView

LAN NetView comprises a suite of software products that let LAN users distribute software as well as monitor and control network devices, operating systems, and applications while sharing information with other IBM and non-IBM management systems. It is compliant with DME from OSF and also supports OS/2, DOS, Windows, and Macintosh clients. LAN NetView is capable of supporting both CMIP and SNMP protocols.

LAN NetView has three layers. At the base is the infrastructure that provides the means to manage the LAN. Management applications written to LAN Net-View fall in the middle layer, and at the highest layer, the system administration interface is found. The managing system is expected to run at the beginning on OS/2. Figure 6.5 shows a typical example of resources managed by LAN Net-View.

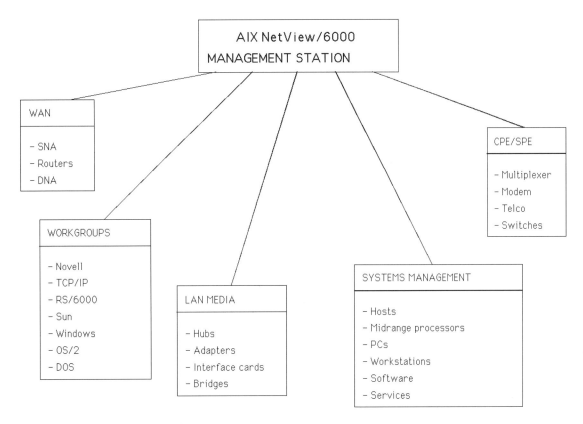

Figure 6.4 IBM AIX NetView/6000

LAN Netview consists of the following key components:

- LAN NetView Manager
- LAN NetView Enabler
- LAN NetView Agents

LAN NetView Manager supports the graphical user interface, and it forms the nucleus of the product. LAN NetView Manage conforms to IBM's SystemView and Systems Application Architecture (SAA). Currently the component supports the following tasks:

- Asset management
- Configuration management
- Logical views of components and connections
- Communications with other components over standardized interfaces

In addition to supporting single LANs, LAN NetView Manage supports remote LANs connected over WANs. The protocols supported include SNMP and CMIP for communications with agents, XMP for communications between management, and CMOT and CMOL for certain OS/2-based communications.

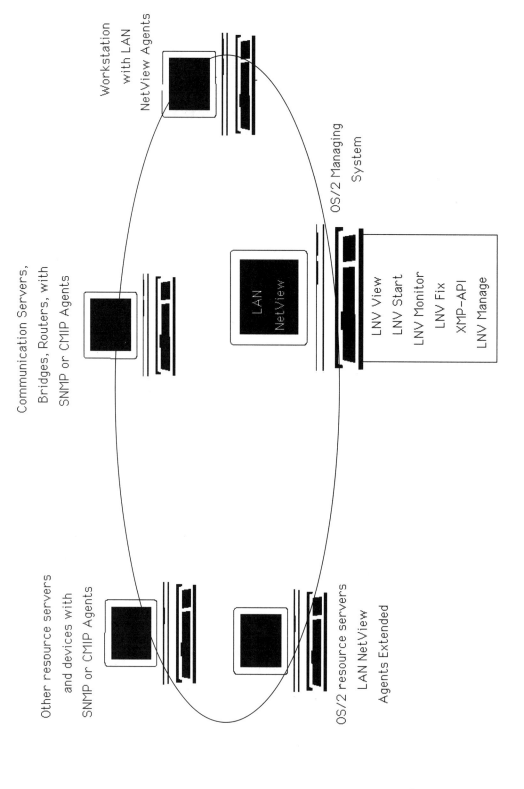

Figure 6.5 IBM LAN NetView for Systems Management

The second component of LAN NetView, LAN NetView Enabler, is the management agent for OS/2-2.X clients. LAN NetView Agents support DOS and Windows clients. The Extended version of the Enabler is designed to manage servers such as IBM LAN Server, DB/2-OS/2 Extended Services-Database Server, and Communication Manager/2.

In addition to supporting basic services such as topology, discovery, event management, LAN NetView Manager also supports several value-added management applications. These include LAN NetView Monitor, LAN NetView Fix, and LAN NetView Tie.

LAN NetView Monitor collects status and performance information, and supervises thresholds. LAN NetView Monitor provides graphics displays, but does not provided extensive diagnostics.

LAN NetView Fix supports troubleshooting by interpreting, correlating, and collapsing events and alarms.

LAN NetView Tie enables bidirectional connections to mainframe NetView. This connection is intended to support large corporations that want to keep mainframe NetView to professionally supervise and manage large distributed LANs and many distributed systems.

6.2 APPLICATIONS FOR THE PRINCIPAL PRODUCT FAMILIES

IBM and third parties are currently writing additional applications for the members of the management family. With the exception of LAN NetView, customers have many opportunities to find the right mix of management applications.

6.2.1 Mainframe NetView Applications

For the past few years, IBM has taken the initiative to introduce a number of new applications for mainframe NetView that offer enhanced automation and integration. These applications include Automated Network Operator (ANO/MVS) and LAN Automated Option (LAN AO), LANRES, OAC/MVS, AOExpoert/MVS, Multisystem Manager, EPDM and Desk/2 for NPM.

In addition, several third parties have developed new applications for mainframe NetView that add significant improvements to host-based SNA management facilities.

6.2.1.1 Automated Network Operator (ANO)

ANO helps automate responses to a large number of VTAM messages. LAN AO expands these capabilities by accepting messages from Token Ring networks via LAN Network Manager.

6.2.1.2 LAN Automated Option (LAN AO)

LAN AO is a mainframe package that lets network managers monitor the physical components of multiple token ring LANs from a centrally located NetView console. LAN AO runs with IBM's Automated Network Operations (ANO), a Net-View program that automates VTAM and MVS operations. It is intended to link LAN AO to LAN Management Utilties/2 (LMU/2), a set of applications that collects information on OS/2 activities.

6.2.1.3   Forthcoming Applications

IBM and other third parties are currently working together to develop new applications that will let users dynamically manage Novell-LANs, AS/400 mini-computers, and LAN NetView. These applications will use new dynamic topology management technology that visualizes topology problems and changes in real-time. The applications will run under the Graphic Monitor Facility, an OS/2-based presentation interface that displays network topologies in a graphical format. In particular, NetView MultiSystem Manager may gain attention from IBM customers for allowing mainframe NetView to manage Novell Networks.

NetView MultiSystem Manager allows an enterprise to combine centralized control through mainframe NetView distributed computing in the LAN environment. This includes supporting facilities management of LAN media and Net-Ware resources on the same enterprise-management console.

NetView MultiSystem Manager dynamically discovers and stores NetWare LAN resource configuration and status data in RODM. The product includes a facility called ACCESS that allows user-written REXX-based applications to interface to RODM. ACCESS supports three packaged utilities, including the following:

- BLDVIEWS, that allows users to build customized views
- A correlation utility that supports physical/logical correlation for NetWare resources and those resources managed by LAN Network Manager
- A task management utility that supports dynamic discovery and monitoring of mainframe NetView tasks and applications

In addition, NetView MultiSystem Manager includes a utility supported command access to the NetWare topology agent from NetWare servers.

6.2.1.4   Applications for Tuning SNA/APPN
Network Performance

To help users increase efficiency of SNA and APPN networks, IBM now offers two products for optimizing NCP: NTuneMON and NTuneNCP. NTuneMON gives users the capability to monitor in real-time major NCP activity, such as line utilization, buffer pool usage and data communication flows. NTuneNCP lets SNA users tune SNA networks without having to take NCP down.

NTuneMON improves the user interface of NetView Performance Monitor (NPM). NPM is a VTAM application that collects SNA and Token Ring data by using VTAM in the host and the Network Control Program in the front-end-processors as information source. Using NPM, various indicators can be monitored, displayed, optimized, and reported. The improvements include an increased number of monitored indicators, such as VTAM-buffers, links between devices, fluctuation of traffic flow, autodiscovery of the configuration, and a new presentation service. Users are able to monitor the networks from a OS/2 Presentation Manager-based graphical monitor communicating with the mainframe via an LU 6.2 connection.

6.2.1.5   Enterprise Performance Data Manager/MVS

IBM has recently released the Enterprise Performance Data Manager/MVS (EPDM) application for collecting and reporting performance data on SNA, CICS, IMS, and other resources and stores it in a DB/2-database.

Under the SystemView umbrella, EPDM replaces IBM's older Service Level Reporter (SLR) product. Like SLR, EPDM collects network-related data from NPM, NetView Hardware Monitor, Network Control Program, VTAM, and from LAN Network Manager (LNM). However, EPDM has improvements such as links to a new IBM application called Reporting Dialog/2. Using a OS/2-based system and Reporting Dialog/2, data may be queried and reported interactively.

6.2.1.6   LANRES

To offer more capabilities to Novell users, IBM has designed and implemented the LAN Resource Extension and Services (LANRES) Series. This product family provides software for IBM PS/2 Micro Channel Servers running under Novell's NetWare Operating System and software for IBM VM and MVS hosts. By means of LANRES, Novell servers can use mainframe resources for printing and for backup. Also, LAN administration tasks may be supported by the product. LANRES fits into the mainframe NetView Multisystem Manager program. This program enables users to manage NetWare and other types of local area networks from mainframe NetView.

6.2.1.7   Third-party Applications for Mainframe NetView

There are several new applications for mainframe NetView now offered by third-party developers. These include EView from NetTech, Inc., Network Performance Powerpack from Blueline, and Net/Overview from Enterprise Systems Software.

Increased NetView operator productivity with decreased operating costs is the goal of the EView family of NetView management tools from NetTech. EView products automate responses to network alerts and eliminate duplicate alarms to achieve significant operating performance improvements.

EView Entry provides all the necessary services, interfaces and automation features for the other members of the EView product family. The interfaces include connections to IBM's Info/Man problem management database, NET-CENTER graphical user interface, and to NetView's Graphics Monitor Facility. EView Entry allows users write commands that mainframe NetView can run automatically. It also contains a NetTech database for storing these commands. Other members of the family are:

- Network Resource Manager: for defining and monitoring critical resources allowing operators to concentrate on particular areas or on individual resources.

- Problem Manager Interface: for filtering duplicate, typical or related messages from the NetView stream. Thus, filtered problems are forwarded to Info/Man.

- Focal Point Manager: Tool to monitor and manage multiple NetView managers from one location supporting maintained remote operations.

- Job/Task Monitors: Tool to monitor and report status of all EView instruments to the NetView operator.

NetTech is now enhancing the EView product family to support dynamic correlation of logical and physical SNA resources. The new products will support SNA management with or without mainframe NetView. Figure 6.6 depicts this new architecture.

Another application, called OpenSNA from Peregrine Systems, can automatically gather and correlate data such as token ring device names and locations and present this data on SNMP-based network management platforms. This technology helps users and vendors build applications to keep records on network topology and to track network resources such as hubs, routers, and personal computers automatically. It could also become the underlying technology for software distribution or trouble-ticketing applications.

After initialization, the application automatically gathers SNA logical units and Exchange Station Identification (XID) data—which verifies the identity of SNA nodes—from SNA mainframes. It also collects hub and router names, port information and the adapter addresses from all devices linked to them. The data is then used to build a database of information containing SNA names, XIDs, physical addresses, hub and router names, and port numbers. The data is maintained in a relational database, and may be connected with several network management platforms, such as Star*Sentry (ATT/NCR), OpenView (HP), SunNet Manager, and AIX NetView/6000 (IBM). Not only configuration data, but also commands, VTAM messages and alerts may be received from the host-agent, residing in various host platforms. The management platform is connected via LU6.2 with the host platform. Arriving messages maybe correlated with SNMP traps and polling-replies, and using an extensible proxy agent, also with messages from nonstandard devices.

The Vital Signs family of products from BlueLine Software provides performance monitoring for VTAM, VM, VM/ESA, CICS, and VSE. Vital Signs helps mainframe specialists track and troubleshoot network performance problems before they interrupt operations. From a single console, multiple VTAMs may be supervised. The monitoring software resides on the mainframe and can detect problems by continuously monitoring key indicators, such as buffers, performance thresholds, and service parameters. When thresholds are reached, an alert is generated, stored, and can be passed on to the operator console. Users can react to the problem immediately or use the information in the database for historical reports.

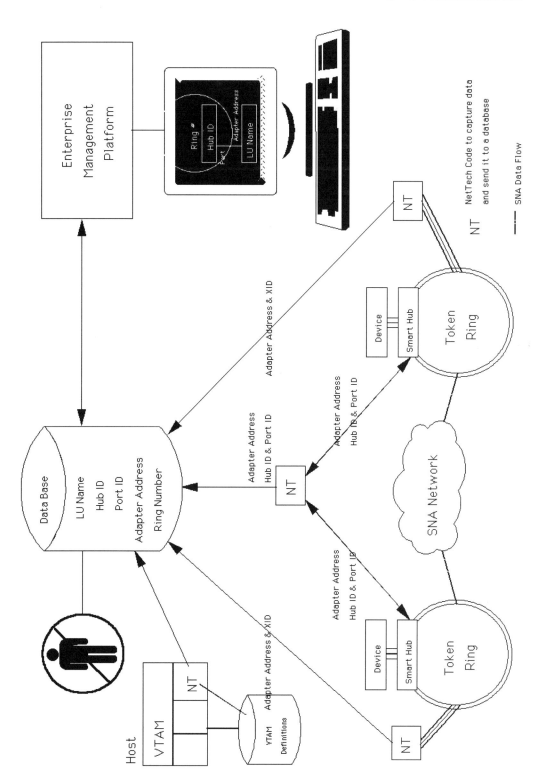

Figure 6.6 Dynamic correlation of logical and physical SNA resources

Net/Overview from Enterprise Systems Software offers extensions to NetView to support end-to-end management and real-time views of SNA sessions, links and devices. The application resides alongside NetView on the mainframe, monitoring SNA traffic coming through VTAM and NetView hardware monitor. Net/Overview supports a dynamic graphical map and status supervision of principal SNA resources, such as physical and logical units. This product is considered a useful extension to NetView.

6.2.2   Applications for LAN Management

In many organizations, most applications are distributed between the LANs and mainframe NetView. Applications for LAN management from third parties include Vital Signs for LANs from BlueLine Software, Network Control Series from Network General, Legent NetSpy and LANSpy, and AlertView from Shany.

BlueLine's Vital Signs for LANs enables centralized management of distributed client/server environments. The product gathers data about application performance on multi-protocol LANs, connected to SNA networks. It is very useful for organizations that are distributing mainframe applications to LANs while keeping management at a central location (Figure 6.7). The product runs as an agent on a workstation running Windows that is attached to Ethernet or Token Ring LANs. LAN performance data is forwarded to Vital Signs for VTAM on the mainframe; the connection is accomplished by an LU-to-LU session. Vital Signs for LANs collects information on response time, configuration data, workstation traffic, segment statistics, login/logout history, and errors. Network specialists can use the data to identify LAN bottlenecks, conduct capacity planning and isolate problems before they impact other users. NetView operators can send NetWare commands directly to the appropriate LAN destination. To a limited degree, data can also be collected on interconnecting devices. Protocols supported include IPX, TCP/IP, NetBios, AppleTalk, Banyan Vines, and others. The product fills the gap between SNMP-based solutions, protocol analyzers, and host monitors.

Legent Corp. offers two products, NetSpy and LANSpy which, in combination, and provide service-level control up to the end user of SNA networks. LANSpy resides on a single personal computer on each LAN segment. It collects LAN performance information such as response time (local and remote), client and server utilization, control-layer traffic, elapsed time from request to reply, inbound/outbound queue length, and sends them to NetSpy residing on the central mainframe. From NetSpy, users can set performance thresholds for LANSpy for any of the parameters. When a threshold is exceeded, LANSpy sends an alert to NetSpy that may be displayed in real time along with host alerts.

Network General's Network Control Series consist of two parts; Foundation Manager and Cornerstone Agent. Both components reside on OS/2-based personal computers. Foundation Manager functions as a concentrator that monitors and analyzes LAN traffic from up to 256 Token Ring or Ethernet LANs. Cornerstone agent runs on PCs attached to remote LANs and can pass performance data to Foundation Manager. The Network Control Series uses LAN Network Manager as broker to communicate information to mainframe NetView; informa-

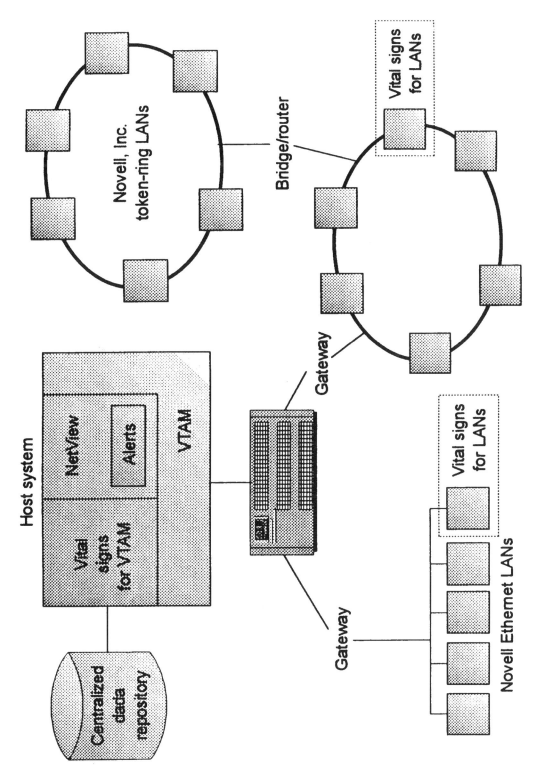

Figure 6.7 Blueline Software Vital signs for LANs

tion is in the format of NMVT messages. This combination of products lets Net-View users monitor LAN network utilization, frames received, total errors, and other LAN performance statistics. Foundation Manager alerts sent to NetView may also contain recommendations for actions. Locally, Network Control Series users can more efficiently gather data on LAN performance via a new Solution Bar GUI. Another valuable feature is the use of out-of-band channel for the exchange of information. The vendor also offers portable versions of the components. This allows the integration with leading network management platforms.

AlertView from Shany, Inc. helps to isolate and eliminate problems in various networks running under various network operating systems. It provides the users with real-time solutions to LAN application problems and report information to mainframe NetView. The tasks are subdivided into four major categories:

- Fault prevention—automated execution of LAN housekeeping tasks, the preventive analysis of application problems, the supervision of scheduled procedures and backup tasks, and the protection against network infection by viruses.
- Reporting—the AlertView agent transmits an alert containing comprehensive, detailed information about each event as it occurs, distributes the report to any location, and ensures that the manager receives complete, detailed reports on the application, files, servers, print queues, and on other indicators.
- Corrections—automatically eliminates recurring problems by analyzing the existing alerts to determine the appropriate corrective procedure for each event, with the initiation of corrective actions in the background, and with the support of remotely accessing devices and applications.

AlertView has been enhanced to provide support for troubleshooting non-IBM bridges, routers, applications, and operating systems from Novell, Microsoft, Digital, Hewlett-Packard, and Artisoft. As platforms IBM mainframe NetView, Novell-NMS, and also SNMP managers are supported. However, AlertView provides the strongest support for IBM operating systems, services, platforms, and protocols.

6.2.3   Applications for AIX NetView/6000

The base AIX NetView/6000 platform provides configuration, fault and performance management. For more information on these basic platform services, see Chapter 4. IBM and third-party applications provide AIX NetView/6000 with the additional functionality needed to manage all types of components an processes in the enterprise network. The following sections describe these important applications.

6.2.3.1   Systems Monitor/6000

Systems Monitor/6000 supports management of IBM RISC System/6000 and HP workstations from the NetView/6000 console. In the near future, IBM plans to enhance Systems Monitor/6000 by adding support for managing other systems such as Sun and OS/2.

The IBM Systems Monitor is a smart agent that provides two important functions:

1. It allows the SNMP management functions to be distributed into the network; and
2. It provides user-configurable systems management capabilities for the critical workstation resources in your network. Systems Monitor/6000 extends the enterprise-specific MIBs on the workstations on which it operates so that hundreds of systems management attributes can easily be managed, including: system configuration, file system status, CPU utilization, disk usage, and user information. Systems Monitor/6000 can also be extended to meet specific customer requirements such as monitoring of critical applications.

As a distributed SNMP manager, Systems Monitor/6000 can be used to monitor a customer-defined set of SNMP devices on a network thus off-loading this responsibility from the network management platform and freeing the platform to manage larger, more complex networks. Systems Monitor/6000 uses sophisticated filtering, thresholding, automation, and analysis to insure that only the most crucial information is forwarded to the SNMP manager.

The product currently runs on IBM AIX. IBM plans to add support for other platforms, such as Digital OSF/1 and Sun Solaris. AIX NetView/6000 is supported by the Ingres relational database, but other databases, including Sybase, Oracle, Informix, and DB2/6000 are expected to be supported in future releases as well.

6.2.3.2   Trouble Ticket/6000

IBM's Trouble Ticket/6000 application supports problem management, trouble ticketing, system inventory, and notification. The product was originally developed by Networx, Inc. (now acquired by Legent).

The Trouble Ticket/6000 application allows users to designate which events received by NetView/6000 should automatically open up a problem record or "incident." The operator also defines all notifications and escalation rules use in problem management.

Trouble Ticket/6000 supports problem management from fault detection to problem resolution, and it supports the ability to help circumvent problems before they occur. The system inventory capability provides detailed information on network devices, software applications, and external services supporting network operations.

Trouble Ticket/6000 tracks the problem history of each device connected to the network, each software program installed on the network, and each service used by the network. This provides users with access to information that can help the network run more efficiently.

6.2.3.3   Hub Management Program/6000

This application displays an expanded view of IBM 8250 hubs including realistic graphics of various hub components. The status of each component is indicated by color.

Hub Management Program/6000 allows operators to assign individual ports or modules to a LAN and to isolate any module from the backplane for trouble-shooting purposes. The product automatically discovers IBM 8250 hubs and their installed modules and forwards this information to NetView/6000. In this way, the application leverages the operating environment of NetView/6000. It also provides network security by preventing unauthorized users from accessing the network. Hub Management Program/6000 can also be used to manage Chipcom ONline System Concentrator hubs.

6.2.3.4   AIX NetView Service Point

AIX NetView Service Point allows AIX systems to exchange network management data with mainframe NetView. AIX Service Point operates in a screenless environment on an RS/6000 or Sun workstation, acting as a gateway to mainframe NetView.

AIX NetView Service Point uses LU6.2 for efficient communications of alerts to mainframe NetView, as well as execution of mainframe NetView commands. The product supports shared libraries, allowing Service Point applications to dynamically link with the Service Point. Thus, applications developers no longer need to coordinate service point modifications with application modifications.

AIX NetView Service Point also reduces network broadcast traffic by allowing remote applications to specify which service point to access.

6.2.3.5   LAN Manager Utilities/6000

LAN Management Utilities/6000 (LMU/6000) is an application for IBM AIX Net-View/6000 that allows users to manage LMU-managed LANs from the NetView/6000 console. LMU/6000 merges and correlates the LMU-managed network topology into NetView/6000. The application adds flexibility to an organization's management structure—for example, users can manage LAN segments locally during normal business hours and switch to a centralized management from the NetView/6000 console nightly and on weekends. LMU/6000 conforms to IBM's SystemView architecture. It can run on IBM and Novell NetWare LANs supporting OS/2, DOS, Windows, and Apple Macintosh user workstations.

6.2.3.6   SNA Manager/6000

SNA Manager/6000 is a new application for managing SNA networks from the NetView/6000 platform. The product requires mainframe NetView to be installed on the mainframe. It also requires AIX SNA Services/6000 or AIX SNAserver/6000, AIX DCE Base Services/6000, or AIX DCE Threads. The product does not work with Sterling Solve: Automation.

SNA Manager/6000 supports automatic discovery of SNA nodes. Physical topology is maintained in mainframe NetView's Graphic Monitor Facility (GMF). The mainframe NetView View Preprocessor updates the SNA physical topology per user specifications. SNA Manager/6000 loads the SNA physical information into NetView/6000's General Topology Manager. Status changes are communicated to SNA Manager/6000 automatically; SNA logical units (LUs) are dynamically discovered through mainframe NetView every time an LU view is requested from the SNA Manager/6000 application. The product can communicate to IBM mainframe NetView using LU6.2. SNA Manager/6000 can use either IBM AIX SNA Services/6000 or SNA Server/6000 to provide LU6.2 communications.

SNA Manager/6000 can be used to send commands from NetView/6000 directly to VTAM and/or to mainframe NetView. The NetView/6000 operator can send any mainframe NetView command or VTAM command, as well as any host operating system command to MVS systems such as a JES command or customized command. A pop-up Command response window is provided for line messages with mainframe NetView V2R4; a pull down menu is available for generic commands such as activate, inactivate, and recycle. SNA Manager/6000 also supports security features that are consistent with mainframe NetView's span and scope security.

6.2.3.7   AIX RMONster/6000 and RMON Agent/2

These applications are based on the SNMP Remote Monitoring (RMON) MIB. RMON lets network operators remotely monitor network segments and then report errors or potential problems to an SNMP-based network management platform, such as NetView/6000.

These applications can monitor all nine groups of data specified in the RMON standard. (For more information on RMON, see Chapter 3.) RMONster/6000 runs on AIX NetView/6000, monitoring network performance gathered from any RMON-compliant agent attached to a Token Ring or Ethernet LAN. Functions of RMONster/6000 include processing statistical thresholds, collecting historical data, displaying real-time LAN status, and consolidating data from multiple RMON agents. The application also allows export of data to other applications for the purpose of compiling reports.

RMONsterAgent/2 is an RMON agent that runs on any OS/2 workstation. Data can be captured and displayed on the RMONitor Agent/2 workstation.

6.2.3.8   Third-Party Applications for NetView/6000

There are over 30 third-party applications currently shipping for NetView/6000 (Faulkner, 1994). These applications provide a wide range of functions. (Many of these applications are discussed in detail in Chapter 5.)

IBM's NetView Association is encouraging third parties to develop more applications for added functionality. NetView/6000 had a late start in garnering third-party support in comparison with HP OpenView and SunNet Manager, since these competing products were on the market about two years before IBM. However, the growth of third-party applications for NetView/6000 has been healthy to date.

The joint participation of both IBM and Digital in the NetView Association will have a positive effect on increasing third-party support for NetView/6000 and Digital's Polycenter Manager on NetView. Although the number of third-party applications shipping on Polycenter Manager on NetView numbered in the single digits as of June 1994, the outlook is expected to improve substantially in 1995 as industry acceptance of Polycenter Manager becomes more widespread. (For more information on Polycenter Manager, see section 4.3.11.)

Perhaps the most interesting new area of NetView/6000 applications development has been the appearance of SNA management applications that use an SNMP framework.

Until recently, SNA and TCP/IP networks were managed with separate tools and frameworks. This is still true in most organizations, although new forces may blur this distinction during the next two years. While most large companies still rely heavily on their older SNA networks, more are moving toward distributed IP networks. IBM has responded to market pressures, and to the growing prevalence of TCP/IP technology, by incorporating SNMP functions into more of its devices; likewise, the vendor is putting more powerful programmatic interfaces into mainframe NetView, allowing greater interactions with the mainframe NetView subsystem from external applications. These developments signal the intrusion of SNMP-based systems into IBM's previously SNA-centric management framework.

In late 1992, Peregrine Systems introduced an SNMP-based alternative for SNA network management called OpenSNA. Basically, OpenSNA is an application that allows management of the SNA environment from Hewlett-Packard's HP OpenView, an SNMP management platform. OpenSNA does not require mainframe NetView nor Solve:Automation since it obtains SNA information directly from the VTAM primary program operator (PPO) interface. As a vendor, Peregrine Systems possesses considerable expertise in the IBM SNA environment; its flagship product, the Peregrine Network Management System (PNMS), has been a strong offering in the mainframe-based change management and help desk arena, outshining its competitors since its introduction. OpenSNA was Peregrine's first major foray into the UNIX-based SNMP management market.

Another impressive new SNA application is Cabletron's BlueVision, which was primarily developed by a start-up firm called NetTech. NetTech's key founders were ex-IBM developers and managers with extensive SNA networking expertise. In less than two years, NetTech has put together a suite of applications for automating mainframe NetView operations as well as the BlueVision product which allows peer-to-peer communications between Cabletron's Spectrum management platform and IBM mainframe NetView. NetTech is currently working on a version of BlueVision which does not require mainframe NetView.

Despite the cumbersomeness and expense associated with mainframe NetView and Solve:Automation, it is unlikely that many customers will abandon these products in the near future. Rather, most customers attracted to SNMP-based SNA management applications will look to unload some, but not all, of mainframe NetView's processing onto the SNMP applications to free up expensive mainframe CPU cycles for other uses. This is exactly the functionality that NetTech (and Cabletron) plan to deliver in the next release of BlueVision, due out in late 1994.

Alcatel Bell ITS in Belgium has just introduced a new SNA management application called SNA-Expert that runs on SunConnect's SunNet Manager. As with the other applications just mentioned, SNA-Expert supports display of SNA and TCP/IP topology from the SNMP management console. SNA-Expert is but one component of Alcatel Bell's larger offering, NM-Expert.

Perhaps the most interesting new tool in the market space is a product called Net/Impact from a small company known as Strategic Solutions International. Net/Impact not only provides SNA device status, but it also provides an analysis of the impact that a device failure has on SNA user sessions. Products like Open-SNA and SNA Manager/6000 are essentially device-specific, in that they portray status of each individual device on the screen, whether that device is an SNA component or a TCP/IP device. While helpful, that type of device-specific approach can lead to a fragmented approach to problem isolation and repair. It requires either entering a lot of rules for rules-based automation (triggering scripts for handling specific device problems) or relying heavily on network help desk staff and operators to correlate and consolidate the vast amount of messages and alerts produced by separate SNMP and SNA management tools.

Net/Impact, on the other hand, includes an Analysis Engine that provides analysis of the impact of network failures on active sessions; this can assist operations staff in setting priorities for handling problems based on the number (or type) of affected network users.

While mainframe NetView can provide some degree of alert correlation and automated handling, the IBM SNA/6000 requires mainframe NetView's Graphic Management Facility, a product that may incur high overhead. Customers are becoming increasingly sensitive to unnecessary overhead, particularly on the mainframe, and that low-overhead solutions like Net/Impact are likely to become popular soon. Right now, IBM is not providing low-overhead distributed SNA network management applications that can communicate with SNMP-based and CMIP-based platforms. However, IBM's introduction of NetView MultiSystem Manager is a step in the right direction, as it provides automatic correlation of logical and physical resources—including adapters, Novell servers, and IP resources.

6.2.3.9 Integration Between AIX NetView/6000 and Applications

The level of integration between the NetView/6000 platform and applications ranges from a minimum level where an application is merely launched from Net-View/6000 to total integration of the application through the NetView/6000 Generic Topology Manager and APIs. The following listing explains the various levels of integration and examples of NetView Associate members that provide that level of integration. (See Table 6-2.)

- End User Interface(EUI)—Launch Level: All members of the NetView Association are required to provide EUI support as the minimum level of integration for their applications. This level includes integration at the menu bar, control desk, tool palette, object menu, and help files.
- End User Interface (Advanced-EUI API): Applications that are integrated at this level make use of the following NetView/6000 facilities:
    events
    dialog boxes

TABLE 6-2 Types of Integration Supported by NetView/6000 and Various Applications

Product	Types of Integration				
	User Interface Launch Level	Advanced User Interface API	Database	Protocol Access SNMP CMIS XMP	Enterprise-Specific Integration
All products of NetView Associates	✔			✔	
Diederich & Associates		✔	✔	✔	
Ki Research		✔	✔	✔	
Evolving Systems		✔	✔	✔	
SNA/6000		✔	✔	✔	
LAN Management Utilities/6000		✔	✔	✔	
Trouble Ticket/6000			✔	✔	
Optical Data Systems			✔	✔	
Network Application Technology			✔	✔	
SynOptics			✔	✔	
Elegant				✔	✔
IBM Systems Monitor				✔	✔
IBM 8250 Hub Manager				✔	✔

    addition of symbols
    add submaps

NetView/6000 Association members supporting this level of integration include:

- Diederich and Associates (Expert Systems)
- Ki Research (DECNET)
- Evolving Systems (Voice Telco)

IBM has several products under development that make full use of the Generic Topology Manager (GTM) and APIs provided by NetView/6000, including:

- LAN Network Manager/6000
- SNA Manager/6000
- LAN Management Utilities/6000

LAN Manager Utilities/6000 is currently shipping; the other products are currently in controlled customer release.

Database Integration: Various levels of integration with the NetView/6000 database are supported, including the following:

- Extract: some applications such as IBM Trouble Ticket/6000 and Accugraph's MountainView physical plant management application extract data from the NetView/6000 database and use it in the application.
- Store information: applications that store data in the NetView/6000 database and create their own objects in the NetView/6000 database include: Diederich,

Ki Research, Evolving Systems, and the IBM applications mentioned above (SNA/6000, LMN/6000, and LMU/6000).
- Add information: other applications just add information into the IBM database of objects that NetView/6000 discovered. These include: Optical Data Systems, Network Application Technology, and SynOptics.
- Enterprise-specific integration: includes items such as:

> configuring trap information
> configuring alert information
> Enterprise specific MIBs
> System error logging

Application vendors that provide event/trap support by either sending or receiving events from NetView/6000 include: Elegant, Evolving Systems, IBM Systems Monitor and the IBM 8250 Hub Management Program.

Several options for application-to-application integration are available. The applications may choose to send events to NetView/6000, or they may register to receive events making use of the filtering and thresholding APIs. In addition, applications may store and access each other's data through the NetView/6000 database. Many applications are integrated at the End User Interface where they take advantage of the EUI API so that the application can be seamlessly integrated with NetView/6000. Via this interface, applications are given the ability to interactively modify information, such as changing a color of a node to modify its status or displaying a graph, specific to the application that is displayed on the NetView/6000 EUI. Applications may also make use of the generic topology manager, here various managers that collect protocol specific topology in the network can send this data in an architected format to NetView/6000 which consolidates and correlates the topology data for display at the EUI. This "open" topology capability is critical to meet customers' requirement for managing heterogeneous networks from a single management platform. Table 6-2 summarizes the depth of application integration.

6.2.4   Applications for LAN NetView

LAN NetView provides a single, integrated view of LAN systems. It supports centralized and/or distributed management, viewing of clients, servers, network devices at a centrally located display, local and remote administration, and integration of IBM and third-party applications under a single user interface. Standard protocols and APIs, such as XMP and SOM are supported as well.

A number of third parties offer applications for LAN NetView, and many more products are in development. Vendors currently shipping applications for LAN NetView include: Central Point Software (LANlord), Novell (NetWare clients), Gradient, ProTools division of Network General, Computer Associates, BGS Systems (Best/1 Visualizer), Dolphin (Ethernet and Token Ring analyzer), Heterosoft (ManageWare), Legato (Networker), Farallon Computer (MASS/2), and Strategic Solutions (Service Point/32, providing REXX-based automated alerts).

The following section discusses one of these applications, Central Point Software LANlord, in detail.

Central Point Software's LANlord product (originally developed by Microcom) for LAN NetView extended LANlord's desktop systems management capabilities for enterprise PC-based LANs to include OS/2 client workstations and to support management of LAN Server and NetWare LANs, through integration with IBM's LAN NetView manager platform and IBM's DOS, Windows, and OS/2 agents.

LANlord for LAN NetView uses the same basic architecture as LANlord server/manager/agent, but utilizes LAN NetView support services for integration. It uses IBM Manager, View, and agents, respectively. In addition to multiple management workstations, LANlord for LAN NetView supports use of multiple managed servers.

All LANlord applications can be accessed from a management workstation running under the OS/2 Presentation Manager-based view environment. This ensures a centralized control facility from which an entire network and its resources can be managed. Using LANlord, the following multiple, integrated desktop management applications may be supported:

- Automatic inventory
- Remote management and control
- Network and PC monitoring
- Software metering
- Reporting and data export

6.2.5   AS/400 and RS/6000 Distributed Management Applications

IBM offers four software packages for automating the operations of IBM AS/400 and RS/6000 machines distributed throughout an enterprise network: Systems Management Automation Offerings (SMAO), Automated Operations Control/ Automated Network Operations (AOC/ANO), NetView Remote Operations Manager MVS/ESA, and NetView Remote Operations Agent/400.

SMAO builds on existing mainframe application products to let users automatically monitor, control, and measure the performance of AS/400 minicomputers and RISC/6000 workstations and servers. The new extensions use Automated Operations Control (AOC) and (ANO) to support automated procedures that can handle problem notification and network performance monitoring and also supervise unattended file transfers. Both products use mainframe NetView screens, and connect to the IBM Information Management (Info/Man) problem management database.

IBM NetView Remote Operations Manager MVS/ESA works with NetView Remote Operations Agent/400 to allow centralized AS/400 management from mainframe NetView. The NetView Operator can send native AS/400 commands to AS/400 systems, as well as use mainframe NetView automation to control and manage the AS/400 systems. While in the past, AS/400 systems could send alerts to mainframe NetView's Alerts Dynamic screen, the NetView operator could not easily take action to resolve AS/400 problems. The Remote Operations products solve that problem. These products are integrated with RODM, NetView GMF, and IBM Command Tree/2. Command Tree/2 allows operators to build commands and to send them to an AS/400.

6.3   COMMUNICATION ALTERNATIVES BETWEEN AND WITHIN IBM PRODUCT FAMILIES

Three primary alternatives are available for enabling products in the different IBM product families to communicate and share management information. These alternatives include:

- Mainframe NetView as the management focal point, using the Service Point for protocol conversion among different product families
- Mainframe NetView as the management focal point, implementing protocol conversion in mainframe NetView itself
- AIX NetView/6000 as the Focal Point manager

The following sections discuss each alternative in detail.

6.3.1   Mainframe NetView as Focal Point—Protocol Conversion via Service Point

Due to the large numbers mainframe NetView installations, many companies look upon mainframe NetView as a true "manager of managers" supporting both IBM and non-IBM management products, as depicted in Figure 6.8. (For more information on "manager of managers" model, see Chapter 4.) When mainframe NetView acts as an integration point (focal point) for management data, it is necessary to convert data (management protocols) from non-SNA entities using Service Point capabilities as offered in IBM's management architecture. Service Point features are implemented by NetView/PC, as well as other third-party applications. The following section describes an implementation using NetView/PC.

Third-party systems, PBXs, multiplexers, and LANs may be integrated using NetView/PC as a service point. NetView/PC is a multi-tasking personal computer subsystem that supplies the facilities to support communication of network management data between a personal computer and mainframe NetView. NetView/PC was designed to be used in conjunction with mainframe NetView to provide services that permit user-written programs to extend SNA Management Services (SNA-MS) to non-IBM communications devices. Using NetView/PC, SNA-MS support can be extended to non-IBM and non-SNA communications devices, voice networks (CBX/PBX), and IBM Token Ring networks. It offers the basic services needed by a device-dependent SNA-MS application program and a network operator (Terplan, 1991).

The NetView/PC protocol conversion process can be described as follows: Management data flows throughout SNA sessions, which provide reliable, connection-oriented network transport. The basic SNA message unit—called request/response unit (RU), which supports network management—is called the network management vector transport (NMVT). SNA-MS can flow on either LU 6.2 or SSCP-PU sessions.

NetView/PC helps automatic protocol conversion by implementing table-driven rules for converting NMVT messages. During the conversion, however, messages and data may be lost. Therefore, IBM has introduced a new alarm

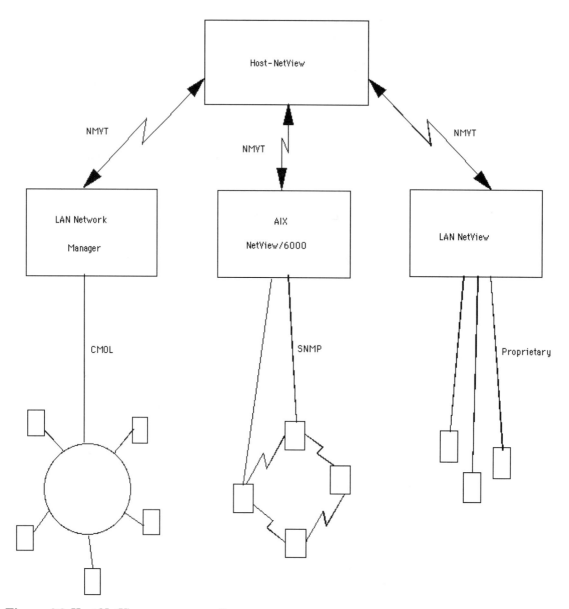

Figure 6.8 Host NetView as manager-of-managers

architecture, called message service units (MSU), which will trigger automated actions without having to convert each MSU into a message.

To bring solutions to market more quickly, IBM has entered into a number of partnerships. For voice applications, TSB's HubView/PC application collects alerts and traffic statistics from a variety of PBX vendors. TSB/HubView also collects and processes call detail maintenance records (CMDR). Carl Vanderbeck and Associates has designed and implemented a development toolkit for Net-View/PC applications. The first implementation was available for Digital VAX alarms. Other NetView/PC implementations include MCI's MCIView (supervising network services) and Lattis-Net NetMap (supervising SynOptics' Ethernet local area networks).

However, the most significant use of NetView/PC is the integration of token ring LAN management with IBM's LAN Network Manager using NetView/PC emulation. Management capabilities supported by this implementation include:

- Automatic detection and bypass of media and station adapter failures through a mechanism embedded in the adapters.
- Control of distributed management servers, which collect error statistics and report on resource utilization, changes, and parameter settings.
- Local LAN management applications, including fault, configuration, and performance management functions for stations and bridges.
- The Host Alert Facility of the IBM LAN Network Manager as service point for NetView.
- Direct centralized management of SNA devices residing on the LAN from NetView, using Service Point Command Facility and optionally SolutionPac for automation.

Another alternative to NetView/PC, offered by Strategic Solutions, is the Service Point (SP)/32. This application supports communication of non-SNA management data to mainframe NetView; commands can also be received from mainframe NetView. SP/32 also supports the same REXX automation programming language as NetView which means that users can implement applications that run locally on the SP/32 platform or on NetView. A dB Vista database is available to store the automation applications.

Other more or less sophisticated solutions are available from Applied Computing Devices, MAXM Systems, Objective Systems Integrators, and Boole and Babbage.

In contrast with third-party approaches, IBM puts more emphasis on service point implementations on the basis of AIX NetView/6000 running on RISC/6000 or SUN Sparc workstations. Service point provides a gateway for network management information between non-SNA devices and mainframe NetView. Applications using the AIX NetView Service Point may be either local or distributed. The Service point also supports asynchronous communication devices and provides a host data file transfer facility for sending and receiving files. Several vendors are writing applications to the service point in such areas as:

- Service management
- UPS management
- Voice management
- Transmission management
- Automation and expert systems
- Database management
- Systems management
- Data backup and recovery management

However, NetView/PC is no longer IBM's strategic solution for integrating non-SNA and non-IBM devices. IBM is instead offering LU 6.2 capabilities in addition to or instead of the NetView/PC platform, bypassing the need for third parties to write special management applications. The LU6.2 interface is much easier to use, offers better performance, and is a more secure base for implementing applications. LU 6.2 is also be used for internetworking mainframe NetView and other solutions such as Sterling Solve: Automation.

Both IBM and third parties have been working to improve the efficiency of protocol conversion. As a result, IBM is offering a LU 6.2 based solution for both AIX NetView/6000 and LAN NetView. LU6.2 supports the exchange of a wider range of alerts. In other words, these structures represent a more cooperative than hierarchial management. The many offerings in this area include solutions from SynOptics, Proteon, Netassist, CrossComm, and Ungermann-Bass.

NetView/6000 also accepts RUNCMDS from NetView which can automatically execute SNMP, AIX commands, and shell scripts. Therefore, SNMP environments can be directly managed by mainframe NetView. LAN NetView also provides the capability to convert traps to alerts which can be forwarded to mainframe NetView via SNA services and OS/2 communications manager. LAN NetView also accepts RUNCMDS from mainframe NetView.

6.3.2   Mainframe NetView as Focal Point using Protocol Conversion in NetView

The second alternative for communications between IBM product families still positions mainframe NetView0 as a Manager of Managers, however, all protocol conversion takes place in the mainframe. In other words, management information is exchanged via native (proprietary) protocols between mainframe NetView and managed objects. Managers—typically OSI and SNMP managers—are implemented in the mainframe to support this configuration (Figure 6.9).

6.3.2.1   OSI Management

Mainframe NetView supports OSI network management via the OSI/Communication Subsystem (OSI/CS). This product provides a full implementation of the seven layers of the OSI model, including the OSI Common Management Information Protocol (CMIP). Thus, OSI/CS can report events to other OSI management systems and/or to receive CMIP messages. OSI/CS can also be able to translate a CMIP event message into an SNA NMVT generic alert, which can be forwarded to NetView.

IBM has also extended this functionality to OS/2 environments via the OSI/CS gateway. This implementation offers a very powerful distributed integration capability at the site level.

6.3.2.2   SNMP Management

IBM supports SNMP at both the agent and manager level. SNMP agents are available for OS/2, MVS, VM, and S/6000 systems. Managers have been implemented on MVS, VM, and on RISC/6000 under AIX.

The AIX NetView/6000 is a graphics-based station with X-Windows, and, as such, is comparable with other SNMP manager solutions. The mainframe-based

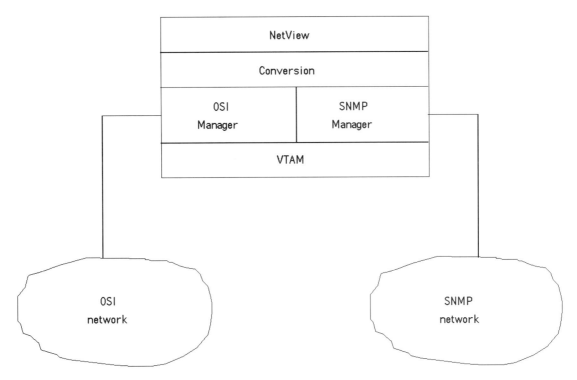

Figure 6.9 Host NetView as focal point for OSI and SNMP management

solution is very important for customers who are thinking about integration. Mainframe NetView is the focal point, and plays the role of an SNMP manager. The gateways between NetView and TCP/IP are Trap-to-Alert and RUNCMD processors. A typical dialog between mainframe NetView and the SNMP manager includes the following steps.

1. SNMP command is issued by operator or CLIST/REXX.
2. SNMP command processor passes the command to the RUNCMD processor.
3. The RUNCMD processor validates, encodes, and creates an SNMP PDU.
4. TCP/IP sends the SNMP PDU to the agent and receives response(s).
5. Response is passed to the Trap-to-Alert processor
6. The Trap-to-Alert processor decodes each response(s) and sends it to mainframe NetView.
7. Each response is sent to operator or to other receiving tasks.

While this second alternative guarantees a high degree off centralization, it pays the price of CPU overhead.

6.3.3   AIX NetView/6000 as the Focal Point

The third alternative is to use of AIX NetView/6000 as the focal point manager (Figure 6.10). In this case, three basic mechanisms can be used for managing SNA objects by the SNMP manager:

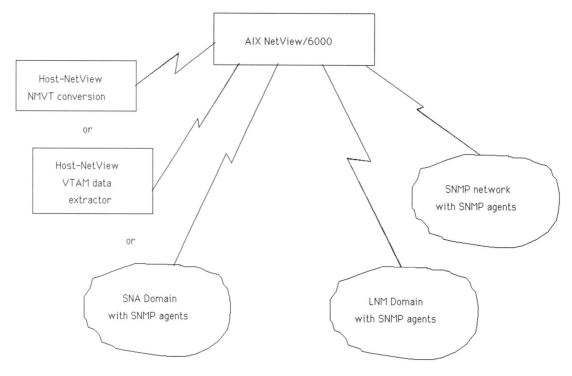

Figure 6.10 AIX NetView/6000 in the role of focal point network management platform

- gateways
- direct interface to VTAM
- SNMP agents

The first mechanism employs a special gateway to collect and convert SNA management related information into SNMP format. IBM offers SNA/6000 for this purpose. SNA Manager/6000 pulls SNA-related data and passes it over an LU 6.2 session to NetView/6000. It allows to graphically display the SNA sub-area network topology and status to the LU level, including terminals and applications. It allows to open a command line interface to send mainframe NetView, VTAM, and MVS commands to mainframe NetView. SNA alerts are converted to traps and sent to NetView/6000 so they can use NetView/6000's event display and filtering.

The disadvantage of this solution is that it requires mainframe NetView and the GMF, potentially resulting in higher overhead and, of course, additional licensing fees. Peregrine's OpenSNA, as well as other new third-party products now appearing from NetTech and Objective Systems Integrators (via Strategic Solutions) obtain the required information directly from VTAM and allow customers to forgo using NetView if they so desire.

The second way is to bypass mainframe NetView and collect information directly from VTAM. Applications using this approach include Peregrine Open-

SNA, Cabletron/NetTech Bluevision, NetImpact from Objective Systems Integrators, and the various SNA-extractors from Sterling Software.

The third way is to implement agents for each individual SNA components and manage them by AIX NetView/6000 or by another SNMP manager. The prerequisite for this is the development of a Management Information Base (MIB) for each SNA component, defining SNA-specific variables of front-ends, logical and physical units, VTAM, and other important components. Usually, SNA-gateways, such as from Synch Research are equipped with an SNMP agent. This type of implementation can also extend to include all components of LAN Network Manager and LAN NetView. This type of integration does not mean that this solution is superior to the individual ones represented by mainframe NetView, LAN NetView and LNM.

6.4   IBM'S DIRECTIONS

6.4.1   APPN

IBM does not want to weaken its position with its customers in sensitive management areas. The extended SNA, based on APPN, has won its battle against other initiatives led by Cisco with APPI. Now, both are working together to promote innovative network management solutions. IBM will incorporate powerful management capabilities into APPN. From today's perspective, mainframe NetView will play an important role in managing APPN. The key enhancements to mainframe NetView are:

- APPN networks will collect and pass information to mainframe NetView through a new management application on the NetView mainframe and an agent on an OS/2 machine running APPN. The two will communicate via CMIP over an LU6.2 transport.
- The NetView Graphic Monitor will be able to accept and display APPN node status information through the OS/2 agent.
- A NetView Resource Object Data Manager (RODM) will let mainframe NetView collect and store APPN node status information in a distributed fashion.
- The OS/2 APPN agent will be able to collect accounting information, such as message and character byte counts, from all attached LU6.2 servers. The data can be passed to NetView for reporting and charge-back to end users.

APPN is well suited for distributed computing. Operations and dialogs between the end nodes (ENs) and network nodes (NN) are completely independent from central control. While this new kind of peer networking has significant advantages for building and maintaining networks, it has forced the development of a new SNA/MS (management services) infrastructure. The requirements are:

- Maximum configuration flexibility for management
- Minimization of network overhead for management
- Coexistence with management in existing SNA networks
- Possibilities for future growth of management application programs

To meet these requirements, the SSCP-PU services must be replaced by LU 6.2 services. The choice of LU 6.2 was a logical choice for the following reasons (Journal of Network Management):

1. LU 6.2 sessions are not restricted by configuration in the way that SSCP to PU sessions are: they are supported in a wide variety of SNA networks, such as subarea networks, LEN networks, and APPN networks.
2. The data encoding method for LU 6.2 transaction programs, the generalized data stream variable (GDS), permits records of up to 32K bytes to be sent and received simply. The LU 6.2 architecture provides the facilities that segment outbound application program data streams and then perform the appropriate re-assembly for inbound data. Data records longer than 32K are sent as a series of 32K records.
3. LU 6.2 sessions may be nonpersistent, meaning that they may be deactivated when no longer needed, and reactivated again when needed, thus minimizing costs in networks using public switched telecommunications facilities. This deactivation and reactivation of sessions is not apparent to application programs using LU 6.2 services.
4. LU 6.2 includes provisions for session-level security (password authentication of session partners), an important consideration in more open peer-to-peer networks.

IBM has evaluated a number of implementation alternatives of LU 6.2. The basic solution was named multiple-domain support (MDS) because it provided a mechanism for communication between domains. MDS is implemented as a layer above LU6.2.

An examination of SNA networking trends leads to the conclusion that future APPN networks may be very large. In those networks, the ratio of APPN end nodes to network nodes will be high, i.e., each network node will serve a large number of end nodes. It is also expected that the end nodes will produce relatively small volumes of management services records. In that environment, the number of LU 6.2 sessions required to support direct connectivity between focal point nodes and APPN end nodes for MDS would be comparatively high, and the utilization of those sessions would be comparatively low. This situation is undesirable for the end nodes, since APPN generally relieves end nodes of as much SNA control overhead as possible, and this is undesirable for the focal point nodes, which must activate and maintain very large numbers of relatively unproductive sessions.

The ultimate goal is to encapsulate "CP-CP" control sessions into existing LU-LU sessions that are required in any case between network nodes in APPN. The results of the optimization are (Journal of Network Management):

1. Management services data is sent between an APPN end node and its serving network node over existing CP-CP sessions. Separate sessions for management services are not required.
2. APPN network nodes provide routing of management services data for both their local MS applications program and for management services application programs on server end nodes.

3. Focal point nodes send management services data destined for APPN end nodes over LU-LU sessions to the appropriate serving network nodes, which then forward that data to the end node over the CP-CP session.

4. All management services routing decisions are based upon dynamic information available from the APPN directory of network resources. No statically defined routing information is required.

Figure 6.11 shows the reduced number of CP-CP sessions in an APPN-network. The management data for MDS are encoded into Management Services Major Vector structures. Their structure is an enhanced and extended version of NMVTs from hierarchical SNA.

The focal point concept remains from "old" SNA. It allows for APPN for centralized management. A focal point is an SNA node supporting an application program or set of application programs that provide centralized control. The focal point may be implemented in practically any of the nodes. There are many topologies with a single focal point, with multiple focal points and also with nested focal points. The initialization of establishing the control structure, MS capabilities (MS CAPS) messages are exchanged between the focal point and entry points. The focal point is flexible allowing explicit, implicit, and default sphere of control. Usually this high level of flexibility is limited during optimization. The application concept with MS CAPS is shown in Figure 6.12. The focal point optimization results for APPN are illustrated in Figure 6.13. Practical implementation of these ideas may use different existing protocols and products. IBM is experimenting with both CMIP and SNMP to embed MS. Also, mainframe NetView is under consideration as a focal point. Many of the users with mainframe NetView will migrate gradually to the new SNA. In such cases, the existing mainframe NetView services are very useful.

APPN management is supported by NetView APPN Topology and Accounting Management (APPNTAM) that automatically discovers all nodes and links in an APPN network and helps to build an object-oriented database. The product consists of manager code, which runs on the mainframe, and agent code, which transmits APPN, device and link information to the manager using CMIP encapsulated in an LU6.2 session. Based upon this information, the manager builds an object-oriented topology map of all APPN resources and maintains the data in RODM. RODM displays the topology on NetView's Graphics Monitor Facility. The agent code is running on OS/2, on APPN-nodes, VTAM, and AS/400. A second version of the product is using SNMP instead of CMIP. The accounting part tracks and stores LU6.2 session and conversation data so users can monitor and evaluate throughput and usage. Traffic can be balanced when certain APPN nodes are becoming overloaded.

6.4.2   CMIP and OMNIPOINT

IBM is a member of the Network Management Forum, and is developing interfaces supporting OMNIPoint interoperability between existing network management products and solutions. IBM is also active in AIMS (Action-Team for the Integration of Management Systems). Using the "edge" of AIMS—a special

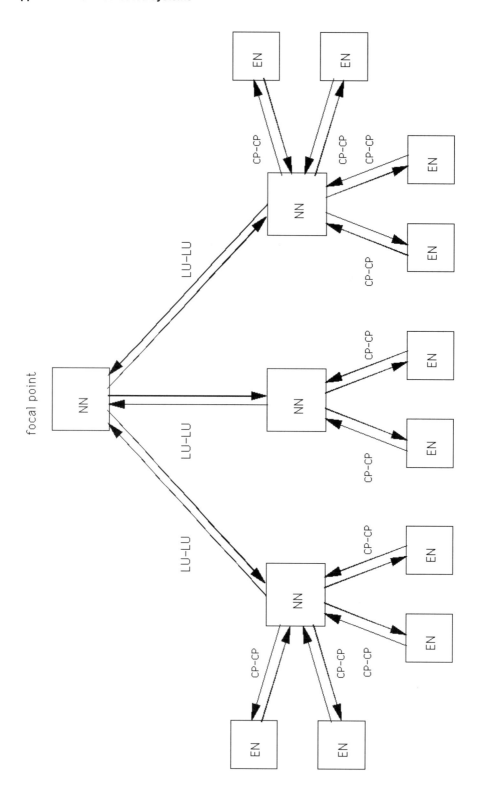

Figure 6.11 Concentration of MDS sessions in an APPN network

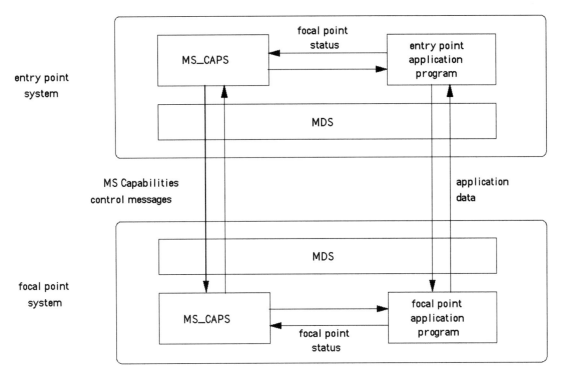

Figure 6.12 MS_CAPS application concept

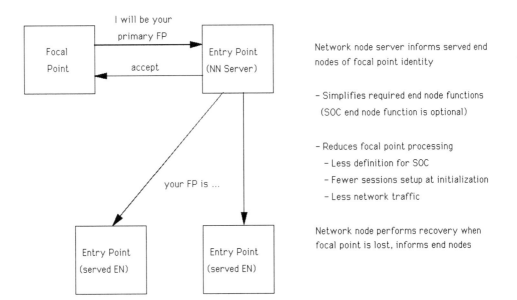

Figure 6.13 Focal point optimization for APPN

extension of management applications—enables IBM management tools to communicate with existing other networks and systems management tools at low overhead. It does not mean however, that the "edge" is going to be used for IBM-internal communications.

OMNIPoint is an agreed set of standards which, used together, provide an open management architecture. OMNIPoint defines how shared information should be stored and how that information should be communicated. Systems designed or extended with OMNIPoint conformance in mind, can easily share information with each other. But, in particular, legacy systems, cannot be easily expanded by OMNIPoint capabilities making integration very difficult. By using generic gateways, such as the Open Management Edge ("edge"), integration is faster and easier. The "edge" is a set of application programming interfaces that allow conforming applications to talk directly to one another and share data. This "edge" is a lightweight management architecture sitting on the periphery of applications (See Figure 6.14), that can act as a translator to other applications. Use of the edge makes full, bilateral, gateways no longer necessary. Each half-gateway talks to the "edge" which contains the protocols and connections for the applications to reach one another and exchange data. Communications are con-

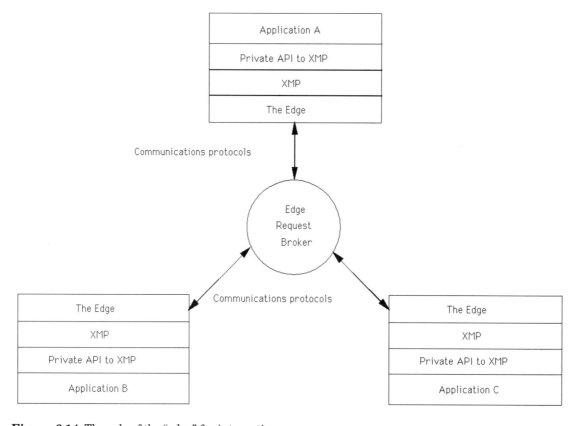

Figure 6.14 The role of the "edge" for integration

trolled by the Edge Request Broker (ERB). ERB shows some similarities with CORBA and DME, but it is easier to implement and to maintain. Initial implementations of the edge produced encouraging results for the following application areas.

* Systems management
* Network management
* Asset management
* Help desk tools
* Modeling instruments

Between the "edges" and ERB, a variety of protocols, such as SNMP, RPC, BSD, SQL, and CMIP may be selected.

6.5 SUMMARY

IBM's vast installed base represents many customers who may require one or more of the products discussed in this chapter. Therefore IBM is a very popular platform for development of third-party applications. Third parties have been writing platform and product extensions for mainframe NetView for many years. Now, they are writing applications for AIX NetView/6000 and for LAN NetView, as well. To date, LAN Network Manager has not attracted many third parties and the product is more or less stand-alone.

IBM's relationship with Digital Equipment Corp. will have an impact on SNA management directions. Digital's licensing of NetView/6000 technology will produce interesting hardware/software alternatives for customers attracted to Net-View/6000. Digital's Polycenter Manager on NetView is the first result of the IBM/Digital agreement. Polycenter Manager on NetView is an SNMP system that supports extensions for DECnet management. The first version of Poly-center Manager on NetView runs on Digital's OSF/1 operating system and Alpha AXP hardware. It provides autotopology, mapping, and autodiscovery of Digital PhaseIV and DECnet/OSI devices management via the Network Information Control Protocol (NICE). Polycenter Manager on NetView also manages Digital terminal servers and bridges. The next release of Polycenter Manager on Net-View will support Windows NT and OpenVMS on Alpha AXP. It will include a hot-standby failover feature and support for Oracle, Informix, Sybase, and Digital Rdb OSF/1 databases. Future version of Polycenter Manager on NetView will offer enhanced reporting for DECnet Phase IV, management of events, and enhanced DECnet/OSI management. These versions will run on OSF/1, Windows NT, and OpenVMS AXP.

Regarding IBM's entire network management product family, communication links do exist between the products and users may customize their IBM-dominated management environment by putting the emphasis on product best suited to their environment.

Many organizations are hoping to reduce operating costs and increase the quality of service by integrating management of SNA networks under a UNIX-based SNMP framework. New applications will emerge in 1994 and 1995 that allow users to accomplish more effective SNA management without using mainframe NetView. Most customers will initially seek to off-load portions of mainframe NetView functions onto the SNMP platform to free CPU cycles and increase operator efficiencies. Very few organizations plan to displace mainframe NetView totally in the near term.

Users may choose to deploy SNMP-manageable SNA servers as they migrate toward integrated SNA-TCP/IP management. Products such as IBM SNA Manager/6000, which act as bridges between mainframe NetView and SNMP platforms, will be important in the short-term as well.

The limiting factor in managing an SNA network from an SNMP-based (or any non-IBM SNA) management platform is IBM itself. While there is a shift in the industry towards SNMP-based management of the SNA environment, it is clearly not in IBM's best interest to see substantial decreases in the expensive mainframe NetView licensing fees.

IBM's high-performance routing (HPR), also called APPN+, is sure to impact SNA management directions. It will be one or two years before APPN+ creates inroads in most organization's management strategies, since the industry traditionally waits for connectivity technology to prove itself before management solutions appear. In summary, the status of integrated SNA-TCP/IP management indicates the progress the industry has made in merging the two worlds. It is happening, slowly.

7

HP OpenView Integration

7.1 INTRODUCTION

Hewlett-Packard's HP OpenView is one of the leading platforms for both Windows and UNIX environments. HP has designed the HP OpenView Management Platform Architecture as the foundation for an open, modular, distributed solution for network and system management.

The HP OpenView Management Platform Architecture decomposes the network and system management problem into several components: a distributed management infrastructure, a graphical management user interface, management applications, management services, and managed objects. These cooperating components are all accessible through standard, well-documented APIs.

7.2 OPENVIEW PLATFORMS

The clear separation and the definition of multiple application programming interfaces allow third parties to integrate their applications into the platform. Figure 7.1 shows the various layers of the HP OpenView management platform.

HP OpenView offers multiple platform services, depending upon the needs of users. SNMP agents are best supported by the SNMP-management platform (Figure 7.2). HP OpenView supports a range of basic management services; in this respect, there are many similarities with other SNMP platforms. Management applications reside in the middle between the direct SNMP-API and the user interface APIs. Third-party vendors may choose to implement either Windows or MOTIF as the user interface. HP has application examples for both.

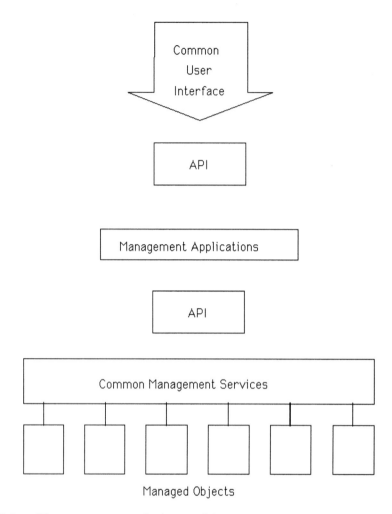

Figure 7.1 HP OpenView management platform architecture

The Distributed Management Platform (Figure 7.3) offers SNMP and additional application interfaces (SQL-APIs) to databases and to XMP-based management APIs. Figure 7.4 clarifies the boundary lines between platform services, development kits, and one of the principal applications called Network Node Manager.

7.3   INTEGRATING HP OPENVIEW WITH APPLICATIONS

In an effort to meet customer demands for integrated management, Hewlett-Packard has been particularly aggressive in developing partnerships with key third-party applications developers. The following section describes some results of these partnerships thus far, including these applications (see Figure 7.5):

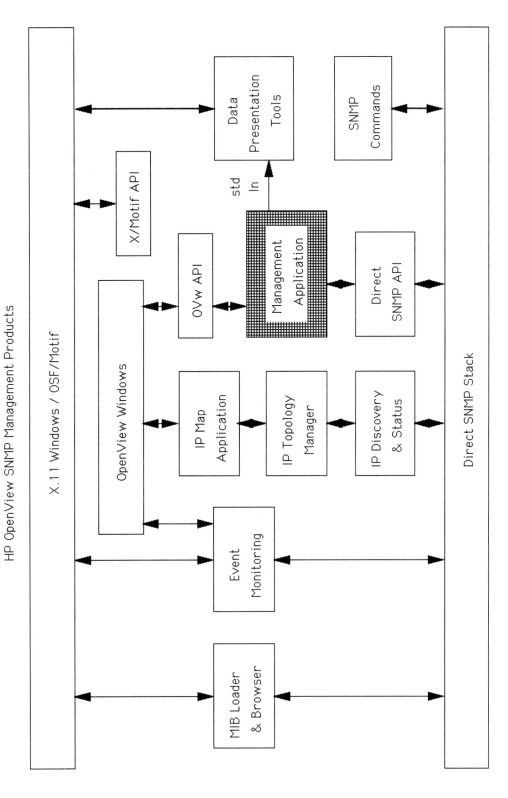

Figure 7.2 HP OpenView SNMP management platform architecture

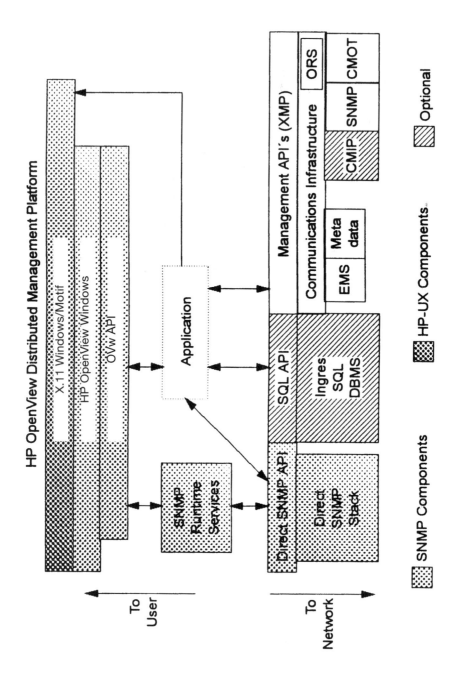

Figure 7.3 HP OpenView]

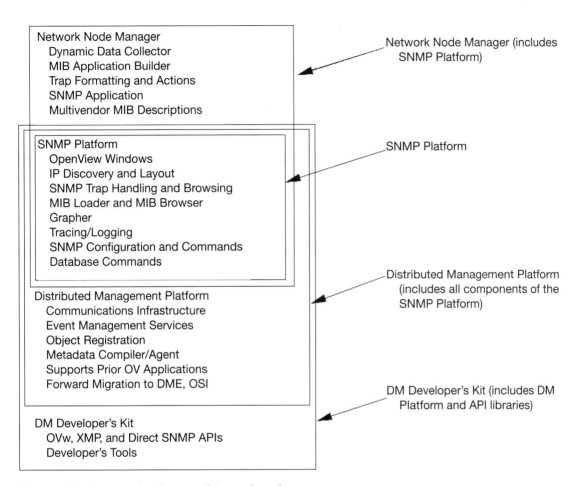

Figure 7.4 Services, development kits, and products

- Isicad Command 5000
- Remedy Action Request System (ARS)
- Peregrine Systems OpenSNA
- Ki Research OpenDNM
- HP (formerly Metrix) NetMetrix
- Peregrine StationView and ServerView
- Legent Paramount
- BGS Best/Net Modeling

The integration of the NetMetrix application is expected to grow tighter in the future due to the Hewlett-Packard's acquisition of Metrix Systems, which developed NetMetrix. Also, HP's decision to resell the Peregrine products implies that HP will ensure tighter integration between HP OpenView and OpenSNA, StationView, and ServerView.

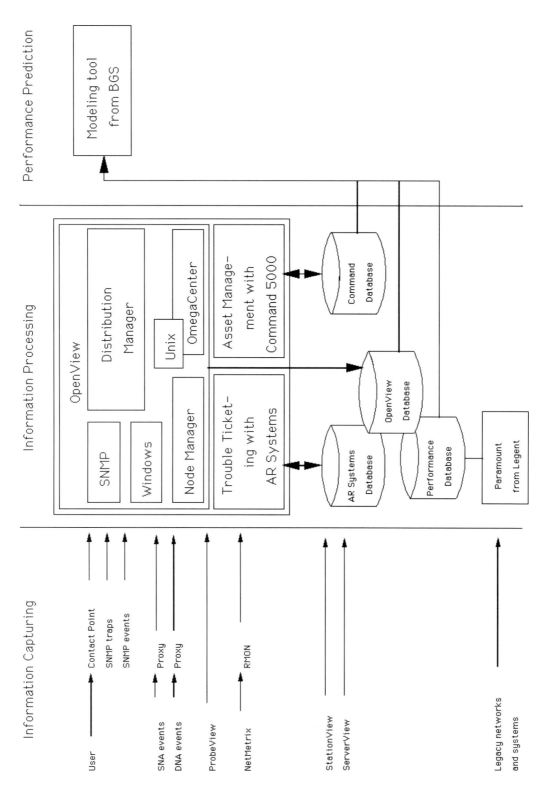

Figure 7.5 Depth of integration under OpenView

7.3.1   Integration of Command 5000

Isicad's Command 5000 is a leading physical asset and cable management application. Command 5000 is integrated into the HP OpenView platform at the level of HP Network Node Manager and is fully incorporated into the menu-hierarchy of HP OpenView. Command 5000 supports user interface integration including icon tools and maps. HP OpenView Network Node Manager is consistently supervising the logical status of the networks and systems. When HP OpenView operators require detailed information about the physical network, the Isicad application is invoked by launching from the menu bar and forwarding the necessary parameters, such as address and/or name of the component. At this moment, the Command 5000 and HP OpenView databases are not yet synchronized.

7.3.2   Integration of Remedy Action Request System

By virtue of integration with the underlying platform, Remedy AR System trouble tickets can be opened by any of the redefined events generated by HP OpenView. AR System is connected to the Network Node Manager but the level of integration is still low and considered as a combination of "drop-in" and "cut and paste." In other words, the AR System is accessible from the Network Node Manager screen, and the operator can view both simultaneously. Information of selected fields can be cut and moved from Node Manager to AR System. But tracking the fault resolution process is independent from Network Node Manager.

7.3.3   Integration of Peregrine OpenSNA

The purpose of Peregrine's OpenSNA is to connect HP OpenView to mainframe NetView applications. This integration is targeting the UNIX version of HP OpenView and guarantees a real dialog with IBM-hosts. Both native VTAM and mainframe NetView messages and commands are used. The integration is accomplished by an SNA proxy-agent under UNIX. (See Figure 7.6.) The proxy-agent communicates with the SNA-agents residing in MVS-hosts. The proxy is the go-between that connects the TCP/IP-interface and XMP-interface. (See Figure 7.7.) The manager includes the XMP interface that is providing the link of carrying events and commands between OpenView and MVS-hosts. (See Figure 7.8.)

Integration between OpenSNA and HP OpenView is partially at the event level and partially at the protocol level. There is no database or map integration available yet. However, the user may cut and paste the SNA and TCP/IP-configurations together. So far, drop-in capabilities are supported, as well.

7.3.4   Integration of OpenDNM

OpenDNM from Ki Research is similar in purpose to OpenSNA, except that it connects the Digital DECnet environment with HP OpenView. VMS- and Ultrix-based management systems are connected to the UNIX version of HP OpenView. (See Figure 7.9) There is bilateral dialog between the two management systems.

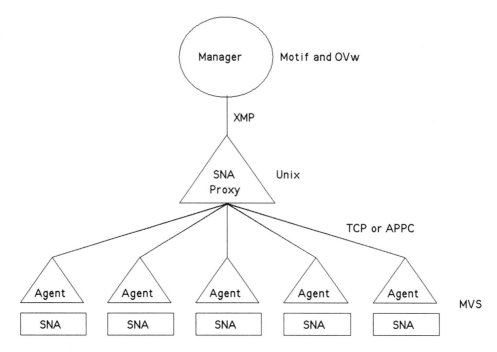

Figure 7.6 Peregrine OpenSNA design

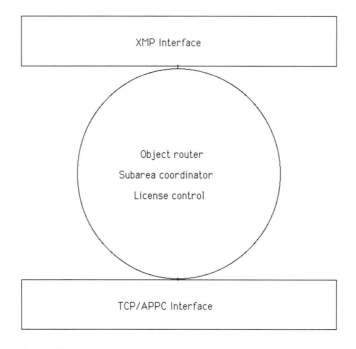

Figure 7.7 Peregrine OpenSNA proxy design

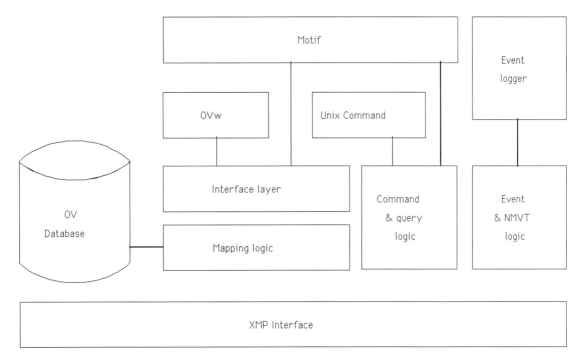

Figure 7.8 Peregrine OpenSNA manager design

The integration is accomplished by a proxy agent under UNIX. The proxy agent communicates with the agent residing in VMS and Ultrix hosts.

Integration between OpenDNM and HP OpenView is partially at the event level and partially at the protocol level. (See Figures 7.10 and 7.11.) There is no database or map integration available yet. However, the user may cut and paste the DNM and TCP/IP-configurations, together. So far, drop-in capabilities are supported, as well.

7.3.5   Integration of HP NetMetrix

Hewlett-Packard's Test Division has marketed a hardware-based traffic monitor called LANprobe for several years. With the acquisition of the NetMetrix product from Metrix Systems, HP now has a software-based monitor in its product family. While the HP OpenView applications for integrating NetMetrix and LAN-Probe are still separate at this time, the two products will soon converge and there will be one management application offered instead of two.

NetMetrix is considered one of the best performance and traffic monitoring tools in the industry. It fully supports RMON, enabling OpenView to unify monitoring and management on the same platform. The integration is at the SNMP protocol level. The NetMetrix suite of applications, including the Load Monitor, NFS Monitor, Traffic Generator, and Protocol Analyzer, can obtain data from

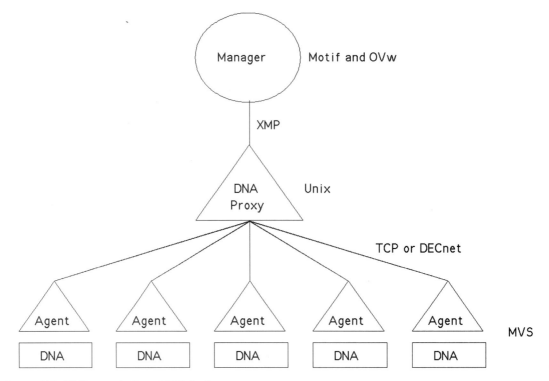

Figure 7.9 Ki Research OpenDNA design

RMON agents in hubs, RMON probes, the HP LAN Probe, or the NetMetrix Power Agent. The Power Agent supports an Internetwork Monitor and provides extensive filtering; it runs on a UNIX workstation that can support processing of quantities of data collected.

HP OpenView uses SNMP to access data from an RMON agent (either the NetMetrix Power Agent or the HP LANprobe.) Alternately, an X window system can allow a remote segment probe to project its display back to the central monitoring station.

Unlike many traffic monitors which require installation of an expensive hardware-based probe on each monitored LAN segment, NetMetrix is a software implementation. Users can install NetMetrix on any available UNIX workstation on the LAN to obtain full-function traffic monitoring and analysis. In addition, NetMetrix includes applications for load monitoring across the internetwork.

In the future, HP will position NetMetrix as a Network Analysis Server, capable of running a wide variety of agents and applications, and serving as an integration point for monitoring and analysis processes. For example, the Network Analysis Server may run the NetMetrix Power Agent to continuously monitor the segments to which it is attached. It could also run SNMP proxy agents that communicate with local devices in the domain using proprietary protocols and convert this to SNMP for use by HP OpenView. The Network Analysis Server

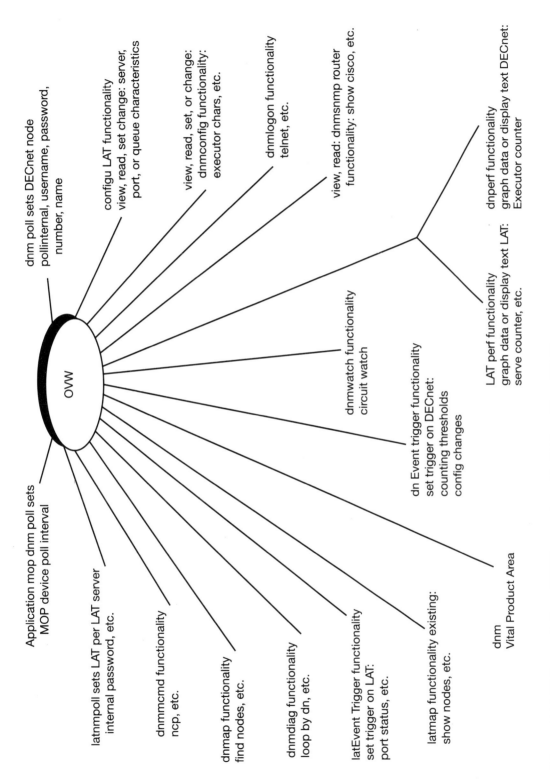

Figure 7.10 Ki Research Open DNM integration with HP OpenView (OVW)

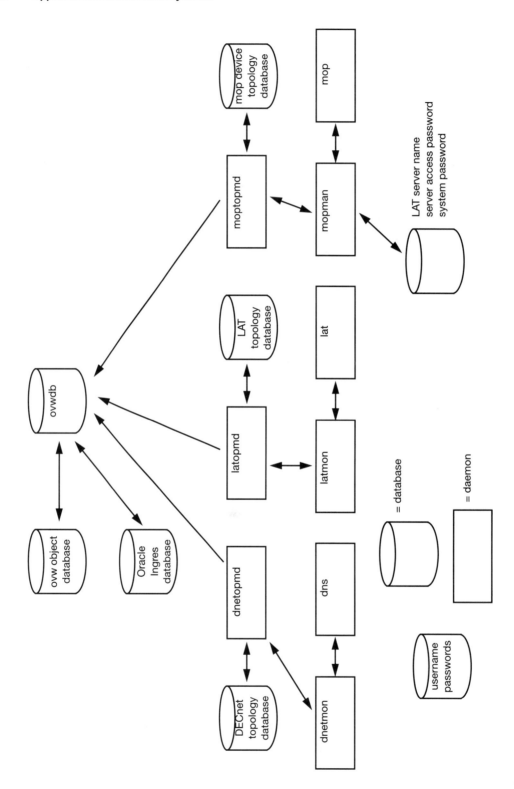

Figure 7.11 Ki Research Open DNM Design

could also run expert system applications which draw from an integrated database. HP is expected to develop intelligent applications that run on a Network Analysis Server, and make sense of a consolidated set of data from many devices on the network. HP plans to fully integrate NetMetrix into the Probe Manager system configuration. The resulting product family will be called NetMetrix. Figure 7.12 shows the present structure. In the future, NetMetrix will assume the roles of both ProbeView and ProbeManager.

7.3.6   Integration of Peregrine StationView and ServerView

Peregrine's StationView manages DOS-clients by detecting faults with DOS clients, allowing configuration changes to boot files, and providing hardware/software inventory. StationView is helping user organizations manage Novell networks from the UNIX-based HP OpenView console. It is composed of:

StationView/OV

    IP map integration
    IPX map
    StationView management windows

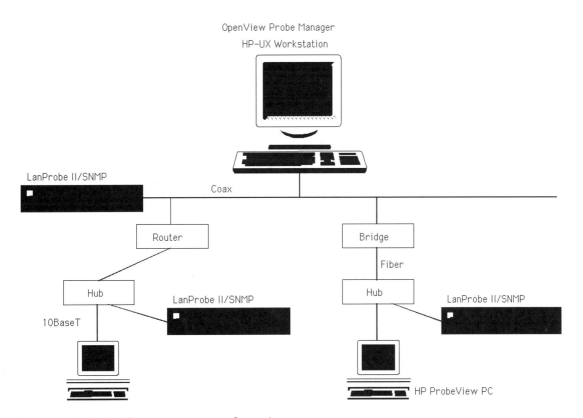

Figure 7.12 Probe Manager system configuration

StationView Agent

StationView proxy agent NLM

StationView collection software for PC (not a TSR)

StationView/DOS

StationView management windows faults, network hardware, software printers

The integration is supported on the MIB level.

Peregrine ServerView manages NetWare servers by monitoring the performance of key server parameters, by supervising users and configuration files, by invoking OpenView actions through NetWare server events, and by providing hardware/software inventory. It is comprised of:

ServerView/OV

IP map integration

IPX map

ServerView management windows

Faults	Summary
Performance	Network
Configuration	Hardware
Security	Software
Accounting	Printers

ServerView Agent

Suite of NetWare loadable modules (NLMs)

Real time polling and alerts

The integration is supported on the MIB level.

7.3.7   Integration of Legent Paramount

To support integrated enterprise-wide resource and performance management solutions, Hewlett-Packard will be integrating Legent's Paramount architecture with HP PerfView and other HP-UNIX performance products.

The scope of integration is:

HP PerfView distributed performance management

Legent Paramount architecture

HP Performance Collection Software

Legent MICS reporting

HP GlancePlus Online performance monitor with expert advisor

Legent performance, IS financial management, capacity management, storage, networking MVS solutions

Figure 7-13 shows how these modules are going to be unified under LCM (Legent Communications Manager). The level of integration supposed to be the database. It is very likely, that the database provided by Legent will be tailored to HP OpenView. Besides SMF and SAS, other databases can be considered; each of them is more a flat file then a real database.

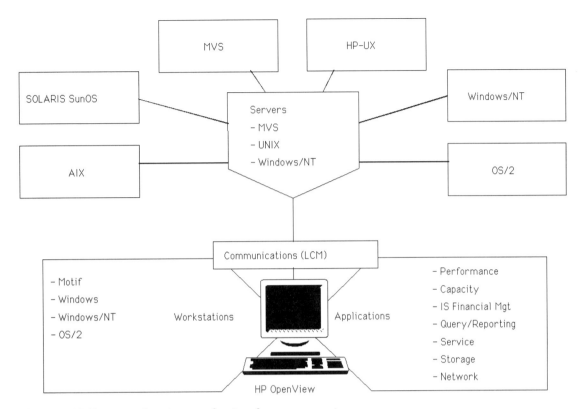

Figure 7.13 Integrated systems and network management

7.3.8 Integration of Modeling Tools

Modeling tools such as Best/Net from BGS currently do not support integration with HP OpenView. When integration is introduced, it will be minimal in the beginning. The most likely scenario is the ability to exchange datafiles containing topology, inventory, and utilization data. In this case, HP OpenView would initiate the export of information, and the modeling product would answer "what if" queries. Invoking the modeling application can be programmed into a tool on the user interface; drop-in may be used to modify the model and to watch modeling results. In particular, configuration and change management functions will be tightly coupled with modeling instruments.

Table 7-1 summarizes the types of integration targeted with the products addressed in the segment.

7.4 SUMMARY

Platforms and applications from Hewlett-Packard and third parties are very attractive to users targeting early and broad integration for very heterogeneous environments. In particular, HP offerings are best suited for organizations in

TABLE 7-1   Integration between HP OpenView and Various Applications

| Product | User Interface | | | | Protocol Access | | | |
	Drop-In	Tool	Map	Database	SNMP	CMIP XMP	Event	Product Support
Isicad Command 5000	✔	✔	✔					
Remedy ARS	✔							
Peregrine OpenSNA					✔		✔	
Ki Research OpenDNM					✔		✔	
HP NetMetrix					✔			
Peregrine StationView				✔				
Peregrine ServerView				✔				
Legent Paramount				✔				
BGS Modeling	✔	✔						

which proprietary architectures, such as SNA, DECnet, or NetWare play a dominant role. It is interesting to observe that HP OpenView offers both dimensions of integration; horizontal for element managers for systems and networks, and vertical for test instruments, diagnostic tools, traffic monitors, element managers, and integrators. The variety of HP OpenView applications now available from third parties enables users to select, customize, and implement the right mix of applications. Case studies involving these applications are addressed in Chapter 8.

8

Application Integration Case Studies

As Chapter 5 describes, more than 100 different third-party management applications are now shipping for open management platforms such as SunConnect SunNet Manager and Hewlett-Packard HP OpenView. Currently third parties must retool these applications for each new platform supported. However, in the future, applications developers will be able to take advantage of high-level application programming interfaces that will allow porting of applications from one platform to the next. This technology will encourage a "plug-and-play" management applications market, as well as a certain level of tighter integration between applications and platforms. These developments will make it easier for end-user organizations to control the management of distributed client/server networks around their management platform of choice.

Even as the industry moves toward this higher level of integration and centralization, customers still have immediate needs for achieving interoperability of existing applications and existing products. This chapter concentrates on several case studies demonstrating integration that is possible today, primarily as a result of alliances or agreements made between applications providers and platform vendors. These case studies reflect the types of integration typically required by organizations today—such as the integration of management platforms with physical asset or cable management applications, trouble ticketing systems, traffic monitoring and analysis tools, performance analysis applications, and fault diagnostic tools. In particular, this chapter emphasizes solutions based on HP OpenView, SunNet Manager, OSI NetExpert, and AT&T StarSENTRY, and includes applications from networking vendors such as Cisco, SynOptics, Wellfleet, and WilTel and independent software vendors such as Accugraph, Isicad, OpenVision, and Remedy, Tivoli.

Many users, systems integrators, and consulting companies are working with manufacturers on various integration projects. The number of products under consideration for integration may differ, but basically the following types of products play a principal role:

- The platform or umbrella product supporting the integration effort
- The database for storing and maintaining asset, connectivity, status, and performance data
- Graphical application for visualization
- Asset or infrastructure management application
- Trouble ticketing application
- Element management products or device-specific applications
- Various utilities to improve communications within the network management organization.

This chapter shows four generic examples. The first example deals with OSI NetExpert as an umbrella product for a large organization in the financial industry. The second addresses AT&T Star*SENTRY as a platform for integrating various products from the perspective of an outsourcer. The third case study shows the integration direction for a WAN services provider. The last is a special integration example from a military application.

8.1 CUSTOMIZED NETWORK MANAGEMENT INTEGRATION USING NETEXPERT FROM OBJECTIVE SYSTEMS INTEGRATORS

This case study involves an integration project for a large financial services firm. The firm is struggling with typical network management problems, including a high degree of equipment complexity, the use of multiple management protocols, the fragmented maintenance of management-related data, the existence of multiple management platforms, and increased pressure to deliver improved service quality to end-users. This firm did not start from "scratch"—it has been using management platforms and management applications for several years. However, these solutions were device- and service-specific, resulting in a fragmented approached to management. The network management integration project for this firm has the following principal objectives (Hart, 1994):

- Integrity between fault and configuration management processes
- Seamless access to multiple physical and logical network views
- Use of a common database to ensure a single network view across multiple applications
- Simple access to applications from a tool bar
- Compliance with standards as far as meaningful
- Easy maintenance of the solution and the tools involved
- Integrated handling of trouble-ticketing and service order processes to reduce the number of different types of processes
- Increased levels of automation

- Increased efficiency of operations
- Decreased mean time to restoring service and to repair

To accomplish these goals, the resulting integrated solution must have a product supporting the following requirements at its core (Hart, 1994):

- A comprehensive development environment, including libraries and application programming interfaces (APIs)
- Compliance with Motif to ensure a consistent user-interface
- Support of extensible object and attribute data structures
- Support of client/server technology
- Availability of an expert engine
- Support of industry-standards, such as SNMPv1, SNMPv2, CMIP, CMOL, or at least subsets of them
- Ability for vendors or users to customize the solution

These requirements cannot be met by any single application or platform available today. Therefore, successful implementation of this project requires the combination of multiple products, including (Hart, 1994):

- NetExpert (Objective Systems Integrators) as the umbrella integrator (for more information on NetExpert, see Chapter 3)
- MountainView (Accugraph) to support asset, cable and configuration management
- MotionMail (Accugraph) to support communications within Network Management Groups
- Remedy Action Request System (AR System) to support trouble-ticketing and service order processing
- OS/Eye*Node from Digital Analysis Corporation to play the role of a generic SNMP manager
- HP NetMetrix to collect and to process performance metrics in LANs
- Crossroads to design and to maintain graphical user interfaces
- Informix for storing and maintaining data in a relational database management system (RDBMS)

The financial services firm worked with a systems integrator to arrive at this combination of tools. The solution is open-ended, and allows for the future inclusion of other products as well. The decision for an umbrella manager was strategically the most important part of the integration management direction.

8.1.1   OSI NetExpert

NetExpert is a powerful integrator for various types of managed objects and element management systems. In this integration project, the NetExpert tool is responsible for the following functions:

- Central repository of equipment, inventory, circuits, and users by supporting multiple MIBs in a relational database.
- High-level view of the network topology where each managed object may be addressed individually.

- Central control by the expert engine to correlate various events from various sources, transporting trouble information to the ticketing system, issuing service orders, and issuing work orders.
- Gateway to other management systems supporting receive-only, dialog, and cut-through applications.
- Platform to integrate applications using state-of-the-art application programming interfaces.

As an alternative to NetExpert, the firm may have chosen IBM NetView/390, Sterling Solve: Automation, Maxm Systems MAX, or Allink's Operations Coordinator. However, these products were found to be less flexible than NetExpert, in particular because they lacked applications programming interfaces (APIs) for supporting third-party products.

8.1.2   Accugraph MountainView

MountainView from Accugraph is a typical cable and asset management system responsible for the following functions:

- Site level design using CAD-technology.
- Management of the physical inventory.
- Visualization of physical views by taking/pursuing managed object IDs and by offering colorization driven by the operational state of objects.
- Linkage to the central database by its RISE-module, by attributes updates, and database updates.
- Linkage to multiple SNMP managers, such as OpenView, AIX NetView, Sun-Net Manager, when the project is going to be extended toward SNMP subintegrators.
- Platform supporting development of customized applications.

Isicad's Command 5000 application Isicad provides similar functionality, as does Konfig from Auto-trol.

8.1.3   Accugraph MotionMail

MotionMail from Accugraph is helping to exchange information between network management support personnel. In particular, the following functions are supported:

- Creating messages to be exchanged
- Cutting and pasting between multiple windows which represent different applications
- Adding annotations including draw and write, post-its, and voice comments
- Attaching documents to the core message

8.1.4   Remedy AR System

Action Request System from Remedy is the basis of the trouble tracking solution for this integration project. In particular, the following functions are supported by AR System:

- Opening trouble tickets
- Setting parameters for filtering
- External access and launch
- Notification of progress
- Application programming interfaces to customize ticket formats, filters, operating environments, and notification services

Legent's Paradigm application represents an alternative to the Remedy AR System.

8.1.5   Digital Analysis OS/Eye*Node

OS/Eye* Node from Digital Analysis Corporation supports SNMP agents from various manufacturers. OS/Eye*Node is capable of supporting distributed management. In particular, this tools is responsible for:

- Gateway-level integration with NetExpert using the generic gateway protocol conversion applications
- Polling SNMP agents
- Supporting distributed management applications

Other SNMP managers such as SunNet Manager, HP OpenView, IBM Net-View/6000, and AT&T StarSENTRY are also capable of acting as subintegrators.

8.1.6   HP NetMetrix

For this integration project, HP NetMetrix is the performance monitor for LANs. It supports a client/server structure in distributing, monitoring, and processing tasks. NetMetrix supports a rich set of performance indicators. These indicators may be used individually or combined with RMON data when the application runs under the SNMP manager.

In addition to HP NetMetrix, many other traffic monitoring applications are available. Distributed monitoring applications are offered by Network General, Concord Communications, Network Application Technologies (N.A.T.), Armon Networking, and Axon Networks. All of these products support the RMON MIB, making data consolidation and processing easier. Technologically, these products offer similar capabilities and could actually be used instead of NetMetrix.

8.1.7   Crossroad Systems Crossroads

Crossroad from Crossroad Systems is a utility program for building graphical user interfaces. These serve as the basis of visualization of physical and logical topologies and of applications integration on the tool bar level.

8.1.8   Informix Relational Database Management System

In this integration project, Informix RDBMS is used for storing and maintaining data in a relational format. In particular, the following items are stored.

- Alert files
- Performance indicators
- Accounting data
- Call detail records
- Trouble tickets
- Service orders
- Documentation sequences

Informix is the center of all relevant information that is centrally maintained. Local databases are still supported by all the other applications and tools just listed.

In addition to Informix, a variety of relational database management systems (RDBMSs) are on the market today. These include Oracle, Sybase, Ingres, Access, and Unify. The project team decided to use an existing RDBMS product instead of waiting for an object-oriented database, even though the latter may have been more efficient. The life-cycle management of this integration network management project includes the evaluation of emerging products, however, including particularly those from IBM and Tivoli. Future project phases are likely to address a combination of relational and object-oriented technologies.

8.1.9   Levels of Integration

The financial services firm mandated that this integration project was to be completed within a reasonable timeframe. Thus, waiting for each chosen product vendor to supply detailed and well understood application programming interfaces was out of the question. Instead, the decision was made to implement tools bar integration as displayed in Figure 8.1.

This minimal level of integration makes maintaining the solution and control change management of all tools involved easier, without impacting the umbrella product or other applications. "Cut and paste" is supported for all tool combinations. In certain bilateral combinations, the linkage of tools is deeper and uses real application programming interfaces and/or de facto standards such as SQL between Informix and database or file structures. Figure 8.2 displays how the tools are connected to each other. Crossroads is not shown; it is responsible for background work.

The integration project does, however, support a close relationship between tools solving fault and configuration management problems. In these two cases, two components, NetExpert IDEAS and GENERIC GATEWAY, are combined, as well as Remedy ARS and the inventory control capabilities of MountainView.

Trouble-ticket processing includes the following steps (Hart, 1994):

After receiving an event by the NetExpert gateway, the event will be displayed on the graphical screen automatically. At the same time, the attributes of status indicators will be updated. Selected events will launch the ARS applications and populate the trouble report fields by porting event data from the gateway to ARS. Trouble reports may also be created by manual inputs. In both cases, ARS is expected to send a message to the gateway and to update the object attributes with the trouble report number.

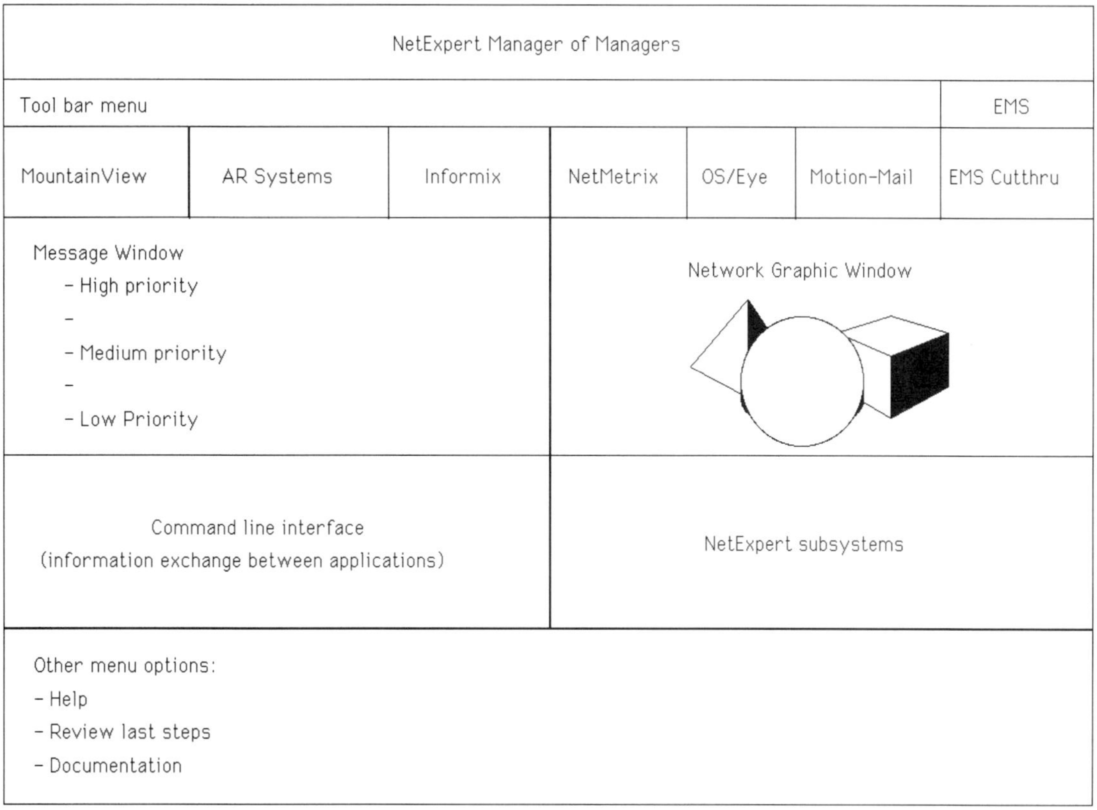

NetExpert Manager of Managers						
Tool bar menu						EMS
MountainView	AR Systems	Informix	NetMetrix	OS/Eye	Motion-Mail	EMS Cutthru

Message Window
  – High priority
  –
  – Medium priority
  –
  – Low Priority

Network Graphic Window

Command line interface
(information exchange between applications)

NetExpert subsystems

Other menu options:
– Help
– Review last steps
– Documentation

Figure 8.1 Tool bar level integration

IDEAS from NetExpert evaluates trouble reports and decides whether a trouble ticket would be opened by checking the object group for existence of a ticket. If it does not exist, a new ticket is created using the AR System API. If more information is needed, MountainView is contacted to port additional attributes to selected trouble ticket fields. The object attributes are updated with the ticket number, and the trouble reports receive the ticket number to which they belong.

If the ticket does exist, then the trouble report will be correlated to the object group ticket. As a result, the report receives the ticket number, and the problem resolution priority is updated if appropriate through the API. The trouble tickets are routed to the right destination using Remedy Notifier services.

After eliminating the problem, clear events or manual input will invoke the closure process. First, NetExpert determines whether a trouble report is still open on the object under consideration. If yes, and if the report or ticket is automatically (system) generated, then they will be closed automatically by the AR System. This fact is communicated to the gateway that changes the status attribute on the report and on the ticket via the API and clears the attributes through the gateway. If the report was manually created, the Remedy notifier routes it to the creator for closure or rejection.

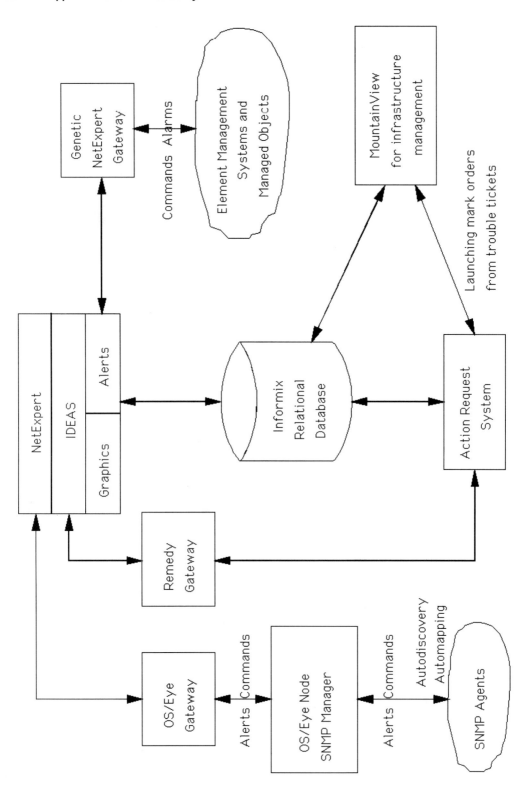

Figure 8.2 Integrated architecture

Escalations are routed to NetExpert gateway by ARS and treated as events. Escalation decisions are part of the fault tracking process and are handled by ARS.

Figure 8.3 illustrates the major process steps to create trouble reports and trouble tickets indicating the export/import of information between the tools.

Service order processing includes the following steps (Hart, 1994):

Upon receipt of the work order by the gateway, the gateway updates the object attributes, which include:

- the administrative state
- date for implementing the workorder
- checking and if necessary updating the workorder number
- vendor name

After having completed the updates, the gateway sends the work order as an event with special attributes to IDEAS. IDEAS is then expected to check the object status that may indicate:

- repair
- maintenance
- move, add, or change

Depending upon the state, IDEAS decides whether the target date indicated in the work order is acceptable or not. If yes, the work order is confirmed for implementation. If not, a new date is recommended by IDEAS. Usually, alerts and status changes for work orders are not displayed on the NetExpert graphical screens.

In both cases, IDEAS of NetExpert plays a key role in the integration of:

- repair and fault management
- service and fault management

8.2 NETWORK MANAGEMENT INTEGRATION USING AT&T STARSENTRY

This integration project was undertaken by a large firm offering outsourcing services to multiple clients in various countries around the world. To remain competitive, the outsourcing firm must establish a global presence. Global presence can be demonstrated by establishing networked network management centers. Locally, network management centers are more likely to support systems management as well. In addition, the need to manage multiple clients makes the requirement for integrated network management all the more critical.

Because of the need to manage multiple clients in either a shared or dedicated fashion, the following requirements arise:

Unified processes and procedures: Operators cannot afford to use different processes and procedures for managing client's networks. In particular, when network management resources are shared, unification is required.

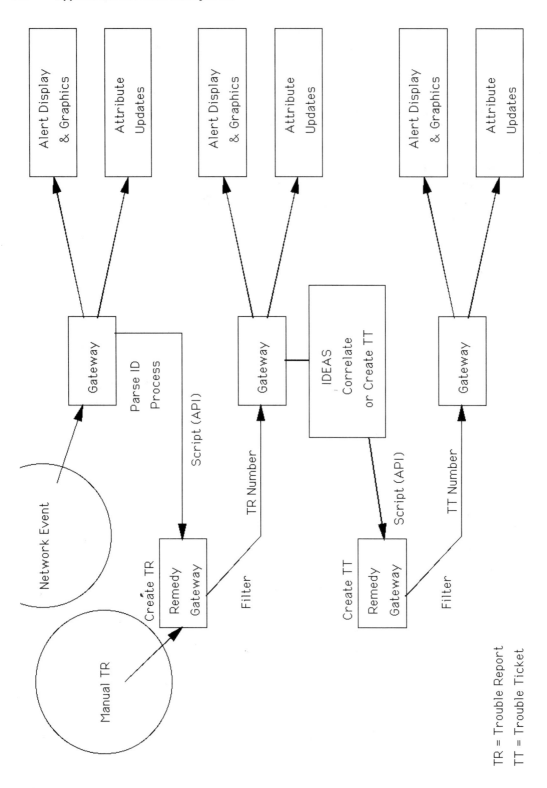

Figure 8.3 Trouble tracking procedure

TR = Trouble Report
TT = Trouble Ticket

Well defined lines of demarcation for clients: Unification in this area is extremely difficult. If different, the scope of management responsibilities is different, too. The outsourcer is expected to unify the bids with the following few alternatives:

- Management up to the wall
- Management up to half of the routers or bridges
- Management including/excluding the servers
- Management including/excluding PABXs
- Management of the backbone only

Volume of messages and alarms: If multiple clients are managed together, the volumes of messages and alarms may be substantial. The network management product must have a programmatic interface to write filtering applications.

Connections to various managed objects and element management systems: The clients' networks will have various networking components and management systems that may have been manufactured in different countries. Also in such cases, the bi-directional link must be built. As far as possible, standard and open protocols are expected to be used.

Scalability of the products selected: Not only the message and alarm volumes, but also the number of connections to managed objects and element management systems is growing. As a result, the CPU and storage capabilities of the products should cope with the changing and growing requirements.

Shareability of resources: Some clients will insist on partitioning the management products for security reasons. This means, that databases, displays, views, and reports should be separated from each other. Still they can share the same resources.

Powerful performance reporting: To better quantify the indicators of service level agreements, performance should be measured and reported periodically. At minimum, the network management product should collect and provide raw data.

Education and cross education of staff: The staff of the outsourcer must know all the networks and network management products taken over from clients. This may require substantial know-how extension for the personnel. As a result, however, the outsourcer will have a network management staff with over average skill levels.

The basic requirement is information sharing among the network management centers in order to support configuration, fault, and performance management processes in an environment in which multiple network management centers located in different countries operate as peer centers.

The basic functionality of networked network management centers includes:

1. Trouble ticket entry and tracking:

   Four different types of tickets need to be supported, trouble tickets (TT) for faults, configuration change request tickets (CC) for planned configuration changes to clients' networks, information tickets (IT) that may be opened in response to suspected problems for proactive management action, and quality assurance tickets (QA) that are opened to analyze and fix the root cause of recurring problems. The client service point supports related functions.

2. Asset management:

This function supports configuration management activities by maintaining information about customer network inventory, physical, and logical configuration. Accessibility is guaranteed to both customer and network management centers making change management tasks efficient.

3. Network graphics:

In order to guarantee up-to-date information on network status, this function integrates the ticketing and asset management systems. If desired, network graphics may be partitioned by customer.

4. Integrated database:

The database is supporting an integrated view of the assets as well as the tickets so that correlation of the two applications are facilitated. The database is expected to include the MIBs and RMONs for real time management of intelligent network elements and element management systems.

5. Flexible reporting:

The integrated solution needs to support several reports. Some of them are standard reports to evaluate the internal operations. Others are contractually required to be provided to the customers. Also, ad hoc reports may be required by customers or operating personnel.

6. Links to element management systems, operations support systems (OSS), and external systems are required to ensure a high level of correlability of events, alarms, and messages. Information export and import are supported using both in-band and out-band technologies.

7. Managing multiple interfaces:

Each network management center must manage its interfaces to its customers, suppliers, and peer centers. These interfaces involve network and systems management functions, processes to implement these functions, and systems used to support the process. The need to support a range of customer premises equipment and their respective management systems requires highly skilled human resources.

These functional requirements can only be met by using a combination of various instruments and by deploying multiple management centers. The network management centers are linked together as shown in Figure 8.4. The dedicated outbound lines ensure that management information can be exchanged without impacting the clients' networking traffic.

The proposed high-level architecture is shown in Figure 8.5. The administrative platform operates on a distributed network computing environment. Each location is equipped with LAN-based workstations, applications, servers, and routers. The workstations and servers are linked together by an Ethernet network. All applications can be downloaded from the application server on the workstations. The workstations are used to perform all the network management functions required by the clients.

The database that contains the inventory, tickets, network status, performance data, topologies, and vendor data is centralized and physically located in

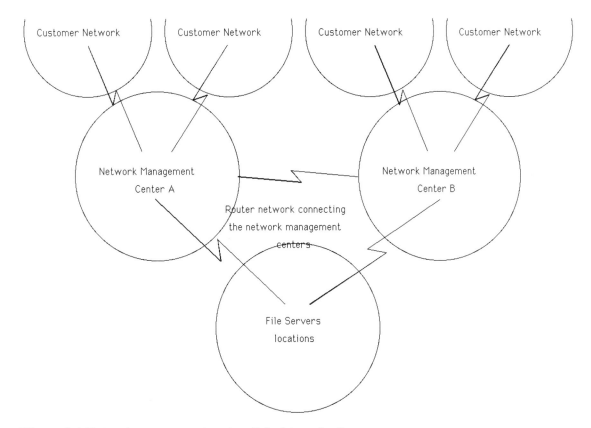

Figure 8.4 Network management centers linked to each other

a file server. A second file server is used as a hot backup to the main file server. The backup server mirrors all information in the main server (Figure 8.6). The servers are located in one of the centers and connected to the other centers by the communication network consisting of private lines. This backbone network has a ring architecture supporting a primary and a secondary path to reach each of the centers.

The network management applications are running on an open standard platform. The applications are comprised of three main management tools:

- AT&T StarSENTRY acts as a platform and for logical network management
- Isicad Command 5000 supports asset management, graphics, and for the management of the physical network
- AR System from Remedy supports trouble ticketing

These tools run on UNIX workstations supporting X-Windows based graphical interfaces, such as Motif. Networking of the workstations and servers is via the TCP/IP protocol. SQL is used by the application to communicate with and retrieve information from the Sybase database management system over the TCP/IP network. NFS (Network File System) is supported to share files in the

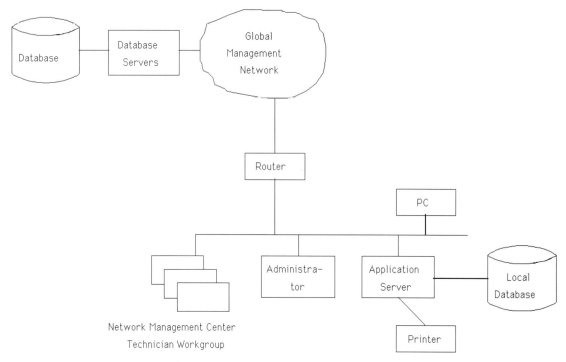

Figure 8.5 Architecture of network management centers

servers and workstations. Finally, PCs may be connected to application servers via TCP/IP. Figure 8.7 shows the various application layers in the servers and workstations.

Reporting is supported by various tools. One alternative is to use the capabilities of Sybase with built-in EZSQL front-end for ad-hoc-reports. Users have also the opportunities to generate pre-built reports by Isicad and Remedy using SQL/Accell. For reports that require business graphics, the raw data are processed by Lotus 123. Figure 8.8 shows the process of report generation.

Information export and support with element management systems is supported via TCP/IP. Arriving data is stored in Sybase. In special cases, flat files must first be filtered and converted. Reporting applications can be applied to this data as well.

As an alternative to AT&T StarSENTRY, the firm could have chosen other products to support the administration of its network management centers and the exchange of management information with customer-owned element management systems. These alternatives include HP OpenView, IBM NetView/6000, and SunNet Manager. Alternatives to Isicad Command 5000 include Accugraph MountainView or Autotrol Konfig. Also, Legent Paradigm could have been selected instead of Remedy AR System.

As mentioned in section 8.1.8, the RDBMS alternatives include Informix, Oracle, Ingres, Acell, and Unify. Theoretically, applications are becoming platform-independent however, the preferred combinations are still IBM NetView/6000

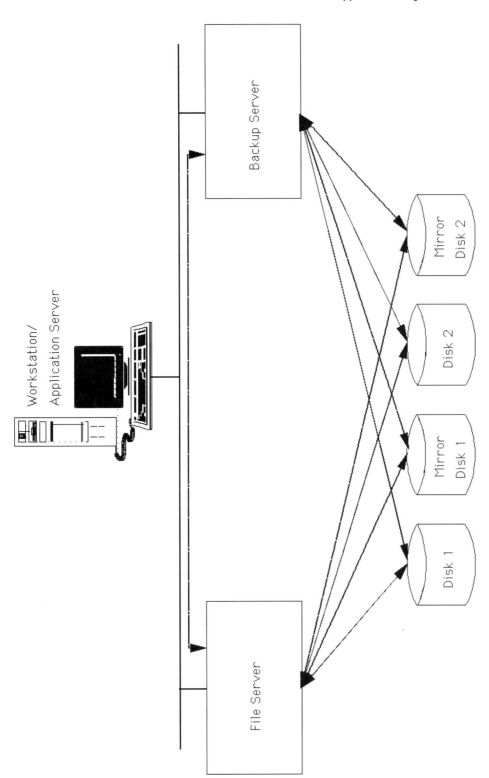

Figure 8.6 High-availability file servers

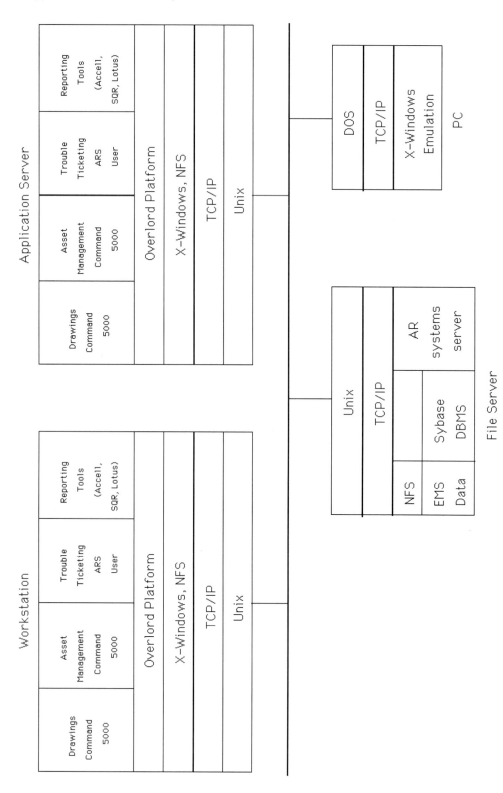

Figure 8.7 Software architecture of the integrated solution

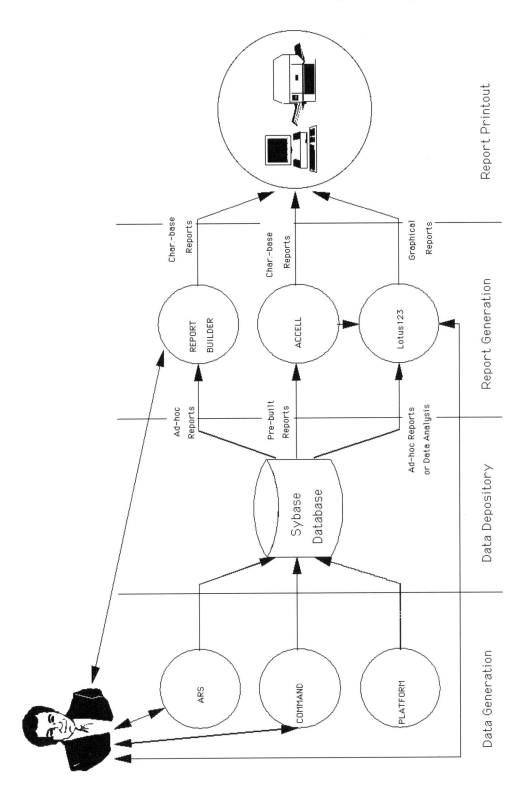

Figure 8.8 Report generation process

and IBM Trouble Ticket Manager (an OEM version of Legent Paradigm), OSI NetExpert and NetImpact from Strategic Solutions, and HP OpenView and Peregrine OpenSNA. In addition, each platform typically provides off-the-shelf links to only one or two RDBMSs. IBM's NetView/6000 Version 3.0 will be among the first platforms to offer links to several RDBMSs.

Another alternative for enhanced reporting is DbPublish. This product generates presentation-quality reports, and can operate with several relational databases; it does not require knowledge of SQL.

The integration solution is updated and expanded as soon as needed due to customer requests. Additional features will be integrated into the solution in the future, including:

- Partitioning by customer
- Accounting by customer
- Expert like problem determination
- Console emulation to support cut through to element management system

Scalability is an overriding concern for the implementers of this integrated network management solution. On the one hand, the suppliers may be tempted to fine-tune the solution for a special mix of customers and for a specific workload volume. However, the long-term capacity limits of the project are not yet known. During the next project phase, the firm plans to conduct stress testing of multiple element management systems and varying administrative workloads, in an attempt to assess the scalability of the solution.

8.3   INTEGRATED APPLICATIONS FOR MANAGING WAN SERVICES USING WILTEL AND SUNNET MANAGER

The market for interexchange carrier (IXC) services, such as private line, 800/900, frame relay, and virtual private networks is increasingly competitive. Carriers are responding to competitive pressure by offering customers better "windows" into the management systems that monitor and administer these services. These windows take the form of element management systems that connect to the carrier's operation support systems (OSSs).

Virtually all IXCs now offer some form of customer-premise based access to management functions. However, only WilTel and MCI are providing this access in the form of applications supporting multiple SNMP-based "open" management platforms. WilTel has been particularly aggressive in integrating its WilView product with other vendor's applications, such as Remedy's Action Request System (ARS) problem management software and Ameritech's MultiProtocol Network Manager.

WilTel is the fourth largest provider of telecommunications and wide area interconnect services in the United States. The WilView product family includes the WilView/X network services management application, the WilView/SNMP agent (providing performance and configuration management data on WilPak frame relay circuits), WilView/EDI (electronic data transfers) and WilView/IMS messaging application.

8.3.1   WilView/X Integration

WilView/X has been integrated into both HP OpenView and SunNet Manager. WilTel expects to integrate WilView/X into IBM NetView/6000 in the near future.

Because WilView/X is integrated with the underlying platform, WilTel-provided WAN links (such as frame relay connections and private line circuits) are represented as icons on the network map of the user's SNMP management console. This is significant, as it extends the reach of SNMP beyond internetwork devices to the actual WAN links which were previously unmanageable via SNMP—thereby providing an end-to-end view from the console. Operators can initiate the WilView/X management application by clicking on a WAN icon. Once initiated, WilView/X provides users with a direct link to WilTel's operational support systems. The WilView/X software does not actually execute on the customer's workstation, but rather on WilTel's host.

Figures 8.9 through 8.11 show connection alternatives between the WilTel host and the customer's workstation. There are four primary options for connectivity:

1. WilPak Frame Relay: WilPak provides the easiest and least expensive option for both WilTel and the customer if the WilPak node already exists. It also provides for the greatest flexibility to the customer if access to WilView from multiple workstations is required. The basic configuration is shown in Figure 8.9.
2. DDS (dedicated digital service/private line) with combined CSU-Synch/ Asynch Converter: This option should be used whenever possible for private line customers, as it provides the simplest and least expensive DDS configuration for both the customer and WilTel. The basic configuration is illustrated in Figure 8.10.
3. Internet access for commercial Internet users (see Figure 8.11).
4. Dial-up using the Network Control Devices (NCD) Xremote X-Windows compression protocol

The display and control of the application is passed across the WilTel network to the end user's workstation. One advantage of this approach is that customers can use any X11-compliant device to support WilView/X, including UNIX workstations (running SNMP management software) or DOS, Windows, or OS/2 PCs (in which case, WilView/X would be operating as a stand alone application, independent of any underlying SNMP platform).

8.3.2   WilView/X Features

For Private Line, WilPak, and WilNet Bandwidth-on-Command customers, WilView/X supports the following functions: circuit inventory, service order tracking, trouble ticket entry and tracking, and messaging. Circuit inventory provides basic circuit parameters, such as type, termination locations, status, and service dates.

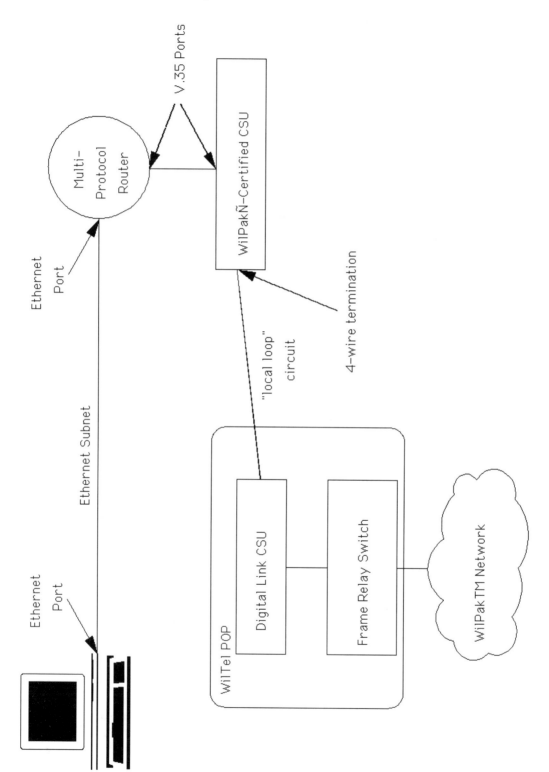

Figure 8.9 Customer connections for WilView™ access (from a PC using WilPak™ access)

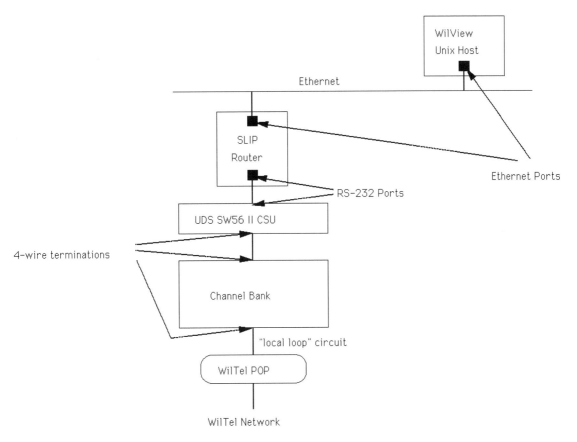

Figure 8.10 WilTel™ connections for WilView™ access (using DS-O access)

In addition, commercial private line users can obtain graphical circuit routing and performance reporting. Using the graphical circuit routing feature, an operator can visually confirm that WilTel has configured the network to meet specific service needs, such as geographic route diversity or some unique routing requirement. Subscribers to WilNet Bandwidth-on-Command can also access WilTel's reservation system through the WilView/X console to reserve bandwidth for videoconferencing or disaster recovery purposes.

WilView/X also supports DS-1 and DS-3 alarm reporting for commercial private line users, and utilization reporting for WilPak frame relay ports and PVCs.

One of WilView/X's major benefits is that it saves network managers time in determining the status of service orders and problems. Major IXC outages are rare for any carrier, but they usually happen at the worst time for commercial businesses. When an IXC has a major failure, it can only handle so many calls from worried customers; if the carrier can not answer customers' calls they can not find out about the status of their network lines.

Integrated trouble ticket support is another time-saving feature of WilView/X. WilView/X has been integrated with Remedy's Action Request System (ARS),

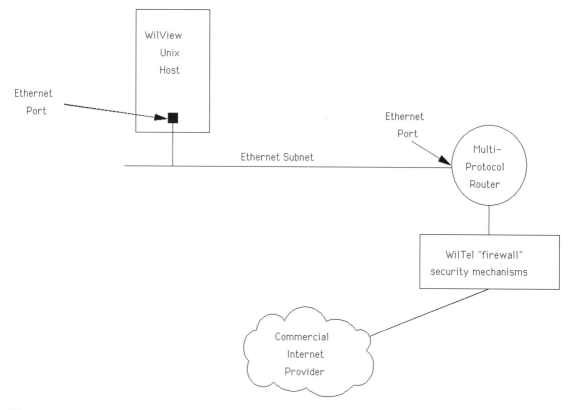

Figure 8.11 WilTel connections for WilView™ access (using Internet access)

providing a single point of contact between WilTel and the end-user organization's help desk, for the purpose of tracking and resolving problems on WAN links. For example, if the operator at a SunNet Manager console pings a remote router and gets no response, but determines from other means that the router is fine, the operator can use AR System to open a trouble ticket and submit it to WilTel, calling up the WilView/X application from the ARS screen.

8.3.3   Application Integration

WilTel has invested its own resources into integrating WilView into other environments. Two examples of this include integration with MultiProtocol Network Manager (MPNM) from Ameritech and the AR System from Remedy.

The MPNM model is as follows: MPNM incorporates four major element management systems: SNMP for TCP/IP networks, IBM NetView for SNA networks, Asychronous Manager for asynchronous devices, and WilView/X for circuits and frame relay connections.

As described previously in this chapter, AR System from Remedy provides trouble ticketing and problem management facilities. The following scenario describes how AR System and WilView/X work together:

1. An end-user calls the client contact point (or help desk) to report that its client/server application is no longer working. The technician quickly attempts to poll the server, but gets no response. There is also no response from the router at the same location.
2. After checking the local management system and getting no indication of failure, the technician opens a trouble ticket using AR System and assigns the problem to WilTel.
3. The technician selects the WilTel button from the main menu of AR System. This opens a new window on the screen, providing access to the WilView system.
4. The technician creates a trouble ticket for export from the menu.
5. The technician identifies the frame relay PVC between that location and the remote location as the problem, enters the appropriate symptoms, and submits the ticket directly to WilTel from the WilView screen.
6. WilTel receives the trouble ticket, resolves the problem, and notifies the client service point.

WilView is also integrated with SunNet manager, allowing SunNet Manager users to identify the WilTel-provided network components as those components fit into the end-to-end network view, and to directly access the WilView application to manage those components. Figure 8.12 shows a simple network where WAN connections from WilTel are labeled. The WAN icons are active and accurately reflect the circuit and WilPak components of the network that are just as critical and just as important to manage as the other elements shown.

To add a component to the SunNet Manager map, the user selects "create component" from the Edit Menu and selects the type of object to be added. With the WilView/Link for SunNet Manager software, the WilTel circuit and WilPak objects appear as types of objects that can be added to the network. The user is expected to enter component-specific information. To manage WAN components, WilView is activated from within SunNet Manager by selecting the WilView option from the Tools menu. Selecting the WilView option will connect the user to the WilView host, where the user can log onto the WilView UNIX-based applications. Other WilTel applications may be integrated the same way.

8.3.4   WilView/SNMP

The WilView/SNMP agent enhances management of WilPak frame relay service from an organization's existing SNMP management platform. WilView/SNMP includes an implementation of the Frame Relay Network Service Management Information Base (MIB). This MIB provides raw service data describing network utilization and performance. To support troubleshooting, WilTel's implementation supports access to historical data up to one month old. WilView/SNMP also allows operators to define custom views into the network based upon selection of specific ports and permanent virtual circuits (PVCs). Custom views can allow for secure distribution of network management tasks in a distributed computing environment.

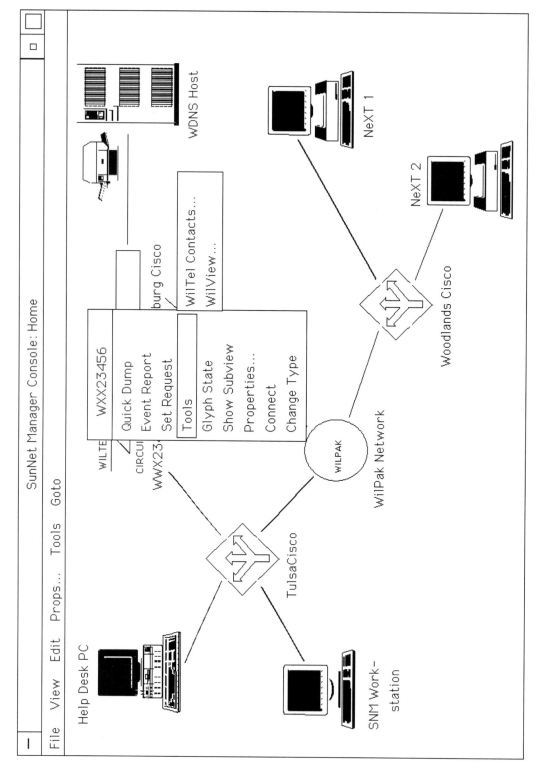

Figure 8.12 WAN connections from WilTel (circuit WXX23456) labeled on the SunNet Manager screen

Scalability of this solution is extremely important for the following reasons:

- The depth of services offered by carriers is increasing.
- The variety of devices at the customer premises is growing.
- Customers are demanding more and more information details about the services to which they subscribe.
- Carriers have more pressure to deliver timely information.
- Customers are demanding support of multiple interfaces to databases, applications, element management systems, and management platforms.

WilTel's selection of SunNet Manager as the SNMP management platform has been well received, and this choice has given the carrier an advantage in many competitive bid situations. Another management platform such as IBM NetView/6000 or HP OpenView may also be supported in the future, however, and trouble ticket application alternatives such as Legent Paradigm may also be considered.

In the future, users can expect to see other WAN services supported in a similar fashion via SNMP. This would, of course, increase the usability of SNMP-based management platforms such as HP OpenView and SunNet Manager. The WilView product family is one of the few management applications shipping today that integrated management of WAN resources with open, SNMP-based management platforms. MCI's Hyperscope is the only other WAN services application now offered from a major carrier that supports multiple platforms. AT&T is in the process of releasing a frame relay management service for use on the StarSENTRY platform.

8.4 INTEGRATING NETWORK AND SYSTEMS MANAGEMENT: A CASE STUDY OF INTEGRATION AT THE U.S. ARMY

The U.S. Army is now in the process of improving its information processing and communications infrastructure. In the past, the subsystems of this infrastructure have had limited interoperability, portability, and scalability. These systems have been independently managed on a mostly piecemeal basis.

Now, however, the Army is in a state of change because of increasing fiscal constraints, downsizing, and changes in doctrine requiring the Army to work "smarter." In particular, recent Department of Defense (DOD) directives have placed additional emphasis on providing more efficient systems and network management services, with increased coordination and interoperability among military departments.

As part of an effort to improve the ability of end-users to support the overall mission, the Army is migrating many of its key applications to a more interactive, modular client/server implementation. Some of these applications include activity scheduling, personnel processing, and education and management information systems. These applications integrate day-to-day support functions processes that are generally found on all Army installations.

8.4.1 Reasons for Integrating Network and Systems Management

The integration of both network and systems management under a common enterprise management framework is an integral part of the Army's modernization effort. Figure 8.13 depicts existing "boundaries" between network and systems management.

The Army anticipates deriving cost savings by implementing centralized network and systems management for remote locations. This centralized support will be supplemented by "lights dim" management—meaning that the use of local support personnel will be minimal.

The goals of the overall Army network and systems management (NSM) effort are as follows:

1. Improve the quality of information services provided to the Army Commander or Joint Task Force Commander and their forces—anywhere, at anytime, and with the least possible number of forward-deployed assets
2. Minimize the labor, and hence the costs, required to manage the information systems assets, without degrading user service

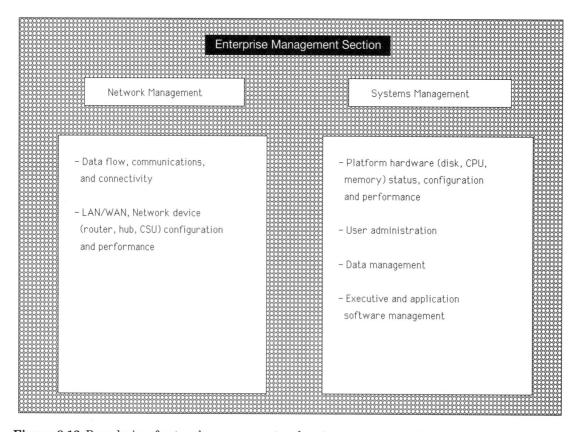

Figure 8.13 Boundaries of network management and systems management

Specific objectives of improving network and systems management include:

- Supporting lights dim operations
- Reducing personnel costs associated with operation and maintenance
- Reducing the level of expertise required for daily operations
- Minimizing network and system downtime through performance monitoring and fault detection and identification
- Enforcing system-wide standards for configuration and performance
- Implementing fully functional non-proprietary standards for network and systems management
- Using currently-available hardware and software

In addition, end-user satisfaction is a primary goal of the Army's NSM project; therefore, an effective local help desk is a focal point of the integration effort. Early on in the project, automated trouble ticketing/help desk applications were identified for originating, tracking, resolving, and analyzing user needs at all sites. This included handling user support requests ranging from the need for a new account ID or password to tracking and reporting system trouble or new user equipment.

The Army wants to centralize network and systems management solutions and move operations to a "lights dim" environment whenever possible to minimize personnel costs. This would allow a core set of experts to be at a central location, managing devices remotely. With the technology that exists today, the concept of centralized management with distributed control can be readily implemented. The following management architecture was developed by the Army to address that concept.

8.4.2 Organizational Structure for Supporting Integrated Network and Systems Management

The Army's network and systems management integration project encompasses as computers, peripherals, systems software, applications, and communications networks connecting 28 selected Army installations in the continental United States.

The overall management architecture is shown in Figure 8.14. A central Network and Systems Management Center (NSMC) oversees many aspects of remote systems management, database administration, and network management. The NSMC is responsible for overall network and systems management functions down to, but not including, user workstations and printers at all locations, and voice information network assets. The NSMC has end-to-end management responsibility—including the following:

- Controlling, monitoring, and maintaining end-to-end network and systems configuration
- Initiating and terminating remote processes (network and systems software downloading, backups, and archives)
- End-to-end fault isolation (excluding end user devices such as PCs and printers)

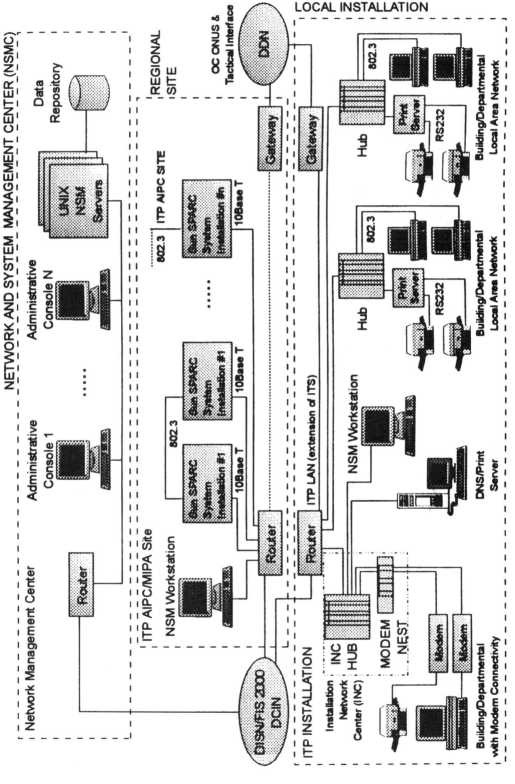

Figure 8.14 Conceptual architecture for the Army network and systems management (NSM) integration project

- Monitoring and analyzing end-to-end utilization and performance
- Monitoring and controlling access
- Identifying and assigning action requests
- Initiating and controlling software maintenance releases

Centralizing control at a Network and System Management Center (NSMC) enforces system-wide standards for configuration control, performance, and fault analysis.

Regional processing centers responsible for Designated Army installations are managed by one regional site. These regional sites, formerly called Army Information Processing Centers (AIPCs), are now called Multifunctional Information Processing Activities (MIPAs). These regional sites are responsible for physical loading of backup tapes, physical asset and facility management, and user processing.

While the central NSMC site shoulders most of the management burden, regional MIPA sites and local Army installations also use selected network and systems management applications to perform local domain management and trouble ticket management. (See Figure 8.15.)

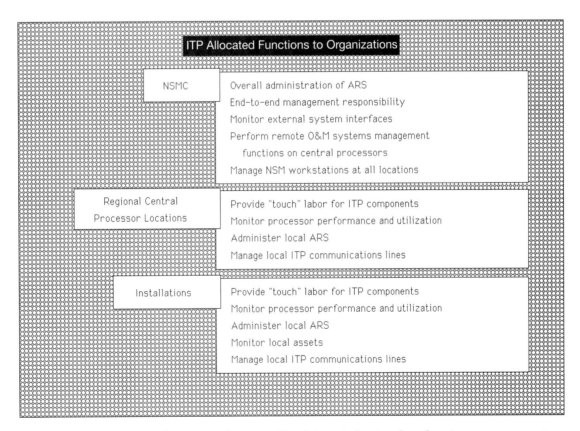

Figure 8.15 Organizational structure for supporting integrated network and systems management

8.4.3   Product Evaluations

The Army evaluated more than 50 applications for inclusion in the NSM project. The applications were evaluated according to their ability to support the following functions:

- action request management (ARM)
- configuration management
- fault management
- performance management
- security management

Accounting management, including charge-back and the assignment of costs to the user of network and system resources, will be implemented after the U.S. Department of Defense and the Department of the Army complete their studies of accounting management criteria. (See Figure 8.16.)

Specifically, the Army looked for management applications capable addressing the following components of the information processing and communications infrastructure: servers, gateways, routers, channel services units/data service units (CSU/DSUs), intelligent hubs, internetworked bridges, modems, RS-232

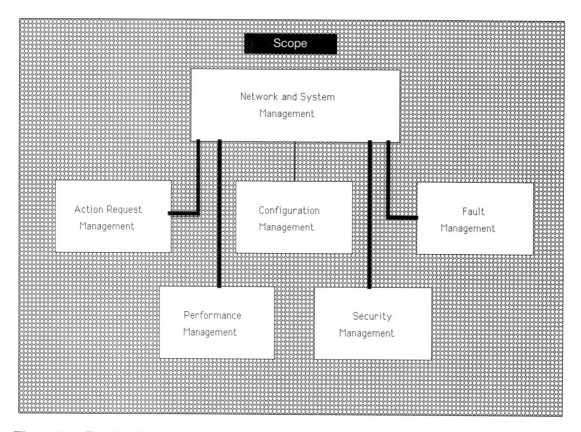

Figure 8.16 Functional scope of integrated network and systems management

interface modules, local area networks (LANs), workstations, device servers, hubs, and printers.

Table 8.1 is a matrix of the products evaluated for this project and the functional areas they support. As shown in Figure 8.17, the central network and systems management center (NSMC) uses hardware from two primary vendors—Sun Microsystems' Sun SPARC 10, and Hewlett-Packard's HP 9000 750. The Army chose to implement network and systems management applications on both hardware platforms. In addition, several software packages for each of the functions were selected for each platform. Because each package performs different functions and satisfies specific criteria, many of the packages must be integrated together to fulfill functional requirements.

The Army has chosen HP OpenView as its primary management systems at the NSMC. However, SunNet Manager is also implemented currently and will be retained for some functions. The NSMC management hardware configuration is as follows:

SunNet Manager (Sun SPARC 10, SunOS, OpenLook)
HP OpenView (HP 9000 750, HP-UX, X11 OSF Motif)
HP OpenView and Ingres RDBMS (HP 9000 750, HP-UX, X11 OSF Motif)

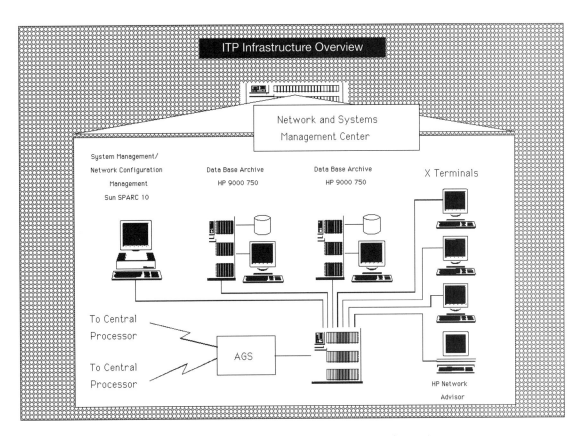

Figure 8.17 Network and systems management center hardware configuration

TABLE 8-1   Products Evaluated for Network and Systems Management

Product	Net Mgmt.	Sys. Mgmt.	Overall Config. Mgmt.	Security Mgmt.	Trouble Ticket Mgmt.
Accugraph Mountain view	✔		✔		
Alcatel TITN NM Expert	✔				
Alida, Inc. Gurutape		✔			
AT&T Comsphere 3600 (CSU/DSU)	✔				✔
AT&T Comsphere 6800 (CSI/DSU)	✔				✔
Boole Babbage Command Post	✔				
Break Away Software Picus	✔				
Cabletron LANView (hubs)	✔				
Cabletron Spectrum	✔				
Cisco CiscoWorks (routers)	✔				
Computer Associates CA Unicenter		✔	✔	✔	✔
Concord Trakker (Tap/LAN)	✔				
DEMAX SecureMax for UNIX				✔	
HP Distributed Management Platform	✔				
HP Distributed Management Development Kit*					
HP Glance Plus UX	✔[1]				
HP LAN Probe II & Probe Manager (Tap/LAN)	✔		✔		
HP OpenView Extensible SNMP Agent	✔	✔	✔	✔	✔
HP OPenView Node Manager	✔	✔[6]	✔	✔	
HP PerfView	✔[1]				
HP RXForecast	✔[1,2]				
HP Laser RX/UX	✔				
Isicad Command Help Desk			✔[7]		✔
Legato Networker		✔[3]			
Logicon Ultrasystems Network Security Manager				✔	

Notes: [1] Performance management only
[2] Modeling
[3] Fault management only
[4] Device management only
[5] Software management only
[6] Extensible agent
[7] Local domain
[8] Third-party implementation
*Applications development kit

TABLE 8-1   Products Evaluated for Network and Systems Management *(continued)*

Product	Net Mgmt.	Sys. Mgmt.	Overall Config. Mgmt.	Security Mgmt.	Trouble Ticket Mgmt.
NetLabs Assist	✔[1,2,3,4]				
NetLabs Discovery	✔				
NetLabs Manager	✔[4]				
NetLabs Service Desk					✔
Net Metrix	✔[4]				
Networx Paradigm			✔		✔
Objective Systems Integrators net Expert	✔				
Open Vision Technology Lights Out		✔	✔		
Peregrine Network Management System	✔				
Raxco Backup Unet		✔			
Raxco Security Toolkit				✔	
Remedy Action Request System			✔		✔
Remedy Health Profiler	✔				
Silicon Graphics Net Visualizer	✔[4]		✔		
Sun Microsystems SunNet Manager	✔		✔		
Sun Microsystems SunShield				✔	
SynOptics Lattisware Solutions (hubs)	✔				
SynOptics Optivity	✔		✔[5]		✔
Tivoli Courier			✔		
Tivoli Sentry				✔	
Tivoli Works		✔	✔		
TransARC AFS		✔			
Wellfleet Site Manager (routers)	✔[4]		✔[4]		
Woodside Technology Inc. Fortress				✔	

Notes: [1] Performance management only
[2] Modeling
[3] Fault management only
[4] Device management only
[5] Software management only
[6] Extensible agent
[7] Local domain
[8] Third-party implementation
*Applications development kit

Table 8.2 lists the primary supporting management applications selected by the Army for each management platform at the NSMC. The following packages were selected for further evaluation on the SunSPARC station:

SunSPARC Hardware

Network Management

SunNet Manager or NetLabs (DiMONS, NetLabs/Assist, NetLabs/Discovery) are recommended as basic managers to perform configuration device manage-

TABLE 8-1   NSM Software Summary

NSM Software Category	Sun SPARCStation	HP Platform	Intel Platform
Network Management	SunNet Manager Concord Trakker Cisco Works Cabletron LANView SynOptics LattisWare NetLabs Assist NetLabs Discovery NetLabs Manager	HO OpenView Node Manager HP Distributed management Platform HP PerfView Break Away Software Picus HP GlancePlus UX HP LANProbe II & Probe Manager Remedy Health Profiler HP OpenView Extensible SNMP Agent HP Laser RX/UX	
System Management	Tivoli Works TransARC AFS Alida Gurutape/GTBackup Leato Networker	Computer Associates CA Unicenter	OpenVision Technology Lights Out (port this to HP when Tivoli ports to HP)
Overall Configuration Management	Tivoli Center Networx Paradigm	Networx Paradigm Remedy Action Request System Wellfleet Site Manager Accugraph Mountain View SynOptics RiskViews1	
Security Management	SunShield Tivoli Sentry Woodside Technology Fortress DEMAX Software SecureMax Raxco Security Toolkit	Computer Associates CA Unicenter DEMAX Software SecureMax Logicon Ultrasystems Network Raxco Security Toolkit	
Trouble Ticket Management			

ment for Cisco and Cabletron equipment. Concord Trakker (traffic monitor) will be integrated to monitor continuously all LAN protocol layers in realtime. Cabletron LANView will be used to manage network devices and diagnose network problems at the physical layer. CiscoWorks will provide router management for Cisco routers. SynOptics LattisWare will provide diagnostic tools for managing SynOptics hubs.

Systems Management

Tivoli Sentry will be integrated on SunSPARC hardware initially until an HP port is available. Tivoli Works or Alida Gurutape provide an automated systems administration. TransARC AFS architecture will support the distributed computing environment and assist in systems administration functions. Legato Networker or Gurutape will support tape backup capabilities.

Overall Configuration Management

Tivoli Courier will be evaluated for its use in automating software configuration and distribution (see Figure 8.18). Networx (now Legent) Paradigm trouble ticketing software will also assist in configuration management by taking actions upon fault detection.

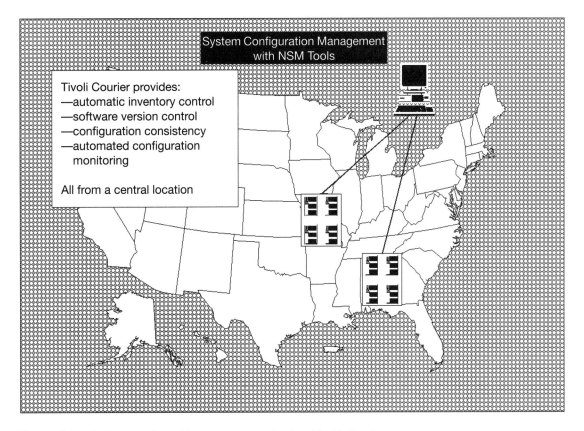

Figure 8.18 System configuration management using Tivoli Courier

Security Management

SunShield, Tivoli Sentry, Security Toolkit, and OpenV*Secure Max and Fortress will be evaluated for security mechanism support.

Trouble Ticketing

HP will support trouble ticketing as the primary management platform.

HP 9000 750 Hardware Platforms

Network Management

HP OpenView Network Node Manager and HP OpenView Distributed Manager are the basic network management packages. HP OpenView Extensible SNMP agents will be integrated in remote workstations to continuously monitor HP platforms and Sun SPARC stations. HP LANProbe II will be used to manage network devices and diagnose network problems at the physical layer. HP PerfView, HP Glance Plus, Breakaway PICUS, and Remedy Health Profiler will be evaluated for performance management.

System Management

Alida Gurutape and CA Unicenter will be evaluated for providing automated systems administration.

Overall Configuration Management

Legent Paradigm, Remedy AR System, and Accugraph MountainView will support configuration management process by taking actions upon fault detection. Wellfleet Site Manager will be used to control and manage Wellfleet routers.

Security Management

OpenVision OpenV*SecureMax (formerly Demax), Raxco Security Toolkit, and CA Unicenter will be evaluated for providing security mechanisms to supplement utilities in the operating system.

Trouble Ticketing

Remedy AR System, Legent Paradigm, or Isicad Command Help Desk will be selected to provide general trouble ticketing capabilities.

Currently, Remedy ARS acts as the integration point for various network and systems management products (see Figure 8.19). Trouble tickets may be generated automatically by integrated applications, using command line integration. Trouble tickets may also be generated manually by technicians at the central or regional sites or by local installation personnel (see Figure 8.20).

8.5 SUMMARY

The case studies covered in this chapter show that integration of many applications into platforms can be accomplished. The depth of integration and the ele-

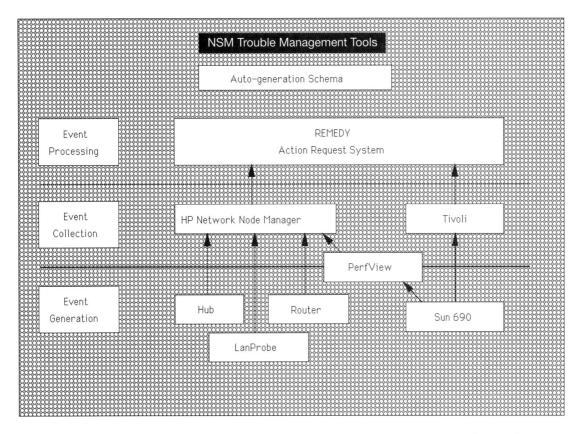

Figure 8.19 Remedy AR System acts as the integration point for various systems and network management products.

gance of solutions may differ from case to case, but the integrated product is working. These examples demonstrate that various vendors can work together, even in cases when one of the vendors is assigned to the integration. Practical experiences show that the biggest barriers are with database integration. Each vendor usually has a favorite relational database with some proprietary implementation flavors; to convince vendors to sacrifice these solutions and port them to the common database is difficult. In some cases, the vendors agree to connect their databases using SQL-capabilities and to synchronize updates but not to port populated databases into a common database. Using multiple databases is not necessarily disadvantageous; it may offer a distribution capability ensuring a sort of load sharing between databases. The result may be a better performance and a higher level of security.

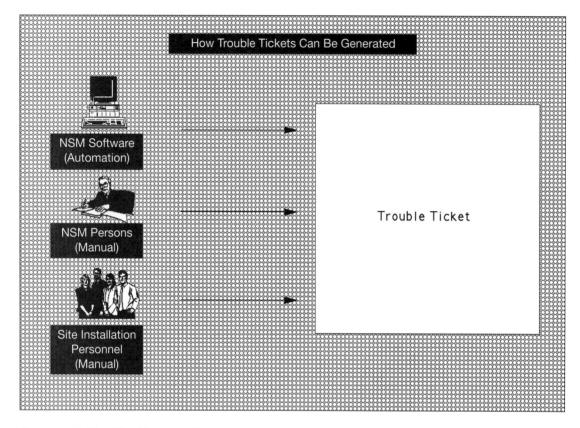

Figure 8.20 Trouble tickets may be generated automatically, or manually by operations center or site personnel

9

Managing Client/Server Structures

The client/server computing model has become popular because it matches the business needs of today's increasingly competitive global economy, and because client/server structures take advantage of the significant decreases in the cost of processing power enabled by technological advances. However, the accelerated pace of client/server deployment creates new and complex challenges for network and systems managers. This chapter describes the client/server computing model within the context of distributed systems and open systems and then explains the unique problems associated with managing client/server structures.

9.1 DEFINITIONS

The terms "client/server," "distributed computing," and "open systems" are often loosely used to characterize today's enterprise networks and information technologies. Actually, these phrases describe specific aspects of current computing and networking technology. Each of these aspects adds a new layer of complexity to network and systems management.

9.1.1 Distributed Systems

The term "distributed system" refers to the ability of multiple, autonomous processors, or CPUs, to share processing tasks. Accordingly, a terminal-to-host network is not actually a distributed system, even if some of the terminals are X-terminals. Today, "distributed system" is often used to describe a collection of workstations interconnected through a network in which the communications delay is not noticeable (Tanenbaum, 1993). Strictly speaking, a true distributed system is one that uses interprocess communications to share low-level processing tasks. However, this book takes the middle ground by referring to distributed systems as multiple independent, autonomous, communicating CPUs that present a single-system image to the user—e.g., processors that support processing in such a way that location transparency is achieved.

Critical problems that arise in the management of distributed systems include handling partial failures (e.g., failure of one processor among many); the impact of moves, adds, and changes in a dynamic environment; and synchronization of processes. The sheer increase in the number of computers in a distributed environment—as well as the increase in the variety of computers—compounds the complexity of the management problem. Methods for dealing with complexity include object-orientation of management applications and domain management.

Object-oriented programming techniques allow developers to encapsulate the behaviors of various network devices and systems components into classes, thereby shielding developers from the complexities of the underlying infrastructure. In addition, object-oriented modelling allows developers to start with a more abstract focus than is possible using procedural-oriented methods. As a result, designers can focus more on the purpose of an application—WHAT it does, versus HOW. The application is modelled in terms of objects, which are externally visible things with which an operator or network administrator interacts. This helps developers to capture the essence of what the system will do for the end-user—instead of becoming distracted with implementation issues. It is important to model the object in an abstract fashion BEFORE making decisions about how to implement the object.

An object-oriented design makes isolating and debugging the application's programming entities (e.g., the objects) and testing them easier for developers. Debugging the interaction between objects is also simpler. Since each object encapsulates its own data and behavior, other software components are restricted to access and manipulate an object through its well-defined, public interface. As a result, developers do not need to have as much detailed knowledge about the overall system to locate and fix bugs.

An object-oriented approach can facilitate the creation of reusable code. However, software reuse is not free. A lot of up-front effort is required to design code for reuse, but the effort pays off generously in the end. When developers spend time making a careful design, they can understand the problem more deeply. Then the implementation process goes faster because the developers have already learned a great deal about the problem. As a result, maintaining or even reducing the time required for one cycle of applications development is possible. More importantly, because the software has been designed from the start with maintenance, extension, and reuse in mind, the time required for any subsequent modification effort is dramatically reduced.

An object-oriented approach is particularly valid when the target application is complex, which is very true for the distributed systems environment. Another good example is an application that a carrier might develop for supporting a new value-added services (such as customer-accessible alternate routing or traffic analysis features). Object-orientation is a very natural way to describe or model the various switches, circuits, alarms, users, services, and other physical and logical components that must be managed in a telecommunications network. For years, standards bodies such as ISO and CCITT have consistently used the concept of objects for specifying interoperable protocols such as Common Management Information Protocol (CMIP) and for defining information models, such as Signalling System 7 (SS7).

Another method for dealing with the complexity of distributed systems is the grouping of objects into domains. Once objects are grouped, administrators can define common policies for managing all objects in the group. Domains themselves can be viewed as objects, and they can be members of other domains (Moffet, 1993). In other words, objects can be members of more than one domain, to reflect overlapping responsibility or different types of management responsibility for the same object. For example, the administrator responsible for the security of a group of UNIX workstations may be different than the administrator responsible for doing backups.

9.1.2   Open Systems

Open systems generally refer to computers supporting the UNIX operating system, and its many derivatives (AIX, Ultrix, SunOS, HP-UX, etc.). Typically, these systems are interconnected via internetworks supporting the Transmission Control Protocol/Internet Protocol (TCP/IP) or Open Systems Interconnect (OSI) protocols, and perhaps other protocols as well. Open systems also employ other published standards, such as Structured Query Language (SQL), for relational database queries. In contrast with proprietary systems, open systems have published interfaces and much of the code lies in the public domain.

Advantages of open systems include the ability to interoperate (at least theoretically) with other open systems and the notion that no one vendor controls open systems technology. While open systems free end-user organizations from being locked-into artificially high license fees and one vendor's view of the universe, they are not without their disadvantages.

The lack of manageability is among the most serious limitations of open systems. Proprietary protocols and architectures have built-in management support; such protocols include IBM's Systems Network Architecture (SNA) and Digital's DECnet. Open protocols—and TCP/IP in particular—include little or no inherent management support. Management must come from external protocols, such as the Simple Network Management Protocol (SNMP), as well as a much greater reliance on external tools such as traffic monitors and analyzers. In particular, for file transfer and virtual terminal facilities of open systems—specifically, FTP and telnet—users must purchase after-market tools to market these protocols of the TCP/IP protocol suite.

SNMP is now the predominant protocol for open systems management, although several management systems also support the OSI Common Management Information Protocol (CMIP). SNMP is optimized for managing LAN interconnect devices, including bridges, routers, and wiring concentrators. SNMP is used to exchange management information between management systems (stations) and agents (network devices or components). SNMP is primarily poll-driven; the manager continuously sends out polls at defined intervals to obtain status from remote agents.

9.1.3   Client/Server

As the name implies, client/server systems consist of client processes (applications) and server processes (which provide system services such as printing, faxing, and access to files, modems, etc.). Client/server systems use a request/response mechanism, whereby multiple clients are able to initiate a request for service (such as access to a file) and a server will respond to that request. Typical servers include:

- database servers
- file servers
- print servers
- document/image servers, fax servers
- mail servers
- gateway/communications servers

Client/server systems (see Figure 9.1) offer transparency and scalability. Ideally, system changes in the client/server system are transparent to the user. In other words, the user is unaware that the application is divided into front-end and back-end processes residing on different computers (e.g., a distributed system). Furthermore, the user remains unaware of the addition (or deletion) of PCs to (from) the LAN, or the addition of extra data storage or the partitioning of data.

Scalability is achieved because client workstations can be added or eliminated with minimal impact on total system performance. Server processes can be moved to larger or faster machines as needed. Additionally, server processes can be replicated at various locations on a network, providing the equivalent of multi-processing and multi-tasking.

In client/server systems, distributed client, and server processes use remote procedure calls to communicate. This creates two types of management problems: lack of global state information, and the need to synchronize processes and databases.

9.2   SPECIAL PROBLEMS WITH CLIENT/SERVER MANAGEMENT

Client/server computing is an attractive alternative to mainframe-based computing because the initial cost for hardware and much of the software is dramatically less expensive. However, follow-up costs for implementing client/server computing in the organization—including network and systems management costs—can be very high if a coordinated strategy is not in place. Client/server computing immediately places a new burden on the network, with unpredictable traffic loads and performance. Systems management is also more complex when compared to traditional proprietary systems that include integrated hardware/

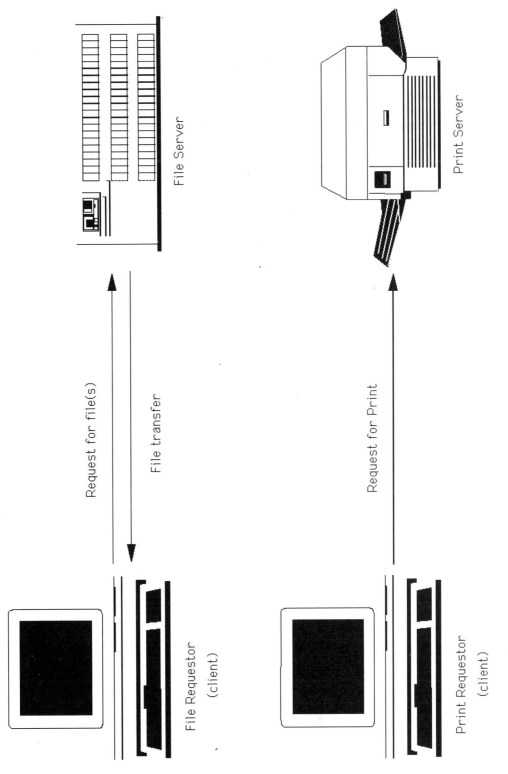

Figure 9.1 Client/server processes

operating systems packages with many systems management capabilities built-in. Systems management alone can represent from 10 percent to 40 percent of the total overall cost of implementing client/server structures (Ryan, 1993). Partial solutions to client/server systems management have been introduced by major vendors including Hewlett-Packard, SunConnect, IBM, and Computer Associates. However, compared to systems management in the mainframe environment, these solutions are incomplete, focusing more on hardware and less on performance reporting, predicting failures, and dynamically optimizing resources.

Critical administrative tools for the client/server environment include a mix of both network and systems management applications, targeting the following areas:

- user administration
- systems administration
- software maintenance and release
- network performance and tuning
- software distribution

The following list highlights several areas in the traditional network management disciplines of fault, configuration, performance, security, and accounting management where there are special needs for client/server structures.

Fault Management

A management system should allow administrators to set conditional thresholds to account for interdependencies among the many client and server processes and network components. To help manage the complexity of the client/server environment, the management system should allow administrators to set thresholds on groups (classes) of items and apply complex criteria to filter out secondary or unwanted alarms when thresholds are crossed. Thresholding on both network device status and status of system components (computer CPU utilization, memory, disk usage, swap space, etc.) must be supported by the collection of management applications. Trouble ticketing should be flexible enough to adapt to the dynamic client/server environment.

Configuration Management

Automatic discovery of nodes should be supported, as well as continual ongoing discovery at user-specified intervals, to maintain configuration of complex, changing client/server systems. Change management should cover both physical and logical resources; support for electronic software distribution is essential. Ideally, software distribution should support both "push" (centrally triggered distribution) and "pull" (distribution triggered by users/administrators at remote sites), as well as backout routines in case of error.

Performance Management

Management applications (in particular, traffic monitoring applications and systems monitoring applications) must be capable of establishing baseline measurements on utilization (network bandwidth, system utilization) at average and peak levels. Baseline measurements must include typical error rates for daily, weekly, and monthly periods as well as typical protocol breakdowns. Trending and analysis should be done at regular intervals to determine whether reconfiguring (repositioning servers or workstations) may improve network and system performance. Unfortunately, the complexity of distributed, client/server networks has resulted in fewer good network design tools. Reporting applications can assist in the collection and presentation of data to support design and optimization, however.

Security Management

External security applications must be added to bolster the rather weak internal mechanisms of UNIX client/server systems. Security audit trail support is important, as is the implementation of security domains across distributed systems. Enforcement of security policies can be provided by systems management applications.

Accounting Management

System resource usage and chargeback is supported by some systems management applications. Internetwork accounting tools are still under development, and they are expected from leading traffic monitor vendors soon.

9.3   CONVERGENCE OF NETWORK AND SYSTEMS MANAGEMENT

Traditionally, network management and systems management have been separate disciplines. Network management focused on maintaining efficient traffic flow across network links by monitoring devices such as network interface cards, connectors, bridges, routers, and hubs. In contrast, systems management concerns performance of software and end-user hardware, as well as user administration. Systems administration tasks include hardware and software configuration management, job scheduling, backup, and data center accounting.

Now, however, customers are seeking integrated network and systems management tools than can present the status and behavior of complex distributed, client/server environments in a graphical format that is easier to comprehend. The driving factors behind integrated network and systems management include improved fault isolation and diagnosis, cost reductions due to higher levels of automation and decreased need for staff, and the need to reduce complexity.

Network management, systems management, and even data management are definitely converging into a new discipline which may be called infrastructure management. The distributed, client/server computing model has created interdependencies—therefore, it is impossible to manage these areas separately and do an effective job in total (McGovern, 1994).

For example, previously it was important to optimize performance of individual host computers to satisfy user demands for specific response times. Now, however, if a user calls the help desk to say that an application is running slowly, the set of possible causes is much greater—the application may talk to several different servers and/or databases across a complex internetwork. Therefore, performance tuning of individual elements in isolation is ineffective. To solve the problem, it is imperative to merge network, systems, and data management into a cohesive solution.

Key vendors are now developing solutions to address this problem. Legent, for example, has created a special layer of middleware software that acts as a backbone into which customers can snap in interoperable applications. This middleware software allows applications to work synergistically (see Figure 9.2). Legent has defined an API for each of the seven management applications areas defined in Figure 9.2. The middleware layer uses a message service that can run over LU6.2, SPX/IPX, or TCP/IP. Versions of this middleware will run on MVS, DOS, UNIX, and other operating systems. In this scenario, it is possible to view performance management as encompassing a collection of distributed computers, network components, applications, and relational database management systems (RDBMSs), rather than just the isolated performance of one host.

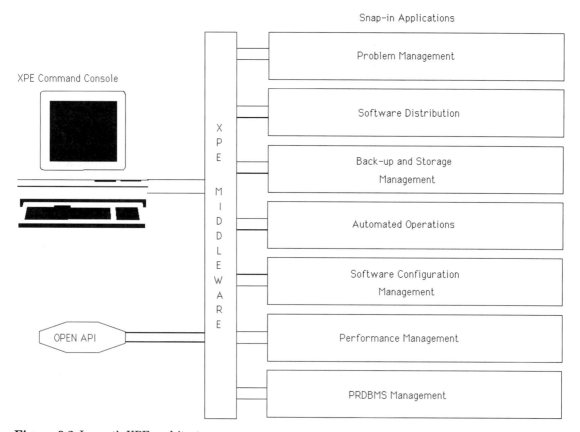

Figure 9.2 Legent's XPE architecture

9.4   SUMMARY

Although client/server computing is fast becoming the dominant computing model, the architecture is inextricably tied to new and difficult management challenges. Aspects of distributed computing and open systems also make network and systems manager's jobs much more difficult. Object-oriented management applications are one possible method for shielding operators and developers from the underlying complexities of these new structures. The convergence of network and systems management is happening as a result of new architectures in which networks and systems are viewed as a single entity, encompassing the information technology resources of the organization.

10

Trends

Client/server structures have become increasingly complex. Their management is becoming an incredibly challenging task. Wide area, metropolitan area, and local area networks are becoming mission-critical to many corporations. Businesses depend on these networks to provide reliable links between servers and clients, to provide end users with computing power, and to supply bandwidth for integrating communications and databases. It is incumbent upon these networks to support better service levels, decrease risks of severe outages, and speed up application implementation.

Technology is evolving to solve these problems, and several trends are becoming evident. These trends include the emergence of comprehensive management frameworks, increased use of intelligent agents, refinement of switching technologies including asynchronous transfer mode (ATM), increased use of object-oriented technologies, advances in expert systems, and improvements in standardized network management protocols. The overriding issue of cost constraints will continue to drive and to moderate these trends.

10.1 MANAGEMENT FRAMEWORKS

To successfully manage the complexities of distributed, client/server architectures, organizations must unify systems and network management under a common framework. A framework is essentially a management platform that adequately addresses both network and systems management by gathering management data from all network and systems components, sharing it across a wide range of applications (Jander, 1994). While today's management platforms, such as SunConnect SunNet Manager and Hewlett-Packard HP OpenView, can provide a single graphical interface for multiple applications, each application still has its own map—creating separate views of different aspects of the network. In the future, frameworks will allow every application equal access to all management data.

More than two dozen network and systems management vendors are now developing management frameworks (Jander, 1994). However, the industry really requires only a handful; a shakeout is expected to occur rapidly, even before many of these platforms are completed. IBM is one of the strongest contenders for survival in this respect; it has already established alliances with key database vendors to form a data hierarchy model supporting a comprehensive network and systems management framework.

10.2 SMART AGENTS

Information processing is undergoing massive change. Advances in computer technology and decreasing hardware prices enable networks and systems managers to endow systems with higher levels of intelligence, and to create networks supporting multiple management protocols and applications.

Smart SNMP-agents, also called super agents or mid-level managers, are but one example of this trend in network management. Among other things, this enabling technology of intelligent agents is capable of better supporting more efficient and localized polling, localized processing of data, and continuous performance supervision. From a management perspective, clients and servers will function as element management systems. This is particularly valid for UNIX-based clients and servers.

Currently, major implementers of smart agent software, including IBM, SynOptics, Cabletron, Hewlett-Packard, and NetLabs use differing methods for communication between smart agents. Some of these vendors use the SNMP Multiplexing (SMUX) protocol, an experimental draft standard; others use early versions of SNMPv2; while still others use proprietary mechanisms (Jander, 1993). It is not clear at this time which if any of these methods will prevail.

10.3 ATM AND SWITCHING TECHNOLOGIES

Networking technology is also undergoing dramatic change. Several important developments are on the horizon, including the race to provide "total connectivity," supported by emerging WAN transport and value-added services. These transport services include fast packet (frame and cell relay), SMDS, B-ISDN, T1/T3. The ultimate goal is to bring all types of WAN-offerings under the umbrella of Synchronous Digital Hierarchy (SDH).

On the LAN level, Ethernet technology will remain entrenched, but the market share of Ethernet technologies is expected to dip over the course of time. Use of token ring and newer switched technologies will increase. Asynchronous transfer mode (ATM) and LAN switching will start to replace routing in campus environments. Over the wide area, however, newer, more efficient source routing algorithms may delay this process. Interconnecting devices will house multiple functions, integrating the capabilities of a multiplexer, router, packet switch, ATM switch, and eventually of a matrix switch. Efficiency may be substantially improved by collapsing many logical network architectures and protocols into one company backbone. From the management point of view, WAN and LAN devices will offer multifunctional, integrated element management systems with or without full enterprise-wide integration capabilities.

10.3.1   Impact of ATM on LAN structures

As users soak up more and more bandwidth, network managers are forced to segment the network to keep utilization levels down. The fundamental problem is that users are sharing the same wire, and thus sharing the bandwidth available on that wire. As the network is segmented, it becomes necessary to add more monitoring probes to maintain the same level of monitoring. This segmentation process can, therefore, become expensive from a management standpoint. In addition, it can be difficult deciding where the bridge or router should be placed to optimize LAN utilization.

The long-term solution to this problem is to use a "LAN switch," in which each node becomes its own segment, and port switching hubs as well as ATM hubs can switch every node. The use of ATM hubs will allow creation of virtual workgroups whereby traffic flow, as well as access to servers and other resources, is implemented as a network management activity rather than as a manual task done at the wiring closet. In this scenario, implementation of moves/adds/changes becomes a simple management application function—drastically reducing the time involvement of staff, and supported by automated record keeping and impact of the changes on the network management map.

10.3.2   Impact of ATM on Traffic Monitoring

Also, in a fully switched network, the function of the traffic monitor or probe changes. Instead of providing promiscuous-mode listening of shared media, the probe monitors the hubs and routers providing the interconnectivity—tapping into specific connections between nodes to investigate problems and traffic flow.

Thus, the advent of LAN switching is creating a new paradigm for monitoring and analysis. This is similar to the need for distributed management and dividing the complex enterprise network into domains. The local domain management system keeps track of its domain, and only presents highly condensed data up to the enterprise management system. The enterprise manager is responsible for end-to-end connectivity between local domains.

Vendors such as HP will seek to position their high-level traffic monitors as domain network analysis servers. The network analysis server will provide extensive visibility of its domain, processing and integrating information from the domain and forwarding it to the central management platform. Stand-alone protocol analyzers will be of some use, but automated management from continuous intelligent analysis servers will become more commonplace.

10.4   IMPROVED NETWORK
MANAGEMENT PROTOCOLS

The growing size and complexity of distributed, client/server networks makes the overhead associated with polling-based protocols intolerable. The use of smart-agents is one method for reducing polling overhead. However, changes to the SNMP protocol itself were also necessary to improve management efficiencies. SNMPv2 includes several improvements targeting management of large, distributed computing networks, including:

- manager-to-manager communications
- bulk data retrieval
- enhanced security

Manager-to-manager communications allows separate copies of management software to share data efficiently without incurring enormous overhead associated with sending bit-mapped X-window graphics across the network. When separate managers can share data efficiently, there is no need to have redundant applications and processes.

Similarly, bulk data retrieval can speed up the time it takes to transfer management data to where it is needed; this can save on transmission costs. Enhanced security is critical in client/server structures where information resources are scattered across multiple, insecure locations. New techniques for simplifying the configuration of SNMPv2 security are currently under development, and are expected to accelerate acceptance of the protocol.

In addition, there is a slow, but growing acceptance of CMIP for managing complex telecommunications networks. CMIP is much more difficult to implement than SNMP, but it offers a wider range of features. British Telecom, AT&T, Objective Systems Integrators, Bull, Siemens, Hewlett-Packard, and NetLabs are among the first vendors to offer CMIP-based products.

10.5   INCREASED USE OF OBJECT-
ORIENTED TECHNOLOGY

Increasingly, management applications will model systems and networking elements as objects. Objects interact by sending messages between each other. The called object (e.g., any network element) executes the processes prescribed in the message against its attributes (configuration data and status), and reports the results back to the calling object (e.g., network management station). Object-oriented databases are supporting this type of dialogue with high efficiency. For some applications, such as configuration management, object-oriented databases offer considerable better performance than relational databases. On the other hand, fault and performance management are better supported by relational techniques.

For programmers who are used to traditional procedural-oriented programming techniques, object-oriented technology is very difficult to learn. The human learning curve will continue to impede acceptance of object-oriented technologies for the next few years, at least.

10.6   EXPERT SYSTEMS

To support proactive network management, many measurements must be taken at different points in the networking segments and at interconnecting devices. These measurement results must be correlated and analyzed in real time. The neural network is a fundamentally new form of computer processor, capable of collecting and correlating high volumes of measurement data, providing appropriate input to the rule-based expert system. Unlike traditional processors, neural networks are trained to recognize patterns by running simple data through them. They can also process many inputs simultaneously.

For network management, neural networks can correlate multiple measurement data streams against preprogrammed measurement data ranges that will cause network faults unless corrected proactively. The output from the neural network is then used by the rule-based expert system to select a corrective action. The use of neural network technology for network management is expected to increase gradually over the next few years.

10.7   COST CONSTRAINTS

In most organizations, upper-level management has always been concerned with cost of capital and improving the efficiency of operations. Various factors will make cost containment even more challenging in client/server environments:

More Sophisticated Systems

Increasingly sophisticated intelligent wiring concentrators (smart hubs) are expected to incorporate many other components, such as servers, clients, routers, bridges, switches, etc. They will include built-in management capabilities; however, beyond a certain volume, the coordination, synchronization, and administration of these intelligent boxes may become more difficult.

Growth of Networks

Enterprise networks continue to expand, both domestically and internationally. In particular, the number of interconnected LANs will grow substantially. In the network management control center, this growth adds to the volume of status and alarm data that an operator must monitor and analyze. Network management instrumentation must allow operators to easily and comprehensively monitor WANs, MANs, and LANs, determine the trouble, and rapidly focus on a magnified portion of the network. At the highest level of monitoring, a several-hundred-segment network must be reduced to a graphic display with well-designed icons and key symbols.

Continuous Operations

Increasingly, many systems and networks must operate continuously. The challenge for vendors is to create user interfaces for platforms and applications that are capable of maintaining an operators' attention, focusing their activities on the most relevant events, actions, and emergencies.

There are several other ways in which vendors must respond to the challenges just listed by providing cost effective management solutions, including the following:

Adherence to a Comprehensive Management Framework

Vendors' offerings must support an efficient model of data hierarchy.

Tighter Integration of Applications into Platforms

The number of networked applications is steadily growing. The depth of integration between these applications needs to grow as well. The solution to tighter integration lies in vendor support of well-understood and well-published APIs.

Automation

Management systems must begin to automate routine functions by improving their capabilities for immediately deciding on systems and networks events. This capability can be implemented both at the manager and agent levels. However, certain agents (e.g., switches in wide area networks) cannot wait for human managers to initiate alternate routing or other recovery procedures. When automation is successful, network administrators can focus more on strategic activities such as traffic analysis, trend evaluation, and planning.

In the near future, management structures will follow of two basic alternatives for integration of management products:

Manager of the Managers:

This is a hierarchical network management structure with a network management station at the top. This station supervises element management systems that are responsible for managing a family of managed objects, such as hubs, segments, routers, bridges, multiplexers, modems, and switches. A manager-of-manager's structure allows investment in an installed base to be preserved. The interfaces between the element management systems and the manager-of-managers are well-defined, however, the number of element management systems in the network operations center are not reduced. Current examples of popular manager-of-managers include IBM NetView/390, Sterling Solve: Automation, OSI NetExpert, MAXM Systems MAXM, Cabletron Spectrum, and Allink Company's Operations Coordinator.

Management Platforms

Management platforms differ from manager-of-manager structures in that they provide only basic management services. Also, clearly defined application programming interfaces are published by the platform vendor, enabling third-parties to develop, implement, and port applications. Examples of leading platforms are: Hewlett-Packard HP-OpenView, Network Managers-NMC 1000 3000, and 6000, Objective Systems Integrators-NetExpert, NetLabs/DiMONs; SunConnect SunNet Manager, AT&T Star*Sentry, and Cabletron Spectrum. (Both Spectrum and NetExpert are capable of supporting both platform and manager-of-manager structures.) Platform vendors do not, typically, offer products for the element management system level. The platform's main goal is to offer integration capabilities.

Currently, most organizations are unwilling to pursue the ideal of integration at any price. Many small to medium-sized network management centers are fully equipped with element management systems only. However, as networks grow in size and complexity, reliance on element management systems will not be sufficient.

10.8 SUMMARY

As a result of more advanced database and platform technology, client/server-structures will be implemented to support distributed network management. Network management clients are workstations or PCs accessed by authorized network management staff; they may be geographically distributed. Network management servers are integrators or element management systems supporting certain physical and logical objects that interact with clients, with managed objects of the networks, and with one another.

The distribution of human responsibilities will follow the same path as the functions of network management. Depending on the size of systems and networks, staffing will vary greatly. In terms of management teams, two concepts are paramount: building the team, and keeping the team together. These require considerable managerial skills. The systems and networks supervisors report to the service manager, who may report to the information system manager or to the chief information officer of the corporation. In a completely decentralized environment, systems and networks supervisors will most likely report to business unit management.

Systems and networks management will be integrated, first by SNMP, then by CMIP; dual support is expected by integrators and platform providers. Integration will take place in multiple steps. We may expect more centralized management that will centralize control, but distribute certain functions. In particular, monitoring, filtering functions, and reactions to routine messages will be distributed to remote sites. The practical implementation may follow OSI standards or hierarchical SNMP standards.

Due to limited human resources, automation of routine systems and networks management functions is absolutely necessary. Vendors are expected to offer new products that will meet this demand. Automation packages may migrate to expert systems that can be used off-line and then on-line, off loading management personnel from routine tasks.

The future implementation of more powerful databases as support for systems and networks management stations will consolidate many templates from various MIBs. Increased use of object-oriented databases is an obvious trend, however, relational databases will not lose their importance, in particular, not for fault management.

We may expect a slow move to outsourcing of systems and network management functions. The decision to outsource will depend on the country, the industry, and the importance of networks for critical applications. The expenses of managing systems and networks will increase due to the demand for constantly improved service levels and enhanced management capabilities. The networks and systems management market is expected to face a serious shakeout; only products and companies with the best responses to strategic direction demands will survive over the next couple of years.

A

Appendix A

ACD automated call distributor
ACSE association control service element
ANSI American National Standards Institute
API Application Programming Interface
ARPA Advanced Research Projects Agency
ARPANET ARPA computer network
AS Autonomous system (connection between IGP and EGP)
ASN.1 Abstract Syntax Notation One
ATM Asynchronous Transfer Mode
B-ISDN Broadband ISDN
BU business unit
CAD computer aided design
CATV coaxial community antenna television
CAU controlled access unit
CCITT Commitee Consultatif International Telegraphique et Telephonique
CLNP Connectionless Network Protocol
CMIP Common Management Information Protocol
CMISE common management information service element
CMOL CMIP over logical link control
CMOT CMIP over TCP/IP
CORBA Common Object-Oriented Request Broken Architecture
CSMA/CD carrier sense multiple access/collision detect
CSU channel service unit
DARPA ARPA of DoD
DAS double attached station
DCE Distributed Computing Environment (OSF)

DEE data circuit-terminating equipment
DES Data Encryption Standard
DDN Defense Data Network
DME Distributed Management Environment (from OSF)
DMI Desktop Management Interface
DMTF Desktop Management Task Force
DNA Digital Network Architecture (DEC)
DQDB dual queue dual bus
DSA Distributed Systems Architecture (Bull)
DSU data service unit
DTE data terminal equipment
EDI electronic data interchange
EGP Exterior Gateway Protocol
EM element management system
FDDI fiber distributed data interface
FDM frequency division multiplexing
FIFO first in first out
FTP file transfer protocol
GGP Gateway Gateway Protocol
GNMP Government Network Management Profile
GUI graphical user interface
HDLC High-level Data Link Protocol
IAB Internet Activities Board
ICMP Internet Control Message Protocol
IEEE Institute of Electrical and Electronic Engineers
IETF Internet Engineering Task Force
IGP Internet Gateway Routing Protocol
IIVR integrated interactive voice response
IMP interface messages processors
IP Internet Protocol
IPX internet packet exchange
IS intermediate system (ISO for IP-router)
ISDN Integrated Services Digital Network
ISO International Organization for Standardization
LAN local area network
LAT Local Area Transport Protocol (DEC)
LED light emitting device
LLC logical link control
LM LAN manager
MAC media access control
MAN metropolitan area network
MAU media attachment unit or multiple access unit
MIB management information base
MIS management information system
MO managed object
MSU Message Service Unit (IBM)
MTA message transfer agent

MTBF mean time between failures
MTOR mean time of repair
MTTD mean time of diagnosis
MTTR mean time to repair
NCE network control engine
NCP network control program
NCL network control language
NE network element
NetBIOS network basic input-output system
NFS Network File System (Sun)
NIC network interface card
NMF Network Management Forum
NMM network management module
NMP Network Management Protocol
NMS network management station or network management system
NMVT network management vector transport
NOS network operating system
OMG Object Management Group
OSF Open Systems Foundation
OSI open system interconnected
OVW OpenView Windows
PAD packet assembler disassembler
PBX private branch exchange
PDU protocol data unit
PC personal computer
PCM pulse code modulation
PHY physical layer (FDDI)
PIN personal identification number or positive intrinsic negative
PING packet internet grouper
PLS physical signalling
PMD physical medium dependent
PSM product specific module
RFC request for comments
RFS Remote File System (AT&T)
RISC Reduced Instruction Command Set
RMON Remote MONitoring standard for SNMP-MIBs
RODM resource object data manager
ROSE remote operating service element
RPC remote procedure call
SAS single attached station
SDH synchronous digital hierarchy
SGMP Simple Gateway Monitoring Protocol
SLIP IP over serial lines
SMAE systems management application entities
SMAP specific management application protocol
SMF systems management function
SMFA specific management functional area

SMI structure of management information
SMDR station message detailed recording
SMP Station or Simple Management Protocol (FDDI)
SMTP Simple Mail Transfer Protocol
SNA Systems Network Architecture (IBM)
SNI Systems Network Interconnected (IBM)
SNMP Simple Network Management Protocol
SRB source routing bridge
SSAP source service access point
STA spanning tree algorithms
TB token bus
TCP Transmission Control Protocol
TDM time division multiplexing
TDR time domain reflectometer
TFTP Trivial File Transfer Protocol
TME Tivoli Management Environment
TMN Telecommunications Management Network
TR token ring
TTRT target token ring rotation time
UA user agent
UDP User Datagram Protocol
UI Unix Internation
ULP Upper Layer Protocol
UPS uninterrupted power supply
VNM Virtual Network Machine
VT virtual terminal
VTAM Virtual Telecommunication Access Method (IBM)
WAN wide area network
XNS Xerox Network Services

B

Appendix B

Addresses and phone numbers for vendors whose products are discussed in this book are listed below.

3Com Corp.; 5400 Bayfront Plaza; Santa Clara, CA 95052; (408) 764-5000

Accugraph Corp.; 5822 Cromo Dr.; El Paso, TX 79912; (915) 581-1171

AIM Technology; 4699 Old Ironsides Dr., Suite 150; Santa Clara, CA 95054; (408) 748-8649

Alcatel Bell ITS; Excelsiorlann 44-46; 1930 Zaventem; Belgium; (32/2) 718 70 11

Allerion (formerly the Ultimate Corp.); 1717 Ridgedale Ave.; E. Hanover, NJ 07936; (201) 887-1000

Answer Computer, Inc.; 1263 Oakmead Pkwy.; Sunnyvale, CA 94086; (408) 739-6130

Applications Plus, Inc.; 122 W. Carpenter Fwy. #535; Irving, TX 75038; (214) 541-1771

Arche Communications; 18, Av du Quebec; ZA Courtaboeuf BP 742; Les Ulis Cedex, 91962 France; 33169 83232

ARMON Networking; Atidum Technological Park, Bldg. 1; P.O. Box 58030; Tel-Aviv, Israel 61580; 97 23 490702

Aston Brooke Software, Inc.; 610 W. Germantown Pike, Suite 300; Plymouth Meeting, PA 19462; (215) 834-3960

Atlanta; Parc Technologique du bois; Chaiand; 20 Rue du bois; Chaland - C E 2934; 91029 Evry Cedex, France; (33) 1 69 11 1540

Aule-Tek, Inc.; 1223 Peoples Ave.; Troy, NY 12180; (518) 273-0983

Autotrol Technology Corp.; 12500 N. Washington St.; Denver, CO 80241-2400; (800) 233-2882

Axlan, S.A.; Centre d' affaires; 1 rue de petit Robinson; 78353 JOUY en JOSAS; (1) 34 65 94 44

Axon Networks; 199 Wells Ave.; Newton, MA 02159; (617) 923-2205

Boole & Babbage, Inc.; 510 Oakmead Pkwy.; Sunnyvale, CA 94086; (408) 526-3000

Breakaway Software, Inc.; 165 Post St., Suite 415; San Francisco, CA 94108; (415) 989-3600

Bridgeway Corp.; 8585 145th Ave. NE; Redmond, WA 98052; (206) 881-4270

Brixton Systems, Inc.; 125 Cambridge Park Dr.; Cambridge, MA 02140; (617) 661-6262

Bytex Corp. (subsidiary of Network Systems Corp.); 4 Technology Dr.; Westborough, MA 01581; (508) 366-8000

Cabletron Systems, Inc.; 35 Industrial Way; Rochester, NH 03867-5005; (603) 332-9400

Calypso Software Systems, Inc.; 134 S Mast Rd.; Goffstown, NH 03045; (603) 497-5112

Cayman Systems, Inc.; 26 Landsdowne St.; Cambridge, MA 02139; (617) 494-1999

Chipcom Corp.; 118 Turnpike Rd.; Southborough, MA 01772; (508) 460-8900

Cisco Systems, Inc.; 1525 O'Brien Dr.; Menlo Park, CA 94025; 415 326-1941

Cisco Systems--Crescendo Workgroup Business Unit; 930 Arques Ave.; Sunnyvale, CA 94086; (800) 283-3629

ComConsult Kommunikationstechnik GmbH; Pascalstrasse 25; D-52076 Aachen; Germany; 49 2408 149150

CompuWare Corp.; 31440 Northwestern Hwy.; Farmington Hills, MI 48334; (313) 737-7300

Concord Communications, Inc.; 753 Forest St.; Marlboro, MA 01752; (508) 460-4646

ConWare Computer Consulting GmbH; Killisfeldstrasse 64; W-7500 Karlsruhe 41; Germany; 49 721 94950

Crosscom Corp.; 450 Donald Lynch Blvd.; Marlboro, MA 01752; (508) 229-5475

DataStaff Ingeniere; 15 avenue du Quebec; BP 646; 91965 Les Ulis Cedex France; (33-1) 69 18 18 69

DeskTalk Systems, Inc.; 19401 S Vermont Ave., Suite F-100; Torrance, CA 90502; (310) 323-5998

Diederich & Associates; 625 Fair Oaks Ave., Suite 290; South Pasadena, CA 91030; (818) 799-9670

Digital Analysis Corp.; 1889 Preston White Dr.; Reston, VA 22091; (703) 476-5900

Digital Equipment Corp.; 146 Main Street; Maynard, MA 01754; (508) 493-5111

Dornier GmbH; Max-Stromeyer Strasse 160; Konstanz, 7750; Germany; 49 7531-830

Eakins Open Systems; 67 E. Evelyn Ave.; Mountain View, CA 94041; (415) 969-5109

ECS Associates, Inc.; 20725 S. Western Ave., Suite 113; Torrance, CA 90501; (310) 320-2002

Elegant Communications, Inc.; 4 King St West, Suite 1101; Toronto, Ontario; Canada, M5H 1B6; (416) 362-9772

Evolving Systems, Inc.; 8000 E. Maplewood Ave.; Englewood, CO 80111; (303) 689-1347

FiberMux Corp.; 9310 Topanga Canyon Blvd.; Chatsworth, CA 91311; (818) 709-

6000

Fore Systems, Inc.; 1000 Gamma Dr., Suite 504; Pittsburgh, PA 15238; (412) 967-4040

Frontier Software, Inc.; 1501 Main St., Suite 40; Tewksbury MA 01876; (508) 851-8872

Gandalf Systems Corp.; Cherry Hill Industrial Center, Bldg. 44; Cherry Hill, NJ 08003; (609) 424-9400

Gensym Corp.; 125 Cambridge Park Dr.; Cambridge, MA 02140; (617) 547-2500; Graphael; 1-3, Rue Stephenson; 78182 St. Quentin; Yvelines, 78182, France; 33 130587800

Hewlett-Packard Co.; 300 Hanover St.; Palo Alto, CA 94304; (415) 857-1501

Hirschmann GmbH; Richard Hirschmann Strasse 19; Postrach 110, D-73726 Esslingen; Germany; 49 7113101545

Hummingbird Communications; 2900 John St., Unit 4; Markham, Ontario Canada; L3R 5G3; (416) 470-1203

IBM Corp.; Old Orchard Rd.; Armonk, NY 10504; (914) 765-1900

Independence Technologies, Inc.; 42705 Lawrence Place; Fremont, CA 94538; (510) 438-8729

ISICAD, Inc.; 1920 W. Corporate Way; Anaheim, CA 92803; (714) 533-8910

JNA Network Services; 16 Smith St.; Chatswood NSW 2067; Australia; (02) 417 6177

Johnson Control Network Integration Services; 5430 Van Nuys, Suite 400; Van Nuys, CA 91401; (818) 906-3066

Kaptronix, Inc.; 332 Lincoln Dr.; Haworth, NJ 07641; (201) 385-0992

Ki Research, Inc.; 6760 Alexander Bell Dr.; Columbia, MD 21046; (410) 290-0355

Kodiak Technologies; 11754 West Line Industrial Dr.; St. Louis, MO 63146; (314) 993-4300

Landmark Systems Corp.; 8000 Towers Cresent Dr.; Vienna, VA 22182-2700; (703) 893-9046

LANNET Data Communications; 7711 Center Ave., Suite 600; Huntington Beach, CA 92647; (714) 891-5580

Legent Corp.; 575 Herndon Parkway; Herndon, VA 22070-5226

Legent (Networx Division), Inc.; 11911 NE 1st St., Suite 302; Bellevue, WA 98005-3032; (206) 646-1850

Matrix Technology Development Group; 15 Spinning Wheel Rd., Suite 410; Tinsdale, IL 60521; (708) 920-0055

MCI Communications Corp.; 1650 Tysons Blvd.; McLean, VA 22102; (703) 506-6000

Metrix Customer Support Systems, Inc.; 20975 Swenson Dr.; Waukesha, WI 53186; (415) 798-8560

MicroData Systems, Inc.; 2656 S. Loop West, Suite 103; Houston, TX 77054; (713) 660-9771

MicroMuse, Ltd.; Disraeli House; 20 Putney Bridge Rd.; London SW18 IDA UK; +44 (0)81 875 9500

Motorola, Inc.; Mobile Data Division; 11411 No. 5 Rd.; Richmond, British Columbia V7A 4Z3; (604) 277-1511

Motorola Codex; 20 Cabot Blvd.; Mansfield, MA 02048; (508) 261-4000

NCR Corp.; Networks Products Division; 307 Middletown Lincroft Rd.; Lincroft, NJ 07738; (908) 576-5451

NetLabs, Inc.; 4920 El Camino Real; Los Altos, CA 94022; (800) 525-5645

NetManSys; Centre d'affaires Multipole; 41, chemin du Vieux chene; 38240 Meylan, France; 33 76903400

NetTech, Inc.; 4040 Barrett Dr.; Raleigh, NC 27609; (919) 781-7887

Network Application Technology, Inc.; 1686 Dell Ave.; Campbell, CA 95008; (408) 370-4300

Network General Corp.; 4200 Bohannon Dr.; Menlo Park, CA 94025; (415) 473-2000

Network Management Forum; 1201 Mt. Kemble Avenue; Morristown, NJ 07960-6628; (201) 425-1900

Network Partners, Inc.; 2290 North First Street, Suite 310; San Jose, CA 95131; (408) 526-9200

Network Solutions, Inc.; 505 Hunthmar Park Drive; Herndon, VA 22070; (703) 742-4733

NYNEX Allink Co; 4 Gannet Dr.; White Plains, NY 10604; (914) 644-7662

Objective Systems Integrators; 110 Blue Ravine Road, Suite 100; Folsom, CA 95630; (916) 353-2400

Open Network Enterprises; Via Torricelli 34; 20035 Lissone (MI); Italy; 39 245-8101

OpenVision Technologies, Inc.; 7133 Koll Center Pkwy.; Pleasanton, CA 94556; (510) 426-6400

Optical Data Systems, Inc.; 1101 E Arapaho Rd.; Richardson, TX 75081; (214) 234-6400

Oscom International Pty Ltd; Level 25, QV-1, 250 St. George Terrace; Perth W.A. 6000; Australia; 61 9 481 3444

Patrol Software; 100 Marine Pkwy., Suite 465; Redwood Shores, CA 94065; (415) 508-2900

Peer Networks, Inc.; 3375 Scott Blvd., Suite 100; Santa Clara, CA 95054; (408) 727-4111

Peregrine Systems; 1959 Palomar Oaks Way; Carlsbad, CA 92009; (619) 431-2400

PERFORM; Espace Beauville--Bat B; Chemin de la Beauvalle--13084; Aix en Provence Cedex Z

PHILIPS; Piccoloministr 2; D-5000; Voeln 80, Germany; 49 2216773904

Prolin Automation, B.V.; Van Diemenstraat 76; P.O. Box 831; 1013 CN Amsterdam, Netherlands

ProTools, Inc.; 14976 NW Greenbrier Pkwy.; Beaverton, OR 97006; (503) 645-5400

Raylan Corp.; 2525 E. Bayshore Rd.; Palo Alto, CA 94303; (415) 813-0400

Remedy Corp.; 1965 Landings Dr.; Mountain View, CA 94043; (415) 903-5200

RISC Management; 505 8th Avenue, Floor 23; New York, NY 10018; (212) 695-9494

RAD Network Devices; 7711 Center Ave., Suite 270; Huntington Beach, CA 92647; (714) 891-1446

SAS Institute, Inc.; SAS Campus Dr.; Cary, NC 27513; (919) 677-8000

Sestel, S.A.; 215 rue Jean-Jacques Rousseau; 92136 Issy-les Moulineaux; Cedex, France; 33-1-46-45-65-50

Siemens-Nixdorf Informations Systems AG; Sto NC 434 Orro-Hahn-Ring; Munich 83 D-8000; Germany; 49 8963647545

Software Consulting Company, The; 74 Linden Ave., Suite 4; Darien, CT 06820; (203) 655-4899

SSDS, Inc.; 6595 S. Dayton St., Suite 3000; Inglewood, CO 80111; (303) 790-0660

Stanford Telecommunications; 1761 Business Center Dr.; Reston, VA 22090; (703) 438-8027

SunExpress; 4 Omni Way; Chelmsford, MA 08124; (800) 873-7869

SunSolutions; 2550 Garcia Ave.; Mountain View, CA 94043; (415) 336-1506

Synernetics, Inc.; 85 Rangeway Rd.; North Billerica, MA 01862; (508) 670-9009

SynOptics Communications, Inc.; 4401 Great America Pkwy; Santa Clara, CA 95054; (408) 988-2400

Talarian Corp.; 444 Castro St., Suite 140; Mountain View, CA 94041; (415) 965-8050

Teknekron Communications Systems, Inc.; 2121 Allston Way; Berkeley, CA 94706; (510) 649-3677

Telamon; 492 Ninth St., Suite 310; Oakland, CA 94607-4098; (916) 622-0630

Template Software, Inc.; 13100 Worldgate Dr., Suite 340; Herndon, VA 22070; (703) 318-1000

Tivoli Systems, Inc.; 6034 West Courtyard Drive; Suite 210; Austin, TX 78730; (512) 794-9070

Tom Sawyer Software Corp.; 1824B 4th St.; Berkeley, CA 94710; (510) 848-0853

Ungermann-Bass, Inc.; 3900 Freedom Circle; Santa Clara, CA 95052; (408) 496-0111

Unified Systems Solutions, Inc.; 49 Old Bloomfiled Ave.; Mountain Lakes, NJ 07046; (201) 402-2333

Unison-Tymlabs; 811 Barton Springs Rd.; Austin, TX 78704; (408) 245-3000

Unix Integration Services; 11033 Aurora Ave.; Urbandale, IA 50532; (515) 254-3074

UNIX Network Services; 369 Riley St.; Surry Hills, Sidney 2010; Australia; 61 22121963

V.I. Corp.; 47 Pleasant St.; Northampton, MA 01060; (413) 586-4144

VERTEX Systems, Inc.; 12400 Wilshire Blvd., Suite 600; Santa Monica, CA 90404; (310) 571-2222

ViaTech Development, Inc.; 2459 15th St. NW; New Brighton, MN 55112; (612) 636-4033

Wandel & Goltermann Technologies, Inc.; 2200 Gateway Centre Blvd.; Morrisville, NC 27560-9228; (800) 277-7404

Wellfleet Communications, Inc.; 15 Crosby Dr.; Bedford, MA 01730; (617) 280-2411

WilTel; One Williams Center; Tulsa, OK 74172; (918) 588-5791

Xylan Corp.; 9310 Topanga Canyon Blvd.; Chatsworth, CA 91311; (818) 717-3939

Xylogics, Inc.; 53 Third Ave.; Burlington, MA 01803; (617) 272-8140

Xyplex, Inc.; 330 Codman Hill Rd.; Boxborough, MA 01719; (508) 264-9900

Bibliography

Applied Computer Devices. *Network Knowledge Tool Implementation Manual.*
Terre Haute, Indiana: Applied Computer Devices, 1992.

AT&T. *Premises Distribution System, Product Implementation Guide.* Basking
Ridge, NJ: A T&T, 1989.

Autrata, M. "Technologies and support in the OSF/DME offering." Paper presented at Network & Distributed Systems Management '91. Washington, D.C., September, 1991.

Ball, L. L. *Cost Efficient Network Management.* New York: McGraw-Hill, 1992.

Ball, L. L. *Network Management with Smart Systems.* ISBN 0-07-003600-4.

Bapat, S. "OSI Management Information Base Implementation." Paper presented at Integrated Network Management II. Washington, D.C., 1991.

Black, Uyless. *Network Management Standards.* ISBN 0-07-005554-8.

Bloom, G. "An End to Cable Chaos." *Telecommunications* (February, 1990).

Boole and Babbage Inc. *Command/Post Product Description Guide.* Booke & Babbage, Inc., December, 1992.

Brady, S. "Management User Interfaces." Paper presented at the IEEE Network
Management and Control Workshop. Tarrytown, N.Y. 1989. 329-34.

Brigth, J. "The Smart Card: An Application in Search of a Technology." *Telecommunications* (March, 1990): 63-68.

Cabletron Systems. *Managing the Enterprise Network: Command and Control.* by
Roger Dev, Rochester, N.Y.: Cabletron Systems, 1992.

Cabletron Systems. *Spectrum Product Guide.* Rochester, N.Y.: Cabletron Systems,
1991.

Carter, E. H. and P. G. Dia. "Evaluating Network Management Systems: Criteria
and Observations." Paper presented at Integrated Network Management II.
Washington, D.C., 1991.

Case, J. D. "SNMP: Making the Standards Work in Today's Heterogeneous Networks." Paper presented at ComNet '92. Washington, D.C., 1992.

Chiong, J. "UNIX Can Play a Key Role in Network Management." *Computer Technology Review* (Winter 1990): 29-33.

Cisco Systems. *NetCentral Product Guide*. Santa Clara, CA: Cisco Systems, 1991.

Collins, W. "The Reality of OSI management" *Network World* (October 9, 19??).

Comdisco Systems, Inc. *BoNes Product Guide*. Foster City, CA: Comdisco Systems, Inc., 1991.

Concord Communications, Inc. *Trakker LAN Monitor Product Guide*. Marlborough, USA: Concord Communications, Inc., 1991.

CrossComm Corporation. *MS Reference Guide*. USA: CrossComm Corporation, 1990.

CrossComm Corporation. "Understanding LAN Bridge and Router Performance." *CrossComm Corporation. Technical Note* (1990), CrossComm Corporation, 1990.

Datapro Research Corp. *Cable Management Systems, Datapro Reports on Network Management Systems*. NS60-020-101, by M. L. Rothberg. Delran, N.J.: Datapro Research Corp., March 1991.

Datapro Research Corp. *Cable Management Systems: Overview*. NS60-020, Delran, N.J.: Datapro Research Corp., 1992. 101.

Datapro Research Corp. *IBM AIX NetView / 6000*. NS30-604, Delran, N.J.: Datapro Research Corp., 1991. 201-03.

Datapro Research Corp. *IBM LAN Network Manager*. NS30-504, Delran, N.J.: Datapro Research Corp., 1991. 101.

Datapro Research Corp. *IBM SNA and NetView*. NM40-491, Delran, N.J.: Datapro Research Corp., 1989. 101-08.

Datapro Research Corp. *Inventory and Configuration Management, Datapro Network Management*. NM20-300-101, by Lee J. Huntington. Delran, N.J.: Datapro Research Corp., October, 1991.

Datapro Research Corp. *The LAN Troubleshooting Sequence, Datapro Reports on Network Management*. NM50-300, Delran, N.J.: Datapro Research Corp., 1990.

Datapro Research Corp. *A Look at Selected LAN Management Tools*. NM50300, Delran, N.J.: Datapro Research Corp., (1989). 701.

Datapro Research Corp., *The Network Security Management*. NM20-200, by J. A. Cooper, Delran, N.J.: Datapro Research Corp., 1990.

Datapro Research Corp. *OpenView's Architectural Model*. NM40-325, Delran, N.J.: Datapro Research Corp.(1989). 101-07.

Datapro Research Corp. *An Overview of Simple Network Management Protocol*. NM40-300, Delran, N. J.: Datapro Research Corp., 1990. 201-07.

Datapro Research Corp. *SNMP Product Guide*. NM40-300, Delran, N. J.: Datapro Research Corp., 1990. 301-16.

Datapro Research Corp. *SNMP Query Language*. NM40-300, Delran, N. J.: Datapro Research Corp., 1991. 401-04.

Dem, D. P. and J. Till. "Monitoring LANs from a Distance." *Data Communications,* McGraw-Hill, (November 1989): 17-20.

Digilog, Inc. *LANVista Product Guide*. Montgomeryville, PA.: Digilog, Inc., 1990.

Digital Equipment Corp. *LAN Traffic Monitor, Product Guide*. USA: Cambridge, 1989.

Dodson, G. and R. Heidel. "Client/Server Systems Management." *CMG Transactions* Chicago: (Fall 1993), 82:7-13.

Fabbio, R. "WizardWare: An Overview." Paper presented at Network & Distributed Systems Management '91. Washington, D.C., September, 1991.

Feldkhum, L. and J. Ericson. *Event Management as a Common Functional Area of Open Systems Management*. IFIP Congress, 365-76. Elsevier Publisher, 1989.

Feldkhum, L. *Integrated Network Management Systems.* IFIP Congress, 279-300. Elsevier Publisher, 1989.

Ferguson, R. "The Business Case for Network Management." Paper presented at the Distributed Systems & Network Management Conference. Washington, D.C., 1991.

Fisher, S. "Dueling Protocols." *BYTE* (March 1991): 182-90.

Fortier, P. J. *Handbook of LAN Technology.* New York: Intertext Publications, McGraw- Hill, Inc., 1989.

Frederick Engineering. *FECOS Users Guide.* Columbia, MD.: Frederick Engineering, 1991.

Galvin, J. M., K. McClogbrie, and J. R. Davis. "Secure Management of SNMP Networks." Paper presented at Integrated Network Management II. Washington, D.C., 1991.

Gilbert, E. E. "Unified Network Management Architecture Putting It All Together." *AT&T Technology* 3 (No. 2), 1988.

Gilliam, P. A. "Practical Perspective on LAN Performance."*Business Communications Review* (October 1990): 56-58.

Herman, J. "Enterprise Management Vendors Shoot It Out."*Data Communications,* McGraw-Hill, (November 1990): 92-110.

Herman, J., and N. Lippis. "The Internetwork Decade."*Supplement to Data Communications,* McGraw-Hill, (January 1991): 2-32.

Herman, J. "Net Management Directions--Architectures and Standards for Multivendor Net Management."*Business Communication Review* (June 1991): 79-83.

Herman, J. "Net Management Directions--Renovating How Networks Are Managed." *Business Communication Review* (August 1991): 71-73.

Herman, J. "A New View of OpenView."*Network Monitor* 5 (No. 3) (March 1990).

Hewlett-Packard Company. *HP OpenView, NM Server Technical Evaluation Guide.* Palo Alto, CA.: Hewlett-Packard Company, 1989.

Hewlett-Packard Company. *HP OpenView Network Manager Server.* Palo Alto, CA.: Hewlett-Packard Company, 1989.

Hewlett-Packard Company. *HP ProbeView Product Guide.* Palo Alto, CA.: Hewlett-Packard Company, 1989.

Houldsworth, Y. and Co. *Open System LANs and Their Global Interconnection.* Oxford: Butterworth-Heinemann, 1991.

Howard, M. "LAN Management Assessment." Anaheim, CA.:*IDG Network Management Solutions* (April 1990).

Huntington, J. A. "OSI-Based Net Management."*Data Communications* (March 1989): 111-29.

Huntington, J. A. "SNMP/CMIP Market Penetration and User Perception." Paper presented at Interop 1990. San Jose, CA., October 1990.

Infonetics, Inc. *The Cost of LAN Downtime.* Infonetics, Inc., 1989.

Infotel Systems Corp.*LAN Interconnecting Technologies.* Course material. Infotel Systems Corp., 1990.

International Business Machines, Inc.*IBM Token Ring Problems Determination Guide.* Document SY27-0280-1, 1988.

Isicad, Inc. *Command Implementation Guide.* Anaheim, CA.: Isicad, Inc., 1991.

Jander, Mary: "Hot Products of 1993." *Data Communications Magazine* McGraw Hill.

Jander, Mary: "Management Frameworks"*Data Communications Magazine* (February 1994), McGraw-Hill.

Krall, G. "SNMP Opens New Lines of Sight." *Data Communication--LAN Strategies* McGraw-Hill, (March 1990): 45-54.

Lannet, Inc. *MultiMan Product Guide.* Huntington Beach, CA.: Lannet, Inc., 1991.

Legent Corp. *XPE Architecture.* by Robert McGovern. Legent Corp., February 1994.

Leinwand, A. and K. Fang. *Network Management--A Practical Perspective.* New York: Addison Wesley Publishing Company, 1993.

Lo, T. L. "Local Area Networks for Managers." Chicago: *CMG Transactions* (Summer 1990): 31-40.

Lo. T. Leo. "Client/Server Computing and Performance Management." Chicago: *CMG Transactions* 82 (Fall 1993): 15-22.

"The Local Area Network Glossary." *LAN Magazine* New York: (1989).

"Managing Distributed Systems." *Faulkner Information Services* (September 1993).

"Managing Distributed Systems." *Faulkner Information Services* (Jan./Feb. 1994).

Martin, J. *Local Area Networks.* Englewood Cliffs, N.J.: Prentice Hall, 1991.

McGovern, Robert. "Legent's XPE Architecture," June 1994.

Mier, E. "Testing SNMP in Routers." *Network World* (July 1993).

Miller, H. *LAN Troubleshooting Handbook.* Redwood City, CA: M&T Books, 1989.

Miller, M. A. *Managing Internetworks with SNMP.* New York: M&T Books, 1993.

Moffet, J. and M. Sloman. "User and Mechanism Views of Distributed Systems Management." *Distributed Systems Engineering* 1 (No. 1), (September 1993).

Morrison, W. "Ethernet LAN Management: NMCC/VAX ETHERnim." *Integrated Network Management.* IFIP Congress, Elsevier Science Publisher, 1989.

Mouttham, A. et al. "LAN Management using expert systems." *Integrated Network Management* IFIP Congress, Elsevier Science Publisher, 1989.

Mueller, Y. *The Hands-On Guide to Network Management.* New York: Windcrest/ McGraw-Hill, 1993.

NetLabs, Inc. *DualManager Product Implementation Guide.* Los Angeles: Net-Labs, Inc., 1991.

Network General Corp. *Sniffer Network Analyzer Product Family User's Guide.* Menlo Park, CA.: Network General Corp. 1991.

Network Management, Inc. *LANfolio Product Guide.* New York: Network Management, Inc., 1990.

Network Managers Limited. *NMC 3000 Product Specification and Implementation Guideline.* Guildford, United Kingdom: Network Managers Limited, 1991.

Novell, Inc. *LANAnalyzer and LANtern Product Guide.* San Jose, CA.: Novell, Inc., 1991.

Novell, Inc. *NetWare Management Functions.* San Jose, CA.: Novell, Inc. 1990.

The OSF Distributed Management Environment, White Paper. USA: Cambridge, 1991.

Objective Systems Integrators. *NetExpert-Product Description.* Folsum, USA: Objective Systems Integrators, February 1992.

OSI/Network Management Forum. *Forum 002--Application Services.* Bernandsville, N.J.: OSI/Network Management Forum, 1992.

OSI/Network Management Forum. *Forum 003--Objects Specification Framework.* Bernandsville, N.J.: OSI/Network Management Forum, 1992.

Remedy Inc. *Action Request System--Product Description.* Sunnyvale, CA.: Remedy Inc., September 1991.

Rhodes, P. D. *LAN Operations--A Guide to Daily Management.* Reading, MA.: Addison-Wesley Publishing Company, Inc., 1991.

Rose, M. T. "Network Management is Simple: You Just Need the "Right" Framework." Paper presented at Integrated Network Management II, Washington, D.C., 1991.

Rose, M. T. and Keith McCloghrie. "The Structure and Identification of Management Information for TCP/IP-Based Internets." RFC 1155, DDN Paper presented at the Network Information Center, SRI International, May 1990.

Ryan, Hugh. "Sticker Shock." *ComputerWorld Client/Server Journal* 1 (No. 1), (November 1993).

Saal, H. "LAN Downtime: Clear and Present Danger." *Data Communication--LAN Strategies* McGraw-Hill, (March 1990): 67-72.

Sanghi, S. et al. "How Well Do SNMP and CMOT Meet IP Router Management Needs? " Paper presented at Integrated Network Management II, Washington, D.C., 1991.

Schatt, Stan. *Understanding Network Management Strategies and Solutions.* Windcrest/McGraw-Hill, ISBN 0-8306-3727-3

Scott, K. "Taking Care of Business with SNMP." Data Communication--LAN Strategies, McGraw-Hill, (March 1990): 31-44.

Spohn, Darren L. *Data Networks Design.* ISBN 0-07-030360-X.

Stallings, W. *SNMP, SNMPv2 and CMIP.* Redding, USA: Addison-Wesley publishing Company, 1993.

SunConnect/Sun Microsystems. *SunNet Manager Product Guide.* Mountain View, CA: SunConnect/Sun Microsystems, 1990.

SunConnect/Sun Microsystems. *SunNet Manager Solutions Portfolio* (Winter 1993-1994), MountainView, CA: SunConnect/Sun Microsystems, 1993.

SynOptics Communications, Inc. *Lattisnet Product Guide.* Santa Clara, CA: SynOptics Communications, Inc., 1990.

SynOptics Communications, Inc. *Network Control Engine Product Guide.* Santa Clara, CA: SynOptics Communications, Inc., 1990.

Swanson, R. H. "Emerging Technologies for Network Management." *Business Communication Review* (August 1991): 53-58.

Tanenbaum, Andrew S. "What Have We Learned So Far?" Distributed operating systems anno 1992. *Distributed Systems Engineering* 1 (No. 1), The British Computer Society, The Institution of Electrical Engineers, and IOP Publishing, Ltd., September 1993.

Teknekron Communication Systems. *NMS/Core Product Guide.* Berkeley, CA.: Teknekron Communication Systems, 1991.

Terplan, K. *Communication Networks Management.* Englewood Cliffs, N.J.: Prentice Hall, Inc., 1991.

Terplan, K. *Effective Management of Local Area Networks.* New York: McGraw-Hill, 1992.

Tjaden, G. S. "The Allink Approach to Management Systems Integration." Paper presented at Network & Distributed Systems Management '91. Washington, D.C. September 1991.

ViaTech Development Group. "Electronic Software Distribution." a white paper. ViaTech Development Group, 1993.

Index

3Com
  LinkBuilder Vision, 199
  Transcend, 199, 205

Accugraph
  MotionMail, 320
  MountainView, 241–242, 320
administration tools, 38
AIM Technology Sharpshooter, 224
AIX NetView/6000, 122–126, 267–268
  APIs, 180–182
  applications for, 278–285
    AIX NetView Service Point, 280
    AIX RMONitor/6000 and RMON Agent/2, 281
    Hub Management Program/6000, 279–280
    integration between AIX NetView/6000 and, 283–285
    LAN Management Utilities/6000 (LMU/6000), 280
    SNA Manager/6000, 280–281
    Systems Monitor/6000 systems, 278–279
    third-party applications, 281–283
    Trouble Ticket/6000, 279
alarms, 7, 13
  management platform support for, 109–110
Alcatel Bell ITS SNA-Expert, 246–247, 282–283
alert notification applications, 243–253
AlertView, 226, 278
Answer Computer Apriori, 237
APIs (application programming interfaces), 24–25
applications for network and systems management, 191–257
  categories of, 191–194
  examples of
    device-specific applications, 198–210
    platform extension applications, 243–253
    process-specific applications, 233–243
    service-specific applications, 253–255
    systems management applications, 210–226
    toolkits and development environments, 255–257

  traffic monitoring and analysis applications, 226–233
  levels of integration of, 195
  need for third-party applications, 194
  overview of, 191–194
  shipments of, 196–198
ARMON Networking ONSITE, 228
Army, U.S., 341–352
asynchronous transfer mode (ATM) and LAN switching, 365–366
Atlanta David System Hub Views, 199
AT&T
  Frame Relay, 209
  frame relay customer premises application, 253
  StarLAN 10 Smart Hub Manager, 199
  StarSENTRY
    Computer Manager, 211
    LAN Manager Monitor, 224
    network management integration with, 325–334
    Software Manager, 221
    Systems Manager/OperationsAdvantage, 161–164
  third-party support for, 197
authentication
  with Kerberos, 95–98
Autotrol Konfig, 242
Axlan Administrator, 224
Axon Networks LANservant Manager, 228

BlueLine Software Vital Signs product family, 274, 276
Boole & Babbage CommandPost, 247–248
Breakaway Software PICUS, 211
Bridgeway EventIX, 248–250
Brixton Systems BrxOV, BrxSNM, 250
Bull Integrated Systems Management (ISM), 143–145
  APIs, 189
business model, 30–36
Bytex 7700 Series NMS, 200

Cabletron
    BlueVision, 282
    SpectroPhone, 244
    SpectroWatch, 244
    Spectrum, 129–132
        APIs, 185–188
        for Open Systems, 200
        third-party support, 197–198
Calypso Software MaestroVision, 212–213
CA-Unicenter, 157–159
centralized change management, 8
Central Point Software LANlord, 286
change management, 50–54
Chipcom ONdemand NCS, 200
Cisco
    CiscoWorks, 74–76, 205, 207–208
    Crescendo Manager, 200
client-server systems
    definition of, 358
    special problems with management of, 358–361
    transitioning from legacy systems to, 1–3
    trends in, 364–370
CMIP (Common Management Information Protocol), 18, 19,
    21–22, 45, 295–299
ComConsult Kommunikations CCM, 242
Computer Associates (CA) CA-Unicenter, 157–159
CompuWare EcoTools, 213
Concord Communications Trakker, 228
configuration databases, 39, 42–46
    integrated, 43–45
    populating, 42–43
console emulators, 38
console management applications, 245–246
Conware Computer Consulting NEMA, 208
costing and billing, 68–70
Crossroad Systems Crossroads, 321

data analysis and reporting applications, 233–237
databases, 38
DataStaff Ingeniere NetPerf, 228
DeskTalk Systems
    Trendalyzer (Cooperative Reporting), 233
    TrendSystem (Cooperative Consoles), 245
Desktop Management Interface (DMI), 12, 18
Desktop Management Task Force (DMTF), 12, 18
device-specific applications, 191–192, 198–210
    router and bridge/router management applications,
        204–209
    smart hubs, 198–204
    WAN devices, 209–210
Diederich & Associates NetScript/6000, 250
Digital Analysis OS/Eye*Node, 213, 321
Digital Equipment Corporation (DEC)
    Polycenter Manager on NetView, 146–148
DiMONS 3G, 140–143
directory services, 47–48
discovery, 108–109
Distributed Computing Environment (DCE), 97
Distributed Sniffer System(DSS), 230–231
distributed systems
    definition of, 355–357
    management of, 9–17
        fragmentation of management, 9–14
        networks and systems management applications, 14–15
        staffing issues, 15–17
DMI (Desktop Management Interface), 24

documentation tools, 39
domain management, 113
Dornier FNS 7090 Network Manager, 200
DOS/Windows-based network management platforms. *See*
    network management platforms
downsizing
    changes brought about by, 4–9
    from legacy systems to client-server systems, 1–3

electronic software distribution, 76–80
Elegant Communications XRSA, 240
Encompass, 141, 182–185
Enterprise Systems Software Net/Overview, 276
EventIX, 248–250
Evolving Systems ESI Environment and Voice and Data
    Integration System (VDIS), 6
expert systems, 15, 38–39, 84–90, 368
    architecture of, 85–86
    benefits of using, 89–90
    OSI NetExpert, 86–89

fault management, 54–60
    HP OperationsCenter, 159–161
    with smart hubs, 80–83
FiberMux LightWatch Open, 200
Fore Systems ForeView, 209
fragmentation of management, 9–14
Frontier Netscout Manager, 228

Gandalf Passport, 208, 209–210
GDMO (Guidelines for the Definition of Managed Objects),
    45–46
Gensym G2, 256
global operations directors (GODs), 102
graphical user interfaces (GUIs), 111

Health Profiler, 233–236
Hewlett Packard. *See* entries starting with HP
Hirschmann StarCoupler Manager, 200–201
HP Distributed Network Advisor, 228
HP GlancePlus, 160
HP HARMONi, 250
HP History Analyzer/Traffic Expert/Resource Manager, 229
HP NetMetrix, 93–95, 229, 309–310, 313, 321
HP OmniBack Link, 215
HP OpenSpool Link, 215
HP OpenView, 119–122, 301–316
    APIs of, 171–179
        data integration with OpenView Windows Object data-
            base, 174–175
        event integration, 177–179
        HP OpenView Windows API (OVsAP), 172–174
        product support integration, 179
        protocol access integration, 175–177
        relational database support, 175
        SNMP API, 175–177
        XMP and XMP-based APIs, 177
    Distributed Management (DM) Platform, 138–140
    Distributed Novell Manager, 250
    integration of applications with, 302–315
        HP NetMetrix, 309–310, 313
        Isicad Command 5000, 307
        Legent Paramaount, 314
        modeling tools, 315
        OpenDNM, 307, 309
        Peregrine OpenSNA, 307

Peregrine StationView and ServerView, 313–314
Remedy Action Request System, 307
Interconnect Manager/UX, 208
OperationsCenter and, 159–161
platforms for, 301–302
for UNIX, 119–122
for Windows, 150–152
HP OperationsCenter, 159–161, 215
HP PerfRX, 161
HP PerfView, 160, 217
hubs, smart. *See* smart hubs
Hummingbird Communications PC Terminal Emulation,
245

IBM applications, 258–299. *See also* specific applications.
AIX NetView Service Point, 250–251
AIX Systems Monitor/6000, 217
AS/400 and RS/6000 distributed management applica-
tions, 286
Automated Network Operator (ANO), 271
Enterprise Performance Data Manager/MVS, 273
forthcoming, 272
Hub Management Program/6000, 201
LAN Automated Option (LAN AO), 271–272
LAN Network Manager. *See* LAN Network Manager
LANRES, 273
NetView. *See* AIX NetView/6000; mainframe NetView;
NetView/6000
product families, 259–271
communication alternatives between and within,
287–293
tuning SNA/APPN network performance, 272–273
import/export facilities, 48–49
Independence Technologies
iVIEW Event Manager, 218
iVIEW Log Mgr, 244
iVIEW SNMP Agent Kit, 256
System Manager, 218
TM Analyzer, 217
Informix Relational Database Management System,
321–322
integrated configuration database, 4
integrated databases, 43–45
integration of applications, 4. *See also* specific platforms
case studies, 317–354
with AT&T StarSENTRY, 325–334
with NetExpert, 318–325
U.S. Army, 341–352
with WilView product family and SunNet Manager,
334–341
onto management platforms. *See* Management platforms,
integration
Internet Engineering Task Force (IETF), 18
Isicad COMMAND 5000, 242–243, 307

Kerberos, 95–98
Ki Research OpenDNM, 251, 307, 309

LAN analyzers, 38
Landmark Systems Probe/Net, 218–219
LAN element management systems (EMSs), 36
LAN monitors, 38
LANNET Data Comm. MultiMan, 201
LAN NetView, 268–271
applications for, 285–286

LAN Network Manager, 262–267
applications for, 276–278
legacy systems
monitoring and gateway applications, 246–253
transitioning to client-server systems, 1–3
Legent
NetSpy and LANSpy, 276
Paradigm, 238
Paramount, 314
license management, 98–100
Licensing Service API (LSAPI), 98–99
logical business model, 30–36
log management applications, 243–253
LU 6.2, 294

MaestroVision, 212–213
mainframe NetView, 261–262
applications for, 271–276
APPN and, 293–295
communication alternatives for, 287–293
AIX NetView/6000 as focal point manager, 291–293
using protocol conversion in NetView, 290–291
using protocol conversion via Service Point, 287–290
managed objects, 18–21
management applications. *See* applications for network and
systems
management databases, 39–50. *See also* configuration databases
import/export facilities and, 48–49
integrated, 43–45
manipulating, 46–47
structure of management information (SMI) and, 45–46
management functions and processes, 4, 30–70
logical business model for, 30–36
tools for, 36–37
Management Information Files (MIFs), 78
management integrators, 36
management of distributed systems. *See* distributed systems
management platforms, 101–189
basic services of, 107–115
advanced platform services, 112
alarms, 109–110
APIs and developer's toolkits, 111–112
device discovery/network mapping, 108–109
distributed architectures, 115
domain management, 113
graphical user interfaces (GUIs), 111
management protocol support, 110–111
manager-to-manager communications, 113–115
network modeling, 113
SQL database links, 111
station services *vs.* management platform services,
107–108
definition of, 101
integrating applications onto, 164–189
Bull Integrated Systems Management (ISM) APIs, 189
Cabletron Spectrum APIs, 185–188
HP Open View APIs, 171–179
IBM AIX NetView/6000 APIs, 180–182
methods of integration, 165–166
Network Managers APIs, 188–189
SunConnect SunNet Manager APIs, 167–171
Wollongong Management Station APIs, 189
network. *See* network management platforms
systems. *See* systems management platforms
manager-of-managers (MOM) model, 102–105

manager-to-manager communications, 113–115
mapping applications, 253
Matrix Technology Mobile Driver, 245
MCI Communications HyperScope, 255
Metrix OpenUpTime, 241
MIB (management information base), 19–21, 45
MIB browsers, 110
MIB compilers, 110
MIB tools, 38
MicroMuse LegacyWatch, 251
MIFS (Management Information Files), 78
Miror Systems RARS/2, 251
modeling tools, 39
Motorola Mobile Data NMC 5000, 255
MountainView, 241–242

NetCensus, 99–100
NetExpert, 86–89, 318–325
Net/Impact, 283
NetLabs, 350–351
    Assist, 252
    DiMONS, 126–129
        APIs, 182–185
    DiMONS 3G, 140–143
        APIs, 182–185
    ServiceDesk, 238–239
    third-party support for, 197
    Vision/Desktop, 225
NetManSys NMS/FastBench, 256
NetMetrix, 93–95
NetTech, 282
    BlueVision, 251
    EView, 273–274
NetView, 102. See also AIX NetView/6000; mainframe Net-
    View
NetWare Management System (NMS), 148–150
Network Application Technologies EtherMeter, 230
network architectures, 11–12
Network General
    Distributed Sniffer, 230–231
    Network Control Series, 276, 278
Network License (NetLS) Server, 98–99
network management
    business model of, 30–36
    changing scope of, 26–28
    convergence of systems management and, 361–362
network management platforms. See also management plat-
    forms
    DOS/Windows-based, 148–152
        HP OpenView for Windows, 150–152
        Novell NetWare Management System (NMS), 148–150
    models of, 102–107
        global operations director, 102
        manager-of-managers (MOM) model, 102–105
        open management platforms, 105
        platform/applications model, 105
        SNMP platforms, 106–107
    UNIX-based, 115–148
        AIX NetView/6000, 122–126
        Bull Integrated Systems Management (ISM), 143–145
        Cabletron Spectrum, 129–132
        Digital Polycenter Manager on NetView, 146–148
        HP OpenView, 119–122
        HP OpenView Distributed Management (DM) Platform,
            138–140
        NetLabs/DiMONS, 126–129

NetLabs/DiMONS 3G, 140–143
SunNet Manager, 116–119
Wollongong Management Station, 134–138
Network Managers
    APIs, 188–189
    NMC Vision, 132–134
    third-party support, 197–198
network mapping, as management platform service, 109
network modeling, 113
network monitors, 38
Network Partners Trapper, 219
Network Solutions Cabletron MMAC Hub Views, 201
NMC Vision, 132–134
non-preprovisioned change requests, 54
Novell NetWare Management System (NMS), 148–150
NYNEX Allink Operations Coordinator, 252

Objective Systems Integrators (OSI)
    NetExpert, 86–89, 318–325
object-oriented technology, increased use of, 367
OMNIPoint program, 22–23, 295–299
Open Network Enterprises M.O.O.N., 219
Open Software Foundation (OSF)
    Distributed Computing Environment (DCE), 97
    Network License (NetLS) Server, 98–99
open systems, definition of, 357–358
OpenView. See HP OpenView
OpenVision Open V*SecureMax, 220
Optical Data Systems LanVision, 201
Optivity, 80–83
Oscom International Pty OSGATE-700, 252
OSI (Open Systems Interconnect), 18, 20

Patrol Software DDS/Patrol Link, 219
PC LANs, management applications for, 224–226
PC systems, management applications for, 224–226
Peer Networks Programmable Agent & Development Envi-
    ronment, 256
Peregrine Systems
    Cover/PNMS, 239
    OpenSNA, 252–253, 274, 282, 307
    ServerView, 225, 314
    StationView, 225–226, 313
performance management, 90
performance monitoring, 90–93
performance tuning, 60–63
Perform SAGE/X, 253
PICUS, 211
platform extension applications, 193–194, 243–253
    alert notification and log managers, 243–245
    console management applications, 245–246
    legacy systems monitoring and gateway applications,
        246–253
    mapping applications, 253
platforms. See management platforms
Polycenter Manager on NetView, 146–148
preprovisioned change requests, 51–54
presentation tools, 38
Probe/Net, 218–219
process-specific applications, 193, 233–243
    data analysis and reporting applications, 233–237
    help desk/problem management/trouble ticket applica-
        tions, 237–240
    physical asset/cable management/configuration manage-
        ment applications, 3
    service level agreement reporting applications, 240–241

Prolin Automation Pro/HelpDesk, 239
RAD Network Devices MultiVu, 208
Raylan Network Manager, 201
relational database management systems (RDBMSs)
  SQL links to, 111
Remedy
  Action Request System, 307, 320–321
  Action Request System (AR System), 240
  Health Profiler, 233–236
Remote Alert Reporting System/2 (RARS/2), 251–252
RISCmanagement RISCreporter, 236
RMON (Remote Monitoring MIB), 19, 21, 91–92
  NetMetrix and, 93–95
router and bridge/router management applications, 204–209
routers, remote configuration of, 72–76

SAS Institute SAS/CPE for OpenSystems, 236–237
scalability, 8–9
security management, 15, 39, 63–68
  Kerberos and, 95–98
  UNIX systems, 97–98
service level agreement reporting applications, 240–241
Service Point, 287–290
service-specific applications, 253–255
Sestel HubMan, 201
Shany AlertView, 226, 278
Siemens-Nixdorf Bridge Management, 208
smart agent software, 365
smart hubs, 198–204
  isolating faults using, 80–83
SMI (structure of management information), 45
SNMP (Simple Network Management Protocol), 18–21, 45, 46, 367
  remote configuration of routers and, 73–74
Software Consulting Distributed Error Log Notification (DELN), 245
software distribution applications, 220–223
software monitors, 38
Spectrum, 129–132
staffing issues, 15–17
standards, 17–26
StarSENTRY Systems Manager/OperationsAdvantage, 161–164
Strategic Solutions International Net/Impact, 283
Structured Query Language (SQL), 111
SunConnect Encompass, 141
  APIs, 182–185
SunNet Manager, 116–119, 334–341, 350–351
  APIs, 167–171
    Agent Services API, 169–170
    Database/Topology API, 170–171
    forthcoming APIs, 171
    Manager Services API, 167–171
SunSolutions ShowMe, 246
SunSPARC hardware, 350–352
Synernetics ViewPlex, 202
SynOptics Optivity, 80–83, 202
systems management
  business model of, 30–36

changing scope of, 26–28
convergence of network management and, 361–362
standards for, 24
systems management applications, 192–193, 210–226
  PC LAN and PC systems management (including client/server applications 4
  security management applications, 220
  software distribution applications, 220–223
  UNIX systems management, 210–220
systems management platforms, UNIX, 152–164
  Tivoli Management Environment (TME), 153–157

Talarian RT Works, 256
Tally Systems Corp. NetCensus, 99–100
TCP/IP (Transmission Control Protocol/Internet Protocol), 20
Telemon TelAlert, 245
Template Software SNAP, 256–257
third-party applications. See applications for network and systems
Tivoli Management Environment (TME), 153–157
TMN (Telecommunications Management Network), 23–24
Tom Sawyer Network Layout Assistant, 253
toolkits and development environments, 255–257
traffic monitoring and analysis applications, 193, 226–233
trouble ticketing, 7–8, 13
trouble tracking tools, 38

Ungermann-Bass NetDirector for UNIX, 204
Unison Tymlabs Maestro, 219
UNIX Integration Services HeartBeat, 219
UNIX systems
  network management platforms. See network management platform
  security issues, 97–98
  security management applications, 220
UNIX systems management
  applications for, 210–220
  platforms for, 152–164
    Tivoli Management Environment (TME), 153–157

version control, 76
V.I. Corp. DataViews, X-Designer, 257
ViaTech Development Xfer, 221–222
Vital Signs family of products, 274, 276

WAN analyzers, 38
WAN device management applications, 209–210
WAN element management systems (EMSs), 36
WAN monitors, 36
WellFleet Site Manager, 209
WilTel WilView product family, 255, 334–341
Windows, network management platforms See network management platforms
Wollongong Management Station, 134–138
  APIs, 189

Xfer, 221–222
Xyplex ControlPoint, 204